The Form and Technique of

PSYCHOTHERAPY

The University of Chicago Press
Chicago and London

The Form and Technique of

PSYCHOTHERAPY

I.H. Paul

The University of Chicago Press, Chicago 60637
The University of Chicago Press, Ltd., London

© 1978 by The University of Chicago
All rights reserved. Published 1978
Printed in the United States of America
82 81 80 79 78   5 4 3 2 1

Library of Congress Cataloging in Publication Data

Paul, Irving H
  The form and technique of psychotherapy.

  Includes bibliographical references and index.
  1. Psychotherapy. 2. Psychoanalysis. 3. Client-
centered psychotherapy. I. Title.
RC480.5.P34   616.8'914   78-3181
ISBN 0-226-64999-7

I. H. PAUL, professor in the Department of
Psychology at the City University of New York,
is the author of *Letters to Simon: On the Conduct
of Psychotherapy.*

Contents

Acknowledgments

For his astute suggestions and generous help in shaping this book's structure and format, I wish to give special credit and much thanks to Robert Stewart.

For having read parts of the earlier drafts and given me fine criticism, I am grateful to Arthur Arkin, Mary Engel, Stuart Feder, Herbert Nechin, Lloyd Silverman, and Paul Wachtel.

For permission to quote and paraphrase from my *Letters to Simon: On the Conduct of Psychotherapy* (© 1973 by International Universities Press), I thank International Universities Press and Irene Azarien, who edited it. And for permission to reproduce substantial portions of a paper I wrote, titled "Psychotherapy as a Unique and Unambiguous Event" (*Contemporary Psychoanalysis* [Journal of the William Alanson White Institute and William Alanson White Psychoanalytic Society] 12, no. 1:21–57. ©1976 by Academic Press, Inc.), I thank Arthur Feiner and the William Alanson White Society.

The great and invaluable debt I owe to my students—classes 1971 through 1976 of the clinical psychology program at City University of New York at City College—is clearly reflected throughout this book. I dedicate the book to them, with gratitude and affection.

Introduction

Two decades ago a book on psychotherapy technique didn't have to define psychotherapy very precisely, nor rise to the defense of technique. But so ambiguous has psychotherapy grown—probably no professional service in our society is marked by a heterodoxy so great, by theoretical and ideological frameworks so divergent, methods and procedures so variegated—that now such a book must specify carefully what it means by "psychotherapy" and locate its position along a broad, multicolored spectrum. Concomitantly, and perhaps because of that ambiguity, technique has become so controversial a subject—many influential teachers and practitioners have declared it irrelevant to the conduct and effectiveness of psychotherapy or, if not altogether irrelevant, then relegated to a role of minor and incidental importance or condemned it as artificial and formalistic or dismissed it as being essentially unteachable because it is so fluid, idiosyncratic, and unspecifiable—that anyone who ventures to articulate technical procedures and principles has first to argue in favor or the relevance, the significance, and the teachability of "technique." This book, consequently, needs a substantial introduction.

The book's main purpose is to articulate and explicate the formal procedures and fundamental technical principles of a particular method of psychotherapy which is a blend of traditional psychoanalytic and nondirective methods, whose mode is verbal, whose central process is inquiry that focuses primarily on the patient's intrapsychic realm, and whose chief requirement of the therapist is to maintain a rigorous nondirectiveness and neutrality across a wide range of issues which can extend to key aspects of the therapy's procedure. The basic format and clinical-theoretical underpinnings of the method are described and discussed during the course of this book, but there isn't the attempt to give a comprehensive description or full account of the therapy itself, of its substance and its drama. The book's aim is limited and its coverage selective; form, not content, is its central subject. (According to the analogy I like to use, playing the piano is the chief subject, not music.) Thus, there is little about personality differences and dynamics, about psychopathology, aetiology, and symptomatology, nor is much attention paid to such phenomena as emotional insight, reconstruction, acting-out, impasses, and crises. Instead, the focus is on issues of procedure and format, on technique, the craft aspects entailed in conducting a particular kind of psychotherapy.

Neither does the book attempt to examine all of the technical aspects. Since I intend it as part treatise and part dissertation, since my aim is to write intensively rather than extensively and to be as concrete, as specific, and as detailed as possible, I select those issues of procedure and format which I believe are the most fundamental and salient, and examine them exhaustively. In a sense, my aim is more ambitious than to write *on* technique, or even *about* it; I try to write a basic technique as explicitly as I can.

That's a feasible goal for a therapy which relies substantially on the verbal mode, because the mode is isomorphic in its spoken and written forms. To be sure, the translation of spoken into written language isn't free of serious limitations; spoken language is far more expressive, insofar as it embodies a rich variety of nonverbal signals, such as voice tone and texture, inflection and tempo, along with facial and body gesture. Nevertheless, those aspects of communication can be fairly rendered in written form, at least descriptively. And, though writing about a verbal psychotherapy may not be without certain serious shortcomings, it is free of the inherent limitations that writing about music, for example, or about surgery, where the modality is qualitatively different, where techniques have to be demonstrated.

Well-informed opinions differ on the question of how and when psychotherapy technique is best acquired, but not whether didactic study is ever likely to be sufficient. Apprenticeship and supervision are such clearly necessary prerequisites that few would defend the proposition that technical proficiency can be acquired without clinical practice. The most serious challenge, however, comes from those who question the relevance and role of technique itself. For some teachers and practitioners, it is an arid and useless formality, mechanical and inhuman, a way of keeping distance and playing an empty role—therefore it shouldn't be taught at all. For some it is a necessary evil; it remains subservient to understanding, it emerges quite naturally from a knowledge of the dynamics of human experience and behavior together with a knowledge of the dynamics of psychotherapy—therefore it needn't be taught. For some there's no such thing as a correct technique (not even a good one); all therapists must fashion their own out of the ingredients of their individual personalities and tailor it to their patients' particular personalities and problems—therefore it cannot be taught. With all these points of view I strongly disagree.

Who am I to disagree? On what grounds do I base a conviction that technique should and can be taught? One way to answer is with my credentials, which can serve several functions. For one, the nature of my professional experience is obviously pertinent to my views and opinions; and though I try in this book to rely as much as possible on the cogency of my rationales and the force of my arguments (which can, to a substantial extent, be judged on their own merits), I also make appeal to my clinical experience. For another, my conception of psychotherapy and my convictions with respect to technique have evolved out of personal experiences, principally as student, practitioner, and teacher. Therefore, a *vita* is the relevant way to define myself and can provide an appropriate preface to my definition of psychotherapy and defense of technique.

My formal training began in general and social psychology (McGill University), and continued in clinical psychology (University of Pennsylvania). It was a traditional academic training, of the late 1940s and early 1950s, which stressed breadth of scholarship, research, an objective approach to psychodiagnostics and an eclectic approach to theory and therapy. During my internship I was taught to do orthodox Rogerian nondirective counseling (by Seymour Feshbach), but I neither became indoctrinated nor expert in the method. Then I spent several years in postdoctoral training at a private teaching hospital (the Austen Riggs Center), where I studied psychoanalytic theory (principally with David Rapaport) and learned psychoanalytic therapy (from a staff that included Margaret Brenman, Robert Chassell, Erik Erikson, Robert Knight, and David Shapiro). I completed my formal training at an orthodox Freudian institute (the New York Psychoanalytic Institute), where I was one of a handful of psychologists who had clinical training and supervision in classical psychoanalysis (mainly from David Beres, Bertram Gosliner, Heinz Hartmann, Otto Isakower, Milton Jucovy, and Rudolph Lowenstein); and I also had the invaluable opportunity to learn a great deal from Merton Gill and David Rubinfine. Subsequently, I joined the faculty of a graduate program in clinical psychology (City University of New York at City College), where I became largely responsible for teaching student therapists—out of which experience this book has directly grown.

Though my conception of psychotherapy—combining as it does a nondirective with a psychoanalytic orientation—has its roots in my formal training, it wasn't there I became so convinced of the saliency and importance of technique, and neither was it in my clinical work; it was in my role as teacher of student therapists. And since students are typically less interested in learning about therapy than in learning therapy, this book is largely the product of what I learned from, and with, them.

I have dedicated this book to my students for two main reasons: (1) their work is contained in it; (2) their attitudes and opinions, their needs and biases, and, most of all, their searching questions and hard challenges, provided the basis and background for most of the text. Furthermore, not only did they cause me to formulate and articulate many of my principles and technical procedures, they helped me discover some of them. All teachers know how much can be learned in teaching, how reasons and rationales have to be sharpened in the process of striving to explain and persuade, how trying to make something clear forces one to be clear; and teaching psychotherapy requires an examination of basic assumptions and first principles along with their actual application to concrete conditions and clinical circumstances. My students have required of me a clear and coherent set of reasons (rationales and principles), a clearly defined set of boundaries (limits and conditions), and a logically consistent and psychologically articulate set of methods and procedures (techniques). Consequently, many of the lessons that are contained in this book were taught to me in a significant way by students, despite the fact that they hadn't yet had any firsthand experience doing psychotherapy. The course on which this book is based was given when they were preparing for their first experience at doing therapy; its objective was to prepare them for their first supervised work. And the fact that they already knew a good deal about psychotherapy—they had a reading familiarity with the relevant psychological issues and theoretical concepts—has had an important influence on the book's selective content and narrow focus.

Someone in the position of academically preparing students to assume the responsibilities of conducting psychotherapy must make a number of critical choices in deciding what to teach, in what sequence, and how to teach it. To teach everything isn't possible, and neither can everything be taught at once; the teacher has to decide what issues and lessons have priority, what can be taught and what can only be acquired in the doing, and—perhaps most important of all—how to teach the craft. To be sure, those decisions will be vitally influenced by the teacher's conception of what psychotherapy is, but they will also be shaped by a fundamental attitude concerning the role and relevance of explicit methods and procedures. And my attitude toward explicit methods and procedures (technique) also has some significant roots in my experience as a pianist.

"Can you play the piano?"—"I don't know, I've never tried," is an interesting joke; it can easily be transposed into, "Can you surgically remove an appendix?"—"I don't know, I've never tried," without losing its incongruity and humor. Consider, however, "Can you do psychotherapy?" The joke is no longer so funny because there's a popular point of view that all one has to do is try, that anyone with certain talents and interests can go right ahead and be a therapist. After all, don't people regularly help one another with emotional and psychological problems? Don't they hear each other out with patience and compassion, giving understanding, comfort, and advice? What else is psychotherapy but the good ministrations of one person to another, helping him endure, overcome, and change? What specialized skills are required that most people don't already have?

My conception of psychotherapy leads me to claim that the difference between a therapist and a friend (who gives good counsel) can be no less significant than the difference between a surgeon and a friend (who removes a splinter), that the discipline of therapy is no different in principle from the discipline of playing the piano. And the difference isn't merely an operational one—that is, a psychotherapist is someone who is professionally engaged in providing the professional service of psychotherapy—it is substantive. My main thesis is this: just as the surgeon and the pianist are defined by the fact of possessing technical skills, by being craftsmen, so the psychotherapist can (and should) be defined.

Consider the simple scale, one of music's basic technical components. First of all, music, to a significant extent, is made up of scales and parts of scales, and the pianist therefore needs the skill to play them fluently and automatically in order to be free to pay attention to the aesthetic content and meaning of the music. Second of all, there is a tradition of correct or good scale work that is neither arbitrary nor capricious; there's a correct way to finger each scale that isn't based on intuition or on aesthetic considerations but mainly on the mechanics and physiology of the instrument and the pianist (there is a "science" of scales). This doesn't overlook the fact that playing scales can never be fully mechanical; there are idiosyncracies of hand which require a tailoring of the rules; the nature of the instrument counts (it makes a difference whether the scale is played on a piano or a clavichord), and so does the music's context and purpose (the same scale can be fingered differently when it occurs in a piece by Mozart, by Liszt, and by Debussy). But the fact that modifications need to be made in no way obviates the value and necessity of the pianist's acquiring the skill of playing scales, and neither does it mean there are infinite ways to play them; there is a standard and correct way, perhaps a few of them, and every pianist must learn them at the level of a skill. The same is true for the surgeon. And the same can be true for the psychotherapist—we too must know how to pass the thumb under the third and fourth fingers smoothly, fluently, and automatically; our students must learn it; and there is a correct way.

Furthermore, to be a pianist, it isn't enough to know music, to understand the aesthetic principles and artistic purposes of Mozart, Liszt, and Debussy; neither is it sufficient to understand how the piano is constructed and how it relates to the actions of the fingers, hand, and arm; one must also acquire the craft of playing. Similarly, to be a surgeon, it isn't enough to know anatomy and physiology; one must know how to operate, one must have technique. And similarly, I believe, to be a therapist, it isn't enough to know psychology and psychiatry, the way people's emotional experiences are organized and get disorganized, the way their behavior is motivated, their phenomenal world structured, and the like; neither is it sufficient to understand the dynamics of personality change or behavior modification. One must acquire the technical skills of therapy, one has to learn the craft.

To be sure, my analogies are not without serious limitations. A therapist isn't a surgeon whose technique has to take a great precedence, and neither is he like a pianist who cannot begin to play any music without a certain level of skill and facility. Still, they are relevant enough, I believe, because conducting therapy is part science and part art, and both its parts require a substantial technical foundation: that's the working hypothesis for this book. In addition, it has a thesis.

Perhaps because a teacher is prone to develop a conception or theme around which to organize the pedagogy, perhaps because the process of teaching elicits underlying convictions and gives voice to silent opinions, I have come to profess that the psychotherapy situation can be construed in a way that sets it apart from all socially familiar interpersonal and professional paradigms. Accordingly, psychotherapists can take a stance that doesn't borrow significant features from other professionals who provide human services in our society and can relate to their patients in a way which is uniquely that of a "psychotherapist." Here is how I formulate the thesis: Psychotherapy is potentially a unique and distinctive event, and psychotherapists can define themselves as unique and distinctive professionals.

A further thesis—which I believe stemmed indirectly from the fact that matters of theory and conception can be expounded and argued, case histories and clinical events can be recounted and examined, but techniques can actually be taught and practiced (in the sense that one learns and practices the piano)—is this: Psychotherapy can be relatively unstructured without being concomitantly ambiguous, and a therapist can remain both nondirective and neutral and, nevertheless, function actively and effectively. In fact, it has become my strong conviction that the efficacy of an average-expectable course of psychotherapy can be profoundly enhanced when the therapist remains as nondirective and as neutral as it is feasible to be, giving the patient little, if any, guidance and counseling, as well as little, if any, evaluation and reinforcement; it is then that the therapist can participate actively in the really vital processes of therapy and thereby promote its effectiveness.

And the method that embodies those theses and actualizes those potentials is the kind of therapy I write about in this book. I've already written about it in an informal treatise, titled *Letters to Simon: On the Conduct of Psychotherapy*, where I designated the method with a typographical rendition of the generic term "psychotherapy," namely, *Psychotherapy*. In my opinion, it could well be designated as *Psychoanalysis*, because its orientation is basically psychoanalytic insofar as it relies heavily on the interpretive mode of intervention along with the principal conceptions of psychoanalysis's clinical theory. But there are differences which many analysts would regard as crucial, principally in respect to *Psychotherapy*'s thoroughgoing nondirectiveness, which requires, among other things, a major alteration of the "fundamental rule." The patient is not directed to use the couch, and neither is he instructed to free-associate.

In a recent book devoted to psychoanalytic technique, Charles Brenner sustains the familiar point of view that a "real analysis" is not possible if a patient doesn't use the couch.[1] "Some" analyzing can be done face to face, but there is a "certain point" beyond which it cannot be done that way. In respect to free-association, though he qualifies the term in several important respects—pointing out its inaptness because it doesn't accurately describe what actually happens when a patient "freely associates"—Brenner arrives at a similar conclusion: free-association remains a crucial process for the definition of psychoanalysis as a treatment method.

Insofar as *Psychotherapy* shares the basic orientation and underlying spirit of orthodox client-centered counseling, it could be designated *nondirective*. But the major and pivotal role of interpretations, along with its emphasis on the phenomena of transference and resistance, may, in the opinion of many, vitiate *Psychotherapy*'s nondirectiveness. Harry Bone, however, has argued cogently that psychoanalytic and client-centered procedures have more in common than is generally recognized. "It would be a misleading oversimplification to say that psychoanalysis espouses interpretation and that client-centered therapy repudiates it," writes Bone, "The phrases 'interpretation by the analyst' and 'therapist-facilitated self-integrations by the client' require explication . . . There is less difference than is often supposed, in regard to

1. Charles Brenner, *Psychoanalytic Technique and Psychic Conflict* (New York: International Universities Press, 1976).

interpreting', between the standard psychoanalysis of Fenichel and client-centered therapy.''[2] Similarly, Leon Levy has examined the differences between the practice of psychoanalysis and of client-centered therapy and come to the conclusion that they have been overstated and misconstrued.[3]

I've considered coining a new name—*Nondirective Psychoanalysis*, which I believe would be quite accurate, if clumsy—but concluded it would be presumptuous. Moreover, a significant number of teachers and practitioners will recognize *Psychotherapy* as the kind of therapy they already teach and practice. Rosalea Schonbar, for one, in a searching essay called "Confessions of an Ex-Nondirectivist," describes how she introduced the interpretive mode into the structure of nondirective therapy. She raises the question, "Is it possible to value the patient, genuinely respect him and his capacity for growth, to be empathic and acceptant, to be guided by his inner experience and readiness, and still be an interpretive therapist?"—and answers with a persuasive yes. Schonbar argues that interpretations need not be judgmental the way Rogers insisted they had to be, and neither do they necessarily violate the patient's rate of exploration nor "create" resistances and transferences. And she concludes from her clinical experience that the act of interpreting doesn't require any significant change in the basic attitudinal aspects of nondirective therapy, which "are probably basic to becoming an effective therapist of any kind."[4]

At any rate, I continue to use the typographic solution I arrived at in *Letters to Simon* (where I wrote parenthetically, "If you forget, after a while, that by *Psychotherapy* I do not mean simply psychotherapy, then I'll be far from dismayed; for I won't deny that deep down I believe that its methods and principles apply to all forms of psychotherapy that are good and effective."[5]) In chapter one of this book, and in the context of an examination of the larger issue of role definition for the psychotherapist, I present *Psychotherapy*'s most fundamental features.

Chapter one is a lecture on *Psychotherapy* and may be regarded as a continuation of this Introduction. Beginning with chapter two, I focus most of the attention on matters of technique and procedure and examine them in the context of a series of "paradigms," which consist of a variety of simulated, hypothetical situations and transcripts that were designed to help me teach

2. Harry Bone, "Two proposed Alternatives to Psychoanalytic Interpretation," in *Use of Interpretation in Treatment: Technique and Art*, ed. Emanuel F. Hammer (New York: Grune and Stratton, 1968), pp. 172–73.

3. Leon Levy, *Psychological Interpretation* (New York: Holt, Rinehart, and Winston, 1963).

4. Rosalea Schonbar, "Confessions of an Ex-Nondirectivist," in *Use of Interpretation in Treatment*, pp. 55–58.

5. I. H. Paul, *Letters to Simon: On the Conduct of Psychotherapy* (New York: International Universities Press, 1973), p. 8.

Psychotherapy's technical principles and requirements in a concrete, explicit, and detailed way. (Instead of "paradigms," I sometimes call them "exercises" and "studies," after the model of Czerny exercises and Chopin studies, coherent pieces composed for practicing discrete technical requirements and mastering technical problems in a musical way.) My examination of the paradigms is interspersed with commentaries and digressions; my presentation of the paradigms is interrupted by a lecture on the noninterpretive modes of intervention, chapter five; and the final chapter of the book is entirely given over to three interrelated lectures on formal technical considerations for which I haven't devised any paradigms.

In view of the fact that *Psychotherapy* has already been described and discussed in my *Letters to Simon*, the matter of redundancy and overlap has to be considered. Subsequent to writing that book I've made a number of significant changes and important refinements; my views on neutrality and nondirectiveness are more stringent and consistent, my approach to technique is more rigorous and systematic, and I lay greater emphasis on the issues of role definition and uniqueness. Still, though I now find fault with some of my earlier views (and would want especially to rewrite many of the illustrations I composed, mainly because the interpretations are more confronting than they should be), there isn't really any basic difference between this book and *Letters* in the treatment of *Psychotherapy*. Moreover, though I have tried to minimize the overlap between the books, there is a substantial redundancy that results from my effort to make this book as coherent as possible so that a reader's familiarity with *Letters* would not be a prerequisite for a full comprehension of its contents. There are, to be sure, some important omissions that arise partly from an unwillingness to repeat myself (for instance, I don't discuss the stages of *Psychotherapy* because I have nothing further to add on the subject), but wherever it seemed necessary, I decided to go ahead and repeat or paraphrase what I'd already written, with the hope that the reader familiar with *Letters* won't experience a complete *deja entendu*. I do, however, repeat myself during the course of this book, and I do it deliberately, because my attempts to avoid repetition tended to impair the structural coherence of the text. I've decided to minimize the making of reference to other places in the book, so instead of referring back to something I've already written (or forward to something I later write), I sometimes simply write it out—and later write it out again—occasionally with modification and amplification, occasionally without. (The gain in continuity and comprehensibility outweighs, I hope, the risk of tedium and the flavor of propagandizing.) Often I discuss, at different places in the book, the same issue from different perspectives, and I'll rely on the index to help the reader who wants to examine my views on a particular subject.

There remained, however, the problem of writing with clarity and at the same time with precision and judiciousness. Remarkably few assertions can be made about an enterprise like psychotherapy which can stand free of substantial qualification and significant caveat. For every technical principle and supporting rationale, for every rule of thumb, every prescription and proscription, there are important exceptions and crucial conditions. Perhaps it was little more than an expression of my obsessionality, but the early drafts of this book were encumbered with so many qualifying phrases, so many parenthetical asides and digressions, that the result was a turgid text. I'm not satisfied that the final version is sufficiently free from such encumbrances, but I've tried to strip away as many of them as I deemed prudent. My aim was to enhance readability without oversimplifying or distorting my views and giving the appearance of being dogmatic and high-handed.

In any case, however, it isn't ever easy to write explicitly on technique without slipping into a dogmatic posture. And it's especially difficult when the technique applies to a form of therapy that puts a premium on uniqueness, and whose uniqueness is predicated on the distinctive way the therapist has to behave. Because *Psychotherapy*'s technical requirements are based to such a substantial extent on interventional modes that the therapist has to try and avoid, including many that are used deliberately and freely by qualified and experienced practitioners, I run several kinds of risks in explicating and advocating them. On the one side stands the risk of overstatement and exaggeration (in the interests of bolstering my arguments), on the other is the risk of blurring the focus (in the interests of keeping from seeming inflexible and ignoring the fact that context always counts). And since I'm not only explicating a particular method of therapy but also challenging practices that are so commonly used and widely accepted, there's the danger of oversimplification and misrepresentation. Having acknowledged those difficulties and pitfalls, let me add the following claim: I want to be rigorous, consistent, and forceful in argument and advocacy, without at the same time being rigid, inflexible, and intemperate. The degree to which I've failed is partly a function of my literary technique.

Finally, I wanted to write without the grammatical implications that all therapists are male. Unfortunately, the ubiquitous "he" is enormously helpful; reliance on the plural—as in this Introduction—becomes quite stilted, and to write "he-or-she" is awkward. One way I've chosen to solve the problem is to rely a good deal on the first-person, both singular and plural; another is to address the reader directly as "you." This means I address "you" as if you were a student of psychotherapy, and, in doing so, I intend the term *student* to be interpreted in its broadest sense. I assume we are all students of psychotherapy, even those of us who are experienced practitioners and teachers. When I do employ the third-person singular, however, I clearly intend the masculine pronouns in their nongender sense.

The same is true for all references to "patients." Moreover, every patient who is used for exemplification, both in the paradigms and the lectures, is imaginary, and I have contrived to make gender entirely irrelevant. Instead of arbitrarily designating this "patient" as "male" and that one as "female," I consistently—and purely for the sake of grammatical convenience—designate all patients as "male."

1

On *Psychotherapy* and the *Therapeutic Process*

In his comprehensive and detailed treatise, Robert Langs recommends beginning psychoanalytic psychotherapy with the questions "What can I help you with?" and "What problems have you been having?" Langs's rationale is this: "I thereby immediately communicate my medical orientation as a physician *vis-à-vis* a patient and my role as an expert in helping the patient to alleviate his emotional suffering."[1] How those queries communicate a medical orientation is unclear, but a more serious question is why such an orientation is necessary or desirable in the first place.

We therapists need a professional identity, naturally. To contend, however, as Langs appears to be doing, that our identity has to be of a professional "something"—namely, a physician or a psychologist or social worker or teacher, or whatever one's credentials provide (Langs goes on to write, "Nonmedical therapists can communicate a similar stance")—implies that the role definition "psychotherapist" will not suffice for expertise in helping to alleviate emotional suffering, it needs hyphenation with an already well-established and socially familiar profession. That assumption deserves critical examination because, for one thing, it may have distorted the definition of psychotherapy in ways that affect the intrinsic processes of psychotherapy; for another, it may be responsible for a certain uncertainty about our essential role and function.

1. Robert Langs, *The Technique of Psychoanalytic Psychotherapy*, 2 vols. (New York: Aronson, 1974), 1:66.

The fact that the assumption is likely to be held by many prospective patients is germane but not crucial. To be sure, the average-expectable patient may require of us a socially familiar identity and might expect from us an already familiar kind of professional service. Langs suggests this matter be dealt with only later on in therapy. "I will subsequently make it clear to the patient," he writes in a footnote, "that we will be working together on his problems and this type of help differs from the usual medical model in that each of us have an active, albeit different, responsibility. Initially, however, the patient is seeking help and I am offering it to him; the rest will unfold later." But is it necessary or desirable to begin by promising a familiar kind of service only to break that promise later? Why not establish right away that this service is going to be different, while at the same time holding out the promise that it will be effective in providing the sought for help? In the case of a patient who is uninformed about psychotherapy, or who has reason to be apprehensive about it, it might be unwise to begin with much explication, but is it inappropriate or insufficient to present a professional role without making it appear to be a medical one—or a behavioral scientific or pedagogical or religious one? The answer to these questions, in my opinion, lies not only in our patients' expectations and conceptions; we therapists, too, can have difficulties defining our work in a professionally autonomous way.

At any rate, faced with the question "What are you, really? What is it you actually do?" we cannot answer with the simple, "I am a psychotherapist who provides psychotherapy," and expect that to suffice. Whether for our patient or for ourselves, further definition is required to specify what psychotherapy, and therefore the psychotherapist, consists in. And if we want to articulate a definition that is distinctive and autonomous, that doesn't borrow from other social-professional roles and institutions, we cannot define ourselves as physicians who care for a patient's *psyche* rather than *soma* with psychological instead of physico-chemical treatment, or as behavioral scientists who clinically apply the scientific principles of psychology, or as teachers whose methods of instruction and training are geared to a patient's personality and symptoms rather than to his cognitive-motor skills, or as priests who minister to the human soul but without supernatural concomitants.

I don't mean to claim a necessary disadvantage to accepting a nonautonomous definition; my point is it necessarily influences the vital processes of therapy in ways that need to be examined. And I believe some of the influences are likely to be both unnecessary and unproductive in respect to therapeutic effectiveness and outcome. They are influences which have their roots in history and haven't outgrown their origins. Consider briefly how the history of psychotherapy makes it amply clear why the physicianly role definition has been our dominant one, and how the more recent history shows why that definition has been rapidly losing its dominance and giving way to those of behavioral scientist, teacher, and priest.

Insofar as it is essentially a healing service, psychotherapy can probably be traced back, in one form or another, to the time when people first devised the system of providing human services in exchange for material goods. In the forms we know it today, however, psychotherapy dates from the medical profession's abrogation of what had been a religious function, and it isn't inaccurate to say that when medicine expanded its healing service to include psychological suffering, the profession of psychotherapist was actually born. Thus, our first role definition was that of physician. In order for psychological suffering to fall within the purview of medicine, such suffering had to be part of the natural order; the "disease" categories of neurosis and psychosis had to be formulated, and insofar as patients had a mental "illness," the role definition of physician-psychiatrist was appropriate for the psychotherapist. Even when the treatment method was wholly nonphysiological, that definition could be maintained because the structure of the doctor-patient relationship did not change. The patient continued to be regarded as someone who was innocent of moral and ethical blame, whose suffering was visited upon him by forces of nature and exigencies of accident over which he had little, if any, control, and whose cure entailed a passive acceptance of the ministrations of the doctor. The doctor diagnosed the causes and continuing sources of the disease and then took charge of the patient's life to counteract and reverse the disease process. The epithet "doctor knows best" continued to define the therapist as the learned one, the benevolent authority with license to diagnose, to prescribe, and to administer.

Though the medical model came under serious question when influential voices were raised against the concept of mental illness, that development in itself would probably not have sufficed to undermine it. For good reason did Freud occasionally regard psychoanalysis as interim and temporary, to be replaced eventually by physico-chemical methods; and when psychoanalysis was being launched as a purely psychological form of treatment, Breuer and Freud (in 1895) went to great lengths to theorize about hysteria at the neurophysiological level of discourse. And while it is probably true that the promise of discovering the organic basis of neurosis could not be held in abeyance too long, and the lack of success in isolating the disease process had to invite skepticism and reformulation—and while it was also inevitable that questions should be raised about the fruitfulness of diagnosing all mental disorder, all personality disturbance, and all psychological suffering in purely medical terms—that alone would probably not have sufficed. Moreover, I believe it also took more than the recognition that psychotherapy was highly nonspecific as a "treatment"; medicine was familiar with such nonspecific treatments across a wide range of its professional service. What it took to launch an effective movement away from the model of traditional medicine and uncover the misfit of the physicianly role was, in my opinion, the development of new methods of treatment. (Group psychotherapy is a prime example.)

The rapid evolution and remarkable diversification of psychotherapy methods that occurred, principally in the decades following World War II, is familiar enough to need no documentation. Suffice it to say that the expert-layman, benevolently authoritarian relationship that defines the doctor and patient could no longer endure under the strain of the new therapies. To be sure, many therapists turned back to the older priestly model, and many moved into the roles of scientist and engineer. But the major impetus behind the rejection of the medical model has probably been the fact that psychotherapy grew more and more exclusively psychological. And once the mantle of medicine was cast off, psychotherapists were free to experiment with new and novel ways to serve the psychological and social needs of their clients. That left the task of articulating an appropriate role definition, a task which has generally been ignored— perhaps out of the conviction that it isn't so important.

"If the real issues are not to be evaded," writes David Bakan in a thoughtful and provocative essay in which he challenges the role models of physician, scientist, teacher, and priest, "the psychotherapist has available to him two main role postures, *repairman* and *healer*." Bakan contends that the contemporary therapist ought to emulate the repairman for his craft and the healer for his art, and take those roles as his principal models.[2]

Bakan puts great emphasis on the repairman's central value, technical competency. "Everything is subservient to competence. His craftsman's intelligence proceeds systematically, orderly, efficiently, parsimoniously, economically." The appropriateness of the model is limited, however, by the fact that the objectives of the service must be clear and unambiguous, a limitation that Bakan claims is serious but not insurmountable. In my opinion, what is more serious and less surmountable is conceiving of the patient as a passive object with no inherent responsibility in the process of its repair, because that way of construing his role is inimical to most forms of traditional therapy.

---

2. David Bakan, *On Method: Toward a Reconstruction of Psychological Investigation* (San Francisco: Jossey-Bass, 1969). My citations from Bakan's book are drawn from pp. 122–26, a chapter titled, "Psychotherapist: Healer or Repairman?"

And the conception is related to the fact that a repairman is basically a troubleshooter, a diagnostician, who puts things back into working order—a role that may be fully appropriate only for the behaviorally oriented therapists who rely on the technology of conditioning and relearning.

Nevertheless, the craftsman's values and attitudes are worthy ideals. In Bakan's words:

> When it is not corrupt and vulgar, the role posture is self-effacing ... formal ... The repairman interests himself in matters of fact. He has license to investigate as thoroughly as the situation demands. He is both without squeamishness and without intrusiveness. He gets little pleasure from his work except the pleasure from a job well done ... It is not without respect that I present this image of the repairman. One cannot be a citizen of the contemporary world without valuing this role posture as an ideal. There are many instances in which this role posture is both possible and appropriate. Indeed, where it is appropriate, it would be wonderful if our psychotherapists could come close to this ideal.

In his examination of the healer role, Bakan stresses the process of relieving the sufferer of his burden of guilt. The healer's art is to manage, in one way or another, to deny the correlation between suffering and sin—sin being translatable into the secular terms of responsibility. "The healer may assert a deterministic metaphysics which denies responsibility, assert that the suffering is the result of infantile and, hence, innocent experiences, locate the root of the suffering in the unconscious, and the like. These are latter-day forms for depressing the correlation of suffering and sin." The healer also makes the assumption that there are forces inherent in the sufferer which will alleviate his suffering, and the healer manages to make these forces effective. "As contrasted with the repairman, the healer's agency is not to supply the efficient cause, but only to permit the pre-existing forces in the client to function."

And communication—such a vital aspect of psychotherapy—is integral to the healer's art. Bakan points out that a major aspect of his role is to enhance communication among regions of existence, "whether this be between the holy and the mundane, between one person and another, between consciousness and unconsciousness, or between the scientist and the layman." Opening channels of communication is certainly a germane function that is distinctive to most forms of therapy.

Bakan concludes his essay by drawing attention to two major, and contrasting, obstacles that must be avoided before we can accept the healer model, magic on the one hand, and rigid scientism on the other.

As a healer, one concerns oneself with things that are only limitedly comprehended. Success in these areas makes one feel like a magician. (Freud said this of himself when he began with the cure of certain cases of hysteria.) This is a temptation to be avoided by the healer. A healer should believe in the abiding mystery of what he concerns himself with, but a magician must never believe in 'magic' in the mysterious sense. The magician becomes a failure if he believes the illusions that he creates. A rigid scientism, on the other hand, is so impatient with anything short of well-founded belief that it closes off from consideration the realities which have not yet been encompassed by science. Both of these are to be avoided.

The healer role fits us better than the repairman role does, and in certain respects the fit is very close, but I think the model itself is too broad and encompassing for psychotherapy. Bakan fails to consider what a wide variety of professional positions it covers—the physician's, for instance. In fact, many professional services rely on the comforting techniques of healing. Lawyers apply them when they seek to reassure their clients while helping to solve (repair) their legal problems; even politicians may play the role of healer (successful politicians typically are skillful orators not merely because they succeed thereby in articulating their policies but also because that kind of communication is an integral aspect of their healing technique). A healer, no less than a repairman, is basically a problem solver, and the craft—which consists of a set of psychological techniques that serve to motivate, to reassure, and to advise—can be applied to all sorts of human problems, be they medical, legal, social, psychological, and whatever. The question therefore remains, What kind of healing process is psychotherapy? How is it, and how might it be, distinctive?

Naturally, I would not have raised this question if I didn't intend to answer it. And neither would I have raised it if I didn't feel prepared to defend its significance. I believe I can do both from the vantage point of *Psychotherapy*. Therefore, I return to the question, "What are you and what do you do?" and offer the answers which are available to us when we conduct *Psychotherapy*. Lest the following list of "I do nots" give the impression of a straining after sheer contrast, let me qualify it in advance by mentioning that these proscriptions are meant to be taken as standards or ideals. I have ample opportunity during the course of this book to draw attention to the practical limitations that are typically encountered; still, if you read every "I do not" in the list as "I try my best not to, whenever it is possible, feasible, and clinically advisable," you'll have a more accurate impression of what I intend to convey.

1. "Unlike a physician, I do not prescribe and proscribe; I give no advice and guidance; I offer no nostrums and palliatives to assuage discomfort

and suffering; and neither do I rely on the special properties of 'trust father' in the forms of authority, faith, and suggestion.''

2. ''Unlike a scientist, I do not apply standards of evidence to my patient's report; I don't maintain an attitude of skepticism; and I don't offer a technology for problem solving and for ameliorating maladaptive behavior.''

3. ''Unlike a teacher, I do not instruct and train; I give no reinforcements, and neither do I provide incentives; I don't impart a methodology for self-improvement; and I don't rely on the teacher-pupil relationship (with its overtones of parent-child).''

4. ''Unlike a priest, I do not invoke a higher order of truth, a philosophy or an ideology; and I don't offer the security of a social institution or group in which membership can be gained by making psychological changes.''

What, then, do we do?

''I provide my patient with the opportunity to have a distinctive and unique psychological experience, one he generally cannot have by himself or with other professionals; and that distinctive and unique experience I call the *therapeutic process*.''

I was tempted to coin a new term for this special experience (calling it, perhaps, the ''*theta* [for 'therapeutic'] -*process*,'' the way Max Wertheimer called the apparent-movement illusion the ''phi [for 'phenomenon'] -phenomenon''), but decided to treat it the same way as ''*Psychotherapy*''—simply italicizing the term to indicate that it denotes the event I claim is distinctive to *Psychotherapy*. Insofar as the *therapeutic process* denotes the core event of this therapy, insofar as it is the proximate goal toward which we work in the interests of our patient, I devote a substantial part of this book to it. Now I will try to define it.

Four Propositions toward a Definition of the *Therapeutic Process*

Psychotherapy can be defined in terms of two sets of behaviors and intentions, those of the therapist and those of the patient. There is a natural interaction between the two sets of behaviors and intentions, and most definitions of psychotherapy are constructed around that interaction. Since, however, the interaction of such sets can only be defined in terms quite different from those of each one—the interaction itself cannot be described at the same level of abstraction as the component sets—those definitions tend to be at once too vague and too formalistic. For that reason, I prefer to define *Psychotherapy* in a way that makes no reference to any interactional processes. It seems to me adequate and accurate to formulate a definition that focuses on the distinctive behaviors and intentions that describe the therapist and relies wholly on the concept of *therapeutic process* to denote the psychological experience that the therapy affords the patient. The therapist's behaviors and intentions are then construed in terms of the establishment and promotion the *therapeutic process* and the facilitation of its full development and course.

This definition amounts to a specification of our methods, procedures, techniques, and goals as therapists—and it contains a ruling construct, the *therapeutic process*. Since the definition is formulated in a way that emphasizes how all of our behaviors and intentions are organized around a ruling construct, the *therapeutic process*, that's what requires formal definition. And since it isn't the sort of process one can point to, I won't be able to give it a precise and succinct definition. It requires at least four separate propositions, each of which has to be explicated. But before I do that, I can convey the essential spirit of the *therapeutic process* with a broad description.

Just as the *analytic process* denotes the core event in classical psychoanalysis, the *therapeutic process* is meant to denote the core event in *Psychotherapy*. It refers to a patient's work, as well as to his subjective experience, when he expresses and explores his inner and outer realities, when he strives to articulate and to understand his behavior, his self, and his mind. The *therapeutic process* entails the acts of reflecting and introspecting, of reminiscing and recollecting, and of reorganizing and reconstructing. The realm of outer reality, the patient's world of objects and stimuli, is not slighted, but the major focus is on his inner reality of affects and impulses, of needs and conflicts, of attitudes, beliefs, and fantasies, of habits, defenses, and values. And a special emphasis is placed on the experiencing of his individuality and autonomy as well as on his sense of volition. Finally, it is a process that comes down to the complementary acts of *understanding* and of *being understood*. Thus, the *therapeutic process* is an activity of self-inquiry that strives to articulate, to comprehend, and to discover.

Can all these acts and events be fairly subsumed under a single concept? To encompass so many phenomena is certainly asking a lot of a concept. Whether or not it overloads the *therapeutic process*, my justification rests on the observation that the separate aspects of self-inquiry tend to work together in practice, and they tend to become especially interdependent as the therapy develops. The same is true for the *analytic process*, and some analysts would regard the foregoing paragraph as a depiction of that process. But the *analytic process* is usually construed in a narrower and more specialized way, requiring, for instance, genetic reconstructions and the resolution of experiences and symptoms into component parts and determinants. Furthermore, the *analytic process* relies on the task of free association, not on the exercising of choice and decision, and it's therefore a more passive experience.

Nevertheless, the two concepts generally refer to the same kinds of acts and events, and since they share the same basic referents as well as the same essential spirit, it doesn't distort my presentation too substantially when you read "*analytic process*" where I write "*therapeutic process*." To be sure, there can be differences, but *Psychotherapy* needn't be significantly different from classical psychoanalysis. When the circumstances and the patient allow it, a course of *Psychotherapy* can become indistinguishable from a course of psychoanalysis, insofar as the patient may slip naturally into the free-association mode, his symptoms and habits may be subjected to analysis, his conflicts and fantasies brought to the surface, a transference-neurosis may burgeon and be resolved, and the rest. There's nothing in *Psychotherapy* that prevents this from occurring, and there are a number of important features of the method that can cause it to happen. The critical difference is that we, as therapists, don't actively cause it to happen. But I want to emphasize that, insofar as we do nothing to prevent it, and insofar as certain key features of the clinical situation, along with our attitudes and behaviors, are consonant with its happening, it can and does happen. It depends largely on the patient (his purposes and his personality) and on the circumstances of the therapy (the frequency of sessions, for instance) how closely a course of *Psychotherapy* will approximate a course of classical psychoanalysis, and whether it will instead take on some key features of other forms of traditional psychotherapy, such as those which can fairly labeled Humanistic and Existential.

Following are four propositions that formally define the *therapeutic process*.

1. It is an intrapsychic and mental process. The *therapeutic process* isn't meant to be construed as an interpersonal and behavioral event. The most commonly encountered definition of psychotherapy centers around the interpersonal relationship between therapist and patient, whether conceptualized in pure relationship terms or in terms of interpersonal communication. For *Psychotherapy*, however, that kind of definition is inapt because the *therapeutic process* is not a relationship event; it occurs not among people but within a single individual (in the same sense that acquiring the ability to play the piano is something that happens within a person). A good psychological model for it is the phenomenon of dreaming, which is an internal and autonomous experience. Such a model may obscure the fact that an interpsychic process, a communication process, may be a necessary condition for the occurrence of the *therapeutic process* (it can facilitate, promote, as well as impede), but it does highlight the fact that the phenomenon itself is conceivable as wholly intrapsychic.

What "intrapsychic" means can readily be explicated in terms of subjective experience, modes of awareness, and the like. The intrapsychic realm is experienced in terms of thoughts and feelings, wishes and fantasies and memories, and also in terms of a palpable sense of sclfness that is essentially autonomous. Intercourse with reality occurs via the medium of perception and action and is phenomenally experienced in terms of subject-object. From the outside, however, the intrapsychic realm is only inferable, not "observable." But there's no insurmountable problem here; I don't believe that epistemological considerations need deter anyone from accepting the reality of another person's intrapsychic realm, nor that we as therapists can be prevented from legitimately claiming to "observe" that realm just because our mode of observation rests upon an act of inference. We need only be cognizant of the fact that our mode of observation is a peculiar one, and one of its peculiarities is that full certainty is never attainable. For that reason, the possibility of error can never be altogether ruled out. Nevertheless, while we may not be able to observe our patients' intrapsychic realm with the same degree of rigor and objectivity that a natural scientist observes his data realm, that doesn't mean we can claim no significant validity for our observations. The intrinsic limitation on our capacity to confirm observations mandates an attitude of reservation and a quest for multiple and convergent information, nothing more fundamental than that. I will sidestep for now the question of knowledge by empathy and simply claim that it is subject to the same limitation of relative confirmability, which is quite different from impugning the potential validity of any and all observation of this kind.

Similarly, no epistemological argument forbids us from postulating the reality of mind. And in the commonly understood sense of the term, the *therapeutic process* is a *mental* event. Mental is not simply synonymous with intrapsychic; it takes its connotation from the distinction between mind and body, where body is represented by behavior. My point is this: the *therapeutic process* is not behavioral in the commonly understood sense of "behavior"; subjective experience is the central mode, and the only activity (that is, "behavior") is verbal. Insofar, however, as we can construe verbal activity to be mental, the process remains exclusively mental activity.

It may be useful, if also more accurate, to say that we are dealing with thought rather than with action. The relationship between them (essentially it's the mind-body problem) can be formulated in a variety of acceptable ways, but however we choose to formulate it, we can legitimately restrict our focus to one or the other. Since my preference is to construe the *therapeutic process* as mental, in the sense that it is fundamentally a phenomenon of thought rather than of action, my position is that *Psychotherapy* makes commerce with mind and trusts that body will follow suit in some lawful way (be it in Interaction, in Transcendental Harmony, in Double-aspect, or whatever).

"I will not be telling you what to do; I won't suggest what decisions you should make or how I think you should behave." That is the fundamental limitation you impose on yourself and make clear to your patient when you conduct *Psychotherapy*. This does not mean, however, that you remain aloof from his actions. "I will try to help you understand your actions and behaviors, and sometimes I may be able to help clarify the reasons for your decisions; but what you do and how you decide will remain entirely up to you." In that sense, then, does the therapy maintain its focus on mental events.

Psychotherapy is contemplative; action is thought about but not taken, behavioral events are examined from a distance, the mode remains phenomenal and mental. What is the basis of that major restriction? Why not deal also with action and body? My answer to this fundamental question takes several different forms, which are given at different places in this book. Here I give its broadest and perhaps most provocative formulation.

The fact that it makes commerce only with mind reflects a critical feature both of *Psychotherapy*'s uniqueness and its effectiveness. For it also to deal with body events—in the form of giving direction and advice in the realm of action, for instance—would first of all obviate its distinctiveness and obscure the vital distinctions I am drawing in this lecture. Second of all, insofar as you devote your mind entirely to the patient's mental domain, it would undermine your effectiveness in bringing about significant changes in his behavior. Perhaps "undermine" is too strong, but I am convinced that the dynamics and goals of *Psychotherapy* require a rigorous neutrality which can only be maintained when we abstain from trying to influence our patient's behaviors and actions.

The first proposition can be summarized as follows. The *therapeutic process* requires of us to make it clear to our patient that we both fully accept the reality of his phenomenal experience and that it is our major focus of interest. In our participation we reveal an effort to comprehend what he thinks, feels, wants, and how he thinks, feels, and wants. As therapists, our basic orientation is to observe a patient's intrapsychic realm and to understand his mental functioning.

2. *It is based on the act of discovering.* We also make it clear, in the way we time and formulate our remarks, that the major goal is to discover. Most of our remarks are organized around the function of uncovering and explaining, gaining better understanding and new insights. And the fact that we work

toward that goal implies that we intend our patient to work toward it also. Before I discuss this implication, it is worth considering the nature of discovering.

The term denotes more than one kind of event. First is the discovering of something which already exists but has been hidden from view. The uncovering of unconscious ideas and of unrecognized or unacknowledged feelings, impulses, and conflicts belongs in that category. Second is the discovering of a new way to comprehend events that were already fully cognized; what is discovered is a different organizing principle. This category encompasses the comprehension of new interconnections among experience, new cause-effect relationships, as well as the discernment of new meanings and significances, and it is more a creative act than an uncovering one. Importantly, there may be a transformation of "knowledge by description" into "knowledge by acquaintance," insofar as the personal significance of psychological events and experiences is comprehended for the first time. Third is the act of reconstruction, of piecing together disparate events (usually from the past) into a new coherence and integration. In traditional therapies this is often what is entailed in remembering the past, and it is part uncovering and part reconstructing.

Typically, all three kinds of discovering are intimately interrelated and work together in the process of therapy, so there's little practical purpose served by drawing distinctions among them. I therefore use the term *discovering* for each of these processes and events, and I draw a major distinction between them and *learning*. My thesis is that the *therapeutic process* is best construed as an instrument of discovering rather than as a method of learning.

The primary goal of all therapy is, of course, change; and even if this change is conceptualized as an alteration of mental events, the process can be called "learning." But the term can blur some vital distinctions. If people "learn" to walk and also "learn" to love, if they "learn" to play piano and also "learn" to control their feelings, then the term has become a synonym for psychological change; and only in this omnibus and unspecific sense can the changes that occur as a result of the *therapeutic process* be classified as learning. If we want to be more specific, however, if we want to put a special emphasis on the process of mental reorganization or of an alteration in phenomenal experience, then we have a term that better conveys the properties of such an event—and that term is *discovering*.

Separating change into the dual processes of learning and discovering can be justified without at the same time obscuring their close interrelationship. When a pianist studies a new piece of music, he learns the notes by acquiring the knowledge of what they are as well as the motor ability to perform them. In addition to learning the piece that way he also acquires the meaning of it, its emotional tone, its sound, artistic purpose, and the like. This kind of acquisition is quite different, and the term *discovering* is a more exact description of it. Just as one doesn't "discover" the notes and the way to finger and phrase them, so one doesn't "learn" the meaning of a piece of music. Similarly, in first acquiring the ability to play the piano, we don't "discover" how to play a *C*-major scale, and neither is it accurate to say we "learn" the feeling of exhilaration at being able to play it. *Learning* is appropriate to the acquisition of knowledge and skills, and *discovering* is appropriate to certain kinds of reorganizations of experience. Thus, we discover, not learn, how it feels to be triumphant or depressed, how our fear of success is influencing our work, how an event that occurred in childhood is still functioning in the present, and the like. And it is that distinction which underlies my assertion that *Psychotherapy* entails discovering as a central event.

The practical implications of this assertion are far from trivial. For one thing, it follows that any efforts on your part at teaching a patient cannot be regarded as intrinsic to *Psychotherapy*. Which doesn't mean, I hasten to add, that you must therefore avoid any learning on his part, that you must never teach; it means only that you cannot conceptualize such experiences as aspects of the *therapeutic process*.

Suppose your patient is a pianist who experiences muscular tension when he practices, and this tension interferes with his work. Suppose further that you happen to know a way to practice with less tension, and you also know a way to teach it (you can describe and demonstrate it or prescribe a program of training for it). So you decide to go ahead and give your patient the benefit of that knowledge. Why not, after all? Won't it be beneficial, perhaps even vital, to his well-being? The question is, however, Should you regard what you've done as "psychotherapy"? Haven't you done something that is properly called "teaching"? What you've done, after all, is something a piano teacher would do, and he wouldn't call it "psychotherapy"—So why should you? Just because you're a psychotherapist?

Pursuing the example, and making it more germane, suppose the patient is tense because he experiences a variety of distressing feelings while practicing, and they are feelings he can't identify. Suppose you recognize them as constituting aspects of the affect of anxiety. Suppose further you judge it might be helpful to him if he could identify, articulate, and label that group of distressing feelings; so you tell him that when he practices he is experiencing anxiety. And he finds the knowledge helpful, even to the extent of enjoying a subsequent improvement in practicing. (We know from clinical experience that this kind of intellectualization can be efficacious in learning to control affective experiences.) But, and this is my point, the event was not an intrinsically psychotherapeutic one; it is best characterized as a teaching (or didactic) event. Again, you have behaved like a teacher, not a psychotherapist. Not that you shouldn't have done it. Why shouldn't you do whatever you can to help him, especially when the problem is psychological in nature? My only contention is that you haven't contributed to the *therapeutic process*; you offered an intellectualization, a cognitive lesson.

I don't mean to imply, however, such a remark cannot bespeak an act of discovering. If, for instance, he was familiar with feelings of anxiety but never recognized that his experience at the keyboard was similar to those feelings, then your suggestion could contribute to the *therapeutic process* insofar as it reflects a true discovery. "Oh, so that's a manifestation of my anxiety!" is importantly different from, "Oh, so that's what's called anxiety!"

Neither do I mean to be implying that a discovery-interpretation is necessarily more beneficial than a teaching-interpretation. It may well be that any discovery-interpretation you could have made would have been less beneficial to him than the remarks you made. The point here is not that discovering is always more efficacious than learning. I am contending that it is something quite different, that there is value in maintaining the distinction, and that its focus upon discovering is an aspect *Psychotherapy*'s uniqueness. And lest my thesis grow absurd, the qualification in the third proposition is necessary to introduce at this point.

3. It does not encompass everything that occurs in Psychotherapy. The *therapeutic process* is the core event but not the sum-total of everything a patient experiences in *Psychotherapy*. For one thing, a substantial and significant part of his behavior may be devoted to an avoidance of the process. The term *resistance* can generally be applied to these avoidance events, and there is a sense in which they can be considered as part of the *therapeutic process*. But there are other behaviors that remain integrally necessary to both the process and its resistance and yet are essentially different. What I have in mind are such acts as the recounting of experiences and events, the exchanging of information, the explaining of certain meanings, and the like. My point here is simply that the *therapeutic process* is the core event, the uniquely indigenous one, but it's far from being the only event in *Psychotherapy*.

The reason I am making such an obvious point is this: I regard the process to be of such critical importance that I believe it is necessary for us, as therapists, to behave as if it were the only event that counted. That doesn't mean we disregard or minimize everything else; it means only that our first priority is the integrity of the *therapeutic process*. We must want to promote and facilitate its full development, and we must strive to avoid behaving in ways that prevent, impede, or interfere with it. And why? To put it succinctly, because that's the process which effectuates the long-range alterations and reorganizations that are the goals of the therapy.

I need to emphasize *long-range*, because short-term considerations sometimes—often, in fact—differ significantly. It isn't uncommon for a certain behavior on our part (the putting of direct questions, for instance) to have a short-term beneficial effect which is at variance with a long-term beneficial effect. The *therapeutic process* can sometimes be enhanced by certain short-term methods but in a way that will impede its long-term development. (Much more about this matter soon.)

Since the major requirements for maximizing the *therapeutic process* are to a significant extent the same as those for maximizing the occurrence of discovering, What are the optimum conditions for discovering? is a germane question. And to answer that question, I find it helpful to turn again to a comparison of discovering and learning. To begin with, both require an appropriate motivation in the form of a felt need and perceived goal—so that is the first necessary condition. Just as one must want to learn, be convinced that learning is a good and useful thing, and take it as one's goal, so must one want to discover, be convinced of its efficacy, and take it for a goal. But once the motivation has been established, the process of discovering differs significantly from that of learning.

For one thing, learning can benefit from instruction and simple imitation—being shown how—in a way that discovering cannot. Discovering is a more autonomous process insofar as it is less dependent on the influence of a mentor and teacher, or at least it is dependent in quite a different way. Furthermore, the results of learning can be demonstrated in a way that the results of discovering cannot. (Compare the way one shows having learned a piece of music with the way one shows having discovered its emotional meaning.) In an important sense, discovering is a more private phenomenon. Not that I believe the results of learning can be directly perceived, whereas the results of discovering must be indirectly inferred. Only the mode of observation is different; otherwise, the results of discovering are fully as palpable as those of learning. But there is this important difference: to appreciate the results of learning, the observer need not be able to perform the act; the fruits of the learning can be observed from the outside, so to speak. To appreciate the results of discovering, on the other hand, the observer has to be capable of apprehending the discovery itself; the observer has to understand the new insight, comprehend the new solution, feel or empathize with the new feelings.

That point deserves elaboration. We can accept someone's having learned to play the piano simply by listening to him do it. We need not be able to play in order to appreciate the results of the learning. The same, however, cannot be said for discovering. Say the pianist has also discovered the serenity of a Mozart sonata or the passion of a Beethoven sonata, can we appreciate that discovery unless we already know those attributes? In order for us to hear them in his performance we must also discover them (either for the first time or in advance). Similarly, someone's discovery of a mathematical solution requires us to share that discovery before we can accept that a discovery has in fact occurred. In order to do that, we must have knowledge of the mathematics because without such knowledge, the discovery will be meaningless to us. But we don't have to be able to do the mathematics, or play the piano; just as we can apprehend the discovery of an explorer without first knowing how to make maps or navigate. Given the appropriate kind of knowledge and understanding, a discovery can be shared by the simple acts of pointing and explaining; no new learning is required.

The relevance to *Psychotherapy* is this: exploration is the central event and discovery the central goal, and the discoveries must be shared ones because it is bound to be insufficient for us to notify a patient of our discoveries until and unless he is capable of making them. So, in an important sense, they are not valid discoveries until they get made by him. What I mean to be stressing is the degree to which the act of exploring and the phenomenon of discovering are autonomous processes that can be shared but not taught. When we offer an interpretation, we seek to share with our patient a discovery, not teach him a lesson. Perhaps we also teach him the lesson of how it's done; though insofar as we make it clear that our purpose is to have him make and share his discoveries too, the main "lesson" involved is that he too can do it.

I am inclined to push the point further and claim that the "lesson" is not merely that he *too* can do it but more importantly that *only he* can do it. What I have in mind is, insofar as it's his self and mind, his inner and outer realities, that are being explored, the discovering is predicated upon autonomy—and not merely on a sense of it but on its actuality. In my opinion, the actuality of the patient as an individual with volition and power, an active agent in the direction of his life, must be the principal subject of discovery that lays the groundwork and provides the framework for the *therapeutic process*.

Autonomy, to be sure, is always relative, and rests on a delicate balance between independence and interdependence; autonomy can become so excessive as to shade into detachment and insulation. We know patients who suffer from an overweening sense of their separateness along with an unrealistic conviction that they are fully responsible for every event in their lives. I mention this only to forestall criticism, to acknowledge the complexity of the issue, and also to admit I am running the risk of serious oversimplification. But the reason I'm stressing autonomy at this point is because I intend in the next paragraph to answer the key question, How do we promote the *therapeutic process*? And my answer is based on the hypothesis that a patient's essential autonomy is the paramount subject for discovery and serves as the main context for self-inquiry. It is necessary, however, to add the qualification, "the limits and boundaries and qualities of his essential autonomy," meaning his *relative autonomy*.

Here, then, are the technical guidelines—my answer to the key question— by which we, as therapists, can best establish and facilitate and promote and sustain and optimalize the *therapeutic process*. We refrain from directing the patient in any way; we don't interview him or counsel him; we don't judge or criticize him; we provide no reinforcements in the forms of rewards, punishments, and incentives of any kind; and we don't share our personal feelings, attitudes, beliefs, and opinions. Instead, though we are caring and tactful, we maintain a position of neutrality and impersonality; we observe without much participation beyond a full empathy along with a degree of warmth and enthusiasm; and we bend ourselves entirely to the purpose of understanding the patient, relying mainly on the instrumentality of interpretation to share that understanding.

These guidelines are weighted on the side of proscriptions. We are free to offer interpretations (which explain, articulate, uncover, reformulate, reorganize, and understand by discovering), and we can allow ourselves a measure of warmth and enthusiasm, but otherwise we strive to avoid a significant number of common interpersonal behaviors and attitudes. Moreover, there is even a major constraint on our use of interpretations: they have to be appropriately and judiciously timed. Only when they are needed for the purposes of restoring and enhancing the *therapeutic process* are interpretations free from constraint.

Each of the principles and guidelines is elaborated and exemplified in the following chapters, but I want to qualify them here by pointing out that they are meant to be regarded as ideals or standards, to be aspired to. Furthermore. not only am I writing here about ideal standards but also about long-range goals, and I don't want to leave the impression that short-range goals have to be so stringently avoided. There is sometimes, to be sure, a one-to-one correspondence between both kinds of goals, but even when they are antithetical, there is no peremptory reason to give priority to the long-range.

Consider again the pianist who experiences anxiety while practicing. I pointed out that you might decide to offer some "nontherapeutic" help with that problem because it could be so important to his well-being. Insofar as it doesn't promote the *therapeutic process* and might in some ways retard it, and insofar as it casts you in a role that might be inimical to its optimal development, you have to take account of the fact that you're risking the sacrifice of a long-term benefit in favor of a short-term one. My point then is this: if you took into account only the long-term considerations, you wouldn't choose to offer the advice or the intellectualization (or even, for that matter, a poorly timed interpretation); weighing it against the possibly great short-term benefits, however, you might decide to forego the long-term benefits, or if not forego them, forestall them. At any rate, to give prioroty only to long-term considerations, to aspire toward an ideal state of affairs, no matter what, is rarely necessary or desirable. Clinical judgment (and wisdom) must never be abandoned to the dictates of any method or system. And with that defense of virtue I turn to the final proposition.

4. It is founded on the psychoanalytic conception of ego-autonomy. To maximize a patient's freedom to express, explore, and inquire, you have to withhold direction and behave in ways that keep to a minimum all forms of control and encroachment. Your principal role has to remain that of observer and commentator, the listener who listens actively and helps the patient understand his experiences by articulating, analyzing, and explaining them. But you offer such help mainly, if not almost exclusively, when you judge that the *therapeutic process* requires it of you. In an important sense, you supervise the process itself, and to the extent that it is construed as an essentially autonomous process, you must keep from shaping it unduly.

Psychotherapy's nondirective and psychoanalytic format is designed to achieve the benefits of freedom for the patient, freedom from "neurosis" (in the broadest sense of the term). Phenomenologically, it is likely to be freedom from ego-alien experiences and compulsions, from inner as well as outer conflicts and maladaptive habits. That goal, which I prefer to conceptualize as ego-autonomy, determines virtually all of your significant behaviors and attitudes as therapist; every technical principle has some bearing on the patient's acquiring greater freedom-autonomy. "My central hypothesis is that he will benefit from the therapy to the extent that he attains greater Autonomy from—and therefore greater control over—the forces that operate upon his Ego from within [his personality] as well as from without."[3]

The concept *ego* is clinically useful and can be construed in two complementary ways: (1) to denote the core of our personality, consisting of our self-image and the so-called executive functions of our behavior; (2) to denote the phenomenal self that we come to recognize as our autonomous sense of "me-ness." Psychoanalytic theory formulates ego as a personality structure that is embedded in a matrix of processes and forces which originate

3. Paul, *Letters to Simon*, p. 14.

both from within the personality and from without. The former may be thoughts, action tendencies, fantasies; they include feelings and needs; they may be experienced as conflicts and ambivalences. Whatever their character, they represent inner processes and pressures that are never in perfect harmony with the core me-ness; and when that harmony reaches a certain degree of dissonance, they are conceptualized as ego-alien. From without, ego is subject to the pressures and demands of reality, which are also never in perfect harmony with the self; and when that dissonance becomes excessive, they are considered maladaptive. "The task of mediating and harmonizing these relatively independent configurations of processes and forces (which can, but need not, be conceptualized as Id, Superego, and Reality) is one of Ego's chief functions. Add to this the hypothesis that Ego too has substantial interests and claims upon behavior, and we have a picture of a complicated and dynamic interplay and counterpoint. This interplay and counterpoint are what the concept of Ego-Autonomy—and its essential relativity—denotes."[4]

Psychotherapy's central hypothesis is this: ego-autonomy is supported and enhanced by unfettered self-confrontation and understanding, which entails and promotes a fuller sense of authentic selfness; by coming to know himself better, by becoming more familiar with the full range of his inner and outer reality, and by experiencing himself as a relatively independent and volitional being, a patient will gain a stronger, firmer, more modulated and realistic control over his experiences and actions. (And with that gain will come the "cure.") Accordingly, the basic goal of the therapy—and it is also the way we conceptualize the *therapeutic process*—is the gradual freeing of ego from the excessive grip of both inner and outer conflict and compulsion.

Construing the *therapeutic process* in terms of ego-autonomy provides a theoretical basis for the thesis that *Psychotherapy* can be—indeed, must be—a unique experience for the patient. His experience in *Psychotherapy* is hardly possible under ordinary interpersonal conditions where autonomy cannot be exercised so freely. He can express himself and communicate his mind with a degree of freedom which is either impossible or inappropriate in situations where the other person's feelings and reactions must be taken into account, and where the results can have a variety of real implications they don't have in therapy. That degree of freedom is far from an unmixed blessing, and certain aspects of it can be painful and anxiety-provoking (especially during the early phases). Furthermore, a patient isn't likely to want the kind of freedom that *Psychotherapy* offers him, and neither is he likely to want the kind of relationship with you which that freedom requires. It requires of you a nonevaluative

4. Ibid., p. 15.

attitude, a position of neutrality, that is not only unfamiliar to him but also can be quite discomfiting. And your neutrality has to be supported with a stringent impersonality.

Neutrality and impersonality are subjects that require careful, detailed, and concrete examination. Since, however, I regard them more as technical, or practical, issues than as conceptual ones, I don't discuss them here. (I do in chapter nine.) But before I end this discussion of broad theoretical matters I want to make some further general remarks about technique, to supplement those I included in the Introduction.

The *Therapeutic Process* and Technique

Though they are intimately related to the *therapeutic process*, and that process has a substantial basis in theory, the technical principles of *Psychotherapy* did not emerge from theoretical considerations alone. Theory may have had a guiding hand, but the techniques, for the greater part, grew out of purely pragmatic considerations. In fact, I believe it accurate to claim that *Psychotherapy*'s theoretical underpinnings are largely a post-facto context for a set of methods and procedures that evolved gradually out of clinical experience. And the pragmatic experience was that of prac-titioners and teachers from such diverse theoretical persuasions as Andras Angyal's Gestalt-orgasmic point of view,[5] Otto Fenichel's Freudian one,[6] Carl Rogers's nondirective-humanistic point of view,[7] and Hellmuth Kaiser's nondirective-psychoanalytic one.[8] Even uniqueness, as a prime value of *Psychotherapy*, had its origins in clinical experience. Moreover, I came to regard uniqueness as a good-in-itself before I had persuaded myself that it was also an attribute of therapy which promoted important and enduring psychological change and growth. At first it was largely an intuitive sense that a unique and distinctive kind of therapy would have a substantial efficacy.

And as I wrote in the Introduction, the method also grew out of pedagogical considerations and experiences, out of the need to articulate principles that could be acquired by appropriate training and didn't rely too heavily on certain kinds of predispositional personality traits and talents. There was no question in my mind that technique in psychotherapy takes the same kind of

5. Andras Angyal, *Neurosis and Treatment: A Holistic Theory*, ed. and trans. E. Hanfmann and R. M. Jones (New York: Wiley, 1965).

6. Otto Fenichel, "Problems of Psychoanalytic Technique," *Psychoanalytic Quarterly*, 1941.

7. Carl Rogers, *Client-Centered Therapy* (New York: Houghton Mifflin, 1959).

8. Hellmuth Kaiser, *Effective Psychotheraphy* (New York: Free Press, 1965).

disciplined practice it does for any performance skill—it can benefit not only from an accumulation of past experience but also from preparation in advance and rehearsal—but I had to believe it needn't be so dependent on unlearnable skills. After all, I was teaching it.

Because of its emphasis on uniqueness, but chiefly because of the way it construes the *therapeutic process*, *Psychotherapy* requires of us an exact technique, and its constraints allow relatively little latitude with respect to our personal characteristics. In many contemporary forms of therapy, most notably the encounter varieties, it matters a great deal who the therapist is, what personality traits and special talents he has. Consequently, only certain of their technical requirements can be taught; a great deal remains outside the realm of acquisition and learning. That the same is not true for *Psychotherapy*—or at least not so true—is an important advantage, because insofar as we don't "do our own thing," insofar as we don't rely on charisma or even, to any substantial extent, on intuition, we can readily acquire to a sufficient practical level the skill of conducting *Psychotherapy*. It takes work, study, and practice, but the main natural talents we need are sensitivity, empathy, and clarity. The ability to understand and to communicate understanding accounts for the bulk of the variance. That ability is largely a function of comprehending, by learning and discovering, the special dynamics of *Psychotherapy* itself, because the principles of our technique rest upon those dynamics.

When I claim that *Psychotherapy* requires an exact technique, I have in mind a high (or call it microscopic) level of exactitude. Details of wording and of phrasing, of inflection and formulation, these matter (as do also, of course, details of gesture and nonverbal behavior). They matter significantly and substantially, despite the fact that therapy is such a large enterprise in time and in the multitude of verbal and nonverbal exchanges that it's often possible to pay attention only to its macroscopic events. There are good reasons why supervisors might not listen to the verbal details but only to the larger content and sweep of the sessions they oversee, and some justification can be found in the Gestalt-organismic point of view. But a whole can be more than a mere sum of its parts even when the parts are contributing substantially and significantly to that whole. In psychological phenomena, the parts, even the smallest ones, can be intrinsic to the shape and form of the whole. At any rate, I am convinced that every detail of our conduct as therapists counts, both in and of itself as well as cumulatively. And I'm never surprised when a patient points out to me, or recalls, a precise detail of what I said, or exactly how I said it, and claims it has had a significant impact on him.

Then there's the matter of individual style, and the question, Must each of us find his own style, his own stance and approach? Most teachers of psychotherapy would answer yes, thereby taking exception to the kind of pedagogy that is reflected in this book, especially insofar as it often seems to put the words in the student therapist's mouth. It's one thing to suggest that you convey this or that message to a patient, it's quite another to tell you exactly what words to use. My position is not as rigid as it may sometimes appear in the following pages. First, however, let me admit to finding nothing intrinsically wrong with telling a therapist—be he a student in the narrow or broad sense—exactly what to say. I believe that finding and agreeing upon a precise way to word a remark can be very useful. For one thing, it often serves the valuable function of freeing us to devote our full attention to understanding the patient. If, however, the words aren't easily learned, if they aren't natural and congenial, we'll be distracted by the effort it takes to find them, and that can detract from our ability to pay full attention. Furthermore, while our work as therapists can benefit from the discipline of self-consciousness, excessive self-consciousness can interfere with our work; and the requirement to speak in ways that aren't habitual can intensify one's self-consciousness (which is likely to be too great to begin with when we are inexperienced). Therefore, it has to be altogether necessary to acknowledge a degree of latitude in the matter of style and to allow for a range of individual proclivities and differences.

How much latitude and allowance, and what kinds, are difficult questions to answer in a general way. But perhaps it will suffice to point out that words have a vital significance in *Psychotherapy*, and close attention must therefore be paid to them; and while different therapists may choose different ways and words to express the same idea, each must bear scrutiny for its connotations, its surplus meanings, and its unwanted implications. Conducting therapy—especially *Psychotherapy*—requires a great precision of communication on our part: that is one of its basic craft aspects. And I won't resist the temptation of claiming that the ability to communicate accurately is likely to correlate with the ability to understand accurately.

2

The Autobiography
Paradigm

Imagine that during the first session with a new patient—after he has given his reasons for wanting psychotherapy, after you have given a brief explanation of how therapy will proceed, and after schedule and fee arrangements have been made—he informs you that he is writing an autobiography for you.[1] He's been working on it since the time you spoke on the telephone and made this appointment; it's not yet completed, " . . . so I'll give it to you next time."

How you respond to this information—and subsequently to the patient's reaction to your response—will be influenced by various considerations, but it will depend chiefly on the kind of psychotherapy you intend to conduct. If it is a classical (Freudian) psychoanalysis, you would regard a written autobiography as inappropriate; while you'd be interested in the meaning and significance of his decision to write one, you wouldn't want to take a noncommital position toward such a deviation from the formal procedure of psychoanalysis, and therefore you'd probably tell him that for you to read his autobiography could be a serious departure from your preferred way of conducting therapy. Similarly, if you intend to work interpersonally with the patient (according to Sullivanian principles, for instance), you might also regard the autobiography as inappropriate and want to discourage him from submitting it. My point is this: from divergent clinical-theoretical orientations

1. A reminder: since all "patients" are hypothetical, and their gender is irrelevant, I intend the third-person singular pronoun in its generic sense—to refer to a person, male or female.

(and there are obviously more than the two I mentioned), an *a priori* stand can be taken against the autobiography. And the same applies to taking an *a priori* stand in favor of it, because there's doubtlessly a form of therapy being practiced which requires one to be written, and certainly a good many for which it would in no way be dissonant or inappropriate.

If your decision is to reject the autobiography, you can expect that the patient's reaction might pose a problem; but no matter whether you choose to explain your position before you've listened to his reasons for writing it or to wait until they have been presented and discussed, the issue itself is likely to present no serious technical difficulties. There is no reason to expect it will distort your role definition or introduce a note of fresh ambiguity into the therapy. As a matter of fact, the very opposite can be expected: the issue might actually contribute importantly to a clarification and articulation of your role definition, insofar as it gives you the opportunity to further explain the format and structure of the therapy you prefer to conduct, and thereby it can serve to reduce the ambiguity that inheres in psychotherapy. None of this is likely, however, if you choose not take an *a priori* stand—and that's the choice you have to make when you want to conduct *Psychotherapy*.

I don't mean to imply that only one clinical-theoretical orientation requires a therapist to avoid such an *a priori* position and that only one rationale exists for fostering a substantially unstructured therapy. *Psychotherapy*'s rationale is based on its thoroughgoing nondirective orientation, which has to extend quite far into the basic procedures of the therapy itself. The method requires us to minimize the extent to which we impose a structure—to the limits of feasibility and sound clinical practice. Therefore, when *Psychotherapy* is your method of choice, you have to avoid taking a stand either for or against the autobiography without first knowing the patient's motives, expectations, and feelings on the matter; this means you are confronted with at least two technical problems. One is how to secure that knowledge while still adhering to your nondirective principles; the second is how to formulate your decision in a way that won't distort your definition as a therapist and introduce further ambiguity into the format of therapy.

Neither do I mean to say that once you've learned what the patient's motives, expectations, and feelings are, a nondirective orientation mandates whether you accept the autobiography or not. Your decision can still be influenced by your particular preferences and points of view. For instance, you might want to guard against feelings of resentment over the imposition on your time, or you might welcome the opportunity to have the autobiography's information; you might want to take account of the potential "manipulation" that's involved, or instead put a higher priority on the positive motivational aspects; you might be concerned about the possible defensive and resistive implications, or else about the implications for mastery and synthetic-function—the possibilities and considerations are many and diverse. But I'm not going to discuss them here because my intention is to exploit the hypothetical situation in order to examine some fundamental features of *Psychotherapy*. Though it's far from typical that a patient will begin therapy with an offer to provide us with his autobiography, I have found this situation an especially useful one to study, because it brings into focus some basic questions about the process definition of *Psychotherapy* and the role definition of the psychotherapist.

The Autobiography Paradigm is part of the Basic Instruction Paradigms, which are presented and examined in chapter 3. My reason for devoting a separate chapter to it—and examining it at great length and detail, with substantial commentary and digressions—is that it has some far-reaching and instructive implications. For one thing, the paradigm provides a good introduction to my central thesis that psychotherapy is potentially an altogether unique event and, as therapists, we can define ourselves as unique professionals. For another, it concretely exemplifies the way psychotherapy can be relatively unstructured without being concomitantly ambiguous, and a therapist can remain nondirective and neutral and nevertheless function actively, clearly, and effectively.

Before turning to the technical issues, I want to mention one reason you can't rule out accepting and reading the patient's autobiography: you have no way of knowing whether the result will be his deciding to forego therapy with you. And you can't maintain that if it did have such a result, then it was worth it because he was therefore unsuited for *Psychotherapy*. Since the method's reliance on the verbal medium must not be construed as imposing a constraint of this kind, you may not contend that reading the autobiography outside the session (or even within it, for that matter) is so dissonant with the spirit of the method that it must never be done. I don't mean to dispute that it is dissonant, because I do believe it's likely to be better for the *therapeutic process*, all things considered, if you didn't have to read it. But the dissonance is not so serious as to rule it out altogether, no matter what the ramifications may be. At any rate, since nondirectiveness is a vital priority of *Psychotherapy*, if it comes to a choice between your reading the patient's autobiography and your giving him a directive, the choice is clearcut. It boils down, as so many technical matters in psychotherapy do, to a consideration of relative priorities.

My approach would be the following. Though the *therapeutic process* stands a better chance if I don't read the autobiography, I may have to read it in order for the process to stand any chance at all. Therefore, I need to find out how necessary it is, or in what way it may be necessary, and for that reason I'll have to learn more about the patient's attitude—how he conceives of its function, how strong his need to have me read it is, and what the ramifications of my rejecting it will be (and also, to be sure, of my accepting it). Moreover, since I want to learn these things without influencing or prejudicing the matter for him, it is necessary (at least for now) that I keep him from knowing my reticence. But I cannnot remain silent on the matter; this early in therapy such a silence would imply that it raised no special problem. If I were to say nothing about the autobiography for the rest of the session, the patient could surmise that I was fully prepared to accept and read it, which could cause him to complete it; and he would have good reason for being resentful at having done that when I knew all along I didn't intend to read it. As a consequence of these considerations, my short-range goal is to pursue the topic in a way that keeps my options open—and his too—and at the same time clarifies the issues involved in it. Most vitally, the way has to be fully consonant with the terms and spirit of *Psychotherapy*'s basic format and orientation.

The Interviewing Mode

Consider the simplest and most natural way to get the patient to speak about his reasons for writing the autobiography, asking him—"Please tell me why you decided . . . " or "I'm wondering what your reasons are . . . " or "How come?" That straightforward act is, of course, a directive; no matter how I word it, what my inflection is, I am directing him to tell me his reasons. To be sure, the act may define me as someone who wants to understand his motives, but it defines me also as the one who focuses attention and determines what lines of investigation he should follow.

If you were to maintain that a why-question does little more than facilitate the patient's deliberations along lines he himself chose, that I am thereby encouraging and enabling more than directing and leading, I would contend that the possibility is quite remote because there isn't any reason to believe he would have explored his reasons without my intervention (in which case, by the way, it was quite unnecessary); instead, he might have gone ahead to speak about the way he was organizing his autobiography and how he was writing it. It seems most likely, therefore, that the why-question will be perceived as a directive act, an instruction—and that, after all, was its intent.

If you were to contend that a why-question simply defines me as someone who is interested in knowing and understanding the patient as thoroughly as possible, nothing more, I would argue that you are overlooking the fact that I selected my line of inquiry from a range of possibilities. I chose one question out of a number of possible ones. I might have chosen not to ask about his reasons for writing the autobiography but rather about one or another aspect of it: for example, was he doing it chronologically or what kinds of events was he including or was this the first time he had written one. In short, the inquiry is directed, insofar as it is focused in a way that interested me, without regard to what he was interested in. (I have an ulterior motive for putting the question, don't I?)

But most teachers and practitioners, no matter what their orientation, would regard the simple why-question as entirely appropriate and not worth giving a second thought to. Therefore, I need to digress from the paradigm in order to explicate and discuss a fundamental technical feature of *Psychotherapy*, which I can do best by drawing on Erwin Singer's scholarly treatise on traditional psychotherapy.[2]

"Whether a therapist knows it or not, through his behavior he constantly defines and redefines himself to the patient, whether by acts of commission or of omission," writes Singer. "What [he] pays attention to and what he seems less interested in, what questions he asks and what questions he does not ask, whether he asks any questions at all, are only some of the indicators which are communicated and make for the therapist's definition *in the eyes of the patient* ... Inevitably and for better or worse, *therapy starts from the earliest moments of the patient-therapist encounter.*" And Singer speaks to the uniqueness of *Psychotherapy*'s structure and function in these three ways:

> The psychotherapeutic relationship, even though still an expert-client relationship, is completely different [from the physician-patient relationship] insofar as its aim is not to ameliorate a condition for the patient but to aid him in becoming the ameliorative agent—to help him become his own healer.

> The therapist's authority derives from his ability to grasp, understand or—in terms usually employed—diagnose those inner constellations (and their historical bases) which interfere with the patient's attempts to develop a meaningful and satisfying life. Therapeutic authority is also based on the ability to engage the patient in collaborative behavior designed to remove those roadblocks to self-fulfillment and active living.

> Both patient and therapist are engaged in a collaborative search concerning the patient's genuine inner situation, the therapist being skilled in the *methods* of searching and *methods* of helping patients learn the ways of *self*-inquiry

I have chosen to quote Singer because he articulates the issue with such explicit clarity that it is possible to examine critically a basic feature of his

2. Erwin Singer, *Key Concepts in Psychotherapy* (New York: Random House, 1965). My citations from Singer's book are all drawn from pages 133–37, and the italics are added for my own purposes.

technique (his *methods*) in the light of his therapeutic aims. And I see a fundamental dissonance there, a basic technical problem (a dilemma perhaps): How can a therapist participate in the collaborative effort whose aim is to promote his patient's active self-inquiry while at the same time not be directive? Without losing sight of the fact that Singer construes *authoritative* broadly, and I prefer a narrower construction (restricting it to mean "skilled in the methods of promoting active and free self-inquiry"), I contend that any interrogation has to be a technique of last resort because it can be inimical to the fundamental goal.

Consider the following aspect of Singer's technique, which he presents in close connection with the above quotations. To illustrate his points, he offers the clinical example of a patient who sought therapy because he frequently felt the urge to masturbate. "He considered this abnormal, experienced guilt feelings about such urges and even more profound guilt and shame when he gave in to them. Recently there had been a decided increase in his masturbatory impulses and activities and he believed that this was decidedly pathological and hence was seeking the aid of a therapist to counteract what he thought were manifestations of mental illness." At this juncture, writes Singer, "The therapist, after listening to the patient's statement for a while, inquired about the man's reasons for thinking that this behavior was so pathological." Then, commenting on this "inquiry," Singer makes the following claim: "The therapist had of course neither denied nor confirmed the patient's belief, but he had defined himself as an individual who took little if anything as self-evident, as a person who deemed inquiry important and was eager to hear the foundations of the man's belief."

Putting aside for the moment the question of whether the patient was in a position to recognize that definition and whether in fact he might more readily arrive at a quite different one ("in the eyes of the patient"), Singer's way of construing the therapist's inquiry is potentially shortsighted. To claim he was not passing judgment on the patient's belief, that he merely "inquired" into it, is quite indefensible. Would he have done the same if the patient were speaking of suicidal or homicidal thoughts and impulses? Would he have asked about the man's reasons for thinking his behavior was pathological if that behavior consisted of hallucinations?

Even if his intentions were entirely neutral—and I'm being unfair to Singer because he introduces this illustration by pointing out that the therapist's response defines a great deal about his value orientation, which could include his own attitude toward the pathology of masturbation—the fact that he chose to inquire implies more than a mere interest in knowing why. Every why-question runs the risk of expressing some doubt, and in certain contexts—notably the kind that Singer's illustration typifies—chances are good it will be perceived as containing an implicit challenge. The patient's reaction, in fact, amply confirms my contention: "[He] looked up with amazement, as if he thought the therapist were insane. It never occurred to him that any person in his right mind would question what seemed to him self-evident truth; that masturbation at his time and station in life was a reflection of pathology."

At the very least, Singer's therapist confronted his patient ("Please look at your reasons"). Like most teachers, Singer believes that confrontation is consonant with the goal of promoting self-inquiry. Whether it's a valuable therapeutic mode or not—and I don't intend to argue it on those grounds until chapter five—the fact remains that a confrontation is a directive. Insofar as it directs the patient to examine and explore, and insofar as a therapist who is striving to remain nondirective cannot rely on the instrumentality of any kind of explicit directive, other means have to be used to achieve those goals.

Returning to the Autobiography Paradigm, my point is that the simple and straightforward expediency of asking the patient why he is doing it will have implications that go beyond inquiry and the intent to promote useful exploration. The patient can legitimately infer from my question that I have doubts about the autobiography's utility and appropriateness. And if he raised this issue, or simply put the counterquestion ("Why do you ask?"), for me to claim, "I asked only because I thought it might be useful to you to examine your motives and expectations," might be duplicitous. After all, if I thought the thing was altogether appropriate and was fully prepared to accept it, would I have asked why?

Do we therefore have to conduct *Psychotherapy* without ever asking a direct question? No, but we do have to try to avoid questions which are directive in a way that circumvents or undercuts a patient's free self-inquiry—those which impose a topic of deliberation by asking for facts and probing for feelings. However, we can draw a sharp distinction between such questions and those that ask for the meaning of what the patient is saying. For one thing, clarification questions are not directives to explore but, rather, directives to explain ("Tell me what you mean to be saying"); for another, they subserve our intention to understand what he is telling us (" . . . because I'm not sure I understand"). To avoid a duplicitous use of the clarification question (that is, the use of it as an indirect directive to explore), it is necessary that we truly not have understood, and/or that our patient's utterances be open to several constructions, so that when he challenges our contention that his meaning wasn't clear, we are in a position to suggest several possible meanings.

Accordingly, I can imagine saying to the patient (and it is a question despite its declarative voice), "It isn't entirely clear to me what you mean when you say *I'll give it to you next time*." If he responds, "Please tell me what is unclear," I can answer that he might be meaning for me to read it now or he could intend for me to file it away for later use. Since the latter is such a remote possibility, and can strike him as farfetched, I probably wouldn't want to choose that clarification question. And here's my main point: I have another option available to me, another way of learning what I want to know, another way of asking—I can *ask* the question in the form of an interpretation, by remarking, "I take it you'll be expecting me to read it."

To be sure, that remark is little more than a simple guess, if not a simple gratuity. But even if it turns out to be gratuitous, the patient will at least have been understood. (Of course, he's likely to respond with, "Yes, naturally! Wasn't that perfectly obvious?"—to which I could reply, "Yes, I did think that was what you had in mind, but I wasn't entirely sure," and then I would mention the remote possibility if I wanted him to know I wasn't being disingenuous.) On the other hand, if it happens not to be gratuitous but quite incorrect, he will explain and clarify with the aim of insuring that I understand him. At any rate, that will clear up one of the ambiguities, but a second remains: Does he expect me to read it privately? Again, the easiest way to gain clarity is with a remark that has the structure of an articulative interpretation (or call it a mundane guess): "I take it you'll be expecting me to read it privately" or alternatively, " . . . during the session next time."

But I can imagine your groan of impatience at what appears to be a trivial quibble. Will the patient appreciate the subtle distinction between "Why are you planning to give me your autobiography?" and "Are you expecting me to read it privately?" From his vantage point, do they differ in directiveness? Isn't the "interpretation" also a directive? My rejoinder is first to reiterate the conviction that every detail counts; individually it may count for quite little, but details have a cumulative effect that gradually grows significant and substantial. Small differences, in the extended time frame of psychotherapy, have a way of becoming large ones.

Next I can concede that calling those remarks "interpretations" implies a very broad definition of the term, namely, an interpretation is any attempt on our part to articulate a patient's thoughts, wishes, intentions, and feelings. This definition is little more than a loose framework, or first approximation, but nevertheless I think it's useful to count as an interpretation every remark that addresses what is on his mind—even if the remark doesn't seek to explain why it is on his mind, and even if there's no reason to believe it was obscure or disguised or preconscious. To be sure, not every interpretation serves the fundamental interests of promoting active and free self-inquiry in an equivalent way; content and form, as well as context, count substantially. My point here is that the mode defines you as someone whose intention is to understand, and it does it in a basically different way than the interviewing mode—most importantly, in a way that has the potential of becoming relatively free from significant directive properties.

At the very most, an interpretation implies the directive "Pay attention to this!" When it fully resonates with a patient's focus of attention, when it addresses only what he is addressing, that directive becomes inconsequential. But a useful interpretation can be more than a point-for-point articulation: it can raise new issues and fresh considerations, it can draw novel connections and suggest a different way to understand, it can try in various ways to deepen and broaden the scope of the patient's attention—in the several senses of the term, it *interprets*. Insofar as it departs from simply reflecting what is on his mind, and especially insofar as it offers an explanation, the directive to pay attention and take into consideration can assume significant proportions. Whether it does or doesn't assume significant proportions depends largely on its timing.

Timing is the subject of chapter four, and I won't discuss it here beyond making these two claims: (1) an interpretation of any kind can—and should—be timed in a way to keep its attention-deflecting properties at a minimum, if not at a point of relative insignificance; (2) *Psychotherapy*'s technical requirements include the provision, that when its basic format has been carefully and accurately established over time, the patient can feel substantially free to ignore an interpretation if he wants to. The same, of course, can be true of a well-timed question and probe, but to a substantially lesser degree; a question for information and a probe into feelings are more likely to deflect attention, and can never be ignored the way an interpretation can. A direct question virtually demands a response.

At the very least, an interpretation implies the question "Is this true?" In fact, to interpret in a questioning voice—for instance, "What do you think of the possibility that . . . ?"—is generally an effective technique. Nevertheless, to the degree that it resonates with a patient's self-inquiry, an interpretation doesn't entail a significant imposition or deflection of his attention, and insofar as it does ask a question, it needn't imply any directive other than "Correct me if I am wrong." The only question is "Am I understanding you correctly?" and we can make that clear. But we can do the same for questions and probes, make it clear that our only reason for asking is to understand the patient. "I am asking you to tell me why you are writing your autobiography because I want to understand you correctly" can be the message, and it seems insignificantly different from "I am guessing that your reason for writing it is to have me read it because I want to be sure I understand you correctly." Moreover, you can claim an advantage for interviewing when used that way; the query eschews speculation and thereby avoids the possibility of error.

To counter that claim, I first have to discount the risk of error (and postpone discussion of it till chapter five). Secondly, I have to weigh the advantages of speculation, particularly as they pertain to the way you define yourself. My argument then rests on the conviction that the act of speculation defines you in a distinctive and important way: it defines you less as the one who *seeks* to understand than as the one who *does* understand. Moreover, it defines you as the one who understands *sometimes* and *some* things, not who understands everything. Admittedly, the differences here can be quite subtle, but I believe they can also be quite significant. I think it's fair to claim that the interviewing mode can imply that you are steadily wondering why, that you are interested in knowing and uncovering your patient's purposes and reasons; and you thereby define yourself as someone who will seek to discover the motivational bases of his behavior and experience. The interpretive mode, in contrast, need not imply such a ubiquitous kind of interest. You define yourself as someone who wonders why sometimes, and you will seek to confirm your hunches when you believe it might be useful to share them with your patient; you won't be asking out of a special or general interest in motivation per se, only when you have an insight about his motivation—an insight that you believe may be useful (and by "useful" I mean useful for his efforts at self-examination and inquiry)—will you "ask the question." Accordingly, the question may arise, Why (or how) is it useful to promote the patient's inquiry into the autobiography? My answer: because it pertains to the format and procedure of the therapy itself.

Last, but in my estimation by no means least, is the fact that when you speculate instead of interrogate, you establish yourself as someone who doesn't put a patient in the position of having to respond, "I just don't know why."

The Autobiography Paradigm

PT-1:   After I spoke to you on the phone last week and we made the appointment for me to begin today, I sat right down and began writing my autobiography for you. I've been working on it for about an hour every evening before I go to bed, and I figure it should take another few days to complete it. So I'll give it to you next time.

Instructions: Assuming that you do not choose to greet this news with silence, how would you respond to it? Your task is to compose a continuation, a dialogue, imagining what you, the therapist, will say, what the patient would then say, and so on. Your continuation should convey your understanding of the issues as well as your way of handling them concretely. You may assume that the patient has already been given the Basic Instruction for *Psychotherapy*.

Since this exercise is preceded by a discussion of *Psychotherapy*'s basic principles, the students are already familiar with the way I advocate orienting a patient to the method's nondirective format—hence the reference to the "Basic Instruction."[3] The Basic Instruction invites the patient to speak about the things he wants to speak about ("It's up to you") and formulates your behavior and function in terms of listening and trying to understand, adding, "When I have something useful to say, I will say it."

The majority of my students construe the Autobiography Paradigm in terms of the patient's eagerness to expedite therapy.[4] Some emphasize the defensive implications of the decision, some restrict their continuations to a consideration of his expectations about the therapy and therapist, and some formulate it as a simple misunderstanding about the way therapy will proceed. However, the main point of interest here is not the way to understand the event but, rather, how to deal with it: how to begin a dialogue, and how to respond to what the patient can be imagined to say in response—namely, the matter of technique, which refers essentially to the way you actuate your intentions. And the overriding intention is really quite incidental to the autobiography itself; it is to define the therapy and yourself, both uniquely and unstructuredly, yet with clarity, sensitivity, and tact.

My discussion is organized around three example continuations, selected from my students' work, which I interrupt with commentaries and criticisms as well as references to other students' continuations. At the end of the chapter, I present and discuss two "model continuations" of my own.

Example 1

TH-1:   You believe that I will be able to understand you better if you provide me with a *written* autobiography?

PT-2:   Well, there's so much to say, and a therapy hour goes so quickly. And besides, it must be hard to keep all the dates and details straight. Don't you want it?

This *TH-1* is a typical interpretation articulating the patient's reason for writing the autobiography. In one way or another, students focus attention on

3. I discuss the Basic Instruction in the next chapter; so if you interrupt your reading at this point and peruse the first section of chapter three, which explains the way I advocate orienting a patient to *Psychotherapy*, the rest of this chapter might be more comprehensible to you.
4. I am basing my discussion on a total of 123 protocols that I have collected from students over the past six years.

his belief that it will expedite therapy, and many put the emphasis on his wish to have you know a great deal about him from the start. For example, a student puts it this way: "You are assuming that once I have all the facts about your life I will be able to proceed with therapy and help you resolve your problems." To all such *TH-1*s the patient can respond with a mere yes, though students put more words into his mouth at this point—thus avoiding the problem of how to follow up the interpretation. But if he were to respond with a simple yes, you would face the decision whether to remain silent—which could imply the directive "Tell me more"—or to complete the interpretation with, "I take it you feel an oral autobiography would not be as good." As I pointed out earlier, that remark can be construed by the patient as casting some doubt on the soundness of his reason. Moreover, if instead of a yes, he responds with, "Isn't that evident? Why do you draw attention to it?" you can readily respond, "Yes, I did think that was one of the reasons, and I thought it might be useful to focus attention on it." And if he pursues the question, asking, "Useful in what sense?—to raise doubts in my mind?" you can answer with, "No, I didn't mean to raise any doubts; I thought it would be useful because it has to do with your beliefs about how therapy is going to proceed." (That, after all, is always *useful*) This approach, however, is quite likely to put you in the position of soon having to say whether or not you regard the autobiography as "useful."

> TH-2:   If you feel it's important and will be helpful to your therapy, of course I will be glad to read it. In fact, I am interested in doing so. However, I would like to explore some other issues that may possibly be important also. How had you hoped we could use this biography in your therapy?

Before the direct question is asked, *PT-2* contains two interesting points. You could comment on one or the other of them instead of responding to the question. It doesn't necessarily follow, after all, that having a written autobiography will simplify the task of keeping all the dates and details straight, and you can say so. But the student chooses to respond to the direct question, and his rejoinder at *TH-2* fails to respond accurately. An accurate reply would address the question "Don't you want it?" literally. "Yes, I will read it" ignores the *want*. In an important way it may be nonresponsive, perhaps even evasive.

What I would do at this juncture is take the opportunity to tell the patient that my desires will play no part in therapy ("I don't intend to want anything of you, and I don't intend to tell you what to do here, beyond what I said before"), and I might repeat part or all of the Basic Instruction to round things off. Moreover, since the hallmark of therapy is authentic and accurate communication (which, I hasten to insert here, is not synonymous with divulging our thoughts and attitudes), and since my remark begs the question ("Will you take it and read it?"), I would add "I take it, however, that you want to know whether I will read it." Without this comment it is easy to imagine the patient's responding to the intervention with, "Yes, I appreciate that you won't tell me what you want and what I should do, but what I'm really asking is whether you will read the autobiography—wasn't that clear?" And it clearly was.

At any rate, the issue is now squarely joined, and you have little option but to respond directly (no differently than when the patient merely concurs with the final remark I recommended). So the question has to be faced: Yes or No? And I believe that anything other than a yes or a no is bound to be an error; any kind of "maybe" is fraught with potential pitfalls, and any sort of hedging with qualifications may introduce unnecessary complications. Consider the conditional clause that begins *TH-2*, and transform it slightly into "If it is important and will be helpful to your therapy." That's a risky kind of condition to introduce because it raises the questions, Who will make the judgment? and How? Similarly, "I would rather not, but I will if it means a lot to you" may be entirely accurate (though not as accurate as " . . . unless the therapy depends on it"), but it places the burden of responsibility on the patient to prove that it is important; it sets him a task to fail or succeed at, to demonstrate the value of an autobiography. Moreover, there may ensue a struggle of wills, or a difference of judgments, which is not only unnecessary but wholly inimical to the spirit of *Psychotherapy*.

Therefore, once he has put the question (and bearing in mind also that this is a first session with a new patient), there is potential hazard in not giving a direct answer; and the student would have completely avoided the hazard if *TH-2*'s acceptance were not hedged by the opening clause. I realize that the sense of the clause is "*Since* you feel it is important," but even so, the remark would be far better without it. Furthermore, there is no need to compound the reinforcement with, "In fact, I am interested in doing so"; "I will be glad to read it" is more than sufficient.[5] And *TH-2* should end with the acceptance. To have said yes is altogether sufficient; there is no need to direct the patient back to the question of what function the autobiography will serve. In fact, allowing him to react to the gracious acceptance, waiting to learn what hap-

5. After the second sentence of *TH-2*, the student appended this note: "Dr. Paul, I *know* you are going to take this as overly reinforcing. However, I feel it shows an interest and concern for the patient, and I feel from my own experience as a patient that it is *right*." This reflects a problem we often face teaching student therapists a form of therapy that is different from the kind of therapy they themselves experience.

pens after the warm reinforcement, could be instructive and useful. As it stands, *TH-2*'s third sentence can be construed as an attempt to undo an error (it is as if the message were "That was unfortunate though necessary, now let's get back to business!")—and the way the student gets back to business is to commit that most flagrant of technical errors, putting a directive question.

> PT-3:   Well ... You have to know all the details of my life in order to begin helping me, don't you? I thought if I got it all down on paper it'd give you a head start, and I wouldn't have to go over it all again. I mean, *I* know it, it's *you* who has to catch up.
>
> TH-3:   So you feel the autobiography can substitute for talking about your earlier experiences.
>
> PT-4:   Well, I've gone over them again and again—what's the sense of talking about them?
>
> TH-4:   I have the impression you would prefer not to talk about them.
>
> PT-5:   No, it's just a question of efficiency.
>
> TH-5:   Just efficiency?
>
> PT-6:   Well, I guess some of them are rather unpleasant ...

Consider *TH-4*, what a large leap it takes from *PT-4* where the patient questions the value of taking time to give the facts of his life when he can write them for you to read. That's a fair question, deserving a fair answer. It isn't uncommon for patients to feel they're going to be wasting valuable time when they recount events for our benefit. Of course, we can regard it as a necessary use of session time, and we may also believe that they might learn something for themselves during the recounting (that the act of reconstructing the past, for instance, can be an intrinsically useful act of exploration), but we cannot simply ignore the point the way *TH-4* ignores it, and substitute a rather tactless kind of interpretation—in fact, a confronting remark for which there isn't a shred of evidence. Since he is writing the entire script, the student could easily have provided some evidence to justify the interpretation, something most students take pains to do in their continuations.

And finally, when the patient disagrees, saying it's just a question of efficiency, to challenge his opinion with a *TH-5* like that is without a shred of merit. It says "I don't believe you" and "Come off it!" It can only put the patient in an embarrassed and defensive position. It's no way to promote useful self-inquiry. And with that slap on the wrist, I turn to a second example.

Example 2

> TH-1:   I'm wondering why you decided to write your biography for me.

> PT-2:   Well, don't you want to know all about me?
> TH-2:   I am interested in knowing what you want to tell me,
>   but I'm wondering what made you decide to write it
>   down for me.

Perhaps because this study is assigned early in the course, and my students are not yet persuaded about the disadvantages of direct questions (or maybe they're not convinced I really mean it when I proscribe them), many begin their continuations with a why-question in one or another of its forms—and *TH-1* is a gentle version. The patient's counterquestion, however, is interesting and ambiguous. It seems to have a challenging edge, amounting to a kind of "Why not!" But judging from the tenor of *TH-2*, the student probably intended *PT-2* to be read in an incredulous tone of voice. In any event, *TH-2* is nonresponsive.

The question "Do you want to know all about me?" cries out for clarification. As it stands it's plainly impossible. So you could first seek to clarify the question by inquiring into the meaning of "all about" him. The patient probably has in mind "all the *important* facts," and he may be wondering what you believe they are, or he may want to know what facts you need before you can begin to play a "useful" role. Whichever, you can answer the question only after you've understood it; and your answer can then be, "I have no way of telling in advance what I need to know before I can be useful." That statement comes down to—and you may choose to say so in these words—"No, I don't have to know certain things about you in order to be useful in therapy." And you can do your best to prove it as soon as possible.

TH-2 answers the counterquestion by slightly transforming the Basic Instruction, but I will refrain from quibbling with it here. I will, however, quibble with the fact that *TH-2* goes on to repeat *TH-1*'s why-question, even though *PT-2* already contained a clearly implicit answer to it. (The emphasis in *TH-2* seems to be the writing down of it, but this goes by the board.) The patient now obliges by repeating his original answer, adding one element which has a double meaning, and then puts the direct question (as he did in example 1).

> PT-3:   Well, so you would have all the information; so you
>   would have a better picture of me, and understand me
>   better. Don't you want it?
> TH-3:   I want it if you want to give it to me. But I'd like to
>   share with you a thought I have: you seem to be work-
>   ing hard on this biography, and one possible reason
>   may be that you want to please me, and give me not
>   only a better picture of you but also have me think bet-
>   ter of you.

This way of saying yes is interesting; you seem to be saying, "I want it *because* you want to give it to me, not for its usefulness." On the other hand, judging from what comes afterward, a more plausible interpretation of the remark is "I'll take it if you still want to give it to me after I've exposed your true motive for wanting me to have it"—because what follows can only be understood as a flagrant piece of dissuasion.

The interpretation the student gives in *TH-3* is an excellent exemplification of an important misusage of the interpretive mode. It epitomizes poor timing, insofar as its function is not to contribute to any self-inquiry that the patient might be engaged in. Even if it were entirely valid, it is entirely unwarranted because it seeks to explain to the patient something he isn't interested in having explained. Consequently, it amounts to a confrontation, and even as such is badly timed. I could give other examples of this kind of misuse of interpretations (Example 3 contains a flagrant one), but suffice it to repeat that a well-timed interpretation resonates. Even tact, which is necessary, is insufficient. (Consider this tactful but untimely example: "I appreciate your wanting to tell me about your life, but I wonder if preparing an autobiography in advance is your way of trying to stay in control of what happens here.")

My third example is drawn from those continuations in which the autobiography is rejected. This one is a bit more argumentative than most, but it points up some of the typical problems incurred when you take an *a priori* stand within the context of the Basic Instruction. Before examining it, I want to emphasize the pivotal role of *TH-1*, your initial response to the patient's announcement.

TH-1 can be an especially important remark; it sets the tone of the exchange, defines your approach to the patient and the problems he will bring to therapy, and specifies what you meant by "useful." Some students begin with a gratuitous remark that apparently serves little more than the purpose of buying some time (and hopefully some further information too). I count as gratuitous such *TH-1*s as, "You've been spending a lot of time on it," "It sounds like a lot of work," and "You felt a need to write it." They do contain a point of emphasis and focus on some aspect of the patient's experience and behavior, but unless they are quickly followed up with an interpretation, they run the risk of diluting and weakening the effectiveness of your participation in the therapeutic process. ("So what else is new?" is a likely response, and you don't want to define yourself as one who speaks the obvious.)

A reiteration of the Basic Instruction can also serve a wait-and-see function, and that's why some students choose to begin with it. I generally take the opportunity to point out that "when in doubt repeat the Basic Instruction" is not a good rule of thumb. Though it's the appropriate way to deal with a good many issues that arise in therapy, what must not be lost sight of is the context in which the reiteration occurs, because that context can give it an altogether different meaning. In the context of this paradigm, to respond with the Basic Instruction simply conveys the message "No, I will not accept and read your biography," and it's better to say that directly, if that's what you intend, and not use the instruction for the purpose. To repeat it after the demurer has been expressed is all right (a student does it by prefacing *TH-1*'s reiteration with, "I don't believe it would be in the best interests of therapy for me to read what you have written," which is a tactful way of saying no), but to use the Basic Instruction as a shield is not.

Now consider how the therapist in Example 3 uses the Basic Instruction to say no so clearly and so forthrightly. That usage is quite different and has considerable merit. This *TH-1* defines you as someone who means what you say. Notice also the way you focus the attention on yourself, on the way you will work in therapy. (That, as I will soon argue, is the best way to approach the problem.) A comparison of *PT-3* and *TH-3* highlights how the patient focuses on the usefulness to himself of the autobiography, and how the therapist refrains from challenging it but instead focuses on its disutility to himself.

Example 3

TH-1:   When I said you can tell me what you want to, and I would listen and try to understand, I really meant it quite literally.

PT-2:   You mean you don't want the autobiography?

TH-2:   I mean that reading something you have written is not the way I think I can be most useful.

PT-3:   But I'll be much better able to give you all the important information about myself if I write it all out systematically.

TH-3:   I feel that I will understand best if you *talk* about what you want to.

TH-3 is too argumentative, and also fails to acknowledge the important point that *PT-3* contains. At the very least, you should preface such a rejoinder with "I understand that an autobiography can be a good way to give me all the important information about yourself," because otherwise the patient may feel misunderstood (if not unlistened-to). And you can then make it clear that, while it may subserve his wish to be systematic, an autobiography won't subserve your need to understand. Furthermore, since it's far from evident why an oral biography would serve your interests better than a written one, the patient deserves an explanation. In fact, *PT-4* seems to be a request for such an explanation; the patient persists in his belief that it will be efficient for him, and he seems to be missing your main point: for you it won't be so efficient.

> PT-4:   But won't it be much better if I write things down? I mean, this way I won't forget things or block.
>
> TH-4:   Perhaps talking about what you want to is something you don't feel entirely comfortable with.

At the height of the argument, the student falls back on the interpretive mode—exactly the wrong time for it! Any interpretation at *TH-4*, unless it seeks to articulate what the patient is meaning to convey, or unless it says something about the argument itself, is bound to be bad. To try and win an argument by making a diagnostic inference is the epitome of parlor analysis, defining you as the confronting one, if not also the one who takes unfair advantage. (This patient will not feel free to level a challenge or engage in argument.)

Many students begin their continuations with an interpretation, though few are as speculative as *TH-4*. Most deal only with the patient's belief about expediting therapy, but some address the defensive implications (ranging from the mild, "You find it easier to write rather than to tell," to the strong, "You want to avoid talking about certain things"). Such confronting interpretations run the risk of being perceived by the patient as a criticism. No matter how accurate or valid, they convey an undertone of evaluation, perhaps as a result of their speculativeness. "Why such a speculation?" he may wonder, "What does it say about my decision to write the autobiography?"

To justify making any kind of interpretation, the common procedure is first to put suitable words into the patient's mouth—easy enough to do in a study like this, and students who don't begin with an interpretation get around to proferring one after they have had the patient furnish some evidence for it. The technical problem remains, however, how to begin the dialogue. Can *TH-1* be an interpretation which isn't overly speculative and confronting—which doesn't impose an extraneous issue on the patient, doesn't direct him or constrain his freedom of exploration, doesn't valuate or judge him, and, at the same time, affords him the opportunity to explore the issue in a meaningful and potentially useful way? I believe it can.

Two interpretations for *TH-1* sufficiently satisfy the requirements I enumerated: one focuses on the implications of the autobiography for the therapy, the other on its implications for the therapist. The first addresses the question What does it mean with respect to the patient's attitudes, intentions, and expectations vis-à-vis therapy? The second, What does it mean in respect to his intentions and expectations vis-à-vis you? In my opinion, the second line of interpretation is bound to be significantly better than the first.

In order to initiate an exploration of what the autobiography means to him with respect to his attitude toward therapy, you can use this *TH-1*: "I gather you're doing it so you won't have to review your life history here." Perhaps it's too gratuitous, but the remark focuses on an evident function of his decision, and it can readily lead into a consideration of its motivational basis as well as its defensive implications. Whether the remark is sufficiently neutral, whether you've conveyed the message that it isn't a good or appropriate thing to do in this therapy, is a moot point. Still, if he were to respond, "Yes, that's the main idea. Are you implying that it's a mistake to write it out instead of reviewing it here? you could honestly say, "No, I didn't intend to convey that message." If he counters with, "So what message did you intend to convey if not that one?" you can reply, "I asked because I wasn't sure whether you intended it to take the place of reviewing your life history here, that I would read your autobiography on my own time so that you could use your time here to speak of other things." But notice that, not only has this led away from the potential defensive implications, you may as well have begun with the more straightforward remark, "And I take it you will be expecting me to read it," which is the second option for a *TH-1*—and, I believe, a better one.

Before I examine that option, however, I'll continue with the first one. Suppose the patient responds by emphasizing the efficiency of his plan, putting it this way at *PT-2:* "Exactly, it will save us a lot of time. No point wasting time going over all the facts here. And you're going to need to know my life history, isn't that so?" When you make no response to this query, he continues by saying, "I think this way will be the most efficient." What now are your choices? How do you pursue the issue without injecting any evaluation or direction, without committing yourself to the position that the decision is not an appropriate one and you're reticent to accept the autobiography and read it on your own time? The chief danger here is to scold him for wanting to avoid reviewing his life-history during the sessions. If you said something like the following, then it would unavoidably constitute a reprimand: "You regard it as a waste of time to review your life-history during the sessions; I take it, therefore, you don't expect to learn anything new and important while you are doing it." It's virtually impossible to offer that kind of interpretation without implying valuation, and that remains true even if you try to emphasize the defensive function, and even if you formulate it more tactfully.

Remember, this is a first session with a new patient. To claim you intended only to expose a defense and if it implied a piece of direction or evaluation then it was well worth it, is quite facile. And equally facile would be the claim that all you're achieving is a clarification of the Basic Instruction. The integrity of *Psychotherapy* requires you to avoid giving directions as much as you can, to avoid enlarging the Basic Instruction so as to include pre- and pro-scriptions, to keep from advising your patient how to behave in therapy. Now, to be sure, it may soon turn out that you have no choice but to do some or all of that; you might have to inform him what the limits of the Basic Instruction are. But at this juncture there is no reason to believe you have to; this early in therapy you still have other options.

Suppose the patient ponders the observation, says he hadn't thought of it, but agrees, "I guess that's what I believe," and then adds, "I take it from the tone of your remark that you do not agree." Since he is asking whether you implied that his presumption was misguided, you have little choice but to make it clear you didn't mean to be disagreeing in any important sense. You might put it this way: "No, I don't mean to be disagreeing with you, though I can see why you'd think so. What I'm trying to do is understand your thoughts and feelings." And you could show what you mean by *understand* by continu-ing, "You see, I wonder whether you're presuming that the way we're going to work here is that you will give me the facts and then I will give you the interpretations; you inform me about yourself, and I make therapeutic expla-nations."

That's a speculation whose main function is to tell the patient what is on your mind, how you "understand." To be sure, he's given you no evidence for it, but he needn't feel cornered if it turns out to be wrong; he can readily say, "No, I thought nothing of the kind." But even if it turns out to be an accurate guess, it isn't hard to imagine his reacting with some embarrassment and resentment—"When you put it that way, it sounds kind of childish and mechanical; it's true, I guess, but you make it so cut and dried." And sup-pose, before falling into a silence, he adds, "I feel a bit mixed up, and I kind of resent what you said." Now you're going to have to articulate his feelings, which, after all, you were quite directly responsible for, and it will be useful to offer him the interpretation, "I think you feel I've scolded you, that I said you have no right to make those assumptions and expect therapy to work that way."

But where do things now stand? Notice how they've drifted away from the autobiography issue itself. While some useful work has been done, perhaps, the question of the autobiography's fate remains unanswered. That's another reason why I regard this line of interpretation as inferior to the second one, which begins the dialogue with a remark focusing attention on the implica-tions of the written biography for you. However, the main reason I judge that option superior is because you want to avoid having to offer an interpretation prematurely and without sufficient evidence that can be shared with the patient. It seems likely that when you embark on a course that focuses atten-tion on his motives and expectations, you will soon find it necessary to "use" an interpretation—and it will run the risk of being perceived by him as against the autobiography.

Here, then, are two model continuations with the second *TH-1*. Since I composed them for didactic purposes, I deliberately contrive some extraneous issues and complications which introduce further aspects of technique.

Model 1

TH-1:   And I take it you'll be expecting me to read it privately, not during the session.

PT-2:   Naturally! That's why I'm writing it.

If the patient says nothing further at this point, I would continue with, "And you believe my reading it will help the therapy." If he again answers in the affirmative without amplifying on his belief, I will have to continue my articulation of the issue. Since I don't want to direct him to do it (and "I take it you're reticent to speak about your belief that my reading it will help the therapy," even if entirely correct, might amount to little more than a directive encouragement for him to overcome that reticence), and since there is no good way to shift the burden of responsibility back on his shoulders, my only good recourse is to accept the burden myself. I would therefore continue by articulating some of his likely motives and expectations, saying, "I can understand how you regard it as a helpful thing, to have me read your autobiography; it will save time for you and make it unnecessary for you to review your life history here," and I would make sure to add "That could be efficient from your point of view." The reason I want to add that remark is because my main intention is to continue with, "But you are also supposing that it will be equally efficient from my point of view," a remark aimed at bringing the focus of attention back to my role.

I'd be creating the opportunity to convey the idea that the autobiography may not be efficient for me; that's the basis on which I want to cast doubt on its advisability. Rather than take the position that it isn't the optimal way to do *Psychotherapy*, I want the opportunity to explain that it isn't the optimal way for me to proceed—a distinction based on the fact that I know for sure it will not be optimal for me, but I don't know yet whether it won't be the best way for him. If it turned out he believes the latter, then I would be willing to countenance the former; in other words, I will accept the task if he maintains the conviction that for him it may be the optimal way to proceed in therapy.

PT-2 (continued):   It will give you all the important facts about me. And that will save a lot of time; I won't have to take up our time just reviewing my life history. I'm a very efficient person, you know. No point wasting time when there's a more efficient way to do it.

TH-2:   I can see how you would regard it as efficient for you—that it would save you time here. But you're also supposing, aren't you, that it will be equally efficient for me?[6]

PT-3:   For you?—sure. Why won't it be?

TH-3:   Well, for one thing, I'll have to study it in order to remember the things you write.

PT-4:   Sure, but the same is true if I tell you all the facts here, isn't it?

TH-4:   No, I'm not sure it is. For me to remember the things I've read in your autobiography will probably be harder than to remember what you tell me here. And I can ask you questions as we go along about whatever I don't understand. That's what I meant when I said it might not be so efficient for me.

PT-5:   That didn't occur to me. [pause]

Where do we stand? I have raised the question of the autobiography's value from my vantage point and thereby cast doubt on its usefulness; I haven't, however, committed myself on whether or not I will accept it. The patient is probably reconsidering the advisability of it, and I don't want to interrupt the silence to influence the course of his deliberations. (He has to learn that he is free to deliberate in silence if that's what he wants to do.) If, after the pause, he says he wants me to read it, despite my having cast doubt on its value—and if he puts it forthrightly, saying something like, "Look, I appreciate that it may not be so efficient for you, but I really want to finish it and have you read it anyway"—I will say, "Yes, I will," and nothing further right now. However, if he is tentative and conveys a sense of doubt, if he shows concern over seeming to incur my displeasure, or if some other issue of this kind now comes up, then I'll forestall my decision and comment on these developments. If his response is simply, "Okay, I see your point, and I understand how it might not be such a good idea; so I'm going to drop it," I won't respond in a way that might influence that decision. But if his response is simple indecision—for instance, "Look, I don't really feel strongly about the thing one way or the other, and I want you to say whether you think it's a worthwhile idea or not"—I will respond with, "I believe that for me to read it is not likely to be very helpful."

6. Ordinarily I wouldn't interrupt the patient's monologue. But because of the nature of the topic, and because my intention is something more than to understand it, I take (or make) the opportunity to direct his attention back to the autobiography in order to continue with the point I originally had in mind to make. To be sure, I am being directive, but in a sense I'm doing little more than completing my interpretation.

But my model continues on the assumption that he breaks his silence with a recounting of the events that led up to the decision:

PT-5 (continued):   I was a bit surprised when you said I could start therapy this week. It wasn't an easy thing for me to decide to go into therapy. Last year, when I was having a rough time in school and at home too, I thought about it. But I figured it was too expensive, and I could work things out for myself. [pause] And things did get better during the summer when I was working. And I thought all I had to do was make myself a schedule, plan my life better, so that I wouldn't fall behind in my school work like I did. [pause] I did make a schedule and every-thing, but it didn't work out. And before I knew it I was in the same mess again. [pause] And then my mother got sick, and things at home got impossible. And my friend Henry went into therapy. [pause]. I wanted to go into therapy with his therapist, but he said that was not ad-visable, and he gave Henry your number to give me. But he said it would probably not be possible for me to see you right away, and when you said I could start today I was a bit surprised. [pause] But it's what I wanted, because things have been really rough, and . . . [pause]

TH-5:   And you felt under a lot of pressure?

PT-6:   Exactly, I sure did! And getting help is really important to me now. So I don't want to mess it up, like I mess up everything else.

TH-6:   So you felt excited and hopeful when I told you you could begin this week. And that's when you made your decision to write an autobiography?

The main function of *TH-6* is to bring him back to the topic of the autobiog-raphy, to prevent the topic from slipping away and remaining unresolved. I have a special reason for resorting to a confrontation: I don't want him to leave the session with a sense of ambiguity about the autobiography, and perhaps with the conviction that I advised him against writing it.

PT-7:   Well, I guess I was sort of excited, though . . . But I realized that it was important and I should do this right. That's when I realized that you didn't know anything about me, and that I would have to give you all the facts. And that would waste a lot of valuable time. [pause] So I got the idea of writing my autobiography for you.

TH-7: I understand. But it's not entirely clear to me what you mean by waste, when you say it would waste a lot of valuable time.

PT-8: [pause] Well, Henry told me his therapist said he wouldn't be able to tell him anything until he knew a lot about him. And that makes a lot of sense to me. [pause]

TH-8: I see. You're eager for me to tell you things as soon as possible. And you have reason to believe that once all the facts are in, and not before then, I am going to start saying useful things to you.

PT-9: Henry's shrink hasn't said two words to him yet, and he's been seeing him for two months. [pause] Anyhow, what can you tell me before you know a lot about me?

That's an important question, perhaps a loaded one, and perhaps there's a challenging edge to it. But in the context of this dialogue, it is pointless to acknowledge anything more than the fair question, "What sorts of things are you going to be telling me?" And because to a significant extent I have imposed the issue, for me not to answer the question would be quite unfair. What I choose to answer is based on several goals, one of which is to show him the sorts of remarks I'll be making, how I construe "useful." Therefore, I will offer an interpretation, and it's necessarily going to be speculative. (Notice, however, that there's already some evidence for it in what the patient has said.)

TH-9: Well, I can suggest to you that you probably have mixed feelings about the matter: a part of you is sort of excited by the prospect and the anticipation of what I will say, but another part of you dreads it. What do you think of the possibility that the prospect of my one day giving you a full explanation and analysis of yourself also frightens you? So maybe you decided to give me all the facts right away to get the ordeal over with as quickly as possible.

PT-10: [pause] I guess that's pretty much ... pretty much correct, I guess. So ... [pause].

TH-10: So I guess you're wondering whether you should finish it and give it to me.

PT-11: Yes. I gather from your remarks that you don't think it's such a hot idea.

TH-11: Yes, I do think it might not be the best way to proceed here. At least from my point of view, it might be better if you told me the things you want to tell me.

PT-12:   So you're saying I shouldn't.

TH-12:   No, I'm going to try never to tell you what you should or shouldn't do. I can appreciate that now, when I've told you that it won't be so efficient for me to read it, and when I've also suggested that one of your reasons for doing it is to get the ordeal over with as quickly as possible, it makes it harder for you to decide to go ahead with it. But I'd prefer to leave the decision entirely up to you.

And that's the end of my first continuation. The second model is predicated on the patient's reacting with more feeling to my *TH-1*.

Model 2

TH-1:   And I take it you'll be expecting me to read it privately, not during the session.

PT-2:   Well, you can read it ... you can read it whenever you like. [pause] You know, I didn't think of that—that you would have to read it on your own time. [sheepish smile, slight flush, and pause]

If *PT-2* continued, "But that isn't asking such a helluva lot, is it?" my *TH-2* would be "That depends on how long it is; and there's another consideration: I'll have to study it in order to remember everything you've written." If he went on to ask, "Isn't that part of your job? Wouldn't you be doing that anyway?" I would respond with, "Sure, but it might be easier for me to remember the things you tell me here than it is for me to remember the things I read about you; and I can ask you questions about things I don't understand as we go along."

TH-2:   You're feeling embarrassed, aren't you?—because you didn't realize I'd have to read it on my own time.

PT-3:   Yes, and that's something I do all the time—I fail to take the other person into account. I'm always imposing on people. [pause] I should've phoned you back and asked you whether you wanted me to do it.

This is too good an opportunity to let slip past. I think it's technically correct to respond as if he had actually asked the question.

TH-3:   I can tell you what I would have answered: I would have said—because I intend never to tell you what to do and what not to do—that it's up to you.

PT-4:   So I would have gained nothing by asking? Then ... [puzzled look]

TH-4: Then what am I making a fuss about?

PT-5: Exactly! I thought you were implying that I should have asked whether it'd be imposing on you to give you my biography.

TH-5: That's not what I meant to imply.

If he had said, "That's what I thought you said," I wouldn't counter with, "No, I didn't say that." This kind of exchange occurs quite often in therapy, where a patient misstates something you said, and it is tactless to simply deny it. The form I prefer (and it is further exemplified in *TH-6*) has the advantage of avoiding a possible argument. It's quite sufficient to say, "I did not mean [intend] to say [imply] that," and it's usually helpful to preface it with "I can understand why you would think I had said [implied] it."

PT-6: But I . . . but you said that if I had asked you, you would have answered that I should do it if I wanted to. And just before you said I should have asked you. [pause] No, I guess you didn't say that in so many words. But you implied that I should have, didn't you?

TH-6: I can see why you think so, but I didn't mean to. In fact, I mean the opposite. What I'm saying—and it's something I need to make clear to you because you had no way to know it before you came here—is that I'm going to try never to tell you what to do. That's what I meant when I said that it was up to you.

PT-7: You mean . . . [pause] Look, I know you said I should talk about whatever I wanted to talk about. And that I sure didn't expect.[pause] It doesn't make much sense to me, either. I can't see what good it's going to be if I just talk and talk. There must be certain things I should talk about.

The patient has raised a vital topic and asked a crucial question. He is asking me—challenging me—about the extent to which I intend to remain neutral and nondirective: Does it extend all the way to what he talks about during the sessions? I discuss this question at some length in chapter three, and the first two Basic Instruction Paradigms deal with it directly. I could deal with it directly now, in the context of *PT-7*, and perhaps I should. At any rate, there are several different options for a *TH-7*, and the one I choose has the disadvantage of bypassing the important issue, but it has the advantage of redirecting him back to the autobiography. Again, my rationale is that I have imposed the topic of its usefulness, and I want to make sure the matter is resolved before the end of this session. Bear in mind, however, that after the issue is resolved, I can, if there is time, return to this issue by reminding the patient of that statement—"Let me ask you something about what you said before ..." Asking about meaning needn't be done right away; it can wait.

TH-7:   I take it you have in mind the things you've been writing in your autobiography.

PT-8:   Sure! I figured you needed to know all about my past, and everything. So I figured if I wrote it all out for you, you could read it, and then you could tell me what things I should talk about. Otherwise I'd just wander aimlessly all over the place—which I've been doing all my life, you know, and it hasn't got me anywhere. Come to think of it, that's not true; it's got me exactly here! [pause] I really need help, and ... [pause]

TH-8:   And you feel a need for me to tell you what you should do.

PT-9:   Yes, exactly! [pause]

TH-9:   I gather the main reason you decided to give me your autobiography is so I should be in a better position to guide you, at least during the sessions.

PT-10:   [pause] And you're not going to do that, eh? [pause]

TH-10:   And you feel I can't be of use to you if I don't tell you what to talk about, if I just allow you to talk about whatever you want to talk about.

PT-11:   Well, it could make sense for some people, I guess— but not for me. Look, I've been doing my own thing all my life. My parents are these big liberals, and everything, and they believe a kid should ... Oh, you know what I mean. And look what a mess I've made of everything! They should've given me more guidance is what I think. And that's why I'm such a selfish person, and inconsiderate, and everything. I never take the other person into account—like, I didn't even think about the fact that you would have to read my biography on your own time. That's typical of me. And I know it, and I should ... I mean, I want to change it. But ... [pause]

TH-11:   But you feel I'm going to have to be active in helping you to change it. And I seem to be taking the same position your parents have always taken—leaving things up to you.

PT-12:   Yes, and that's pretty damned ironic, isn't it? [pause] Look, let me get straight on something. You are saying that everything's going to be up to me here. That means I can ... I can do what I want, right?

> TH-12: [pause] I gather you're wondering if what I said before, when I pointed out that I'd have to read the autobiography on my own time, meant that you aren't free to give it to me.

Notice how my interpretations—or call them articulations—serve the function of focusing attention on the issue at hand, how I am steering the conversation. You may contend, of course, that I am being directive, and in a sense I am. But I prefer to construe this kind of activity as "supervising" the *therapeutic process*, and claim a basic distinction between that and "directing." Certainly, I have to be careful to keep from overusing interpretations in this way, because there is also a distinction between "supervising" the *therapeutic process* and "facilitating" it, and if I am too active a participant it will incur certain weaknesses.

> PT-13: Sure, I figured you were saying that I shouldn't give it to you. But look here, if it's up to me—if things are really up to me—then it follows that ... that if I really want you to read the damn thing ... [pause]
>
> TH-13: Then I will, yes—because I'd prefer to leave that up to you, too.
>
> PT-14: I see. That's interesting. I'm free to impose on you and be inconsiderate. [pause and impish grin] And how about if I really want you to tell me what I should talk about here?
>
> TH-14: [pause] I could do that too.

I paused to make sure I had to respond. In addition, the pause gives me the chance to choose my words carefully, and it also conveys to the patient the care with which I chose them. The sense of my statement is that I would if he wanted me to, if he believed it was necessary for him. Bear in mind that I've already made it amply clear that I preferred not to, that I believed he might benefit more from therapy if he did the choosing. So what I'm doing is defining myself as someone who is rigorous but not rigid, someone who doesn't back him into a corner, who can be "manipulated," and who maximizes his freedom. There will be ample opportunity in the ensuing sessions to establish the limits of my position and the boundaries of my willingness to accede to his requests, and at this early juncture I want to minimize the risk of an impasse.

Now, it seems quite likely that the patient is testing me—his impish grin is a significant signal. I might therefore articulate with, "I take it you're testing me, perhaps teasing me, to see how far I'm willing to go in allowing you to call the shots here." Incidentally, this remark is a rather diagnostic kind of interpretation whose form is evaluative and nonempathic, clearly made from an outside vantage point. I discuss this important technical issue at several places in this book, especially in chapter five, and emphasize how it tends to cast a patient into a passive position and defines you as a keen observer and troubleshooter. So if I did regard it as timely to address the patient's provocativeness, I'd formulate an interpretation this way: "I think you're meaning to keep me from taking your question seriously; part of you wants me to dismiss it as just teasing." It seems to me such a formulation is less evaluative and more empathic, less likely to be counterprovocative—and it's tactful. But I deliberately make no reference to the testing because the issue at hand is more salient. My intention, after all, is to define the therapy and myself as clearly and unambiguously as I can. Moreover, I see little merit in "using" an interpretation, no matter how valid, which might be perceived by him as serving the function of getting me off the hook, so to speak.

Consequently, I choose to address the patient's question directly, responding to its serious component, bypassing for the moment its provocative component. And it is, after all, a very important question he's asking, because he's in the process of making a commitment to an undertaking that can have profound implications for his well-being.

> PT-15: That's even more interesting! You're willing to leave all decisions to me, even the decision not to make my own decisions. [pause and smile] This is quite weird! I must ask my Logic Professor about this. [pause] But it adds up to my having to decide what I really want, doesn't it? And that's not going to be easy, I assure you, because it happens to be exactly the kind of problem that's been messing up my life. [pause] Maybe I should tell you . . . I mean [sheepish grin] maybe I *want* to tell you something about it.

And it seems to me, that whatever decision the patient eventually makes about the autobiography, he is well started into *Psychotherapy*. Have I contrived too pat a correspondence between the nature of his presenting problem and the nature of *Psychotherapy* itself? Perhaps, but I believe it isn't overly farfetched because I construe ego-autonomy as the central theoretical concept as well as the principal clinical rationale.

3

The Basic Instruction
Paradigms

How to minimize ambiguity and maximize unstructured-ness is the key problem we face at the outset of *Psychotherapy*. Insofar as instructions are necessarily directives, they are bound to be dissonant with a nondirective therapy. But is there any sensible and feasible alternative? Can a patient be given an adequate orientation to *Psychotherapy* that doesn't imply a set of directives?

Suppose he begins with a request for orientation, asking "What is the procedure here?" If we wanted to avoid any instructions and setting of rules, we could follow Hellmuth Kaiser's recommendation and answer, "There is no procedure here," thereby maintaining a thoroughgoing nondirective position.[1] But can we expect the patient to be satisfied with such an answer? Surely he'll ask us to explain what "There is no procedure" means; or he may be puzzled, if not justifiably incredulous, at the implication that there could indeed be no procedure. And even when we want him to discover the procedure by himself and to shape it himself to a significant extent—so we've answered "It's largely up to you"—we have to be ready to give some orientation. Therefore, whether or not we deem it appropriate to spell things out completely at the very outset, we have to be utterly clear about both the essential nature and the boundary limits of our format and procedure. These matters have to be carefully considered and thought through in advance.

---

1. Kaiser advocates no instructions whatever, and recommends this reply, for a form of psychoanalysis he called *Effective Psychotherapy*.

In order for me to do that in this chapter with a minimum of digression, restricting myself to the most fundamental issues and their main technical implications, I'm going to require a set of limiting assumptions. The principal assumption is that *Psychotherapy*, as such, can begin right away. Accordingly, I need to assume that the patient wants a traditional therapy and believes it can be of benefit to him, that he has been referred to us by a qualified consultant who assessed his condition and suitability, and that we have good reason to believe we can verify that assessment without having to conduct a diagnostic interview of our own—by observing the patient's behavior during the initial sessions. In short, we have ample basis to believe that *Psychotherapy* can be inaugurated during the patient's initial session.[2] The chief task we face, then, is how to orient him—how best to answer the question, whether asked or not, "What's the procedure here?"

Instead of inviting perplexity with "There is no procedure," and instead of resorting to "It's up to you" (the hallmark of nondirectiveness), we can offer an explanation of *Psychotherapy*'s fundamental principles and give the patient a description of its basic procedure. I see nothing essentially problematic in doing that. But before we choose that course, we have to take into account the possibility that this isn't the best time for such a discussion because he isn't in the best condition to participate in it, much less benefit from it. He might, after all, be apprehensive about therapy; he might be excited, he might be feeling relief upon beginning, he might be anxious about it, he might have doubts and misgivings and need to disavow them. It seems clear to me that the measure of his conflicting feelings about starting therapy is the degree to which a didactic discussion is untimely. Insofar as we have no prior assessment of those feelings, our most prudent assumption is that he isn't in a good position to apprehend *Psychotherapy*'s conceptions and procedures nor to judge whether the method will be suitable and efficacious for him. I don't mean that a patient hasn't the full right to know exactly what kind of therapy he's getting into; my point is that a formal presentation might be inadequate, if not inappropriate, and the optimal way to discover what the therapy entails is to experience it, to have a trial period.

For those reasons, and under the average-expectable circumstances for the average-expectable patient, I believe that a nondidactic and rather informal

---

2. On pages 160–207 of *Letters to Simon*, I discuss in detail the ways *Psychotherapy* can begin. A variety of possibilities are described, individual differences and average-expectable issues are discussed, and requirements in respect to diagnostic considerations, as well as schedule and fee, are spelled out. My intention there is to show how the therapy can be initiated in a consistent, effective, and responsible way. Even though my presentation lacks the rigor I would now want it to have, it would be too redundant and digressive to take up again the range of practical and clinical issues which are discussed there.

orientation is our best option. We can offer a simple and succinct formulation, a formulation which notifies more than instructs, conveys the essence of *Psychotherapy*'s format and provides a patient with the widest, most feasible latitude to begin the way he wants and deems appropriate. I call it an instruction, the "Basic Instruction," to avoid implying that it is entirely free of directive properties. In my opinion, however, it is sufficiently nondirective, and in my experience it provides an adequate preliminary orientation for *Psychotherapy*. Here's the way I word it: "You can talk about the things you want to talk about. It's up to you. I will listen and try to understand. When I have something useful to say I will say it."[3]

The Basic Instruction

The Basic Instruction informs the patient that he's free to speak his mind as openly and self-directedly as he wants. Notice how its wording keeps to a minimum the element of directiveness, how he's been notified more than instructed or taught. He hasn't been asked to say what's on his mind, nor requested to share his thoughts or express his feelings, and there was no suggestion to tell about himself. He can do any, all, or none of these things—if he chooses to ("It's up to you"). Neither does it say "I want you to ..." or "You should ..."—rather, "You can ...," which means "If you want to."

I don't mean to suggest we have to speak the lines of the Basic Instruction verbatim; to substitute "You may" for "You can," or to begin with "You can tell me the things you want to tell me," won't make a significant difference. Whenever I offer a script in these pages I mean only to exemplify concretely, nothing more. No message, after all, is fully conveyed by words alone; nonverbal signals, such as inflection, tone of voice, facial and bodily gesture, contribute substantially to meaning—and so does context. What counts above all else is the message itself, that it be fully and precisely communicated with as few unintended implications and unwanted connotations as possible. And the Basic Instruction's core message is that the patient is free to decide for himself; if that isn't made sufficiently clear, we must take special pains to make it sufficiently clear.

No mention is made of self-inquiry and exploration. To be sure, the silence may be more apparent than real for a patient who knows in advance that traditional psychotherapy is a place for those activities, but the Basic Instruction avoids directing an instruction at them, in a way that could define them as an

---

3. I learned this instruction from Merton Gill, who gives it at the outset of a classical psychoanalysis.

externally imposed task. And while it may be open to a variety of interpretations for a patient who is relatively naive about therapy (the same is true for a sophisticated patient, who might construe the instruction as no different from psychoanalysis's "fundamental rule"), the fact remains that we haven't mentioned self-inquiry and exploration. I regard this careful avoidance of defining the central activities of *Psychotherapy* as a task as a particularly important feature of the Basic Instruction. They will, of course, be defined as the therapy develops, but principally in the ways we participate—the way we listen and understand, and the ways we share our understanding. The optimum development is for the patient gradually to discover for himself how therapeutic self-inquiry and exploration can be, and thereby define them as tasks for himself—but that's an ideal state of affairs, so I don't want to stress it unduly here. What I do want to stress is how, by virtue of the fact that the Basic Instruction's task requirements are minimal, we define ourselves as one who sets no task.

But even if it does deserve to be called a task, the task set by the Basic Instruction has the important characteristic of being incapable of evaluation in terms of success or failure. It clearly has that characteristic for you, the one who set it. From your vantage point, what can it mean, after all, to fail? Since the requirement is to say whatever he wants to, it cannot be argued that a patient is not fulfilling it when he doesn't say what he "wants to" but, for instance, what he feels he "has to." To contend that he *wants* to talk about the things he feels he has to talk about is no sophistry; we can construe "want" in its broadest sense—and we should, because we thereby reduce the Basic Instruction's task requirements to a practical minimum. And what remains to be considered as an exception to such a permissive formulation is silence.

When he doesn't speak, when he chooses to remain silent, is a patient violating the Basic Instruction? Strictly speaking, he is—and it's difficult to imagine *Psychotherapy* proceeding effectively in the face of utter silence. But short of an utter or excessive silence (and what that means in practice is difficult to specify in the abstract), the Basic Instruction also allows for the decision not to tell and to be silent. At the risk of brushing aside a complicated and interesting subject, I am going to assert here that when your patient falls silent he is not failing at anything—not from your vantage point, at least.[4] You may occasionally break the silence with a directive to tell the thoughts he was having, but you do it only to help him overcome the inertia that a silence sometimes has. Most importantly, you try never to imply that any silence isn't useful or that you need to know his thoughts, though you are prepared to explain how your role as audience to his deliberations, and his role in that capacity as well, can be a beneficial one for the *therapeutic process*.

4. My views on silence are contained in *Letters 12* and *13* of *Letters to Simon* (pp. 113–26).

To be sure, the patient's freedom from constraint is limited to verbalization and the expression of thoughts and feelings; the Basic Instruction doesn't say, "You can behave however you like here." Perhaps a more precise, albeit obsessional, rendition is this : "There are no rules about how you're to behave during the sessions beyond the condition that it be mental behavior; you are free to speak your mind and express your thoughts and feelings however you want, but you aren't free to put your feelings and wishes into action."[5] But that needn't be construed as a task requirement for the average-expectable patient.

Thus, when we conduct *Psychotherapy*, we can assume that we've set no task; consequently, the procedure itself remains both unstructured and immune from judgments of success and failure, which frees us from a certain judgmental and evaluative role and enhances the patient's autonomy. Moreover, the fact that no task has been set for him, that he has been given the most freedom possible to speak his mind, typically makes a significant difference in the quality of verbalization. And we can also regard that feature as a vital aspect of the therapy's uniqueness; it reflects a significant difference from the underlying orientation of most traditional forms of therapy.

Consider the psychoanalytic requirement that the patient free-associate. As part of their "Fundamental Rule," analysts make it clear that they expect a patient to speak his mind as freely and openly as he can. Many analysts define this expectation in the form of a task requirement, and then they use the patient's failures to live up to it as occasions for interpretations aimed at overcoming the failure (that is, the resistance). They thereby cast themselves into the role of judge and mentor and also take on the task of judging whether their patient is free-associating or not or, more precisely, of assessing the quality of his thoughts in respect to their relative freedom from censorship and defense.

Donald Kaplan has written a passionate paper on free-association, extolling its theoretical, clinical, as well as ideological, ramifications. Psychoanalysis

---

5. A lawyer once clarified this point for me in the following way. At the outset of his second session he asked, "Am I supposed to lie on the couch?" Instead of answering directly, I took the opportunity to tell him I planned to give him no advice of any kind, and I emphasized that it included advice about how he should behave in therapy. When he heard my reply he snapped his fingers. During the subsequent sessions he snapped his fingers from time to time, usually after I had made a remark, and I didn't learn what the gesture meant until the trial period was over and he had decided to commit himself to the therapy. He then explained that the gesture meant I had made an error—and he reviewed all of my errors. Why was my response to his query about the couch an error? Because he wasn't asking for my advice. In fact, he added, if I had breathed a word of advice during any of the sessions he would not be continuing with me. What his question actually was, he pointed out, is this: "Is there a rule about the use of the couch?" (He wasn't planning to use it right away in any case.) My response was therefore gratuitous and beside the point, though it did imply the answer, "There are no rules."

is a "scientific" psychotherapy, contends Kaplan, by virtue of its reliance on free-association, yet he never addresses the difficult question, How can the process itself be assessed in a rigorous and reliable, not to mention objective, way?[6] Martin Bergmann, in a study of the history of free-association, came to the conclusion that its value, at least insofar as the process was purported to provide the objective evidence from which valid interpretations could be made, may have been exaggerated. Bergmann believes it is difficult to keep from using a patient's free-associations to arrive at a previously held position, one that merely conforms to our theoretical expectations. He quotes Kurt Eissler's remarkable statement, "In the psychoanalytic process 'saying everything' includes not only reporting every event past and present, every feeling, impulse, fantasy, but also that which is considered by the patient to be a lie, a falsification, unimportant, unnecessary. In order to reach the point of bringing all this material into analysis, certain changes must take place in the patient. Strange as it may seem, to live up to this requirement is one of the most difficult tasks, and it is questionable whether anyone has ever lived up to it completely." According to Bergmann, this raises "some disquieting questions," for if Eissler is right, then "most psychoanalytic patients free-associate, if at all, towards the end of their analysis. By then, the bulk of the work of interpretation has already been made, and it was obtained on the basis of data less trustworthy than Freud had believed."[7]

Be that as it may, my main point here is that the instruction to free associate sets the patient a task to perform, and his freedom of choice has thereby been limited in a significant way. When he is new to therapy, but even when he's not, free association may be a difficult task for him, so that not only will his success at it be limited but his efforts may be marked by failure. This doesn't necessarily make it a stressful task, nor do I mean to imply that it puts him into a difficult or awkward position. As a matter of fact, the task can actually make him feel easier and more comfortable in the therapy insofar as the situation is clearly structured for him; he knows what's expected of him, and he need, after all, only try his best. Furthermore, the task requirement can introduce a congenial element of teacher-pupil into the relationship; it can imply a kind of mentorship both familiar and welcome. Our Basic Instruction, by contrast, and to the extent that it sets no task, avoids implying a congenial mentorship. Insofar as it does imply a unique kind of relationship between therapist and

6. Donald Kaplan, "A Technical Device in Psychoanalysis and Its Implications for a Scientific Psychotherapy," in *Psychoanalysis and Contemporary Science*, vol. 2, ed. B. Rubinstein (New York: Macmillan, 1973), pp. 25–41.

7. Martin Bergmann, "Free Association and Interpretation of Dreams: Historical and Methodological Considerations," in *Use of Interpretation in Treatment*, p. 273.

patient, not only unfamiliar but quite ambiguous, it can put the patient into an awkward, even somewhat uncomfortable, position.

Neither do I want to leave the impression that a patient may not construe the Basic Instruction as having set him a task. Perhaps not at the outset, but at various times during the course of therapy, he can find the requirement of deciding for himself a difficult "task," and might experience a sense of failure over it. At such times, moreover, it may be useful, it not necessary, to offer him the same kinds of interpretations you would give if he were working at the free-association task. I'm referring to interpretations that address resistance, which in *Psychotherapy* can be reflected in analogous forms to those of psychoanalysis; instead of a breakdown in the free-association process, however, it occurs as an impairment of the *therapeutic process*, or the patient's active self-inquiry and exploration.

When it is first given, a patient might react to the Basic Instruction with some disbelief and perplexity, wondering whether there aren't certain appropriate topics for beginning therapy. Even after he hears the negative reply ("I would prefer you to tell me the things you want to tell me"), it's easy to imagine his remaining perplexed, because he took it for granted that a therapist would suggest topics of conversation and ask him questions. In that case, you would probably want to articulate the nondirective position you wish to maintain, and explain how you intend to work without preconceived ideas about what would be appropriate or beneficial for him to talk about during the sessions. But even when he accepts the explanation and agrees to the terms of the Basic Instruction, you cannot (should not) assume the matter is settled; the more prudent assumption is that he will continue to find it hard to believe that a therapist can be—or, indeed, ought to be—entirely neutral with respect to the content of the sessions.

The same is true when the patient receives the Basic Instruction with no special reaction, when—after a gesture of recognition, perhaps—he proceeds to speak about something he apparently "wants" to speak about, either because he had planned the topic beforehand or because he judges it to be an appropriate one for therapy. To assume he's grasped the full import of the nondirective format will most likely turn out to be a mistake; the more prudent assumption is that he believes he'll be given some direction and guidance at certain times and in certain ways. Typically, that assumption surfaces in the form of an avowed expectation during the later sessions (especially when he has finished telling about himself and perhaps recounted his life history), but it isn't unusual for it to emerge right away, when the Basic Instruction is given, and it can take a variety of forms.

"Won't you at least tell me what I should want to talk about? Surely it has to make a difference what I talk about!" That expression of incredulity might be followed by a stronger, "Do you mean to say you actually don't care what I talk about, whether I decide to talk about useful things or not? Look here, surely it's going to make a difference to my well-being what I talk about!" And it might end with an outraged, "If I want to waste my time here I'm perfectly free to? Oh, fine! What's it to you, after all? You get paid whether my talk is useful or not." Such challenges can be anticipated; they pose complex and subtle technical problems, and the Basic Instruction Paradigms were designed to study some of them.[8]

Before turning to them, however, I need to sharpen a fundamental point about the patient's incredulous and contentious reaction. Do you really mean it when you avow having no expectations with respect to what he talks about and no preconceptions about what would be beneficial? What if he chooses to talk about the weather or deliver a disquisition on differential calculus, will you not regard such topics as irrelevant? Aren't you going to intervene with a remark implying such talk is not "useful"? Don't you have some basis for believing that certain topics are likely to be more germane than others, more beneficial? And if so, isn't it duplicitous (if not also unethical) for you to keep those convictions to yourself?

Neutrality with Respect to Content

Every psychotherapist has convictions about the differential fruitfulness of topics (commonly called "material"). Those convictions, based on an amalgam of pragmatic experience, wisdom, and theory, are likely to encompass a wide range and variety of psychologically relevant material. You may believe, for instance, that the average-expectable patient stands to benefit from an exploration of his childhood, of his development, of his memories; you may believe that a balance is best struck between the past and the present, or between the intrapsychic and the interpersonal, or between the affective and the cognitive; you may believe that night dreams and daydreams are especially instrumental in uncovering fantasies, conflicts, attitudes, memories. This list can easily be extended. My thesis is that *Psychotherapy* does not require you to abandon those convictions; the Basic Instruction doesn't even imply that you foreswear having them. Just because you want your patient to choose his own topics doesn't mean you have no preconceptions.

---

8. The problems are by no means exclusively technical. The paradigms, however, deal mainly with technique, with purely formal considerations (the scales and finger-work of doing therapy, not the execution and interpretation of actual pieces of music). Naturally, it has to make a substantial difference who and where the patient is, what his reasons are for seeking therapy, what his psychological condition is, and the like, but I often keep such considerations tacit.

What *Psychotherapy* does require of you in respect to such convictions is a kind of holding them in abeyance: you have to keep them from contaminating or diluting your fundamental nondirectiveness. This means, at the very least, you don't inform the patient about them. But more than that, you try your best to keep them from influencing his choice of topics in a way to maximize the occurrence of the types of material you believe are likely to be the most beneficial—and that is no simple achievement. In fact, because the ways you can shape and steer his choice of topics are manifold and subtle, and because it's altogether unrealistic to expect interpretations can be made without at the same time exerting a selective bias (without some degree of picking and choosing), and also because interpretations of resistance can necessarily imply that certain topics are more germane to therapy than others, the achievement can only be regarded as an ideal goal—worth striving for, though impossible to achieve perfectly.

This is a critical question for *Psychotherapy*, perhaps its key problem or dilemma: Can we participate usefully and effectively without at the same time providing reinforcements and being directive? My overriding conviction is that the question can be answered at the level of practice, the level of form and technique, instead of requiring a theoretical resolution. There's no question that absolute neutrality with respect to choice of material is a theoretical fiction, and even if it weren't, we couldn't achieve it without severely constraining our work. But in practice, I believe, it is altogether possible to achieve a degree of neutrality which is significant, substantial, and sufficient; it's possible for us to keep the element of picking and choosing to a certain minimum, and also to take active steps against the reinforcement effect whenever it assumes significant proportions.

At the very least, as I mentioned, you don't tell the patient what your convictions are; at the very most, you face a conflict of interests. On the one side stands your conviction about the differential fruitfulness of topics, on the other your conviction about the profound ramifications of allowing him to talk about whatever he wants to. You can resolve that conflict in practice by deliberately and carefully giving priority to the patient's freedom of choice. But I'm convinced that those two sets of convictions can also be construed as standing side by side without any inherent conflict between them: you can *wish* or *prefer* that he choose to speak on certain topics, and at the same time *believe* or *know* that for you to direct him toward them will vitiate their fruitfulness. In other words, you can maintain the overriding conviction that before any topic can yield beneficial results, it must be freely chosen; it has to be free from the properties of an externally imposed task. And to bolster that conviction you can accept the working hypothesis that, be it the weather or his childhood, differential calculus or his marriage, whatever a patient chooses to talk about will reflect something authentic, meaningful, and salient for him; the topic will prove relevant in the short run, if not also valid in the long run—therefore, in principle at least, he stands to benefit from understanding it.

In terms of practicality (technique), the matter can be formulated as follows: you take the same stance toward whatever your patient chooses to talk about; you construe the choice as reflecting a wish and intention (perhaps a hierarchically ordered set of wishes and intentions), and you try to comprehend them and discover their meaning. Accordingly, you do nothing essentially different when he speaks about the weather than when he speaks about his childhood: you try to understand the decision. The fact that in one case there is a wish (and likely a conscious, deliberate one) to test you, if not also an intention to sabotage the therapy, is essentially no different from the fact that in the other case there may be a wish (perhaps also conscious and deliberate) to provide you the data with which to explain the genesis of his problems, and perhaps the intention to bring matters to an early head and thereby expedite (if not short circuit) the ordeal of therapy. Whatever the wish, whatever the intentions and expectations, you listen in order to understand; and when you believe you have understood and judge it "useful" to share that understanding with him, you offer an interpretation. Which raises another key question, What does "useful" mean?

The final sentence of the Basic Instruction is ambiguous—How do you construe "useful"? The answer is somewhat tangential to the main point of this chapter, and therefore the Basic Instruction Paradigms don't deal with it. (Instead, the Timing Paradigms of chapter four do.) But for the purposes of this discussion, I want to mention that you may judge it "useful" to share your understanding with a patient when the issue at hand is resistance, or when it's prudent to conceptualize it as a form of defense that is directed against the therapy. Accordingly, insofar as they count as resistances and satisfy that criterion of "useful," the wish to test you and the intention to sabotage therapy can be interpreted to him; and the same can be equally true for his wish to provide historical data and his intention to expedite, because they, too, can be construed as resistances of a kind. To be sure, the fact that both sets of resistances differ in certain important respects—their blatancy, for one—is bound to make an important practical difference in the ways you can deal with them and help the patient understand them and the function they may be serving, but it need make no essential difference otherwise.

Only for the sake of this discussion am I assuming that the patient's reason for beginning with his childhood history reflects a significant resistance. It might, in fact, be based on a desire for a classical psychoanalysis, and he may have reason to believe that's the appropriate way to begin one. (The same applies to a decision to use the couch, to free-associate, to recount dreams, and the like.) I don't want to leave the impression here that I recommend you should in any way challenge that decision and reason; you should want only to know and understand them. Moreover, even if they aren't "good" reasons (based on misinformation, for instance), you can choose to offer an interpretation only if you also have reason to believe the decision was actually serving a substantial resistive function, that it might impair the therapy in a serious way. In other words, your convictions about the differential fruitfulness of topics have to remain in the background until the therapy itself is in jeopardy.

But assuming you're dealing with different forms of resistance, you may even welcome their blatant expression, insofar as such an expression gives you an early opportunity to deal with a central issue, the format and orientation of *Psychotherapy*. Paradoxically, when the patient's resistance is manifested by "good-patient" behavior, as, for example, when he recounts for you the details of his childhood, you may face a greater problem interpreting it to him in a meaningful and convincing way. At any rate, that's what I have in mind with the claim that the difference can be largely a practical, or technical, one— it may implicate considerations of timing and tact, nothing more. And *Psychotherapy* requires of us a full faith in the therapeutic efficacy of a patient's choosing freely what he will talk about during the sessions. We have to be prepared to work not only from the surface of his consciousness but also from the matrix of his decisional and volitional processes.

The Basic Instruction Paradigms

Instructions: For this study you are to assume that this is the beginning of a course of *Psychotherapy*, the first session, and the only instruction or notification you have given so far is the Basic Instruction. Please treat the separate paradigms as independent from each other; assume that each paradigm involves a different patient. Your task for the first four paradigms is to complete the dialogue by composing a continuation of several more exchanges between therapist and patient. Your continuation should exemplify your best understanding of the issue and your optimal way of dealing with it.

Paradigm 1

TH-1:   You can talk about the things you want. It's up to you. I will listen and try to understand. When I have something useful to say I will say it.

PT-1:   You mean it's altogether up to me to decide what I should talk about here?

TH-2:   Yes.

PT-2:   And it doesn't matter what I talk about?

TH-3:   It matters that it's what you want to talk about.

PT-3:   But you're the therapist, surely you must know what would be most useful for me to talk about!

What is the best and most "useful" *TH-4*? How should the therapist (you) continue? Should you stay with the Basic Instruction, reiterating and perhaps amplifying it, or should you address the patient's challenging incredulity, at least articulate it? I believe the latter is your better option. For one thing, there's no reason to infer that the Basic Instruction was not understood; for another, when you "hear" the patient's skepticism and disbelief (and perhaps the overtone of mocking in "But you're the therapist"), you're already keeping your promise to listen and understand.

But perhaps because therapy is so young, and an interpretation might be misconstrued by the patient as contentious, for instance, or as defensive, my students generally choose to stay with the Basic Instruction, and they use the opportunity to amplify it. That can be useful, but it has to be done carefully, because the line between amplification and distortion is a fine one, and the Basic Instruction lends itself readily to distortions both flagrant and subtle. For example, notice how this amplification, "I will be able to say more useful things when you talk about what you want to talk about," which a student gives for *TH-4*, implies that your nondirectiveness is supposed to serve the purpose of better understanding the patient. Not only isn't that altogether true, but the patient might be genuinely puzzled about how it can serve that function—which would be far better served by his answering your leading questions and speaking about topics you recommended.

A variety of modifications in the letter and spirit of the Basic Instruction, some amounting to significant distortions, are made by students in this study. The most common is to add the qualifier "important," thereby introducing a kind of task requirement—to say "important" and/or "meaningful" things—and raising the question of judging and evaluating. Consider the following example continuation from this point of view, the way the Basic Instruction gets corrupted, and notice how the question "Important in what way?" remains begged (so that the patient is likely to fall back on his original query "How should I know what's important?") and how *TH-6* differs from the message "It's up to you to decide what it is you want to talk about."

TH-4:   No, I don't know what you think about, what's important to you. Those are the things that are useful.

PT-4:   But shouldn't I talk about my parents or my dreams or sex?

TH-5:   Are you assuming that I think it's important for you to talk about those things?

PT-5:   Yes. Aren't they the kinds of things that will help you understand me?

TH-6:   I don't think your parents or your dreams or your sex life are necessarily important. They may or may not be. I hope to come to understand you by your choosing to talk about those aspects of your experience that you deem important.

The only elaboration that can safely be made is about giving advice. One student suggests this for *TH-4*: "Anything you decide to talk about will be useful," to which he has the patient respond, "But can't you advise me as to what is most relevant?" And now he amplifies with, "I intend to give you no advice or direction as to what to do or say either here in therapy or outside of it. I can appreciate the awkward position that places you in." The notification about advice is important and useful, and the final empathic remark is tactful, but both can wait until you find out what the patient meant by "most relevant."

He is likely to have some definite beliefs about what he should speak about in therapy, and you have to be interested in knowing and understanding them—but you also have to keep from challenging them, or even seeming to. If you intend to avoid any preconceptions of your own, and you're free from misgivings about that intention, not only will you be content to know and understand his beliefs without feeling any impulse to modify them or defend your neutrality, you'll also be in a better position to hear his challenge. In the following dialogue, the student makes an attempt to articulate the patient's challenge (put in terms of "testing" at *TH-6*), but then quickly retreats to the Basic Instruction—instead of staying with the challenge—when the patient bristles at the interpretation.

TH-4:   I believe it would be most useful for you to talk about what you want to.

PT-4:   You said that already. Can't you give me an idea of what to talk about?

TH-5:   It seems that you are trying to get me to tell you what to do.

PT-5:   What do you mean "get"? All I'm saying is that you have more experience in this sort of thing.

TH-6:   Perhaps you are testing me in a way. You want, in

PT-7: other words, to see if I will really refrain from directing and advising you.

PT-7: Look, is this going to be a battle of wills? Are you going to sit there resting on principle or try to help me?

TH-7: I believe I can be of most help to you by not giving advice and direction, but rather by listening and trying to understand.

Instead of falling back at *TH-7*, I would probably say, "I take it you believe that my method will be unhelpful for you" or "You are finding it hard to believe that I am not being willful and that I truly believe this method will be helpful to you," which is tactful enough and doesn't defuse the patient's challenge or deflect attention from his incredulity.

That my students find it easier to speak for the patient than for the therapist is not surprising. What I have found remarkable, nevertheless, is how often their patient is altogether direct and to the point, while their therapist beats around the bush and fails to respond accurately. If understanding is the hallmark of *Psychotherapy* (as it is for psychotherapy), then accurate communication is essential, and for a therapist to be nonresponsive and evasive undermines the *therapeutic process*. In the above example *TH-5* is a clear non sequitur—unless, of course, it is a clear gratuity—and it seems to be caused by the therapist's determination to stick to his guns. Notice how the promise to understand is already being broken. ("I could but would prefer not to," is the therapist's obvious rejoinder.)

The following example is another in which the fact that a single person is speaking for both parties is easily lost sight of, so marked is the lack of simple understanding on the therapist's part.[9] The therapist begins with a relatively good, though rather gratuitous, remark, "You are not happy with the idea that you must make your own choice; you would prefer that I choose for you," and the patient responds by reiterating his doctor-knows-best challenge, "But you know better than I." The therapist then simply repeats his initial remark, "You would like to be guided, not to make your own decision," which is both nonresponsive and rather confronting; and the patient responds by amplifying his challenge with, "That's what I came here for, isn't it?—for you to help me find out about myself. If I could do it myself I wouldn't be here." The therapist counters with an interpretation which ad-

---

9. I realize that the artificial nature of the study, with the same person writing both parts, may be partly responsible for the apparent lack of "communication." Perhaps because the students are listening to themselves, perhaps because their playwriting skills are limited, the lack of understanding may be more apparent than real. Few supervisors, however, will strongly doubt the validity of the conclusions I am drawing from these data.

dresses itself to what the patient might be experiencing, "You are angry because I don't intend to tell you what to do." Notice, however, how that interpretation fails to deal with his complaint. It is easy to imagine him responding with, "Yes, I am not happy, and yes I am angry—and with good reason too, don't you agree?" Now the therapist will have no choice but to deal with the issue itself and make a remark to clarify that the patient is challenging and disbelieving the method of therapy—that this way of proceeding, with the expert providing no guidance, is likely to be futile.

Many students begin their continuations with an interpretation suggesting to the patient that he is angry, which fails to acknowledge and articulate his more dominant feeling, challenging incredulity. I don't mean to contend, however, that only such an acknowledgement is to the point; it is possible, and may even be preferable this early in therapy, to address the content of his remark (by saying, for instance, "I take it you are finding it hard to believe that it's really up to you—that what you choose to talk about is meaningful—that it is the most useful way of talking"). A student puts it this way: "You seem rather persistent. And since I've already said that it is not appropriate to the therapy to give you directions, perhaps you want to find out if I mean what I say, or if you can get me to change my mind." The opening sentence, however, is quite unnecessary and only strengthens the confronting nature of the interpretation.

What about the advisability of a confrontation in response to the patient's complaints? The temptation to counterattack at *TH-4* is great, and the ways to do it are several. A student responds with, "But you are the expert on you" and continues with the interesting observation, "You undervalue your uniqueness when you assume I can immediately understand you and know what is most important for you to talk about." That kind of response runs the danger of putting the patient on the defensive; given his feelings of outrage, it is quite likely to have an abrasive effect, and something of an argument may ensue. Another student starts with, "How would I know? I have just met you for the first time today," to which the patient responds sensibly, "Do you mean to say you have no theory that you go by, no idea of how therapy should begin?" The student doesn't duck the question, but doesn't give it a satisfactory answer with, "I'm not saying that; but all I ask is that you understand the instructions I gave you earlier." Then ensues this interesting exchange: "Which tells me nothing," "Which tells you everything you need to know, as I see it." Again, it's hard to imagine how the patient will continue; he appears to be backed into a tight corner.

In the following dialogue the student comes on too strongly, with remarks that are overly confronting and insufficiently tactful, and with the result that he has the last word, while the patient is apparently left speechless.

TH-4:   You seem to be contradicting yourself. You said, did
         you not, that I am the therapist and I would know what
         would be most useful for you to talk about?

PT-4:   Yes, that's what I said.

TH-5:   And yet when I told you my only instruction was for
         you to talk about the things you want to talk about, you
         completely disregarded it. On the one hand, you say
         that I am the expert and that you will follow what I say;
         on the other hand, when I say something you simply
         disregard it.

PT-5:   I heard your instruction. I just thought it would go more
         smoothly if you told me which things might be more
         important to talk about.

TH-6:   Then you didn't hear the instruction, or you didn't be-
         lieve I would stick to it. It's up to you what you talk
         about. I think, though, that you feel two ways about
         me, as your contradiction indicates: you feel that I'm
         the healer who knows what's best for his patients; and
         you also feel that I may not be so expert, because you
         don't take my instruction—my "medicine"—too seri-
         ously. That sounds like a credibility gap.

TH-6 is a wholly unnecessary attack and should be replaced with silence. The point, after all, has been made, and the patient has not said he disagrees with it now. He is no longer leveling the challenge at *TH-5*; he is saying only that he thought (before, that is) it might be better the other way. Such features of communication are vital; we must hear what our patient is saying as precisely as possible and not disregard its various meanings—most especially its surface meanings. In this example, *PT-5* can also be construed as an apology and can be acknowledged accordingly—"You are apologizing, I take it; I gather you felt my remark was a criticism."

It isn't uncommon (especially when therapy is young) for interpretations to be taken as criticisms, and for a patient to react to them as if he'd been scolded and evaluated. Those unintended and unwanted side effects cannot be entirely avoided, though we can take certain active measures to undo them (which I examine at various places in the subsequent chapters and especially in chapter nine). Nevertheless, it is an aspect of good technique to avoid interpretations which carry too strong an implication of evaluation.

Paradigm 2

TH-1:   You can talk about the things you want. It's up to you.
         I will listen and try to understand. When I have some-
         thing useful to say I will say it.

PT-1:   You mean it's altogether up to me to decide what I
        should talk about here?
TH-2:   Yes.
PT-2:   And it doesn't matter what I talk about?
TH-3:   It matters that it's what you want to talk about.
PT-3:   But what good will that do me? I mean, if I just talk
        and talk—what good is that?

This paradigm is identical with Paradigm 1 until *PT-3*, where the challenge is directed more squarely at the method. I also intended "just talk and talk" to convey a mocking flavor. Again, however, most students restrict their continuations to a reiteration of the Basic Instruction, and many preface it with an empathic and supportive remark (for example, "I can appreciate that you are puzzled about what will go on here. I can only say that I believe this kind of therapy will be good for you"). And again, many of the reiterations change the spirit and intent of the Basic Instruction, sometimes very subtly but nonetheless significantly (for example, "It will help me to understand you").

A comparison of their continuations to Paradigms 1 and 2 reveals quite clearly that my students find it easier to respond to a challenge directed at their role as therapists than to one that is directed at their therapy method. The continuations to Paradigm 2 are significantly poorer in quality, distorting the Basic Instruction more often and resorting more often to didactic and directive remarks as well as to strong confrontations. For example, "If you felt that talking wasn't going to do you any good, why did you apply for this treatment in the first place?" is how a student meets the challenge, misreading the patient's complaint in a subtle way and forgetting that he had no way of knowing in advance what the Basic Instruction would be. Apparently, students have an easier time countering the charge "But surely you must know!" than the charge "But what good will this do me!" (Defending our therapy is harder than acknowledging our fallibility.)

PT-3 can be taken as an expression of doubt, as the patient's wondering aloud if a therapy which allows him to "just talk and talk" can do him any good. A student addresses the point directly with, "I guess it is difficult to see how just talking will do any good," and another does it indirectly, but probably as effectively, with, "I believe you are asking me what part I will take in the therapy." My inclination, however, would be to emphasize the challenge. "You are challenging this type of therapy, aren't you?—experiencing a sense of disbelief, perhaps even of outrage," I would say. "How can it be an effective way of doing therapy for me to leave it entirely up to you what you talk about? That's your question, I take it."

Now, if the patient simply agrees in a way that continues to press the question, I have the recourse of appealing to my professional experience, though that can be taken for granted. I mean, it has to be obvious, and if it turns out it wasn't then, something more is afoot, that I wouldn't be using a method I didn't believe in. What may emerge then is that he either cannot accept the validity of the method in general or else wants to question its suitability for him. Which raises the important issue of a trial period, a brief course of therapy whose function is to determine whether the method is suitable and congenial for the patient.

Several students suggest a trial period in their *TH-4*—for example, "I appreciate that it's hard for you to see how that may be helpful before you've tried it out. Why don't we consider our first week or two of sessions as a kind of trial period, and at the end of the time perhaps you will have more of an idea whether you think this way of working together can be helpful to you." Though they sometimes raise more problems than they solve, trial periods are usually useful and occasionally necessary. To expect a patient to commit himself to an unfamiliar form of therapy, as well as to a therapist whom he knows only by credentials and recommendation, is to expect a great deal. A trial period can go quite far in helping him decide whether to make such a commitment. At the same time, however, a trial period that is reasonably short will often be insufficient to establish the method's usefulness, something which usually doesn't become apparent until the middle stage of the therapy has been reached. But it needn't take too long to determine whether you and he can understand each other; and you can take pains to offer early interpretations whose main function is to show the patient the way you work, the ways you empathize and articulate and explain.

Two further points: (1) it isn't necessary to raise the issue of a trial period in a routine way, for it's generally better to wait until there is good reason to believe the patient will appreciate the need and appropriateness of the measure (when it can be a solution to an actual problem or question, not one that we impose); (2) it can be important to establish clearly when the trial period is over and when the commitment to therapy is made, otherwise the beginning of therapy may remain ambiguous and unrepresentative.

Consider how the suggestion of a trial period might rescue us from our terrible position at the end of this example. The continuation begins with a remarkable *TH-4*, "All the good in the world" (I'll resist further comment on it); and the student has the patient react appropriately with, "What the hell do you mean, *all the good in the world?*" "I firmly believe your therapy will be most useful to you if you talk about anything you want," we explain. "But I can talk to my friends," cries the patient in obvious outrage, "And it doesn't cost me thirty-five dollars an hour!" Now the student has us cling stubbornly to our moorings with the intrepid reply, "I already gave you the basic instruction for it: that is how I do therapy." Notice how difficult it is to imagine what the patient could say, how anything but an impasse could ensue.

Instead of that final remark, we have two options: the first is to suggest a trial period; the second is to offer the interpretation, "I take it, then, that you have reason to believe that therapy for you will require being told what to talk about." If we've chosen the second option, and the patient has vigorously concurred, we simply have to consider making the necessary accommodation. It should go without having to be said—but I discuss the matter soon anyway—that we must be prepared to make reasonable and judicious modifications in our procedure, and if a patient needs to be told what to talk about, there may be no other good option but to do it. (Though for the patient in the above example, it may be too late, because then it wouldn't be "therapy" in our eyes.)

Another option for a continuation to Paradigm 2 is a clarification question. Is it, after all, clear—or clear enough—what the patient has in mind? Some students think it's not, and their *TH-4* consists of questioning the meaning of "just talk and talk." That's a good idea because, for one thing, it might elicit from the patient the admission or recognition that he meant it in a mocking way. But the question "What do you mean?" should be used judiciously; indiscriminate and/or excessive use of it can transform the session into an interview and define us as troubleshooters. The following example illustrates (caricatures, in fact) the problem.

TH-4:   What good do you think it might be?
PT-4:   Oh, I get it! If I just keep on talking, then you will find out lots of things about me so you can understand me.
TH-5:   Oh, how so?
PT-5:   Well, just by the things I say. Like, for instance, what I've just been saying—how I don't like the idea of just talking and talking.
TH-6:   I'm not sure I understand.
PT-6:   Well, that it kind of makes me feel edgy, the thought of sitting in a room with one other person and doing all the talking.

It's perfectly possible, after all, to continue with, "What do you mean by 'edgy'?" and "How do you mean, 'all the talking'?" And if therapy proceeds any longer this way, the patient is either going to worry about his comprehensibility or about our ability to understand—probably both.

Paradigm 3

TH-1:   I think you're feeling angry. And I think the reason is that you expected I would be telling you what to talk about here, that I'd ask you questions, for instance. So, by not doing that, I've put you in an awkward position, and that makes you angry.

PT-1:   Yes, you're right. I always get angry when I feel embarrassed. And it is embarrassing, you know, to have to talk about anything that just comes to mind.

TH-1 is an interpretation about the patient's reaction to the Basic Instruction, and the paradigm requires us to listen carefully to his response. While he accepts the interpretation, perhaps with a note of contrition, he has altered the Basic Instruction. The alteration should take priority over the contrition, though we may find a way to address both issues together.

Having noticed the alteration, our technical problem is how best to draw the patient's attention to it, while at the same time taking steps to help him understand why he did it. But in order to notice the alteration itself, we have to hear exactly what he has said and not allow the fact that emotions are involved to mislead us. That turns out to be a difficult task for my students, probably because they lean to the belief that it is exclusively in the arena of affects where the struggle of psychotherapy takes place. So it isn't surprising that the majority of them structure their continuation entirely around the issue of embarrassment.

Many begin with an interpretation connecting the patient's embarrassment to his fear of being judged and evaluated. "Perhaps you expect that I'll judge what you say and think unfavorably of you if you don't say the *right* thing," is a typical example; and many move into this issue during the course of their continuations. And though they deal sensibly with what is certainly a central issue in therapy, they fail to recognize that they are dealing with the free-association method rather than with *Psychotherapy*'s. A few students even go right along with the patient's alteration—here is a good example:

TH-2:   Perhaps you are concerned because you feel you have to tell me about particular thoughts you are embarrassed about.

PT-2:   Do I really have to tell you everything?

TH-3:   While the decision is up to you, I believe it can be useful in the therapy if you do.

PT-3:   Now I'll feel embarrassed if I do tell and guilty if I don't.

TH-4:   Your saying that you'd feel guilty implies that you expect me to judge you. That is something I don't intend to do.

But a substantial number of students do recognize the alteration, and I will restrict my discussion to their continuations.

Several repeat the Basic Instruction to begin with and leave it up to the patient to express the alteration. For example, after an empathic remark followed by a reiteration, "I can appreciate your anger and embarrassment; you can tell me the things you want," a student has the patient say, "You mean you don't expect me to tell you everything that comes to mind? I thought that's what you did in analysis." This affords us a good opportunity to clarify the format of *Psychotherapy* and explain how it differs from the kind of "analysis" the patient expected. At the very least, we should acknowledge his expectations and attitudes in order to facilitate a full exploration of this important subject. What the student does instead, however, is show no interest in the patient's expectations; he merely says, "I find it more useful to leave it up to you to choose and decide."

The following continuation has a similar shortcoming. The student begins with, "You seem to be under the impression, then, that you are supposed to say everything that comes to mind," to which the patient responds, "Well, isn't that what free-association is?—that you have to say everything whether it's embarrassing or trivial, or whatever." The student clarifies appropriately by observing, "You seem to think you are supposed to free-associate here"; the patient agrees with, "Well, yes," but goes on to ask, "Isn't that what therapy is all about?" Now, instead of acknowledging that the free-association method is commonly used and allowing the patient to tell about his views and feelings on the matter (and holding in abeyance a reemphasis of the fact that he is perfectly free to use it if he wishes to, but that the decision is his), the student remarks, "You may talk about whatever you wish here."

Some students, after having raised the issue, evade it out of an eagerness to offer an explanatory interpretation. In the following continuation the student allows the patient to do the evading. *TH-2* is, "Although you speak as though you are agreeing with me, you appear to me to be saying something quite different, namely, that you feel forced to say certain things." *PT-2* is, "Oh, no, not at all! It's just that if you think I'm angry because I don't speak up, then I feel as if I have to reassure you that I'm not; I'm just embarrassed mainly." *TH-3* is, "Perhaps it is more reassuring to you to think of yourself as embarrassed; it may even be frightening to be angry." This interpretation is clearly premature; at best it should be focused on the patient's anger instead of his embarrassment. More importantly, however, the student seems to be ignoring the patient's attempt to set the record straight, and at the same time losing sight of the fact that he feels "forced to say certain things."

No student begins a continuation by simply pointing out to the patient that he has altered the Basic Instruction. There may, after all, be an important reason he did it, a reason well worth exploring. Even a confrontation, such as "Are you aware that you have changed the instruction I gave you?" can be justified on the grounds that the issue at hand is the format and orientation of therapy. A few students raise the issue of why, not directly but in an inferential way, mainly by focusing attention on the patient's embarrassment. Here are two good examples: "You want me to take the responsibility for choosing a subject to talk about; in this way, you might avoid saying anything embarrassing—or if you do, it won't be so embarrassing because it was my idea," and "It seems to me that you would like me to demand that you speak about whatever occurs to you so that it would be my fault that you are talking about things that embarrass you." A third example has the patient express the reason (after the interpretation, "You feel under some pressure to talk about things you may not want to talk about") in these words, "Yes, I do. But then, as you say that, I see the contradiction. I mean, I can say just what I want to. Well, what I want to tell you is that I wish I knew what I wanted to tell you [laughs embarrassedly]. I guess this is such a new experience for me." It is now possible for the student to suggest, "Perhaps that is the reason you changed things: you would feel less embarrassed if I instructed you to say everything, wouldn't you?"

Similarly, this continuation makes a good start toward developing a motive for the patient's alteration. The student begins with a careful and accurate elaboration on the Basic Instruction, "You can talk about what you want to. Of course, that would include anything that comes to mind, if that is what you want to talk about. But I will deliberately avoid telling you what you have to talk about—it's really up to you." The patient responds, "You mean I really don't have to say everything that comes to mind?"; to which the student patiently says, "You can talk about what you want to." (I would recommend instead either silence or, "You are finding it hard to believe, aren't you?") The patient then exclaims, "This is certainly not what I was expecting." Now the student makes an interpretation that could evoke a useful exploration of the patient's motivation, "You seem both relieved and a little anxious about the prospect of saying what you want to." Another student gets at it this way:

> TH-2: I'm not sure if you mean that some things you might *want* to talk about might be embarrassing or that you feel *required* to talk about anything that comes to mind, no matter how embarrassing it might be.
>
> PT-2: Well, I guess I was thinking I had to talk about everything that came up, but if it's really up to me, I don't—but maybe I might want to. Oh, shit!
>
> TH-3: I think I may understand your reasons for feeling exasperated. Perhaps you're not sure how safe it is here to talk about things that might be embarrassing.

PT-3:   Well, I know everything is confidential here, but still
         . . .Well, I feel funny talking about some things.

Finally, here's a continuation that succeeds in exploring the issue sensitively, and whose single shortcoming is a lack of emphasis on the patient's having altered the Basic Instruction:

TH-2:   I'm not sure I know what you mean by ''have to talk about anything that just comes to mind.''

PT-2:   Well, I have to say what's on my mind, right?

TH-3:   You don't *have* to. It's up to you to say whatever you want to say.

PT-3:   Oh! Well, what if I don't have anything I want to say, then what will you do?

TH-4:   It's up to you to remain silent if you want. I could be wrong, but you sound almost disappointed that I am not going to make you talk.

PT-4:   Yes, I don't know why. I guess I am disappointed, though.

TH-5:   I wonder if you feel it might be easier for you to tell me things you felt I was forcing you to tell me. Maybe you feel embarrassed not because you *have* to talk about things but because you *want* to.

Paradigm 4

TH-1:   I think you're feeling angry. And I think the reason is that you expected I would be telling you what to talk about here, that I'd ask you questions, for instance. So, by not doing that, I've put you in an awkward position, and that makes you angry.

PT-1:   But how the hell should I have know you'd leave it all up to me? I've never been in therapy. All I know is what Harry told me. His therapist tells him what to do, asks him lots of questions and everything. So why the hell shouldn't I be expecting the same treatment?

When a defense is pointed out to a patient, he sometimes reacts with the defense itself. That's what I tried to exemplify in this paradigm, a correspondence between the content of your interpretation (*TH-1*) and the patient's reaction to it (*PT-1*). Few students, however, reveal in their continuations a recognition that the patient is feeling outraged and angry in response to the interpretation itself. Instead, they construe his feelings as stemming from the expectation (and wish) that you behave like Harry's therapist—and they fail to take advantage of the opportunity to show the patient how you will conduct therapy. Nevertheless, they do respond to what is certainly a germane issue (for example, "You are wondering if I'm any good, whether I know what I'm doing," and "You seem to be saying that you feel cheated by me"); and their continuations go on to examine the issue in a way that will be useful for therapy.

Some simply repeat the interpretation itself, and then their continuation usually leads into a reiteration of the Basic Instruction. Several begin with a didactic remark to the effect that different therapists have different methods, thus evading the issue altogether and failing to acknowledge the patient's indignation. Those continuations that persist in implicating the Basic Instruction tend to grow argumentative, as the following concise example does.

> TH-2: Is it possible that you are angry because I won't tell you what to do?
>
> PT-2: Well, just say I want the same treatment everyone else gets.
>
> TH-3: In order for this type of therapy to be useful to you, you must decide what you want to say in the sessions.
>
> PT-3: Would it hurt if you told me just once so I can get the idea?
>
> TH-4: Probably not, but it wouldn't help either.

In this example the patient is asking to try out his (that is, Harry's) method, presumably because he judges it might be better for him. *TH-4* should simply restate and clarify the point ("I take it you believe that way would be better for you because you need guidance"), without contesting the point. If the patient were to persist in demanding that you tell him what to talk about—just once even—you would have the option of acquiescing. (Though it would be disingenuous, if not worse, for you then to say, "Okay, I will. Tell me what makes you believe you need my help in that way!") You also can persist with, "I would prefer not to alter the form of the therapy right now and would rather proceed without questions or suggestions." At all events, however, you should try to avoid the implication that this type of therapy is better than any other, including Harry's; to convey the message "This is the way I choose to do it" is quite sufficient. *TH-4* carries the distinct implication that Harry's therapist's method is without merit—a bad implication to work with.

Now I will examine four examples in which the patient's indignation is acknowledged and the fact that he is reacting to the interpretation itself is recognized. (The patient has just said "But how the hell should I have known . . . So why the hell shouldn't I be expecting the same treatment?")

"It was quite natural for you to expect the same treatment," the student has you respond considerately and tactfully in the first example. But the implication of "natural" may return later on in the "treatment" in a way that will make you regret having used the word. Now the patient repeats his complaint in its most direct form, "Then why did you chew me out for being surprised at the way you operate?" which provides you with the opportunity to deal with a vital aspect of the interpretive mode; you could offer this rejoinder: "I understand why you would take my observation as a criticism and judgment, that when I point out to you the way you feel, you might regard it as my having said you had no right to feel that way. But I'd like to make it clear to you that I did not intend to scold and criticize you, and I'm going to try my best never to do it." Instead, however, the student has you say, "For some reason you are seeing my description of your embarrassment and anger as *chewing you out*, almost as if my saying you feel these emotions is the same as my saying you are out of line, bad." Now, I recognize that the remark can be read as an indirect statement of the one I suggested, but it can also be read as a further piece of scolding. "For some reason" carries the distinct implication that whatever the reason may be it is not a good (that is, a "natural") one.

"It seems to me that you feel I'm scolding you," begins the second example, "that I expected you to know what type of therapy this would be—and you are even angrier because of this." (Fine! Though the final part is dispensable.) "Why shouldn't I be?" responds the patient, "You are putting all the blame on me. You should have told me what to expect." When?—it's unclear, but the student overlooks the question, and responds instead with an amplification and an interpretation: "I didn't mean to scold you or to imply that you should have known the rules. I only wanted to point out my impression that when your expectations don't materialize, you become embarrassed, angry, and perhaps feel that it's the other person's fault for putting you in that position." The patient responds to this interpretation contentiously; his rejoinder clearly indicates that it had no impact; he says, "Well, I was put in that position. I only had Harry's therapy to judge from." And now the student articulates his feeling with, "And you feel that I should have saved you the embarrassment you experienced by being more explicit in my instructions," without recognizing that the patient is again (or still) reacting to the interpretations as if they were criticisms.

In the third example, the student says, "I can certainly understand that your expectations would be based largely on whatever information you've been able to get about therapy from your friends. You seem to feel, however, that I am criticizing you for expecting the same treatment from me that Harry gets from his therapist." "Damn straight!" responds the patient accurately; and the student continues, "When I said that you were feeling both embarrassed and angry, I did not mean that these were bad or wrong ways to feel, merely that it might be helpful to you to realize what, in fact, you were feeling." That's good and to the point, and what it lacks is only the point that the patient's reaction was understandable and/or justified. But the opportunity to make that point will doubtlessly occur again, so my criticism may be a quibble.

Finally, lest some of the examples I have chosen to present leave the impression that my students are lacking in skill and understanding, I conclude my discussion of the first four Basic Instruction Paradigms with this perfect continuation:

> TH-2:   I think you're feeling criticized, as if I said you had no right to expect that I would be telling you what to talk about.
>
> PT-2:   And now you're criticizing me again, saying I didn't understand you when you said I was angry, and imply- ing I really shouldn't be.
>
> TH-3:   I can appreciate that you hear a criticism and value judgment when I point out to you that you are angry. But when I, as your therapist, say you are feeling such and such a way, I mean only that I believe it's true, and it might be helpful to you to recognize it. I don't mean it's bad to feel or act that way, that it means you're a bad person.[10]
>
> PT-3:   You're saying it was good for me to feel angry, it was a perfectly natural way to feel?
>
> TH-4:   I'm not saying it's good or bad. But I can recognize that I put you in a difficult position, since you expected me to tell you what to talk about here.

Paradigm 5

It's the second or third session, and the patient says, "I had a dream last night. Do you want me to tell it to you?" What are your options for a response? Give three good responses and evaluate each one with respect to its advantages and disadvantages.

This paradigm raises two technical issues: the first is how to respond to a request for guidance about what to talk about, the second is how to respond to a direct question. With respect to the first issue, since I have already discussed the question of neutrality in respect to content, I need only to repeat that we simply don't want to instruct the patient to give dreams priority, no matter

10. I am aware the student cribbed this speech out of my *Letters to Simon* (pp. 98–99).

what convictions we have about their special value in therapy. And bear in mind that to respond with, "No, I don't *want* you to tell me the dream because I prefer you to decide what to talk about, but I do believe that dreams can be valuable in helping to understand your thoughts and feelings," would place him in a somewhat paradoxical position. Ideally, he should discover for himself whether, and how, his dreams can be useful, and we should play the same role in that discovery as we play in all others.

But perhaps that ideal position is excessively stringent, and there are ways to solve the problem that are more practical. One option is to begin with a translation of the patient's "Do you want me to tell it to you" into a request for your professional opinion. ("Are you asking me whether I believe that dreams are likely to be especially useful for you to examine here?"—and the same can be asked about the review of childhood events, of sexual experiences, and the like, and can also pertain to the use of the couch.) Once he has concurred that this is what he had in mind (or if he were to put the question directly in the first place), we have the option of responding conservatively that there's no sure way to know it in advance. But *Psychotherapy*'s nondirective format doesn't mandate that response exclusively, because there are patients and circumstances that mitigate the directive force of any notification. It may be entirely possible, in certain cases and under certain circumstances, to tell a patient about the expectable value of dreams, without at the same time directing him to bring them in. For instance, in response to his direct question, we can say, "I gather you believe it, and you're interested to know whether I share the belief." (That's in order to make sure he indeed believes it, and perhaps it will also reveal the nature and strength of his belief.) Then, when he acknowledges the fact, we can say, "It has been my experience that dreams are sometimes [usually, often] useful," and we can add "I don't mean to be giving you any advice or direction," if we aren't reasonably certain he's not going to take it as a breach of our nondirectiveness. The element of directiveness is there, of course, but it can be quite minimal; and if we regard dreams as potentially of great significance for our patient, the "flaw" we've introduced may be well compensated for.

With respect to the second issue, how to respond to a patient's direct question, it is something of a cliché by now to counterquestion with "Why do you ask?" It should also be obvious by now that I proscribe such a response, and why. But to respond with silence is both tactless and unnecessary, especially the first time the patient asks a direct direction, and our most useful response is to explain to him how we plan to deal with his questions. The explanation I give—and typically it's quite sufficient—is this: "From time to time you may want to ask me a direct question, the way you did now, and what I'll usually do is not answer it, not right away. Even when I intend to answer it, I'll often wait a while."

If the patient asked me why I'd wait, I probably wouldn't choose this occasion to give him a sample of it (that is, by waiting), and I'd frame my explanation in one of several ways. Once his question is answered, his reason for having asked it may be lost sight of because the answer might take precedence over the question, is one way of explaining the delay. Another is to put it in terms of my wanting to consider whether or not the answer I could give would be useful for him and the therapy. But under no circumstances would I couch my rationale in terms of his motivation, for I want to avoid the implication that I'm going to judge the question in any way—if it's a "good" question, I will answer it; if I don't answer, it was a "bad" one.

In response to Paradigm 5, few of my students suggest, as one of their options, a remark whose function is to get the patient to say what he thinks of dreams. On the other hand, no student fails to include the key phrase "It's up to you" among has options, and most of them rate that option as the best and most advantageous of all.

"It's up to you" occurs frequently and regularly in students' continuations to all of the Basic Instruction Paradigms, undoubtedly because it conveys the nondirective message so succinctly. Too often, however, it is used mechanically and in a way that amounts to evasiveness and nonreponsiveness. Paradigm 5 provides a good example of a situation where the key phrase feels somehow altogether right for a response but may prove to be evasive and nonresponsive. It's too easy to imagine the patient's persisting with, "Yes, I know it's up to me, but that's not what I asked you; I asked whether you *want* me to tell it to you." My point is that "It's up to you," while fully appropriate to a variety of situations that arise early in *Psychotherapy*, is sometimes beside the point, and therefore we shouldn't lose sight of the fact that it can fail to address our patient's question.

Consider this response, which a student suggests as an alternative: "I'd rather not say whether I want you to tell it or not; instead I prefer to leave it up to you." That seems on its surface like an altogether innocuous variation on the key phrase, and at the same time it doesn't fail to respond to the patient's question—except I don't regard the variation as so innocuous, because it can convey the distinct implication that you have certain wants (with respect to dreams, at least), but refuse to share them with him. When you intend to respond with the Basic Instruction itself, your safest course is to repeat it without paraphrase or alteration; though in the present context there is little wrong with saying, "I want to leave it up to you whether you tell the dream or not," which takes some account of the patient's actual question.

Students suggest that an appropriate response to his question is one or another variation on "It seems that you need my permission to tell me the dream." Aside from the fact that such a remark runs an appreciable risk of being wrong ("No, I didn't ask for your permission, I asked whether you wanted me to tell you the dream,'' is too likely as a counterresponse, and you've gained little, except possibly to provoke a feeling of resentment and a sense of having been misunderstood), it has the disadvantage of being overly confronting. To respond to a question with a confrontation is generally poor technique because of the implicit message ''So you shouldn't have asked.''

Other responses that students suggest include: (1) ''Do you want to tell it to me?''—which is little more than fencing, and it's the sort of turning around on himself that is best avoided; (2) ''Your bringing it up suggests that you'd like to tell it to me''—which has a gamelike flavor; (3) ''If I answered your question, then I'd be telling you what to talk about, and that is something I've said I'd rather not do''—which is the simplest and most direct response, provided, of course, that you've already said you will try to give no direction. (If example 3 is considered too harsh at this early point in therapy—and an even harsher example is, ''I wonder if you are putting me to a test, to see if I'll give you direction''—it can be softened by first remarking, as several students suggest, ''I can appreciate that it's difficult for you to decide what to talk about here, and that my not giving you any guidance at all could be a problem for you.'')

However, I regard all of these responses to be premature, because the meaning of the patient's question is by no means self-evident. What does his ''Do you want?'' mean? It might be little more than a figure of speech; he might simply be pondering aloud whether or not to tell the dream—and if that were the case, the appropriate response (aside from silence) would be, ''I take it you don't know whether you want to tell it or not.'' But what seems most prudent is to find out first what the question means and what his intention was in asking it. One student suggests doing it this way: ''I'm wondering why you're asking me if I want you to tell me the dream,'' which is a bit off the point. The point is best addressed by a simple what-do-you-mean question, like ''How do you mean 'Do you want me to?' '' It's quite possible, after all, for the question to reflect a number of different concerns. He might be wondering whether it's too soon for dreams, whether it would be better if he told you more about himself first. (Bear in mind that if he responds to the what-do-you-mean question with the counterquestion ''Why do you ask? Isn't it perfectly clear what I meant?'' you can point out that it could have had that meaning.)

What many students do is select one or another of the possible meanings for one of their options, and then they cast it in the form of an interpretation. Usually that's a good technique, but in this situation a request for clarification is better than a speculation. We have no evidence to go on, and to speculate from normative or theoretical grounds alone is usually risky. Therefore, direct steps to find out what the patient meant by the question are particularly appropriate here, and they will have the added advantage of establishing the fact that every remark he makes will be taken seriously.

The same is true for a variety of other kinds of questions a patient might ask early in *Psychotherapy*, for which this paradigm is a prototype, particularly questions about how best to proceed during the sessions; "It's up to you" is sometimes beside the point, and "What do you mean?" is usually to the point.

Paradigm 6

It's the second or third session. The patient begins with a silence of several minutes, then says, "I don't know what to talk about." If you choose not to remain silent, what good options do you have? Give three responses which you believe have merit, and evaluate each one with respect to its advantages and disadvantages.

In one or another of its variations—"I have nothing to say," "My mind is a blank," "There isn't anything to talk about today"—this is a common way for patients to begin a session, and neither is it restricted to the early sessions. "I don't know what to talk about" raises issues that are subtle and complex, in addition to their being important, and therefore we have to be ready for it in a variety of contexts and circumstances. We have to be sensitive to its dif-different forms and meanings and also to the implications of the different ways we can respond to it. I'm going to examine and discuss the issues in the framework of the five major options that my students suggest.

Option 1

The most common option is a reiteration and elaboration of the Basic Instruction, particularly its first part. The advantages are clear enough, but in this particular context it has important disadvantages too. Even allowing for the possibility that the patient has forgotten the instruction, a reiteration is likely to be beside the point because it doesn't respond to what he has said. It was not "I don't know what I *should* talk about," and it wasn't put in question form. Moreover, the Basic Instruction's directiveness depends on context; in certain contexts it is primarily a notification, but in this particular one, it can have the distinct message "Please talk anyway"—which is a prodding, an encouragement at best.

Students acknowledge the fact, but they claim an advantage to giving the patient some encouragement. I don't deny it's a useful kind of help in the short run; I contend, however, that is misses the point of what it means to promote the *therapeutic process*. The directive mode, even when used to offer encouragement and support, is so dissonant with the terms and spirit of the Basic Instruction that it should be used only as a last resort. When he experiences the need for encouragement and support, a patient may feel sufficiently gratified when you've understood his need: that's been my clinical experience. Moreover, he'll also feel it when the meaning and purport of his communications are accurately apprehended, when his intentions and feelings and experiences are well grasped. Therefore, a principal criterion for offering interpretations, particularly when it is early in therapy, is to show him that he is making himself understood and fully conveying his feelings.

Option 2

Many students suggest a clear directive that deviates from the Basic Instruction. Here are three representative examples: "You don't have to say anything until you are ready to," "Sometimes it's best not to prepare what to say," and "What were you just thinking about?" Such remarks can be helpful in the short run, but they circumvent the decision process and implicate the free-association method. (Some do it explicitly: for example, "One possibility that might be helpful in getting you to start speaking is to say whatever comes to mind.") Bear in mind that the patient is free to free-associate, if that's what he wants to do; *Psychotherapy* proscribes your playing a directive role in the decision.

But the directive that can be evoked by a patient's "I don't know what to talk about" is apt to be more subtle than the examples I've given. Consider the following remark: "I take it you are not sure you want to share what you've been thinking." That seems like an altogether tactful kind of articulation, doesn't it? And even if mistaken, it is likely to be well-taken. But notice how it conveys the directive "Please share your thoughts" in a subtle way. (In fact, because of its very subtlety, its directive properties may perhaps be insidious, masked as they are behind a seemingly empathic attitude.) This response, "Perhaps you are uncertain about what is important to talk about here, and you would like me to ask questions," is a speculation that is freer of direction. However, the word "important" carries an unwanted implication which the student hastens to rectify, and he does it by adding, "Whatever you have to say is important, and it is up to you to decide what to talk about," which gives an overriding directive tenor to the response.

Option 3

Students include an empathic kind of response among their options. Here are two good examples: "I can appreciate that you find yourself in a difficult, and perhaps an awkward, situation—to choose what it is you want to say," "I can understand that it is difficult to decide what to talk about. Perhaps the idea that you can say what you want—that it's up to you—makes you uncomfortable." These kinds of remarks have the advantage of being supportive, while at the same time articulating the patient's experience. Moreover, even if the articulation turns out to be inaccurate, they are likely to be well-taken because they restrict their focus to the decision process. Compare them with this example: "I guess it's hard for you to tell me some of the things you are thinking about," which focuses on the defense, and notice how it takes a significant step from the patient's "I don't know what to talk about." Without including any evidence, such a speculation can be taken as a criticism of sorts; even if it happens to be correct, it might put him on the defensive and might even cause him to worry about his suitability for therapy.

When you formulate a supportive remark in a nonempathic kind of way—when you do it didactically, as in, "It is sometimes difficult to decide how to begin," and "Knowing that you can talk about whatever you like sometimes makes it harder to speak"—its understanding component may be diluted, and what remains is little more than reassurance. (Such didactic remarks can have the further disadvantage of being gratuitous, merely reflecting what the patient has said.) To be empathic is often quite different from being reassuring. For one thing, reassurance, unlike empathy, can be unreassuring when its intent is too transparent. ("Why are you reassuring me? Do you think I'm worried? And if so, should I be?")

Option 4

Students include an interpretation as one of their three options. Their favorite is exemplified by, "I take it you are waiting [wishing, hoping] for me to tell you what you should talk about [help you decide, suggest a topic]." Next in frequency is, "Perhaps it's not that you don't know what to talk about, but rather that you are uncertain whether there are things you should talk about," or, "Perhaps thoughts were occurring to you when you were silent, but you weren't sure whether you should discuss them." Finally, some center on their own reaction: "Do you have some misgivings about my reaction to some things you want to talk about?" or, "Perhaps you were wondering how I would react to your thoughts."

The big disadvantage to any interpretation—and students acknowledge it—is that it has to be too speculative. In practice, of course, the requisite evidence may be gleaned from the previous session in a way that removes the interpretation from the realm of pure speculation, and then it becomes a good option. But I believe, as a rule of thumb, that our interpretation is best addressed to what the patient has actually said rather than to the preceding silence. And some students focus on the silence, on its meaning—for example, "Perhaps you believe it is bad to be silent in here." Even when some evidence to support such an interpretation is available, I believe it can be ill-advised to raise this issue so early. Silence in therapy is likely to be so complicated and multidetermined that it should not be dealt with too soon and too superficially; it can wait until both its meaning and its relevancy are especially clear.

Another aspect of the interpretations students suggest is their incompleteness. They seek to articulate how and what the patient is experiencing without attempting to provide a reason, to say why. To be sure, a good interpretation needn't be complete; articulation alone is a major function of the interpretive mode. Nevertheless, an incomplete interpretation has a way of shading into a confrontation, into an observation made from an outside vantage point whose principal function is to show the patient an aspect of his behavior or experience with the implicit but clear directive "And please pay attention to that now." To be sure, the distinction between an interpretation and a confrontation is often only a fine one; but when it's incomplete, seeking only to articulate, then an interpretation is more likely to be confronting—and confrontations, especially early in *Psychotherapy*, run the risk of unwanted implications.

The most common is a scolding, and the following example is a good one: "Perhaps you feel it would be easier if I took charge of the session." Even if the thrust of that remark is entirely accurate, it readily lends itself to being perceived as a scolding; the patient can complete it with, "And I ought not to be feeling that." Many confrontations evoke embarrassment, if not shame; the patient can feel caught short and exposed. Of course, the same can be true for complete interpretations too. However, the fact that they provide an explanation of *why* can go far toward eliminating their judgmental and critical implications and softening their power to evoke embarrassment and shame.

At any rate, this early in therapy we have to try to avoid confrontations, because, more than interpretations do, they tend to put a patient on the defensive—and he is likely to be on the defensive quite enough.

Option 5

Some students suggest a remark whose main function is to clarify what the patient means; but rather than simply "How do you mean *I don't know what to talk about*?" they ask the question by enumerating several of its possible meanings. For example, "Is that because you have nothing on your mind, or that what you are thinking seems trivial, or that there are several things on your mind and you don't know which to talk about?" That can be an effective way to ask for meaning insofar as it avoids the potential disingenuousness of "What do you mean?"

Though I'm sure it's amply clear to you how much stress I lay on our basic and overriding orientation of striving to understand—how that includes striving to know what our patient is experiencing in respect to feelings and needs, as well as an equal if not greater focus on his cognitive meanings and communications—I want to emphasize how this orientation requires you to keep in mind the question "What does it mean?" But before you express that question with the remark "I don't understand," you have to be sure you're not saying "I don't understand why [so tell me more about it]." Your directive should only be this: "Help me understand what you mean to be saying; clarify your thinking for me." Accordingly, you ask after meaning only when your patient's utterance was unclear or ambiguous. And this paradigm provides a good instance of that circumstance, because it isn't clear in what sense the patient means "I don't know what to talk about," and, therefore, to ask him for clarification is appropriate from a number of vantage points. He might be unsure what will be most beneficial to talk about, he might feel the need for direction, his mind might be blank, and the like. So if he responds with a "Why do you ask?" you can explain that you weren't sure you understood his meaning, and then go on to enumerate the different possibilities. The fact that you have such possibilities in mind protects you from the danger of using the clarification question for directive purposes alone.

Paradigm 7

It's the second or third session. The patient begins with a silence of several minutes, and then says, "I am bothered by you sitting there and staring at me." Again, aside from silence, give three good options for a remark and evaluate each one.

Many of the same considerations apply to Paradigms 6 and 7, and the best option is again to seek clarification of meaning, even though it may again run the risk of seeming to be disingenuous. But if the patient responds with, "Isn't it perfectly plain?" when you have said, "It is not clear to me what you mean, what it is that is bothering you," you can list some of the different possibilities: (1) It may be your silence that is at issue, or your passivity; (2) It may be that eye contact is being maintained; (3) It may be that what bothers him is a sense of pressure and expectation, or a sense that your gaze ("stare") is critical, or that you can see what he is thinking; (4) The patient may be bothered out of a sense of vulnerability. One or several of these possibilities can be offered if he balks at the clarification question.

What most students do, however, is proceed with one or another of those possibilities and offer a formulation that is an incomplete interpretation (if not a confrontation). The big disadvantage, again, is prematurity: they are necessarily guessing. They therefore run the risk of imposing an extraneous issue. For example, "I take it you mean that you would rather I didn't just sit here and stare, that I would be active." The patient may, after all, be bothered by the staring alone.

Some students include clarification as one of their options (for example, "What would you want me to do?" and "I am wondering what it is about this that bothers you"—which I am perhaps too generously counting as questions aimed at clarification), but most restrict their options to interpretations. Many interpret "bothered" as "angry" and relate it to the silence; many interpret "staring" as "scrutinizing" or "evaluating"; and many focus on self-conscious and vulnerable feelings. All of them are intelligent guesses, but guesses nonetheless, because there is only a single piece of evidence available, the opening silence, and it hardly provides a basis for any of them. Students do invoke the opening silence in their interpretations, and some thereby incur additional disadvantages. Consider this example: "I wonder if this is a possibility, that what's really bothering you right now is the fact that I've remained silent so far,"and notice the interesting implication that you know better what is "really" at issue—the patient is wrong if he thinks it's the staring. To counter with, "But I am not staring," which a few students suggest, is unnecessarily risky because it may provoke an argument that centers on the definition of "staring." And even a tactful, empathic remark like, "I can appreciate that you feel bothered; this situation is a new one for you and takes a while to get used to. I don't mean to stare, I only mean to listen and try my best to understand," might lead to a disagreement.

My chief motive for including this paradigm is because it raises the interesting question, Should you respond by modifying your glance and reducing your staring? Not a single student of mine suggests it as an option. When I raise this possibility with them, students are convinced I would regard such a response as acquiescing to "manipulation," and they invoke the familiar psychoanalytic injunction against allowing ourselves to be "manipulated." When I refuse to acknowledge such an injunction for *Psychotherapy* and then question its rationale, they challenge me on the grounds that our autonomy is violated when we acquiesce to such a request.

I meet the challenge, first of all, by reminding them that it's the patient's ego-autonomy that needs to be protected, not ours. Then I point out that we are not free in the same ways that our patient is—we aren't free to be late to sessions, for instance, or to express our personal feelings and attitudes. In fact, we are under enormous constraints, especially when conducting *Psychotherapy*, and one of them is a constraint upon preventing the patient from influencing our actions. The key question is this: What considerations determine how and when we shall allow our actions to be directly influenced by him?

That's a large question which has to be examined from a variety of perspectives. Here I will restrict myself to requests for action, which include changing the appointment time and fee, and can range from relatively minor requests, such as shading a light bulb which is shining in the patient's eyes or removing a piece of office decoration he finds disturbing, to relatively major ones, such as dressing in a style that is less offensive to him, reading his autobiography, and staring.

Most practitioners and teachers would take the position that our first move should be to find out what lies behind the request; and I regard that as a good rule of thumb. But they would advocate taking this step no matter what the nature of the request is—and that, I believe, is unwarranted and unnecessary. The rationale is to find out first about the patient's motives and fantasies, but I see no compelling reason why they can't be found out afterward. Therefore, I would amplify the rule of thumb in the following way: you should delay making a decision only when the nature of the request has a significant bearing on the method and procedures of therapy itself.

In my opinion, the critical consideration is whether the *therapeutic process* stands to be impaired or impeded, either from the patient's vantage point or yours (that is, whether your ability to supervise it will be impaired or impeded). So if the light bulb has no relevance to the *therapeutic process*, you can go right ahead and acquiesce without first finding out whether the patient's reason is "legitimate"; and the same is true for "staring." If you need to "stare" the way you do in order to listen the way you listen best, then that counts as a significant request, and you should delay responding to it until you've found out how important it is to the patient. When, however, that isn't the case, when the "staring" has little relevance to your ability to listen and understand, you can make the accommodation without first satisfying yourself that the patient has a "good" reason for requesting it. Protecting our neutrality is far more important than safeguarding ourselves against "manipulation." (Much more about this in chapter nine.) And the ruling rationale is always the *therapeutic process*, in the context of the terms and spirit of the Basic Instruction.

4

The Timing Paradigms

Instructions: This study is made up of simulated transcripts of the
beginning of four therapy sessions, each with a different
patient. Each paradigm is constructed in such a way that
it is possible for the therapist to have said nothing during
it. Your task is to speak for him—to indicate where you,
as therapist, would speak and what you would say. Try
for a minimum of four interventions for each paradigm,
and try to base them on what has gone before (not on
what you see coming). Your remarks should be independent of each other. Pauses are indicated in the transcript
by asterisks; each asterisk represents about five seconds
of silence.

Paradigm 1

[The patient is an inhibited and detached twenty-six-
year-old, who speaks slowly, in an apparent effort to maintain his composure.
This is the fifth session. It starts with a one minute silence]

This morning I was thinking about something that I should tell you.**
It's something I've thought about a lot, and whenever I do, it always
confuses me because I don't understand why I did it, what it was all
about.** And it's something I am very ashamed of.****

During this pause you might have the impulse to signal the fact that you are
waiting compassionately, eager to hear what the patient has in mind; and you

88

might also want to say something to help him get started on the narrative. In fact, any remark here is likely to serve only those two functions. Articulating his sense of shame, or pointing out that he seems reluctant to tell whatever it is he feels he "should" tell, will only convey the message, "Yes, I understand, but please go ahead anyway." And even an interpretation like, "Perhaps because it evokes such shame, you mustn't allow yourself to understand it," can amount to little more than a supportive gesture. Moreover, when you keep your silence at this juncture, making no kind of gesture, you make a significant contribution to the quality and texture of a *Psychotherapy* session: you define it as an essentially self-directed monologue and distinguish it from an interview or conversation. You also establish that you are steadily and always waiting compassionately, eager to hear what your patient has in mind; no special signal is ever necessary because your orientation toward him is unwavering.

But I guess I should tell you about it.**

This is the second "I should tell you," and some students choose to intervene by drawing a connection between the patient's sense of should and the fact that the event is shameful. Though it makes good psychological sense, I doubt whether the patient needs to have the connection drawn for him. He is clearly saying he'd rather not have to recount the event because it evokes shame, and he feels compelled to tell it out of a belief that it might be important for therapy. Drawing his attention to that (by raising the question, "In what sense do you mean *should*?" or "I'm not sure I understand how you mean *I should tell you*") could have some therapeutic value, especially if there is reason to suspect that he has forgotten or misconstrued the Basic Instruction, but otherwise it runs the risk of conveying the message "You ought not to feel you should." My preference, therefore, would be to keep the matter in mind and make no comment now. Chances are good it will be possible later to return to the "should" and use it in a meaningful way. (A number of students introduce an interpretation later in the paradigm with a remark like, "I think I understand now why you said at the beginning that this was something you felt you should tell me," and that is good technique.)

It happened when I was about eleven years old, going on twelve, I believe.** What I did was fake an illness. And I spent almost a whole year—a full school year, I mean—in bed, pretending I was sick when I really wasn't.****

This pause is where many practitioners would ask a question. It would necessarily have to be an interviewing question, and at best could serve the function of facilitating a fuller presentation of the event. Instead of offering that kind of help, I believe you should wait patiently, thereby showing confidence that the patient will continue at his own pace and explain the event adequately enough.

It was a terrible thing to do to ... uh ... * to my parents.

The hesitation is, of course, noteworthy, and if you thought the patient was going to say "to myself," you might choose to remark on it. Again, however, it would be better to wait until its relevance and meaning become clear. I am assuming, of course, that nothing he said before—during the previous session, for instance—has any bearing on it.

The impoverished context of the paradigm gives the study a substantial artificiality. Timing is normally based on the background of the entire course of therapy, and a great deal can depend on the session that preceded. Since, however, the paradigm, along with its brief introductory paragraph, provides our only context, considerations of timing must be limited to that. Furthermore, my commentaries are necessarily selective; by no means am I going to attempt an exhaustive consideration of interventional possibilities. My chief purpose in this study is to illustrate and defend *Psychotherapy*'s central timing criterion, which can be formulated quite simply according to the conception of the *therapeutic process*: in short, we speak when we judge that the process can benefit significantly from something we can say. At the same time, however, we have to decide what kind of remark will best serve that function, and in many instances it will be an interpretation. But I think it needs emphasis that even though interpretations can be construed as bearers (and barers) of insight, in the broadest sense of the term "insight," attainment of insight is not synonymous with the *therapeutic process*. Insightful discovery and reorganization may be the result or outcome of the process, but the process itself denotes the patient's principal way of working. Thus, the fundamental timing question is, How does interpreting relate to the *therapeutic process*? How does our principal way of working relate to his principal way of working?

They were very worried, because I was supposedly sick, and yet the doctor didn't know what was wrong with me.*** It was an easy thing to do, too. It was really quite easy. All I had to do was say I didn't feel well. And the only symptom I had ... I mean, I showed, was a low-grade fever; and I found a way to fake that. You see, what I would do is put the thermometer under my body, under the blankets, when no one was looking, and that was enough to make it go up to around ninety-nine or so. [takes a cigarette, but doesn't light it]****

The moment seems right for a useful remark, and many students choose this break in the narrative for the first of their four interventions. Many offer an observation about the significance of the patient's having been able to fool his parents so thoroughly; many focus on feelings of guilt, and some wonder aloud whether the experience was not frightening. Beyond, perhaps, a kind of empathic support, I recognize no useful function to such speculations. The patient has not alluded to any guilt or fright, and we have to avoid speculations based on theoretical considerations alone (or even, for that matter, those based on common sense alone).

The fact that he takes a cigarette at this point is worth noting, but I don't see what useful comment can be made about it now. Anxiety can be inferred, perhaps—But is it appropriate to say so? "I think your taking a cigarette now might mean you're feeling anxious about the event, or about telling it to me." In addition to considerations I have already mentioned, such a comment only tells the patient how he feels, which is quite different from helping him articulate his feelings. Since he doesn't seem to want any help with articulating his feelings (in no way has he asked to be told), such an interpretation is apt to be gratuitous and might be perceived as an imposition. An interpretation can be both an imposition and a constraint on freedom of expression and exploration; to tell a patient how he feels, or must be feeling, or how he felt, can actually impede the *therapeutic process*. Whether it facilitates or impedes depends on clinical judgment and context—which is why timing is generally regarded as the most ineffable and unteachable aspect of psychotherapy technique.

Finally, a substantial number of students give voice to surprise, and several to disbelief as well, that it could have been possible to fake an illness for a whole year. "I fail to see how a temperature of 99 degrees could have been considered serious enough to keep you at home for a year," is how one student puts it; another challenges with, "I wonder if you truly did not feel well, if not physically then psychologically." I regard such remarks, even when their skepticism is muted, as serious technical errors. Now, it frequently happens in therapy that you hear surprising things and experience a sense of disbelief, but to express such reactions to the patient introduces a fresh element into the situation. For one thing, it implicates your personal opinions and beliefs; for another, it can stir up doubt in his mind, doubt which may serve no useful purpose. You have to keep from defining yourself as the doubter or even as the skeptic. Taking at face value what your patient is taking at face value is altogether appropriate, and good timing requires a sensitivity to those moments when he is ready to experience some doubt and to reconsider the condition of his memory. Notice that the patient has not hinted at any doubts or surprises. And bear in mind that, this early in therapy, it's probably impossible for you to know whether he was truly pretending the illness or whether he was the one who was fooled, and whether his memory of the event is faulty.

Therefore, though the moment seems so right for a useful remark, the question remains, What kind? Now, whenever you sense that the *therapeutic process* requires you to say *something*, you have two options: one is an interpretation, the second is a gratuity. With no interpretation in mind, your options reduce to a simple paraphrasing of what the patient has said. That, however, may still be better than nothing, and chances are good you can add something significant to your gratuitous remark that may turn out to be useful for the *therapeutic process*. For instance, if you remarked, "I gather you discovered a way to appear sick when you believed you really weren't," the idea of "appearing" versus "believing" may turn out to have significant reverberations both for the patient's reconstruction of the past as well as for his construction of the present.

> The way it all started was that when we got back from our summer
> vacation . . . No, I was at camp that summer, I think.** Yes, at camp.
> Anyway, I got sick, truly sick, with a sore throat and fever and . . . *
> And I had to stay in bed for over two weeks. Then I got better. And it
> was the middle of September already, and I had to go to school, into a
> new grade. It was the seventh grade, I think.*

Is this the time to offer an explanation, no matter how superficial? (Should you, for instance, connect the feigned illness to problems he was having at school?) Students think it is, and offer a variety of interpretations. (One goes so far as to introduce sex: "Was there something about entering the seventh grade that frightened you? This is a time when children start maturing sexually.")

A fundamental question is this: Should you be wondering why the incident itself occurred? Or, more precisely, In what way and for what reasons should you be wondering why? Now, to listen to the account of an event like the one the patient is telling without wondering why it happened is virtually impossible, but to keep a certain perspective on such mental activity is not. The temptation is always great to play the role of sage, or detective, to help solve a mystery for your patient (which is likely, of course, to be what he hopes and expects, if not also fears, that you will do). And the key question is whether that is consonant with the timing criteria of facilitating and promoting the *therapeutic process*. I obviously would not have raised the question here if I believed the answer to it was yes. At best, in my opinion, the answer is a "sometimes."

Offering interpretations can be construed as our way of "participating" in the *therapeutic process*. That formulation, however, is potentially misleading, insofar as it portrays us as providing understanding or information about a patient's inner and outer realities, and doing it for his sake; or it implies that we help him make discoveries by making interpretations in order to maximize the occurrence of such discoveries. Instead of that congenial formulation, I prefer a more awkward one: Interpretations are our way of "supervising" the *therapeutic process*. This formulation implies that our main purpose in offering interpretations is to promote the ongoing process itself. Since the process is conceptualized as wholly intrapsychic, as entailing autonomous action on the patient's part, and since the overriding goal is for him to be active—to actively strive for understanding, actively exercise and strengthen his synthetic-function, and thereby maximize his control and freedom—it follows that our chief goal is not to impart information, not to give understanding and insight; it is to provide the optimal conditions for him to examine himself openly and freely, and to experience himself as fully and as authentically as he can. Accordingly, it is dissonant with the goals and spirit of *Psychotherapy* for roles to be divided in such a way that he provides the facts and we the meanings. And it's also somewhat dissonant to conceive of ourselves as participating as a kind of partner in the explaining process. Our function is principally to promote the work of therapy itself, and our promise to speak when we have "something useful to say" really means "useful for the *therapeutic process*." We must try to bear constantly in mind that it is a process and not an outcome.

So, for instance, if you are listening to the account of an incident in which your patient apparently abused his brother cruelly, but he shows no apparent recognition of his cruelty, you won't offer that observation in the form of an interpretation—even if you believe you can explain why the cruelty occurred as well as the reason it remains unrecognized, and even when you have good reason to expect that your remarks won't be taken by him as a criticism or directive. The crucial consideration is this: your only purpose in making the interpretation is to proffer an insight, an understanding, and that purpose is both insufficient in itself and potentially inimical to *Psychotherapy*'s central timing criterion. (But I will have occasion to qualify this stringent principle, and soften it, in subsequent chapters.)

With respect to Paradigm 1, my point is this: you should not be trying very hard to figure out why the patient feigned the illness when he was eleven; what you should be trying to figure out is what the event meant to him then and what it means now—why he is recounting it the way he is, what it might reveal about him, and the like.

Yes, the seventh. And I guess I wasn't happy in school—though I don't remember that part of it too well.***

A student offers the speculation, "I wonder if the reason you don't remember it too well is that it's painful to recall how it felt not to be happy in school," which draws attention to a possible defense. There have already been several points of expressed uncertainty in the patient's account, uncertainty which can reflect the defense of repression; and defenses, especially when they are impeding the *therapeutic process*, have a certain priority with respect to timing. In view of the fact that there is no evidence for the speculation (and the patient might wonder aloud, "What makes you think so?"), it might be better to draw his attention to the matter with a remark like, "Do you notice how uncertain you are of several aspects of the event? You're uncertain whether you were at camp that summer, whether it was the seventh grade, whether you were unhappy in school." That, however, is a confrontation and a directive; it "holds up the mirror" and requests him to pay attention to something he's overlooking. I believe it can be justified by the fact that you have an interpretation in mind. If the patient were to respond with a question amounting to "Yes, but why do you want me to notice the fact?" you could reply, "Because I am wondering whether this kind of uncertainty is typical for your memory of your childhood or whether it is associated specifically with the incident you are telling me about." If he persists with a "So what if it is?" you could suggest he might be applying the defense of repression to this particular event because of profound feelings of shame associated with it. To be sure, this is a diagnostic interpretation, a kind that should be used sparingly during *Psychotherapy*; but my point is that a confrontation can be ventured when you have an interpretation clearly in mind and ready to give.

> And so one morning I decided I wanted to stay home. So I told my mother I wasn't feeling well again, and . . .** And she let me stay in bed.*** And that's when it all started, when I got the idea of faking being sick. I remember she decided to take my temperature, and she left the room while the thermometer was in my mouth. And I just took it out and put it under my body so it would show a fever. [lights the cigarette]**** I couldn't have been sure it would work, but it did. I don't know where I got the idea to do it. I just . . . I just did it.*** My mother never suspected anything, and neither did the doctor. And once it began, once I was into it, I just kept right on doing it.** And the longer it went on, the more impossible, you know, it was to stop.**

Students introduce the theme of guilt at this point, and some suggest to the patient that he must have felt frightened. For example, "And I wonder if perhaps that wasn't very frightening, to have started something and then to find there was no turning back." Again, however, I find it difficult to see what value such interpretations could now have. In my estimation, they come too close to being reassuring, supportive gestures and nothing more. Even a confrontation like, "I noticed you lit the cigarette right after you spoke about putting the thermometer under your body; I wonder if there's something about this detail that makes you nervous," can serve a supportive function.

Several students suggest a clarification question, asking, Why was it more impossible to stop the longer it went on? Of course, if you don't understand, you have to ask; but in this particular context a clarification question might have a challenging edge to it—as if you are questioning the logic, or perhaps doubting the psychological validity of the claim. To avoid those unwanted implications, the question can be formulated this way: "I think I understand why that would be, but I'm not sure I understand it the way you do—so would you please explain."

> So I just stayed in bed and played sick.**** I can remember times when I felt awful about it, mostly because my parents were so worried—and so needlessly too.*** But my mother was really wonderful about it. She was always good when any of us were sick, thinking up all kinds of projects to keep us occupied. She taught me things, and she was always buying me new books. She used to play cards and chess with me; and she even made me do exercises so I wouldn't get too weak, and she would do them with me.* She tried to keep my spirits up, even though . . . even though my spirits were actually quite high anyway.** I wasn't unhappy about staying in bed. Actually, I was . . . very happy.

"Are you saying you're not sure whether it was something distressing about school that made you stay away, or something very appealing about staying home that determined your behavior?" asks a student, and again I question its value. The patient is clearly describing his mother as a willing, if not eager, accomplice. But notice that he is mystified by the event, despite the fact that staying home was so pleasant for both of them. Unless you assume he doesn't recognize the import of what he is recounting, you aren't going to get very far with a line of inquiry that seeks to discover the true reason for the event. On the other hand, since he has spoken in a somewhat tentative manner, you could draw attention to it—"I take it you're not really sure whether you were happy"—because the defense of disavowal could be at work.

Some students stress the mother's role—"It sounds as if she almost encouraged you to be sick." At this juncture the only point of doing that would be to help explain the event, if not also to exonerate him from culpability.

> There was plenty to do, and I was never bored.** I kept up with my schoolwork: my teacher would send me workbooks, and my parents would help me with my lessons.** And my father would come home from work and spend time with me. He would even read the newspaper to me—the *New York Times* [small smile]. And that's when I started being such a devoted newspaper reader; I have to read the *Times* every day or else my day isn't complete.****

I inserted this piece of "material" deliberately (and maliciously) in order to lure the unwary student into a neat interpretation of the patient's *New York Times* habit. Patients do that too—provide us with the grounds for an interpretation they already know full well (set us up, so to speak, and watch us do our stuff). At any rate, most of my students are unable to resist the temptation. I won't present any of their interpretations; they are varied and interesting, but suffice it to say they could only have the aim of spoiling the patient's habit of reading the *Times*, and, fortunately, it's unlikely they would be successful in doing so.

> So it was really very nice staying home all that time.** All except for the fact that I was pretending and making them worry for nothing. That used to make me feel bad, sometimes.*****

The account is now complete, and the patient is apparently considering the mixed feelings it evokes in him. If you have an idea about the account's current meaning, if it occurs to you that he might be experiencing the same kind of conflict right now (with his current parent-doctor), then you can lay the groundwork for an important piece of therapeutic work, a potentially vital transference interpretation. To make a transference interpretation now, as several students do (for example, "The thought occurs to me that in telling me how easy it was for you to fool your parents, you are expressing some concern that you may be able to fool me," and " . . . perhaps you feel guilty that you are not telling me things you feel you should"), is apt to be premature. For one thing, the patient might be taken aback or find the idea farfetched. For another, he may arrive at the realization himself if you give him time. But a preliminary interpretation, formulated in a way that is congruent with the transference or can later be translated into transference terms, might be resonant and useful.

A good possibility is conveyed by this succinct example: "Perhaps you felt that only by pretending to be ill could you get the help and attention you wanted and needed." Another is, "Perhaps on some level you enjoyed being able to assert yourself, even indirectly, and control the situation—to manipulate their actions and even their feelings. That's a kind of power you might have enjoyed, even though you felt guilty about it at times." And here's an example that articulates the conflict in a way that is most congruent with the transference: "Do you think it possible that part of you wanted your parents to help you go back to school? Perhaps feeling bad had more to do with the fact that you felt they allowed you to fool them than with playing sick." As they stand, and out of their context, these interpretations can be faulted for seeking to explain the event in purely historical terms. However, the fact that such formulations are likely to have significant implications for the present, that you have a transference interpretation in mind (and it's a transference issue that is bound to have a profound effect on the way the patient construes therapy and relates to you), can take precedence in respect to timing.

There is a point of view, especially prevalent among analysts, that transference has the highest priority with respect to timing, that every manifestation of transference requires active interpretation. Some teachers qualify the point this way: transference requires interpretation only if and when it is also serving the function of resistance—otherwise *Keep the transference in the background!* Some resolve the issue by maintaining (as Freud originally did) that transference is intrinsically a resistance phenomenon (a substitute defense against the remembering and redintegrating of early experiences with important parent figures). Because resistance can so readily be formulated in terms of the *therapeutic process* and therefore translated into the terms of our central timing criterion, I am tempted to accept the view that all true transference is *a fortiori* resistance—and that if it isn't resistance, it doesn't deserve to be called true tranference. But I believe there are few, if any, valid regularities of this sort in the field of human affairs—even psychotherapy. Transference phenomena cannot routinely be regarded and treated as if they were nothing more than a variety of resistance against the essential work of therapy; sometimes they are and sometimes they aren't. When they are, whether by cause or by effect, we can satisfy our central timing criterion; we can formulate the transference in a way to highlight its resistive function, and our decision to offer the interpretation will be based on the goal of restoring the *therapeutic process*. It matters little whether we construe the transference as intrinsic to the naturally functioning *therapeutic process* or as based on our impersonality and neutrality, the fact that it serves to impede the process is what counts. But when they are not serving a resistive function, then we must choose whether to base our interpretation on another criterion altogether.

Moreover, even when you accept the point of view that all transference is resistance, there is your patient's point of view to consider. In order for theoretical formulations to be clinically useful they must be capable of translation into the terms of his experience; the critical test, after all, is how meaningful and valid they are to him. Resistance phenomena pose no intrinsic problem in this regard, though they do pose difficult technical problems. They can, in principle, be interpreted and explained to a patient in ways he can accept as valid. Transference experiences, on the other hand, frequently have a special quality that sets them apart from resistance, and it is far from uncommon for him to experience them as an integral part of therapy and in no way an impediment. For instance, if the transference is "positive" (insofar as he regards you as a nurturant, loving, and perhaps all-powerful, figure), then it may strike a patient as farfetched to entertain the possibility that the transference is serving a defensive or resistive function. And even "negative" transference can have an apparently facilitating effect on therapeutic movement (for instance, viewing you as a demanding, even critical, figure could spur a patient on in the work of therapy). So it's quite possible, and also quite common, to encounter a fullblown transference which can only be formulated, but not interpreted, as a resistance, because it does not in fact accompany a tangible or phenomenally experienced kind of "resistance."

Faced with this situation, you have to judge whether the central timing criterion should maintain its precedence, or whether interpreting the transference (because it is there) has an overriding benefit. If you prefer to keep the transference in the background, you will opt for the former and let the patient figure things out for himself, so to speak—and that is generally the position I advocate. I don't believe, not as a general rule at least, that transference must be given an overriding priority. A certain and special priority, yes; but when a patient is "working well" we don't necessarily have to "work with" him on transference issues (as we do on resistance), we can allow them to "work themselves out" the same way we do for other kinds of issues (not including resistance). For one thing, we have to avoid teaching him that the way to elicit our active participation is by focusing on feelings and fantasies about us and/or the therapy; and for another, we should not want to foster the transference and cause it to assume an artificially exaggerated significance. Therefore, we have to avoid taking steps that could artificially bring it into the foreground.

There are, however, certain patients for whom special factors must be considered to outweigh the advantages of keeping the transference in the background. And though I deliberately sidestep the issue of individual differences among patients in this book, it is misleading to give the impression that it doesn't matter who and what the patient is. In certain key respects, it has to matter a great deal, and this is one of them. Because the exception I have in mind involves a diagnostic consideration, the category of *narcissism*, and the observation that patients with significant narcissistic features tend to form a transference that assumes a special significance of its own. Rather than serving the traditional functions (namely, transference in the service of recall and redintegration), such patients typically use us as "objects" with whom they play out a variety of intrapsychic processes (incorporative and projective); we become, in a certain way, an actual part of their intrapsychic structure. Moreover, that a resistive function is thereby being served is by no means evident; rather, the so-called narcissistic transference tends to become the arena within which the crucial therapeutic issues take place. And when that's the case, it may be necessary to take serious exception to our fundamental timing criterion; it may be necessary, in other words, to work with the patient's narcissistic transference for its own sake. A substantial body of opinion among analysts holds that this is equally true for every genuine transference-*neurosis*. Brian Bird has written an interesting essay on this subject, titled "Notes on Transference: Universal Phenomenon and Hardest

Part of Analysis,'' in which he eloquently states that the transference-neurosis—which he distinguishes from transference-*reactions*—as a fully intrapsychic process, is the *sine qua non* of psychoanalysis.[1]

In addition to such diagnostic considerations, there are certain clinical situations and circumstances which mitigate against keeping the transference in the background, and Paradigm 1, in my judgment, is one of them. The form of the patient's transference, the way it pertains to his underlying attitudes toward therapy, happens to be crucial to the way the therapy is likely to unfold. And to the extent that it is crucial, active measures have to be taken to uncover it as soon as possible. But, as I've said, to do anything more than lay the groundwork at this point is apt to be premature.

> I was able to fool them so easily. It was really such a simple thing to do. And sometimes I would worry that they would find out what I was doing.*

A student takes note of the patient's repeated "sometimes" by asking for clarification with "Sometimes?" The patient seems to be suggesting there were times he enjoyed worrying his parents for nothing, and times he wished they would find out what he was doing, and this can be a useful issue to articulate.

> I also thought I would have to tell them sooner or later—that I would just have to, you know.***

A student takes this opportunity to draw a connection with the way the patient began his narrative, saying, "I wonder why you are telling this secret to me. I remember your saying before that you feel you *should* tell it to me, as if something or someone were forcing you," which is an interesting possibility, suggesting that the present recounting is designed in some way to undo the fact that he didn't ever tell his parents. As it stands, however, without the full interpretation, its tenor is confronting and its purpose unclear. On the other hand, the following example is very much to the point: "Perhaps you feel that in telling me, you have satisfied the sense of obligation you felt then—that you would have to tell them sooner or later—and that maybe in some way I am taking the place of your parents."

> Sometimes I remember even thinking that they must really know I was pretending . . .* You know, that they did know it . . . after a while, anyway, but they decided for some reason or other not to say anything to me about it . . .* to go along with it.***

1. Brian Bird, "Notes on Transference: Universal Phenomenon and Hardest Part of Analysis," *J. Amer. Psychoan. Assoc.* 2, no. 20: 267–301.

I can't resist the temptation of presenting this remarkable example because it so flagrantly violates every principle I've been defending: "Because you were probably too young to remember what really happened, perhaps you were feeling guilty about causing your family concern because you were ill, really ill, for so long—in fact, in great pain, particularly your joints, which your mother exercised so your muscles wouldn't atrophy. And you probably denied this fact then, as you are denying it now, because you felt the pain was a punishment for fooling them and was not a part of your illness. I assume you had rheumatic fever, which many children contract after strep throat, but because you associated it with not wanting to go to school, to you it was not an illness at all; and any symptoms related to this illness, rather than your temperature, was viewed by you as a punishment."

I don't know why I thought that.***

Some students show an interest in the fantasy that his parents knew all along. ("Perhaps your feeling that they really knew you were pretending was a way of easing your guilt about fooling them; by thinking they weren't fooled, you could be sure of not being blamed for fooling them.") The fantasy may be relevant to the transference meaning of the account, and several students take the opportunity to introduce that transference meaning here—for example, "Perhaps you also think that I see through you, and I realize that you are not telling me things you feel you should, but I am going along with that and not saying anything about it for my own reasons." A tentatively formulated version of the same idea is, "Can it be that you are wondering the same way about therapy? It occurs to me that it may seem like another situation in which you have the same kind of control, and that may be worrying you." I'm not sure that this may not be the best and most tactful way to introduce the idea. Tentativeness should not be confused with gingerliness, and it can reduce the potential shock, which I feel is always worth trying to do. In fact, you might tell the patient how tentatively you held the idea, and add perhaps that he was likely to find it farfetched.

But then, there's so much about the whole thing that I don't know: Why did I do it in the first place? Why did I keep it up so long? What was really going on? [puts out cigarette butt and falls silent]

The narrative seems finished—the paradigm is—and the patient has again expressed his mystification. The moment seems right for a useful interpretation, for a remark that can open fresh avenues of exploration. You face a number of choices and decisions. The main one is whether to attempt a direct answer to the patient's questions, and if so how to do it in a way that can promote the *therapeutic process*.

Instead of offering any answers, you have the option of addressing his sense of expectancy—for example, "I take it you are waiting for me to provide you with some of the answers, now that you have provided me with the facts." That, however, seems a little harsh and sounds too much like a scolding, implying that he ought not to have such expectations. The best way to deal with this kind of issue is first to wait out his silence and then make the interpretation after he has reacted to your nonresponsiveness—for instance, "I think I understand why you're now feeling disappointed [upset, irritated, angry]; you were expecting me to provide you with some of the answers once you had provided me with the facts, and I didn't do that." In other words, allow the patient's expectancy to run its natural course.

A student formulates the expectancy issue in transference terms with, "Perhaps you are concerned that, like your parents, who may have known what was going on and didn't tell you, I may have some knowledge about you which I don't tell you," and I think the patient would reject this suggestion, feeling it was beside the point. (He might also feel that you are gratuitously injecting yourself in an artificial, game-playing way.) But perhaps I am now being too harsh, and there is more merit to the interpretation than I am allowing. I am probably being influenced by the belief that there are at least two other options which are better than addressing the expectancy issue.

Another option is to comment on the fact that he seems more mystified than he "needs" to be. He has, after all, given some substantial reasons why he feigned the illness, as well as why he kept it up, and you might wonder why his sense of mystification remains so great. No student follows this line, but I believe many practitioners would, with an observation like, "You know, you've spelled out many good reasons, and still you feel so mystified; I wonder if you sense that you've left something out, something possibly important, something perhaps so painful and forbidden that it has to remain a secret." Instead, what many students do is spell out the advantages and benefits as the patient has presented them, and I see little point in doing that. Even an interpretation which adds a significant dimension, as this one does, "I wonder if you and your parents each had a need to have you be a little boy again at that time, a time in most boys' lives when they are becoming men," is weak because it stays focused in the past and aims only at explaining the event.

Many students offer a lengthy, summarylike interpretation. Here's one example which adds a remark at the end to give the matter some contemporary significance: "Here's the way I understand what happened: perhaps you initially started feigning illness because you were angry at them for sending you off to camp. It was your way of refusing to be sent off again, this time to school. At first the attention and concern pleased you, it pleased you to worry them; but then there was no turning back—you had created a monster; and I think it frightened you that nobody understood you enough to know that you were fooling, and nobody could stop you; and you couldn't stop your self-created game either because you began to fear what they would do. You probably felt grownups would be angry at being fooled by a little boy. I wonder if you still feel that you successfully fool people today—that they also won't understand or know you enough—and that they also would be angry after being fooled.'' Such detailed summaries can be defended on the grounds that they provide a patient with a variety of possibilities to consider and offer him the free choice of what to pursue and explore. ''Here are the different possibilities, as I see them'' is the message, ''You may choose what is most meaningful and important in your judgment.'' In principle, that can be an effective technique, but in practice it has at least two important shortcomings that weaken it. First, it runs the risk of fostering an intellectualized approach to experience; particularly when used frequently, it can establish the pattern of figuring things out in purely intellectual terms. Even when used only occasionally, my experience has been that long and complicated interpretations tend to close things off, rather than open them up for further exploration, and rarely do they lead to important insights—which is the second shortcoming. In general, therefore, I regard interpretations like the foregoing example as poor options.

Its final sentence—which could stand as a separate interpretation—raises another problem: it may deflect attention from what the patient himself was considering. In my estimation, it runs the risk of changing the subject. Only when a clear inference is drawn to the therapy situation itself (that is, to a resistance-transference implication) can such a deflection and change of subject be considered advisable, because then it can be justified in terms of the *therapeutic process*.

At any rate, I think the moment is now right for the transference interpretation itself, especially if some groundwork for it has already been laid. Therefore, I regard the following interpretation, which is a representative example of what a substantial number of students give, to be the optimal intervention: ''I wonder if what you've just told me is somehow analogous to what you are feeling about therapy: as a child you found you could command a lot of love and attention by faking an illness; perhaps you are feeling that the problem which brought you here is also somehow a fake, a bid for attention; and perhaps you are afraid that I'm on to you, but I'm pretending, as your parents did, to go along with it.'' The chief drawback is that it may come as too great a surprise to the patient. To be sure, there are some hints in the material that it may not be far from his awareness. His repetition of ''I should tell you'' can be regarded as such a hint, particularly since it matches his remark that he thought he would have to tell his parents ("that I would just have to, you know"). Nevertheless, there is the risk of his being taken aback, perhaps even shocked, by the interpretation; and if that happens, he might fall back on his defenses. But that risk, in my opinion, is well worth taking, because the potential gains are so substantial and significant. This is, after all, an important matter, and could have a profound effect on the therapy.

Furthermore, aside from bringing a vital transference issue to the surface, it introduces the concept of multiple messages and of several-layered meanings, a concept which is central to all communication and especially important in therapy. If, for instance, the patient were to acknowledge the interpretation's validity and at the same time experience a sense of shame over having been "devious" and "found out," you would have the opportunity to do two things: (1) you could relate that feeling to the incident itself, and (2) you could draw attention to the processes of overdetermination and multiple messages. When you do the second, however, you must be careful to avoid suggesting that the underlying message is somehow the "real" one, as if conscious meanings and intentions are somehow less important than those which lie at or beneath the boundaries of consciousness. And in addition to avoiding the implication that unconscious events are the ones that really count, you have to avoid giving the impression that you're going to be the one who uncovers them. You can convey the idea that they do matter and also that you will listen for them and sometimes draw attention to them; but there remains a mutuality between conscious and unconscious mental events, as well as between your role and your patient's, in the process of *Psychotherapy*.

Paradigm 2

[The patient, a college senior, has been enthusiastic about therapy and involved. This is his twelfth session. Lizzy is a girlfriend of about two months; Harvey is an old friend. The patient begins speaking right away today—ordinarily he doesn't begin as fast.]

Lizzy sends her love. [grins broadly and a bit foolishly]* I was over at her place just before, and when I split she said, "Give your shrink my love." [loosens collar] She said that once last week too, but I didn't tell you. She's been bugging me lately about what goes on in here—asking me what you tell me, and things like that.* But she says therapy is not her bag. Her mother wants her to see a shrink, and she's been hassling her about it for over a year; and I think she can use it too. I told you about these downs of hers; they can last for weeks at a time. But she says she can handle her own problems herself. [slouches down]**

"Perhaps you are wondering about that yourself now—whether you can, or should be able to, handle your problems yourself." This is a representative example of an interpretation that many students give here. Insofar as it articulates important feelings about therapy that may contain the seeds of a resistance, such an interpretation is timely. My inclination would be to convey it succinctly with a half-questioning "And you can't?"—as if to acknowledge that I was merely completing his thought.

What about the slouching down? Should you use it as evidence for an interpretation, and say so? ("The way you slouch down suggests to me that ... ") Most practitioners and teachers will disagree with my answer, which is no. I believe it's a good rule of thumb *not* to comment on a patient's physical behavior and appearance, not even when it has contributed to the formulation of an interpretation. My reasons are several, and they revolve around certain unwanted side effects and consequences—one is that drawing attention to his actions and gestures can make a patient self-conscious (as distinct from reflective) and cause him to worry about (as distinct from reflect upon) the signals he is sending unwittingly, or even wittingly, for that matter. But I'm going to avoid the big digression that this important subject deserves by simply making two relevant points: (1) verbal utterance is likely to be in more active control than nonverbal behavior, and therefore a patient can experience a sense of greater command over what he says than over how he says it and how his body behaves; (2) the Basic Instruction promises that he will be listened to, not watched. Not that we don't remain fully observant as we listen, not that our interpretations won't be significantly influenced by what we see and hear, but it is usually possible to restrict our remarks to the verbal content and style of his behavior and to keep everything else in the background; and to do anything more is usually unnecessary. At any rate, this restriction, in my opinion and clinical experience, can make a profound difference.

> A couple of days ago she asked me what you thought about my going into business with Harvey, into the shop he wants us to set up. And she didn't believe me when I told her you didn't say one way or the other. I explained to her how you don't ever tell me what to do, or anything like that.* I don't even know whether you think the scheme is cool or not.** She doesn't buy that. Her friend Amy's shrink is always telling Amy what to do.**

A variation of what most students suggest at this point is, "Perhaps a part of you wishes that I would tell you exactly what to do," which qualifies as a timely interpretation for reasons I have already given. The way the example is formulated is worth noting: instead of saying "you wish ...," you say, "A part of you wishes ...," implying thereby that the patient has conflicting feelings about the wish. I regard the form as useful and tactful, insofar as it allows him to acknowledge the wish without having to fully embrace it. It has shortcomings too; a sense of disavowed or disowned responsibility is the biggest, and overtones of a split personality or divided self is another. But when you use it only to articulate conflict, and more as a stylistic device than a theoretical formulation, it can be free of significant unwanted implications; my experience with it has been that a patient will appreciate its tact and sensitivity, without at the same time misusing it in the interests of externalization and disavowal. (You must, of course, remain alert to such misusage.)

Some students focus on the indirect way the patient has expressed his wish. "You prefer me to do the same thing, tell you what to do, though you don't feel you can ask directly," says one; and another puts it more strongly, "I wonder if by telling me what Lizzy thinks, you're not really telling me indirectly how you feel about it. Perhaps you resent the fact that I won't tell you what I think of the scheme, and I wonder if you don't find it easier to tell me that Lizzy *doesn't buy that* than to say that you don't buy it." My preference would be to go easier—at first, anyway—and not suggest anything more than embarrassment, saying, "I think you're finding it difficult, embarrassing perhaps, to say you wish I'd tell you what I think of the scheme; I wonder if you are aware of expressing that wish in a indirect way." This reduces the risk of my playing the role of detective, the one who looks beneath or behind the manifest content for hidden meanings and implications. I don't mean to imply that I won't try to understand the different meanings and implications of the patient's utterances, including the hidden ones; but when he is not concerned with them at the moment, when he is not actively trying to discover them, there is the risk of a kind of prosecutor and defendant arrangement.

Finally, to start a didactic discussion on differences among therapists, which several students do here, is quite gratuitous. The temptation is always there, but it's best resisted. Anyhow, the patient isn't saying he doesn't know about such differences, he is expressing a wish that you be like Amy's therapist in this respect. And it is safe to assume that "part of him" also appreciates the value of your neutrality.

> I spoke to Harvey on the phone last night. He needs to know this week whether I'm in or not. He wants to get the shop started already. I told him I wasn't sure still; I need more time.** My father is still dead set against the idea. He thinks it's hairbrained and I'll get stung.* Harvey's going to go ahead with it no matter what; and he said he'll get someone else if I cop out.* Lizzy thinks it's a bad scene, too. But she gets all the bread she wants from her father, so she doesn't dig what's in it for me. All she's hung up about is the time, the evenings and Saturdays I'll have to be at the shop.** You know, that part of it seems really cool to me. It's some-

thing I've never done before. I guess it's like my father, working late at the store and then coming home all filled with it.* You know, my old man never rapped about the store. He just never talked about his work at all. All he ever said was that he didn't want for me to work like he had to. I would have a profession and keep decent hours and make lots of bread.* I guess I must have resented that, you know.* I remember playing store a lot when I was a kid, pretending I was a storekeeper like my father.** One time, it was a rainy day I remember, a Sunday. Anyway, I set up my play store in my room. Boy, I remember how hard I worked at setting it up, all elaborate and everything! I must have worked for two hours getting it all set up. Then I called my father and asked him to come and be the customer, and—typical!—he refused.* Wouldn't tear his ass away from the fucking TV.

Students take this opportunity to suggest that the patient wanted to be like his father and that his father didn't let him. But since there's no reason to suppose he isn't perfectly aware of that, the only nongratuitous function of such an interpretation would be to show some understanding. Even an interpretation like the following one is gratuitous, in my opinion. "Maybe one reason the business with Harvey is appealing to you is that you think it may be a way of communicating with, or getting closer to, your father—by being like him, just as you played being like him as a child." It has the further disadvantage of coming close to being an explaining-away of the wish to go into business (even though the student is careful to say "one reason" instead of leaving the impression it could be the whole reason). Moreover, for reasons I discussed in my comments to Paradigm 1, you have to avoid trying to explain the wish to go into business with Harvey; that particular piece of therapeutic work can be left to the patient.

A few students draw a transference implication at this point, and in an interesting way. For example, "Perhaps your telling me about this possible business venture is similar to your asking your father to play store with you; if I don't show interest or encourage you, I'll be like your father," and "Perhaps you feel that if you asked me to give you advice about it I also— typically!—would refuse." Such interpretations could be useful, but not right now; they would probably be more timely later on in the session when they don't interrupt any reminiscences and you don't interject yourself into the patient's deliberations so abruptly.

And my mother got into a big hassle with him about it. "Alex, why don't you go and play with him? You never play with him anymore!" And then they were off into one of their regular yelling bouts.* I hated it when they hassled each other. Before you knew it, she would drag in the kitchen sink—every fucking complaint in the book. Like how he never took her anyplace, never talked to her, never bought her anything—the whole fucking deal. And then he'd sink into one of his slow burns. "Leave me alone, for god's sake! I'm tired! I work hard all week. Get off my back!"** What an awful scene!**

The parent's argument has several noteworthy aspects, and some students choose to remark on it. Two good examples are, "Your mother was using you to get back at your father?" and "I take it you were upset because you had wanted to please your father by being like him, but instead you felt responsible for a fight in which he expressed dissatisfaction with his work and therefore with what you were imitating." My choice would be, "Do you notice that in your account, your mother begins by fighting your fight, but soon she is fighting her own?" (It suggests that she encouraged a kind of identification with the patient, an alliance against the father.) But my inclination would be to formulate this interpretation for myself and save it for a more timely moment. I'd want to wait and see whether the patient already knows it, and if so, what he makes of it. And I wouldn't worry about having missed an opportunity, because if he changed the subject (or returned to the original one), that might entail nothing more than a postponement. Such a central issue is not likely never to be repeated, and whenever it makes its reappearance I can say, "What comes to mind is how you once recounted the way your parents used to argue . . .''

Now, in view of the fact that my commentaries are growing repetitious (perhaps also tiresome), insofar as I steadily criticize the timeliness of interpretations and recommend a wait-and-see attitude, I want to emphasize that *Psychotherapy* doesn't wholly restrict us to the timing criterion of promoting the *therapeutic process*. It has to be our principal timing criterion, but that doesn't mean it's our only one.

The principal criterion of timing in orthodox psychoanalysis centers on the patient's readiness to comprehend and apprehend; the critical consideration is his state of mind as reflected in the condition of his transference and resistance—when they are optimal, the time is right. Accordingly, the analyst may draw no practical distinction between the criterion questions Can the patient use this interpretation? and Does he need it? The latter gets more or less taken for granted. (If he can use it he needs it.) In *Psychotherapy*, however, not only must we keep from taking the second criterion question for granted, we have to elevate it to a central position. Whether the patient can use and assimilate the interpretation becomes a secondary consideration. Before I take steps to qualify this position and also to stress how I haven't contended that the criterion is the exclusive one, I'll illustrate its implications.

Imagine a patient's dealing with his relationship to his brother and talking about his long-standing hostility; and imagine him doing it well—speaking openly, expressing genuinely felt feelings, reminiscing and reconstructing, freely associating, sticking to the subject. Suppose you get an idea about why he is hostile toward his brother, or suppose you see something important in that relationship which he is overlooking. Suppose even further that you have reason to believe your insight and observation will affect his hostility and perhaps improve his relationship with the brother. Should you offer the interpretation or draw the patient's attention to what he's overlooking? It's obvious my answer isn't a yes; it's a no, at best a "not necessarily." And why not? Because you don't have the requisite reason to. The *therapeutic process* is proceeding optimally, and *it* has no need for an intervention. Admittedly, the efficacy of such a criterion is open to serious question; allowing an opportunity to pass that may contribute to a patient's well-being seems questionable, and my formulation is liable to the criticism that it looks all right on paper but won't work well in practice. My rejoinder is this: clinical experience has convinced me that it can have a great efficacy and contribute substantially to a patient's long-term well-being.

How then should you then proceed? What should you "do" with your insight and observation? Instead of offering it in the form of an interpretation, you say to yourself "Let him arrive at it himself! Let him discover what it is he's overlooking!" After all, if he is working so well, you have reason to expect that in due course he will achieve the insight himself or discover what he's overlooking. And if and when he does, that achievement is bound to be more meaningful and effective that if it was passively received; in the long run it may benefit his relationship with his brother far more. That's my chief working hypothesis. And I base it on the conviction that changes in behavior, in attitudes, and in experience are a natural consequence of the naturally functioning *therapeutic process*. You need not insert your mind into the process, needn't share your thoughts and insights, unless and until the process itself requires it of you. It's the process that needs your special attention; when it breaks down, then your insights and observations can be used with maximal effectiveness.

Accordingly, if the patient experiences an impasse, if he blocks, becomes defensive, feels a pang of anxiety, it is then that you can "do something" with your insight. Then you can most usefully intervene with, "I think I know why you blocked [why your thoughts drifted away from what you were talking about, why you feel defensive and anxious], it's because you came face to face with a painful thought about your hostility toward your brother," or " . . . you might have caught a glimpse of something you've been overlooking." And if he remains unaware of what you're alluding to, you can go on to tell him what it is. An interpretation of that form is far more effective than one which begins with, "I think I know why you are hostile," or "I see something you've been overlooking," because the patient can learn something vital about himself that will not only benefit his relationship with his brother but will enhance his work in therapy. The latter consideration corresponds most directly to our central criterion of "useful."

But there are two major difficulties with that criterion: one has to do with specifying the optimal level of the *therapeutic process*, the second with the potential reinforcement implications of applying the criterion too stringently. The first refers to the fact that it is always possible to improve on the process, in principle at least, and, therefore, always possible to justify an interpretation on those grounds. When we feel the impulse to offer an interpretation, we can usually persuade ourselves that it might improve our patient's level of work—and that judgment is difficult to prevail against. In any event, there is clearly the danger of using the criterion so loosely as to render it highly elastic and "theoretical."

The second difficulty is indirectly related to the first, insofar as it can be cast into the same terms: there is a good probability that a patient will notice how you offer him substantive help only when he isn't speaking freely and openly; he can learn that to evoke your participation he has only to slip into an impasse or into a defensive attitude. To be sure, that happens naturally enough in the normal course of events, but if you speak only when he isn't working well, then he has a powerful incentive to avoid working well. Interpretations are likely to have a limited effect against this kind of reinforcement, and, consequently, you must also time interpretations so that they don't always coincide with an interruption in the *therapeutic process*.

I suppose this consideration can be formulated in the terms of our central criterion in the following way: "I offered the interpretation because the *therapeutic process* needed it, in the sense that it would have been negatively reinforcing to withhold it." But that way of construing the criterion stretches it beyond recognition, and can make it so elastic as to be quite useless in practice. Consequently, I see no way of avoiding the conclusion that the central timing criterion can only be regarded as the principal one but by no means the exclusive one. There must be others we use and give substantial weight. Two such criteria are relevant to Paradigm 2 and the interpretation which provoked this digression.

The first is related to the stage of therapy. Interpretations gradually change their function as therapy proceeds and develops; during the beginning phases they can serve a number of useful functions which become quite unnecessary and even gratuitous during the later phases. For instance, at the beginning, a patient may have to learn how you participate—how you listen to him both empathically and dispassionately, how you formulate understanding without judgment and criticism—and you may offer interpretations in order to show him. (In a sense, your aim is to demonstrate how you construe "useful.")

Another lesson that has to be learned early is that there will be relatively little conversation or dialogue; you may therefore time your interpretations in such a way as to actualize your freedom of choice—for example, by paying special attention to his efforts to solicit remarks from you and by interpreting his reactions to your nonresponsiveness. Then there are "lessons" having to do with dreams (the value of associating to their elements, paying attention to day-residue, and the like), with the genetic orientation and reconstructions (like how the patient construed his parents' arguments)—all having more or less to do with the way therapy will proceed.

The second criterion is difficult to conceptualize and specify in other than negative terms—that is, in terms of avoiding the reinforcement effect, or the sheer monotony and tiresomeness, of only interpreting the *therapeutic process* itself. Perhaps a positive way of putting it is this: there is value in variety, especially in the use of interpretations. Rigor with respect to timing need not shade into rigidity; an occasional "lapse" or deviation from the principal criteria can have some positive value. Therefore, you occasionally have to allow yourself to offer an insight or discovery "for its own sake"; you can sometimes participate directly in the *therapeutic process* as a kind of partner, the one who makes discoveries too. You do this not so much to show the patient how it's done, not to direct or lead him to discoveries, but more in the spirit of active participation. "Look, I've noticed something about the argument! Your mother begins by fighting for you, and right away she's fighting for herself; that's intriguing; that could help us understand some things about you."

But I need to stress balance here, the fact that this should not be overdone, because this kind of participation has deep implications and consequences (it may foster a symbiotic transference, for instance), and, therefore, has to remain secondary to the principal criteria. To be sure, as the therapy proceeds and develops, it can assume a larger role—more of your interpretations can be made for their own sake—but even then the ubiquitous transference (and role definition) implications have to be kept in mind.

> You know, sometimes when Lizzy hassles me I feel just like my old man. I even tell her to get off my back, like he tells my mother.*
> And that time two weeks ago when I hit her ... I mean, I hit Lizzy [shoulders jerk up].*

This speech disruption (and startle reaction) indicates a kind of slip of thought; he was probably about to say, "When I hit my mother." If you thought so, in practice, you'd find it difficult to keep from wondering aloud, "Did you suppose I'd think you hit your mother?" Nevertheless, my opinion about interpreting such involuntary actions, which I alluded to in an earlier commentary, extends to slips of tongue. To foster a patient's interest in them, to have him reflect on them, is one thing; it is another to foster a kind of quasi-therapy game-playing ("Wow, just like the movies and the textbooks!"). At best, therefore, we have to be judicious and selective and not seize every opportunity to interpret these involuntary (unconscious) acts.

I told you about that, didn't I?

Simply answering yes or no ("I don't recall it") is better than, "Perhaps you cannot remember whether you told me about it because you were feeling embarrassed by it." This kind of speculation is justified only in the case of a patient who regularly resorts to repressive defenses.

> Well, she was hassling me about the time I spend rapping with the guys at the student lounge. I told her what I do with my time is my business, and she can split if she doesn't like it; and she said I was a selfish bastard; and she started in yelling. And without really meaning to, or realizing what I was doing, I hauled off and slapped her—pretty damned hard too.***

The argument with Lizzy has a formal similarity to his parents', that's sufficiently clear; and his striking her was probably what he wished his father had done to his mother. Students spell it out for the patient—for example, "This is what occurs to me: perhaps the reason why Lizzy's actions got you so angry is that they set off the anger you felt toward your mother for intervening in something that was primarily between your father and you." Many emphasize the possibility that he is identified with his father and Lizzy is a displacement for his mother. I think such interpretations are likely to be premature unless they allude to, or lay the groundwork for, a transference implication—that it is now Lizzy intervening between him and you. Otherwise, the crucial consideration is whether he is thinking during the fifteen-second pause about why he struck Lizzy, because, unless he is searching for an explanation, for you to offer him one is apt to be pointless.

Several students offer an interpretation that is not only pointless but pointed in the wrong direction. "Maybe you were so angry and hit her so hard because you thought she could be right about your being selfish, and you didn't want to accept that," is bound to bring on more sheepish grinning. And if the following interpretation didn't cause the patient to become defensive, it would cause him to be puzzled. "If you had the store, there'd be a new subject to hassle with Lizzy about. It's not like spending time in the student lounge, Lizzy couldn't call you selfish; after all, you'd be working for bread, and that's okay, even necessary. Then you'd really be able to put her in her place, just like your father did your mother."

I wish I could make up my mind whether to go in with Harvey or not. He says all I have to do is commit myself for a month, and then if I don't like it I can get out. Just a month, so what've I got to lose?* I'm in good shape in school; the Philo paper is almost half finished, and I can do the rest of it in a day if I really work at it. [big sigh]***

The problem is stated, relevant aspects of the conflict have been articulated along with relevant historical antecedents; now the question is, What, if anything, should you say? Should you say something about the patient's expectation of you? Should you say something about why the decision itself remains such a difficult one? Should you try to be of some help in resolving his conflict and facilitating a decision? Most students offer an interpretation at this culmination point, and they select one or another of these questions to address.

Consider, "Perhaps it's so difficult to make a decision because the situation contains so many elements of past family conflicts. You are still trying to set up shop like your father, he is still withholding his approval, and the woman, this time Lizzy, is the complainer about how the desire to earn money is depriving her of attention," and "It sounds like you're really following in your father's footsteps. Like him, you'll manage to be so busy between school and work that you won't have any time to deal with Lizzy," and "Perhaps your problem is not so much deciding whether you want a job like your father's but whether you really want to be like him or not." For reasons which need no repetition here, I regard such interpretations as ill-advised. You shouldn't set yourself up as the problem solver, the one who figures out what the patient's problem "really" is; insofar as your main function is to facilitate the *therapeutic process*, he is best served by your focusing on those elements of his conflict that contribute to the difficulty he's having exploring the problem and/or by your focusing on the transference-resistance issues that might be involved. If you haven't already done it, you can now address the transference the way this example does: "It seems to me you feel pressured by Harvey and Lizzy and your father, everyone telling you what to do. And along with that, I wonder if you don't also have some wish that I would tell you what to do, like I promised I wouldn't, and like Amy's therapist does." But I can't see what other kind of transference issue is at hand that could outweigh the advantages of simply remaining silent, which I regard as the best course of action here.

Consider the advantages. The patient is apparently waiting for some help from you; he wants help in deciding what to do. Silence conveys the message "I will not help you to make that decision, excepting insofar as I can help elucidate the reasons for your difficulty making the decision." Would it be better to convey that message explicitly? Not necessarily. For one thing, since he already knows it, the explicit message might convey the additional message "So please stop wanting help with the decision itself"—and there is the risk of its being taken as scolding or defensiveness or both. Similarly, putting it in the form of an interpretation ("You want me to help . . .") is also a potential scolding insofar as it may be far too gratuitous—again, he knows it, so why tell him? The most judicious way to convey the message is by actualizing it.

If the patient breaks the silence with a show of resentment, for instance, that could provide the occasion for a useful interpretation. But there's the chance that he won't, that he'll return to his deliberations and explore his problem further and deeper. If that ideal thing happens, it will have been your silence which permitted it—and thus will silence have promoted the *therapeutic process*.

Paradigm 3

[Since the beginning of therapy, over four months ago, this twenty-two-year-old has been a "model patient"—never late, never impertinent, always the good boy. Today he is ten minutes late and appears flustered and flushed.]

I'm sorry . . . I'm sorry for coming late.** I'm very upset. I'm sorry.**

Should you comment on the apology? Only two students do—one with a clarification question, "It isn't clear to me if you are apologizing for being late or for being upset," and the other with an articulation, "I take it you feel being late is some kind of transgression against me." While the issue is undoubtedly important—an apology is essentially inappropriate in *Psychotherapy* and might be the manifestation of an underlying attitude worth uncovering (especially in the case of a "model patient")—I believe this is probably the wrong time to explore it. The lateness, after all, is unusual, and the patient is most likely going to talk about it; so the clarification question is unnecessary. Furthermore, his reply would probably be that he's apologizing for being late (and later it becomes clear that he regards being upset as an equivalent offense, since, like coming late, it interferes with the session). What would you "do" with that explanation? Bear in mind that it will have been you who has imposed the topic—the patient was obviously not planning to discuss his apology—and that's a risky thing for you to do when he has something else on his mind, when he's about to recount what caused him to be upset. So better to store the apology and keep it in mind for a future timely opportunity.

I just had a terrible experience, and I feel . . . [averts gaze]** I'm very upset.

The patient's difficulty articulating his feeling, and again falling back on

"I'm very upset," is noteworthy. What feeling is he having such trouble with? To probe the feeling is impermissible; and it is probably too early, and would be too speculative, to offer a comment or observation about it. The most you can do is make an empathic remark like, "I gather you're having difficulty expressing the way you are feeling." But since that remark can amount to an indirect probe, your best option is to wait and see whether he continues to need help articulating the feeling, and, most importantly, why.

> I came late because I was at the Motor Vehicles Bureau trying to get my
> learner's permit. There was a long line at the window, and it took
> forever. And then, when I finally got to the window, the man told me I
> had filled out the application wrong and I would have to do it all over
> again. I tried to correct it, but he wouldn't let me. He gave me a lecture
> and said I'd have to go fill out a new one and then get back in line again.
> And . . . and I was so . . .* so upset, I felt like throwing the damned
> application form right in his face.**

The problem of articulating his feeling is now repeated, and since the event that provoked it has been described, it may no longer be premature to comment on the problem. But now the question is What sort of comment is most appropriate? It's clear enough that the unexpressible feeling is anger—rage, in fact—and many students simply say so. For example, "You say you were upset; it sounds as though you were angry." But only a few students wonder aloud what prevents the patient from saying he was, and still is perhaps, angry.

If there's a vital distinction between articulating an affect and naming it, and I believe there is, it can only be a fine distinction. In this case, however, it may be an especially significant one, and I can't see what you can do beyond naming the feeling. Moreover, you have good reason to suspect (n.b., "always the good boy") that the patient may be quite accurate when he says he feels "upset"; perhaps he actually doesn't experience "anger" because it is too dangerous a feeling. If that happens to be the case, exploring why anger is so unacceptable and examining the ways he defends against its recognition are bound to be more therapeutic. The technical problem is how to help him begin such an exploration and examination.

Consider, "It sounds as if you were very angry with him, yet you say you were *upset*. Perhaps you didn't describe yourself as angry because you feel that being angry with someone is unacceptable." The trouble with that approach is its failure to invite an exploration; it offers the explanation and invites the patient to concur. (And I can easily imagine his accepting the explanation and proceeding to substitute "angry" for "upset.") Another way students approach the problem is this: "I'm wondering what else you feel.

Whenever you try to tell me, you pause and fall back on the description *upset.*" My main quarrel with that remark is the implication that anger is "something else." The patient did, after all, feel "something else"—"I felt like throwing the damned application form right in his face." He may not want to call it "anger," but his cognitive experience was fully appropriate. In fact, if he were to fall back repeatedly on "I felt angry," I might well choose to offer the interpretation, "I take it you felt like throwing it in his face," and perhaps follow it up with, "You felt like hurting the man." Isn't that what it means to be "angry"? The English language, in using "feel" both for the affect and the impulse, captures this point beautifully.

Students assume "anger" and offer the patient an explanation, for example, "He made you feel like an incompetent child, and it angered you," and "You felt powerless, and that made you very angry." Such suggestions would be helpful if he himself was wondering why he was so "upset." But even more important is the fact that he hasn't said "angry." Throughout this paradigm many students speak about the patient's anger and rage, and they do it without seeming to notice that he never uses such terms; they simply assume he knows he was, and still may be, furious. But I composed the paradigm carefully with a patient in mind for whom the recognition of anger is so dangerous and unacceptable to his self-image that he is self-deprecatory, inhibited, and always the "good boy." Moreover, he might also be a person who provokes others to anger, judging from the fact that so many students express a good deal of anger at him in their interpretations. What they do is make interpretations that are critical, scolding, lecture-ish, and confronting (something they do far less in the other three paradigms). Such countertransference feelings are instructive and can be useful signals to us. In this case, they remind us that many passive and incompetent people provoke anger, and an angry response is often rewarding and reinforcing for them.

> So I had to fill out another application, and when I got back to the line it was even longer than before. It was obviously going to take at least a half hour to get to the window, and I saw I was going to be late here if I waited that long.* And I just didn't know what to do. I began to shake . . . my legs began to shake, like sometimes when I'm practicing the piano.

"Perhaps you feel the same way at the piano when you are not able to play something just the way you want to," suggests a student—To what useful purpose?

> I kept looking at the clock and trying to figure out whether I should wait and get the damned thing finished with, or whether I should leave it for next week and come here on time. I didn't know what to do.** I knew

I'd be late if I waited any more, and ... and ...** And typically,
I ... what I did was wait in line for another fifteen minutes, until I knew
I was going to be late here anyway. And then I left without getting the
application in.** So look what I did! I screwed myself up both ways; I'll
have to go back next week and start all over again, and I came late here.*

Throughout the paradigm students look for an opportunity to suggest to the
patient that he chose his behavior quite deliberately and came late because he
wanted to. One suggests it here with, "I wonder what you think of the
possibility that a part of you wanted to come to therapy on time, and thereby
be a good boy, and a part of you wanted to be late and be a bad boy." Since
the evidence is a bit shaky, the student seeks justification in this charge, which
precedes the interpretation: "It does seem to me that you behaved, as you
said, *typically*. You set the situation up in such a way that you did not have to
take responsibility for the choices: you waited until it was too late to decide."
I doubt whether the patient would find that a convincing proof, though being
such a good boy, he would probably acquiesce to it and use it as further
ammunition for his self-deprecations.

And I'm so upset now, feeling so shaky and everything, that ... that I
don't know what good this session is going to do me.** If I'm feeling so
upset, what good is ...***

Is the unspoken word "therapy"? If it is, he has made a startling statement.
Therefore, students speak up. "You don't believe anything can be accom-
plished here if you are not calm and in control of your feelings?" Some go
further—"It's frightening for you to be here when you are feeling so
upset? Perhaps you are afraid of what you'll do or say when you feel so
shaky," and some include "angry." Another possibility is, "I'm unclear why
you feel that your being upset would lead you to question the good of the
session. One thing that comes to mind is that you are feeling like a *bad*
patient, due to your lateness, and perhaps you feel that I have the same
opinion." These are timely remarks, though they tend to go too far or too fast.
My inclination would be first to ascertain whether the missing word is
"therapy" (or perhaps it's the phrase "talking about it here") and allow the
patient to elaborate on the thought. If he didn't, I would postpone speculation
and ask him to explain ("It's not clear to me what you mean when you say, *If
I'm feeling so upset, what good is therapy*," or "I take it you mean to say that
talking about your feelings will do you no good when you are so upset"),
though it's going to be difficult to suppress my incredulity.

The issue at hand, the patient's underlying attitude toward therapy, has a
high priority in timing, calling for active steps on your part to explore his

beliefs—and, hopefully, his underlying fantasies and fears also—now that they have surfaced. In view of the fact that he's such a "model patient," the opportunities are likely to be limited. You have good reason, therefore, to pursue the matter vigorously—though caution and circumspection must, of course, never be thrown to the winds, and tact remains an indispensable element of good technique.

A possible approach is to draw attention to the apparent equivalency for the patient of his having missed fifteen minutes of the session and his having to return to the bureau and repeat the time-consuming procedure (both "screw me up"). The question is, How are they the same? In what way is coming late an equivalent inconvenience? Is it perhaps you who is inconvenienced, and therefore perhaps angry? Does he believe that his having come late and being so upset has affected your feeling for him? The answer might emerge when you make a comment like, "I see how it screws you up to have to go back to the bureau and repeat the unpleasant procedure, but I don't see how it screws you up the same way to come late here." Another possibility is to make reference to the apology which began the session, to say something like, "I think I understand now why you apologized at the beginning; it may be that you believe coming late has screwed me up in the same way," though this might emerge spontaneously when he has had the opportunity to explore his attitude toward therapy. At any rate, you have to take some initiative in promoting that work.

> What a stupid mess! [in a whining tone of voice and close to tears]***
> On the subway I felt like pushing people out of my way.* And I felt like crying too.****

In describing his impulse to push people out of his way, he gives a vivid account of the ideational content of rage, but instead of experiencing the affect, he feels like crying. Explaining this to him is likely to be both didactic and gratuitous. Moreover, not only will little be gained by trying to explain to him why he felt like crying when he himself isn't wondering why, but he's bound to apprehend the explanation as either an exoneration or a scolding (perhaps even both). Therefore, such interpretations as, "You felt like crying because you were enraged," and "You cry rather than get angry," are apt to be a mistake. They may even be perceived by the patient as being reassuring and supportive.

On the other hand, there can be value in articulating the affect in its current form, in the way it might be alive right now. "You were very angry. Maybe crying would have partially hidden that from you, because a part of you really feels very uncomfortable about being angry," observes a student, but instead of stopping, he continues importantly with, "I think you're still feeling angry right now, and you are trying to keep it from yourself in a similar way." That can be a good interpretation at this time.

This only proves that I can't do anything right. Just like my father has always said: I can't do anything right.**

"You mentioned that you felt like crying and also like pushing people out of your way, and I wonder if perhaps these are the two feelings you are expressing now: a feeling of despair and helplessness—as if your father is correct in saying you can't do anything right—and also a feeling of rage at this helplessness," is a fine interpretation that I think is well-timed. My inclination would be to focus more on the impulse to push people out of his way, in order to explore its substitute function and perhaps also the underlying conflict.

But consider this example, and notice how it violates the proscription against scolding a patient in the guise of "understanding" him: "I think I understand why you waited in line for fifteen minutes when you knew it would screw you up both ways. It provides you with a way to not be the good boy, which you have consistently been in therapy, and it gives you a reason to be upset and to tell yourself that it's no use trying." Several students, in their zeal to offer an explanation, make a similar kind of remark, and this underscores a common abuse of the interpretive mode.

So what's the use of even trying if ... if ...** So what can I do? So I come here and I tell you how I'm all screwed up, and you ... you ...*

"Don't help you get unscrewed up," completes the thought. Or you might say, "You're hesitant to complete the sentence, aren't you? I wonder if that's because you're afraid it will make me angry at you." But none of my students say anything at this juncture.

You just want me to talk about it. What's the good of that? I just can't do anything right, and that's all there is to it. I prove it all the time—the simplest things ...***

The patient is apparently saying, "What good is therapy?"—a sentiment that generally provokes us to defensiveness. So it's no surprise that students intervene here with a remark that apparently betrays their indignation, and they deliver a little scolding. Some do it in the form of a didactic, school-teacherish lecture ("It might be that one of the reasons you always seem to set yourself up in a situation in which you fail is because then you don't have to take the responsibility for your actions; as if you say to yourself, 'I always screw things up, so therefore, I don't have to try' "), others with a diagnostic formulation ("You seem to be expressing anger and despair at your not being more decisive, and this appears to make you feel sorry for yourself, which further supports in your mind that your father was right," and "You are leveling a lot of criticism at yourself; maybe that helps you avoid directing your anger at other people, because that's something that makes you very uncomfortable").

An interpretation that avoids those implications and pitfalls is "You seem to be trying hard to convince me that you are totally incompetent; perhaps one part of you wants me to agree with your father and prove you totally inept, while another part of you wants me to reassure and comfort you," and many students give it in one form or another. My inclination, however, would be to make no remark at all—not yet—because it isn't sufficiently clear what's up, whether the patient is saying that therapy is ineffective for someone so inept at it as he, or whether he's struggling with feelings of disappointment at you (combined perhaps with anger). The best way to find out is to wait, a moment or two at the very least.

> You don't even seem to care that I came late. But maybe that's only because you won't say. You are probably saying to yourself that I shouldn't have screwed up the application in the first place—such a simple thing and I can't do it right; and when I saw the time was getting close, I should have . . . I should not have gotten back in line and waited another fifteen minutes. I should've left and gotten here on time.**

Here is a matter of vital importance: how the patient construes your basic attitude toward him and his problems—Do you care?—which is a profound and complex matter that deserves as much attention as possible. This is an opportunity, then, that shouldn't be allowed to pass, and students don't let it. Many, however, miss the point by merely emphasizing that he expects them to be angry ("Perhaps you expected to be scolded for being late, and since you weren't, you're doing it yourself." "I wonder if on some level you want me to be critical of what you've done; you want to prove that you're incompetent, and that I, as an authority figure, should confirm that proof, saying 'Yes, you really are incompetent' "), and but for their failure to implicate the issue of caring, they make good interpretations. The following example gets closer but still falls short: "You seem to expect me to view you as your father did—perhaps you wish I would"; and this one gets closest: "You appear to assume that I am as critical of you as you feel your father is; and on the other hand, if I am not critical, then I don't care about you."

There is more at issue here than the equation of caring with scolding-criticizing; the patient is also implying that if you cared—as his father cares—you would tell him what he should have done. A student captures this point well with "You seem annoyed that I took no steps to help you out of your predicament, and now you wonder if I even care about you. Perhaps you think that if people care about you, they ought to step in and get you out of frustrating situations." In order to lessen the criticism inherent in such a remark, I would divide an interpretation into several parts and begin with, "I take it you assume I do care, I care that you came late, but I simply choose not to tell you; and that means I feel like scolding you, but I'm keeping myself from doing it." Then I would be ready to follow that remark with, "And you assume that I'm thinking to myself the same things you are thinking, and it is what your father has always said to you: that you shouldn't have been so incompetent." When the patient has concurred, and perhaps elaborated on the suggestion, I would offer this speculation: "Telling you what to do, and scolding you for being inept—that means caring for you, doesn't it?" Finally, I would seek the opportunity to add, "And, as your father shows his caring for you by telling you what you should do, so you believe I must show my caring by telling you how you should be competent."

> God, I hated that stupid man! What a mean old bastard! Making me fill
> out another application form instead of making a few corrections. He did
> it on purpose, the sonofabitch! The bureaucratic mentality is horrible.
> That's what we deserve for electing Nixon.

Our political sentiments must play no part in *Psychotherapy*. Students, however, though they may share the patient's convictions about Nixon and government bureaucracy, are struck by the illogic of his statement, and especially by the aura of externalization of blame (though "internalization of blame" might be a more accurate designation). They comment about it, and every one of these comments is without significant merit. I see no useful purpose in drawing the patient's attention to the illogic of his remark, and, again, it runs the risk of being a scolding. (Consider, "You seem to be moving the center of power in this situation farther from yourself; first it was the clerk who controlled it, and now it's Nixon," and "You seem to be tying what the man did to you to a more general social-political phenomenon; maybe that's helping you limit how personally angry you feel at him," and notice their diagnostic, critical tenor.) Even the following one, which is likely to be a helpful explanation and not a scolding, is not worth making: "It sounds as if one reason you are so upset is because you felt helpless and impotent against the man—as if you were up against the entire Nixon administration."

> You know something, I feel like just dropping the whole thing, just
> forgetting it. So I won't learn how to drive. I probably won't be able to

learn it anyhow. And Peter will just have to do all the driving this summer on our trip out West—that's all.****

What kind of silence is this? Does it reflect a break in the *therapeutic
process*, an impasse, or is the patient deliberating silently on his resolution of
the problem, his passive resignation? If you judge it to be a deliberative
silence, a contemplative pause, then remaining silent is your best course.
Most students, however, choose to make a remark (probably also because it is
the end of the paradigm), and many articulate the patient's sense of passive
resignation—which is difficult to do without scolding, or seeming to scold. "I
can appreciate how annoying this incident must be for you, but at the same
time, it seems to have provided you with a convenient way of avoiding the
responsibility of having to learn to drive," is a representative example. You
can respond without seeming to scold, however, provided you take the trouble
to formulate your interpretation carefully, as this example does: "I can understand your feelings of rage and helplessness, and I wonder what you think of
this possibility: that your feeling that it's no use trying, either in the session or
in learning to drive, is a reaction to these feelings." Notice how this interpretation does more than simply articulate the defense, more than simply say his
passive resignation is a "cop out"; it offers an explanation in terms of his
affects. The explanation itself is open to criticism, and may well be invalid for
the patient, but its form goes far toward precluding evaluation and criticism.

Many students see transference implications in letting Peter do all the
driving. "Perhaps you'd like me to do all the driving here," and "I think you
want me to reinforce your feelings of incompetency, like your father," are
succinct examples; and a student offers this interesting formulation, "I wonder if that is not also what you are feeling now about your therapy; a part of
you has been feeling anger toward me, which is frightening and unacceptable
to the rest of you. To keep these angry feelings in check and out of your realm
of responsibility, you must feel yourself powerless and want me to do *all the
driving*." But I believe the patient is probably setting you up to demonstrate
your competency by making an interpretation. If that's the case, you stand in a
paradoxical position: even if you interpret it to him, you are fulfilling the
expectation and satisfying the need. To say, "You want me to do all the
driving here," is to have taken the wheel. This, then, is another reason for
your choosing silence, or at least choosing the option of making no remark.

If you feel that silence may be too harsh and that the patient need some help
(the *therapeutic process* needs some sustenance), you can inquire into his
thoughts ("What are you thinking?"). That, as I've already indicated (and
discuss in detail in chapter five), is a permissible directive, and this is a good
instance where it can serve several functions. For one, it can express your

interest in learning whether he is dwelling on his passive resignation, whether he is becoming aware of the transference implications, or whether he is simply waiting for you to take some action.

Paradigm 4

[The patient, in his mid-thirties, is seeking therapy mainly because he fears becoming like his alcoholic father. Therapy is in its sixth month.]

> I had another great dream last night. You know, I never dreamed as much as I've been dreaming since I started seeing you. I used to have a dream, oh, once a month on the average, if not less, but now I have one at least every week.* I'm not complaining, mind you, but I do ... I wonder why I'm dreaming so much.**

A student suggests this response, "It seems to me you are trying hard to please me, and having a lot of dreams is one way you think you can." The evidence can come only from having read the entire paradigm and inferring that the idealized transference has not suddenly appeared today. But it would probably suffice, at any rate, to remark, "It must have a lot to do with the fact that you come here, don't you think?" and allow the patient to explore the reasons further—if that's what he wants to do at this point.

In practice, it could be useful here to make the patient aware of the defensive possibilities, provided the previous sessions have given evidence that he could be using dreams, for instance, to avoid a direct expression of his feelings and conflicts. You have to be careful neither to encourage nor discourage the bringing in of dreams, and the danger is that an interpretation will have that effect. Therefore, the best (and perhaps the only) time to offer such an interpretation is when it can be put this way—and the beginning phrase is critical: "I think you are wondering whether your dreams are taking up a lot of your time here, and that they may be serving to keep you from talking about ... "or "I think you're sensing that the reason you're not dreaming these days is because you are worried what your dreams might reveal about how you're feeling about ..."

> I guess it must have a lot to do with coming here, don't you think?
> Your interpretations are so very interesting. And I find them very helpful. Like what you said last week, that my father looked so big in the dream because I was seeing him from the position of a child. I guess I've always seen him as being bigger than he really is.**

This doesn't impress me as a good time for any kind of remark. "You see me bigger too," and "Perhaps finding my interpretations so interesting and helpful makes me appear bigger than I actually am, and makes you feel like a child as well,'' have a gratuitous ring to them, despite the fact that they deal with an important transference issue. Insofar as they are incomplete formulations, their implicit critical edge is sharper than it should be. In response to the second example, the patient may actually feel childish, as if you had said it was childish of him to find your interpretations so interesting and helpful.

> Anyway, here's the dream I had last night. I was in a very large room, and ... Hey! I guess that means I was a child again.* That's very interesting!* The room was like a gymnasium or an auditorium. There were lots of rows of wooden chairs that faced a sort of a stage. It wasn't a real stage, just a raised platform of some kind.**

To interrupt a dream (or, for that matter, a narrative account) with an interpretation is poor technique. A student chooses this moment to observe, ''Perhaps you feel somewhat as if you're on stage here; but here if you look for signs of approval from the audience there aren't any.'' It is far better to wait until the dream is recounted and the patient is engaged in trying to understand its meaning.

> Anyway, I was looking for something, or maybe I was looking for someone. I don't remember that part of it too well. And there was no one there except for this one man, who was walking around the place, maybe also looking for something. And he was walking funny, as if he were sick or something.** I kept thinking he was going to fall down.

Students notice that the man behaved as if he was drunk, and they draw the patient's attention to it. For example, ''One possibility is that the man in the dream may represent your father, since you've described him as walking around funny and stumbling, which may be similar to the way someone on alcohol behaves.'' Again, this is not the best time; better to wait until the dream is finished. After the dream has been recounted, and the patient has put the question, ''So what do you think?'' a student suggests, ''I'm wondering if your father didn't often *walk funny* when he was drunk.'' Another purpose in waiting is to see whether he arrives at the hypothesis himself. (Many practitioners would encourage him by asking whether the way the man walked brought anything to mind, which is the free-association method. The patient is instructed to slip into that mode at this moment, for the purpose of uncovering the meaning of that dream element.)

> Then he walked up to this raised platform, and he started to do some kind of a strange dance. And I couldn't figure out what it was or anything.** The next part I don't remember so well. He may have motioned me to come up on the platform with him—maybe he didn't, I'm not sure. But the next thing I remember, I was standing on the platform with him, and ... No! Now I remember. He was gone, and I was alone up there.

> Yes.* And I started to take my clothes off, as if I was doing a striptease
> or something. And then ...* And then I did the ... the weirdest thing,
> and it embarrasses me to have to tell you.** Boy! I knew it was going to
> be hard for me to tell you this part, but ...* but I didn't expect I would
> find it this hard. I'm feeling funny about ... embarrassed, actually.
> That's weird! Here I tell you everything in here—the most embarrassing
> things—and I'm feeling ashamed to tell you this.**

"Perhaps you are feeling very exposed here right now, like when you
had your clothes off in the dream," suggests a student. Another tries a more
ambitious formulation, "It's interesting that the part of the dream just before
this part seemed to express the opposite of shameful feelings, the part where
you were taking off your clothes. Maybe a part of you is not ashamed and
wants very much to expose yourself." These interpretations can be justified
on the grounds that the patient is experiencing difficulty in proceeding with
the account of the dream and that some help might be facilitating. The first
example, in that case, is apt to be quite sufficient; the second introduces a
fresh topic that may actually serve as a deflection. But my inclination, once
again, would be to offer no help at this juncture and to maintain a patient
expectant attitude. For one thing, I may not want to foster his childish position
by defining myself as guide and mentor; for another, there is no reason to
think he won't overcome his embarrassment and continue with the dream. A
silence can convey a sense of faith in his ability to deal with the problem.

> Anyway, what I did in the dream was urinate. Yes, I started to piss. And
> then I woke up and went to the bathroom because I had to piss.*** So
> what do you think?****

To remain silent in the face of this question at this juncture in a session
seems to students a difficult, perhaps a tactless and pointless, thing to do. It
should come as no surprise, however, that I believe it's an integral aspect of
good technique. What is the patient asking?—for you to take an active role, to
tell him what the dream means and thereby rescue him from his embarrassment. The optimal way to meet such a request is to remain passive (actively
passive, I might say). Notice, moreover, how even a "good" interpretation
to that effect—like " ... so you can be the little boy and I can be all-
knowing"—has the paradoxical effect of assuming the all-knowing position
even as that fact is being interpreted.

Only a minority of my students make no response. Among the majority,
a handful are deflections of the question (like, "I wonder what thoughts you
have about it"), and the rest are evenly divided into those that deal with the
transference implications and those that deal with issues centering around

the father ("Perhaps your dream has to do with your fear of becoming like your father, taking his place as a man who sometimes loses control of himself or acts incomprehensively," and "Perhaps the man on the stage represented your father; as you said, it may have been an incident in your childhood. Children sometimes believe that drunk people are sick, because of their gait and manners; and it's possible that though you didn't know why your father was different than other fathers, you were embarrassed that he was different"). The transference interpretations range from such simple ones as, "And now you would like me to explain it all to you, give you interesting and helpful interpretations," to such complicated ones as, "It sounds as if the shame and embarrassment you mention about disclosing yourself to me are partly a reaction to the pleasurable excitement of being looked at while you strip and show yourself." Some focus on the formulation that dreams equal gifts, "It sounds as if you would like an interpretation in return for telling the dream, almost as if we were exchanging gifts," and "I wonder how this seems to you: your dream has to do with feelings you have about therapy, possibly feelings of being exposed or of giving me what may be unacceptable gifts which may be embarrassing to you." Some emphasize the defensive nature of the question, "You know, you said at first that you had a great dream, but now you are feeling ashamed and embarrassed about what you reveal to me; I'm wondering if you are looking to me to tell you what the dream means in order to avoid your feelings about it"—and here is a very good defense interpretation: "You had a great deal of difficulty telling me that part of your dream, and I have a thought about why. My thought is that urinating in your dream represents a loss of control; and I think you fear that you might lose control of yourself in here, and that you would feel embarrassed and terrible." Finally, several students interpret only the shameful impulse, "I think it is possible that what you did in the dream represents on some level your wish to expose yourself and let yourself go here."

> I don't know who the man in the dream was, but he looked kind of familiar.** Hey, you know something! I think he could've been the patient who comes here before me on Wednesdays. I usually see him when he leaves, and I guess I sometimes watch him ... watch him walk out. He does have a funny walk, you know, and ...* Yes, come to think of it, it could have been him. And that's weird! Why would I dream about him?**

Again a question has been put, and again many students respond to it. Naturally, they speak of jealousy, rivalry, and competitive feelings. A typical example: "Could it be true that you are jealous that I have other patients, with whom you share the stage, so to speak?" A student offers, "Perhaps you see him as having something wrong with him, his strange walk, and you feel there's something wrong with him; and since you both come here, perhaps you wonder how you appear, how you perform on the stage,'' an interesting interpretation. Another takes things a step further with, ''When you told the part of the dream where you got up on the platform, I got the feeling you were very glad to take the other man's place on the stage; and maybe that is a feeling you have toward some man, like the patient who comes before you on Wednesday, or your father.''

In practice, I would probably not want to answer the patient's direct questions until the overidealized transference had been resolved; I wouldn't want to reinforce it with shows of cleverness and wisdom. And an additional consideration, over and above this one as well as the other I mentioned, is that I might want to reserve my interpretative work for the underlying homosexual theme that appears to be burgeoning.

> I think the gymnasium was the one we had in school. We had assemblies there, and it had wooden chairs like in the dream.* But why would I be dreaming now about that place?***

Again, an invitation to a transference interpretation, which students accept. ''Perhaps you feel like a child here, as if you are being evaluated for your performance as you once were in school,'' and ''Perhaps you feel on stage here; your dream suggests that you feel as if you're exposing yourself to me, and that this both excites and embarrasses you,'' are typical examples. Some students take this line: ''I wonder if you are waiting for me to say something about the dream or waiting for me to compliment you for being such a good patient; I say this because of your compliments to me and your mention of another patient of mine.'' Several implicate the act of urinating, ''Maybe the dream expresses some of your feelings about the man who comes before you; that in a sense you don't like sharing the stage with him; and urinating expresses some of your feelings toward me for allowing him to share your position,'' and ''Is it possible that part of you wants to tell me your secrets, to be a child again, but another part resents it and would rather be more independent. Your urinating in the dream may be a way you can express some of your hostile feelings.''

Construing the urinating as an act of defiance and hostility is surprisingly common for my students. But there isn't any evidence that the patient construes it that way, and it's inappropriate to speculate from purely theoretical considerations. On the other hand, there is some evidence that he regards it as an act of giving and pleasing, and a few students formulate it that way. Such a formulation, however, is likely to be too farfetched in this context and for this patient, and it might turn out to be little more than an exercise in clever intellectualization. Moreover, he will probably contend that it was the fact that he really needed to urinate which accounts for this dream element.

It's strange, isn't it?**

"Perhaps it's not so strange," counters a student, "If we compare the situation in your dream with the one right here in therapy," a response which has substantial merit and strikes a good compromise among the considerations I've been discussing.

I guess the taking off of my clothes represents what I do in here, doesn't it? I certainly tell you all my secrets.* That's interesting. But ...* But why would I do a thing like urinate?** That ... that doesn't figure at all.* Maybe I wasn't going to urinate. You know something, I'm not actually sure whether it was that or whether I was going to ... uh ... to shit. You see, I failed to mention that I squatted down, and maybe that's because I was going to make a BM.** Now, that's really embarrass- ing!*** Well, I'm waiting for you to say something, and ...** And I'm feeling ... I'm feeling a bit ...** a bit tense.***

Again, as in the previous paradigms, the culmination point is regarded by students as the occasion for a useful remark. In this case, however, the central timing criterion is satisfied: the *therapeutic process* seems significantly inter- rupted, the patient is feeling tense (probably more than his minimization would imply), and a transference issue is clearly in the foreground. So the main decision you face is what kind of remark is most appropriate and likely to be most useful: in my opinion, an interpretation that focuses on the patient's affect and seeks primarily to articulate it. Anything else is too likely to be a deflection and to subserve both the defense of intellectualization and the overidealized transference image.

To simply offer a dream interpretation without articulating the disrupting affect, which many students do, runs the risk of colluding in the patient's defense by complying directly with his request ("I'm waiting for you to say something [because] I'm feeling tense"). Here's a good representative exam- ple which can be faulted on those grounds: "I have an idea about what this dream might mean. I wonder what you think of the idea that taking off your clothes and urinating might stand for a loss of control that part of you desires and another part of you fears. This loss of control is similar to what you ob- served in your father when he was drunk. Perhaps these feelings are being re- activated by feelings of rivalry you may have toward anyone who takes up my attention—other patients, for instance." Some students stress the exhibi- tionistic aspect of the dream; some speak of the patient's secrets as "dirty and therefore shameful'' (''I wonder if you feel there is a hidden or dark side of yourself that is shameful to expose here''); some focus on a simple conflict between exhibitionism and shame; and some articulate only the transference aspect (''You perform for me by producing dreams, as you used to please your parents by making a BM when you were a little boy,'' and ''Perhaps you feel you not only expose yourself in here but also you give me parts of yourself—like when you tell me your dreams—parts you have created or made''). These are good and interesting dream interpretations, but this happens not to be the moment to give one. The patient may ''need'' one, but the *therapeutic process* ''needs'' something different. What it needs is best formulated in terms of his state of tension.

Incidentally, because I judge it important to avoid an interpretation that provides support for his overidealized transference, I regard the first example in the above paragraph as far too definitive, much too ''good'' (and also overly diagnostic) for this particular patient. And here's a perfect example of a nondream interpretation that in itself is very good, but not for him, not now: ''I have a feeling that today's session was like a performance, meant to hold my attention by producing an interesting dream; and now you are waiting tensely to see whether I will approve. The actions in the dream, dancing and stripping, are meant to be watched, just as when you were little you wished to hold your parents' attention and gain their approval by urinating and defecating for them.'' (''That's just brilliant!'' I can picture the patient's responding, ''And so true! How do you do it?'')

Some students do focus directly on his affect, but they tend to make the error of assuming it needs no further articulation, that it's clear enough to him what he is feeling, and instead what he needs is an explanation. ''Could it be that you feel tense because you expect me to find what you were looking for?'' is a succinct example. And ''Perhaps you are feeling tense because you are uncertain if I will accept the parts of you that you consider repulsive and embarrassing; I wonder if you are afraid that by showing those parts, you will become like your father,'' is an excellent interpretation, but it should be offered only after the way he is feeling has been articulated and elaborated upon.

The distinction I am drawing between articulating and explaining the affect is not a sharp one, and some of the students' interpretations combine the two functions. Nevertheless, there can be substantial merit in trying to separate the two, at least in time, in order to be sure the explanation doesn't apply to an affect that is either mistakenly inferred or that the patient is unaware of. The danger of inferring to affects is greatest when a patient is suggestible, as this patient appears to be, and he will ''feel'' what you say he is feeling. Consider these three interesting interpretations, and notice how they infer various affects in the context of seeking to explain his tension: (1) "Maybe you feel embarrassed and tense because of your basic loss of control in your dream. Urinating and making a BM might be seen as expressions of anger toward me. Perhaps it is so difficult for you to express your anger because you fear you would not be able to control its expression or yourself," (2) "Perhaps you feel compelled to take your clothes off in here and tell me everything, however embarrassing. After you tell me, though, you resent the fact that you felt forced, and you get an urge to express your resentment. This is represented in your dream by urinating and making a BM," (3) "The defecation might be seen as an act of defiance, as though you'd decided not to dance like the other man, but instead to express a less cooperative attitude toward therapy. Maybe that's why you were embarrassed to tell me about it and why you are feeling tense now—because you are waiting to see how I'll react now that you've revealed the defiant, childlike part of yourself to me." In my opinion, each example should be preceded by a simpler articulation or a more succinct explanation, like (1) "I wonder whether you're angry at me right now," (2) "I think you are aware of feeling some resentment toward me, and that's making you so tense," (3) "You feel tense and embarrassed right now because you recognize some feelings of defiance in yourself?"

Simple articulations have certain drawbacks which an explanation can help to eliminate. Commonly they have a confronting edge, and a more complete interpretation can blunt it. Whether in this particular context, for this patient, an explanation would incur other disadvantages that would outweigh its ameliorative function, is a difficult judgment to make. We have to balance two or three countervailing sets of considerations, including his suggestibility, his idealized transference image, a possible homosexual and/or symbiotic undercurrent. So the matter of timing is particularly delicate and complicated here.

This is a good place to end the chapter, because timing is far from simple—and there is substantial justification to the often-heard claim that it's the most ineffable aspect of the psychotherapist's art.

5

On Questions, Probes,
Directives,
and Confrontations

My purpose in this chapter is to examine closely the noninterpretive modes that are available to us when we conduct a traditional form of psychotherapy and to show the ways they can fail to promote the *therapeutic process*, and even impede its development. Therefore, I stress the kinds of roles they cast us into, and the kinds of positions they put our patients into. I argue that the interviewing mode tends to define us as diagnosticians, troubleshooters; and the same applies to the confronting mode, which, in addition, defines us as alert observers. Both modes tend to put the patient into a passive and objective position. By contrast, the interpretive mode defines us as observers who try to understand and empathize, whose aim is not so much to uncover a patient's problems as to apprehend and comprehend them; and insofar as our interpretations embody the act of sharing rather than giving, we allow him to take a more active and subjective position.

But that doesn't mean we have to avoid interviewing and confronting entirely, that we must only interpret. For one thing, it is very difficult in practice to draw a sharp distinction between the various modes and to keep them separate from one another. For another, my thesis is best expressed this way: when interviewing and confronting become excessive, which constitutes a purely clinical kind of judgment, they can rob the interpretive mode of its cogency and power. Moreover, when I argue that in the face of steady interviewing and confronting, the patient can fall into a passive posture which may be inimical to the optimal development of the *therapeutic process,* I don't mean to overlook or minimize the fact that the same can also be true for excessive interpreting.

130

And I know the dangers of extreme positions, especially when it comes to actual clinical situations. I know, but can only take for granted in much of my discussion, how much has to depend on who the patient is, the stage of therapy, what matters are at issue, and the like. Consequently, these prefatory remarks are aimed at establishing a well-tempered tonality,[1] and the underlying spirit I wish my discussions and arguments to have is reflected in the wording of the following claim: insofar as well-formulated and well-timed interpretations have the property of shared discoveries rather than of one-sided observations, they run less of a risk of defining you as the active and controlling one, and they maximize your patient's short-term freedom and long-range autonomy. Moreover, despite the fundamental inimicality of the directive modes, there are circumstances in which a directive is wholly appropriate because it promotes the kind of activity which is necessary for the *therapeutic process* to function. One such circumstance, for instance, is when a patient falls silent (and notice how this circumstance is not exceptional, insofar as it's the exceptional patient who never falls silent); to direct him to tell what his thoughts were during the silence may be altogether necessary, and I'm going to argue that it isn't really dissonant with the principles and goals of *Psychotherapy*.

My overriding premise is this: rationales, in the context of the patient's essential well-being, are what govern our behavior as therapists in all forms of psychotherapy no less than in *Psychotherapy;* practical guidelines in the form of rules of thumb are necessary and useful, but they aren't actually rules. In fact, *There are no rules, only good techniques* should be our first rule, and, consequently, the only one.

The Question and the Probe

Perhaps the most distinctive, and at the same time most problematic, of *Psychotherapy*'s technical features is its requirement to avoid the interviewing format.[2] This requirement is difficult to defend, because questions for factual information and probes into feelings are natural ways to achieve some valuable goals, ranging from the purely diagnostic to the purely therapeutic, and it will often be the case that a question is our simplest and most straightforward way to facilitate and sharpen a patient's inquiry and

---

1. A well-tempered scale consists of intervals that are systematically imperfect. By compromising with perfection, and spreading out the imperfections equally among all the intervals, a well-balanced scale, which can be used for every tonality—not ideal for any single key, but sufficiently good for all modulations—is achieved.

2. In *Letters to Simon* I used the term *interrogation* and spoke of the "interrogative mode." The term *interviewing*, however, is accurate enough, and doesn't have such pejorative, prosecutorial connotations.

self-exploration. Nevertheless, the interviewing format has too many serious drawbacks, effects that can seriously impair the *therapeutic process* and distort the *Psychotherapy* session, so we have to try and forego the instrumentality of questions and probes.

Before I argue the point in detail, I want to amplify on the important distinction between a question asking for information and a question asking for clarification, between a request for something the patient had not said and a request for explanation of what he had said. Since the latter is based on our not having understood what he meant to say, the question can be formulated as a statement of fact: "It isn't clear to me what you said, what your intended meaning is." It needn't, of course, be put in declarative form; the question mark doesn't define a question, nor does voice inflection. An interpretation can be stated in question form—"What do you think of the possibility that . . . ?"—and I generally advocate that form. A question proper is defined by its function, to elicit information; a clarification question seeks to elicit information about what the patient actually said, while a question proper asks after information he omitted. The former is wholly consonant with *Psychotherapy*, even essential to it, because it pertains to a key feature of the Basic Instruction ("I will try to understand"); the latter can also be construed in terms of the Basic Instruction, as providing a basis "to understand," but this implicates a different meaning of the key term *understanding*. I'm going to examine that implication closely, but first I want to be sure it's clear that the question "What do you mean?" is never at issue here.

The question at issue is a directive to provide information (for instance, "How old were you when the incident happened?" and "I'm wondering how come you haven't told me how old you were"); it's called a *probe* when the information solicited is affects and feelings ("How did you feel when it happened?" and "What are your feelings now while you recount it?"). My thesis is this: only when an interpretation is at hand, only when the question and the probe are part of a pending interpretation, is their use problem-free; otherwise they have to be stringently avoided. This thesis puts me at odds with many practitioners and teachers who make active, free, and vital use of questions, and for whom the probe is practically a stock in trade. They would agree that the clarification question is useful in that it conveys an interest in a patient's meanings and intentions, but they would contend that the question proper and the probe are equally useful insofar as they show interest in his facts and feelings.

The easiest way to begin my argument is on a pedagogical note, because pedagogical considerations don't support the usefulness of questions and probes. Probably because it helps them maintain a sense of active participation, and also because to inquire into feelings bolsters their self-image as psychotherapists, beginners are prone to venture a question and a probe each time there's a break in their patient's narrative or every time they feel called upon to say something, and the result is a transformation of the session into a clinical interview. Not only does it tend to cast him into a passive position, an interview format tends to exert a subtle but significant influence on the nature of their interpretations; in the context of frequent and indiscriminate questioning, interpretations tend to become diagnostic, or troubleshooting, explanations. Therefore, placing a constraint on the asking of questions and putting a virtual prohibition on the use of probes—a constraint I place on my students (and on myself as well, for I am convinced that the average-expectable therapy proceeds better without much asking of direct questions and with no probes into feelings whatever)—serves the valuable function of insuring more empathic interpreting and more active listening. In my experience, the discipline goes far toward guaranteeing that the therapy will approximate the spirit of active and relatively autonomous exploration that reflects the essential character of the *therapeutic process.*

Many teachers might agree with me, but only about the direct question. The exploration of affects is so vital to therapy, they may contend, that the probe must be allowed, if not encouraged; because, while factual information may well be therapeutically unimportant, the same isn't true for feelings—they have such an intrinsic importance that uncovering feelings is therapeutically justified across a broad range of circumstances. And I too accept that working hypothesis. I too believe that feelings are never irrelevant—that not only are they a vital aspect of human experience, they have a special usefulness in therapy as guides and markers to important areas of inner reality. Thus, not only are affects intrinsically important, but they serve an invaluable signaling function. But I maintain, nevertheless, that the probe isn't the best way to get at them, and neither is it a good technique for exploiting their usefulness.

Consider how easily the probe can be construed as an invitation to intellectualization, to verbalizing the state of affects, freezing a feeling into a cognitive structure that's essentially conventional, merely labeling it. When I put it this way, I obviously mean to denigrate that function, but I do recognize how it can have the important short-term function of helping a patient gain control over the affect. Essentially, it's an invocation of the defense of intellectualization—which, like all defense, is not in itself a maladaptive measure. So if our purpose is to invoke and strengthen certain of his cognitive defenses, then the probe can be a useful technique insofar as it encourages him to put his feelings into commonly understood words. But many teachers and practitioners use the probe for exactly the opposite purpose; they regard it as a technique for circumventing and weakening the defense of intellectualization, thereby getting a patient to confront his feelings instead of dealing only with cognitions. And here is where I disagree, where I regard the probe as antithetical to the purpose, where it can undermine rather than promote.

If the patient is someone who rarely or never reports his feelings, then the probe can be the wrong technique to use, because the crucial issue is why he rarely if ever talks about feelings—and the probe simply bypasses it. What the probe can do is encourage him to reflect upon feelings and pay attention to them, but it does this at the expense of the reason why reflection and attention was lacking in the first place. That reason can count profoundly. In fact, uncovering the reason may actually serve to make him reflective, as well as feelingful, and serve that function far better than the probe.

Consider what the reason might be for a patient's avoidance of feelings. It can reflect his conviction that we are interested only, or mostly, in his feelings, so he will frustrate our interest by withholding them; it can reflect the conviction that his feelings are too inarticulate and amorphous to be put into words we can understand; he may be ashamed of his feelings or fear they'll incur our valuation or be convinced they'll be found contemptible; and there is also the possibility that he simply doesn't know what his feelings are or were. I needn't belabor the fact that such reasons are important to uncover and understand; my point is that the probe is obviously not the way to do it. Asking why obviously is, and we can do it with observation in question form, "I notice you rarely tell me about your feelings. Have you been aware of that?" or "Though you usually tell me what your feeling is, you omitted it this time. Did you notice that?" These remarks are not probes, but they are confrontations; and since the confronting mode is also hazardous, I advocate formulating the observation into an interpretation, which means we have to offer a reason instead of instructing the patient to wonder why (or doing it indirectly with "I wonder why"). So my recommendation comes down to this: we should wait until we have some basis on which to make an interpretation, and not choose to address the subject before then. We don't probe for feelings, we empathize and articulate; and when we have a hunch about why the patient has or doesn't have, always has or never has, a certain feeling, we offer an explanatory interpretation.

But you can make a strong argument for probing first, before interpreting ("I understand now why you found the feeling so hard to have and acknowledge ..."). That argument is based on the value of avoiding possible error; namely, the probe can be an important safeguard against mistaking the patient's feelings. Here's how the argument goes: when I contend that we don't avoid the patient's affects (we simply avoid probing for them), when I stress how this doesn't constrain us from articulating and interpreting affects, you challenge me for placing a premium on speculation instead of favoring a straightforward way of insuring accuracy. Isn't the probe safer, insofar as it takes the precaution of being correct? Moreover, isn't the danger of error compounded by the likelihood that the patient will not feel so free to countenance our mistake, but instead will fall under the sway of suggestion, feeling what we said he was feeling? The issue seems to resolve into the difference between asking after a feeling and guessing it, and the guess is potentially a loaded one because a patient is apt to be suggestible when it comes to his affects ("Yes, I suppose you're right, I am feeling angry," or "Yes, you must be correct, I did feel guilty"). This danger may not be so great when the guess is about factual information, nor so serious when it applies to explanations and integrations (because they have a somewhat theoretical nature to begin with), but when we venture to tell the patient what affect he is or was feeling, the influence of suggestion is apt to be pernicious—and the probe is an appropriate way to safeguard against error.

That's a strong argument with one main weakness: it fails to take account of therapy's extended time frame. Therapy ordinarily provides ample time and opportunity for us to assess the role that suggestion may be playing. We can and should observe the extent to which our interpretations are accepted uncritically by our patient, and we can and should modulate them accordingly. Insofar as we want to avoid the instrumentality of suggestion, we have to pay adequate attention to its potential influence, and not only when it comes to affects but in all of our interpretive speculations. To be sure, since affects are peculiarly susceptible to suggestion, a special alertness and caution is required. But rather than resolve the problem with the use of probes, we have these two options: (1) to be especially conservative in our speculations about patients' affects, (2) to look for opportunities to deal interpretively with the problem of suggestion itself. After all, if we observe that the patient is prone to accept our suggestions, dealing with it in therapy is bound to benefit him because we can assume it's a significant problem outside of therapy as well. To be sure, while the problem itself isn't likely to be indigenous, it's quite true that therapy, with its manifold potentialities for regression and transference, may accentuate and exaggerate it.

If we have a particular reason to be interested in what our patient is feeling but no basis on which to infer it, or if we judge that the feeling is especially germane to the topic under deliberation but hesitate to risk a speculation because he is suggestible, we can draw attention to it with a simple observation ("I gather you don't know what you're feeling") or a mild confrontation ("You aren't considering your feelings"), which can serve to focus attention without unduly forcing his hand. We have to be quite sure, however, that our interest isn't idle, that we're interested in the feeling merely for its own sake, so to speak; we're interested not simply because it was omitted, but because we have reason to believe the omission is significant to the ongoing *therapeutic process*.

Furthermore, whenever we experience the impulse to interview, we can take it as a signal. If we are free from misgivings about our position as the listener and are not being prompted to ask questions by a sense of not participating actively enough in the session, we can proceed on two assumptions: (1) our impulse is prompted by a significant gap in the patient's account, (2) the gap is being determined by a significant reason. Accordingly, our first priority can be to uncover the reason, and the pertinent question to consider is a why-question and not a what-question. To argue that a what-question must precede a why-question, that before we can proceed to explore the reason for an omission we have to know what the omission is, overlooks the fact that the former will emerge quite naturally when the latter is being explored—so in practice we can readily avoid putting the what-question. What I advocate you do is try to convey to the patient, not a sense of curiosity about what was omitted, but a sense of interest in the meaning of the omission. Commonly, he will simply tell you what was omitted and ignore your why-question; at such times you can continue with, "I didn't mean to ask you what it was you left out, or simply draw your attention to the fact that you left it out; rather, I'm trying to explore the reason you left it out, the meaning of your having omitted it from your deliberations."

Otherwise, what tends to happen is a division of responsibilities between him and you, in which he reports the facts and you inquire after the feelings, or in which you take responsibility for the gaps by choosing when to ask about them. And even if he gets the idea that feelings are important, or that gaps in his account are significant, he can learn to report them in an artificial and mechanical way. In reporting his feelings, or in going over his account and filling in the gaps, he will be complying with your expectations, and might enjoy a sense of satisfaction that both of you are doing the right thing (dealing with feelings and significant omissions). But there's little therapeutic value to this sense of satisfaction, and certainly disadvantages to instituting or fostering a sense of game-playing on the patient's part. (Most patients will do it on their own, and by keeping it a one-person game you can gradually extinguish it.) Also, to inquire after feelings can put him in a more passive position than can empathizing with his feelings; to be subjected to a speculation about what he may be feeling does not render a person more passive than to direct him to reflect, to introspect, and to report his feelings—frequently it's just the reverse. The person's response probably depends largely on context, as well as on his way of experiencing and expressing affects.

Before I can regard the question of probes as settled, I need to consider a special function of affects in therapy which I mentioned in passing, the signaling role of feelings. It frequently happens during the course of a session that a patient's train of thought is interrupted or diverted because of a feeling he experiences. At such moments, the probe can serve at least two valuable functions: it can help the patient understand why the thought was interrupted and diverted, and it can sensitize him to the ways his affects govern his psychic functioning. Sometimes the affect is a subtle one, a minimal feeling, fleeting and difficult to capture; and for him to learn to detect and pay attention to it can be a vital lesson. The probe is certainly the simplest, most immediate and direct, way to teach that lesson.

Experienced practitioners are familiar with the phenomenon. They know how to explore such subtle and fleeting affects, how to press them into therapeutic service. Essentially, the affect is used for its signaling properties rather than for its intrinsic interest, and our message is, "Let the feeling be a guide to the fact that something is up!" By being alerted to pay special attention to them during the course of a session, the patient is taught to use his feelings for the purposes of exploration and discovery. (When he asks, "Why do you want to know?" after we've asked for feelings, the answer can be, "Because such feelings can give us a valuable clue to your inner reality, to your conflicts and impulses and defenses.") The mode is basically didactic; the patient is being taught how to explore and work; we play the role of enabler, if not of teacher, guiding the exploration by using affect as marker and guidepost. When we say, "The fact that you experienced a twinge of anxiety may mean that a forbidden impulse, an unconscious fantasy, or a basic conflict is threatening to emerge," it isn't an interpretation but a didactic lesson. The fact that the lesson derives from considerations of theory or out of our clinical experience, not from evidence derived from the patient, defines the formulation as didactic. And it's no less didactic, though probably more tactful and effective, to put it this way: "Your train of thought was interrupted, wasn't it? I wonder if that didn't happen because something intruded on your mind, a thought or a feeling, and that might explain the interruption."

The probe may not be the best technique to use in these circumstances, but it may be the only one available. If there is any basis on which to infer a particular affect, then an interpretation can be more effective, but frequently there is no such basis—and then a probe is our only recourse. Therefore, when it is used for the kind of phenomenon I've been describing, I must agree that the advantages of the mode are outweighed by the potential disadvantages.

Is there also a circumstance when the question for information may have a significant advantage? I believe there is, though it isn't similar to those circumstances. It's when we have an interpretation in mind, judge it as timely, but need some information in order to make sure it's correct. To defend my opinion that this is the only exceptional circumstance, I'll examine in detail the prototypic situation in which we face the option of putting a direct question and make some further points about *Psychotherapy*'s technical requirements during the course of this examination. Suppose a patient is recounting an event from his childhood and hasn't mentioned how old he was at the time; the question is, "How old were you?"

Let's assume the question can be asked without incurring unwanted implications (such as the criticism, "Your account is deficient" or the scold, "You should've mentioned your age"), and that not mentioning his age was a simple oversight on your patient's part, or perhaps it was his presumption that the age isn't so relevant and important. Therefore, were you to put the question, he would merely take a moment to mention his age, and then resume his account. The situation is simple, and the only question at issue is, Why the question? What useful function could it serve to have the information? How could it support and improve the *therapeutic process*?

You wouldn't have wanted to ask for it unless you had reason to believe the information might be important. There's no need here, for the sake of my argument, to minimize the fact that it may help you in several ways to understand him; it might clarify the developmental issues involved and provide valuable information not only about his history but also about his current functioning. The first question for us to consider, however, is what you're going to do with that understanding. Are you going to share it with the patient or do you plan to keep it to yourself?—that can make a critical difference. If you plan to follow it up with an interpretation ("That information helps me understand the event you're recounting, and also to understand your current problems—and here's how . . ."), then putting the question was not an isolated event, it was an integral part of a pending interpretation. The patient will probably appreciate that you asked it in order to make sure the interpretation was correct; it was more a precaution than anything else. In an important sense then, the question had the same properties the interpretation had; it was part and parcel of the interpretation. Moreover, even if it should turn out the information doesn't provide support for the one you had in mind, your having asked for it can be justified, if need be, by telling what that interpretation was.

So this can be an important exception to the proscription of direct questions: when it's part of a pending interpretation, a question serves an integral function which shares the advantages of the interpretive mode and outweighs the disadvantages of the interviewing mode; it merely establishes the fact that understanding and speculation will be tempered and judicious.

But what if you don't intend to explain the event to your patient or draw any inferences from it about his current functioning? What if you have no timely interpretation in mind? In that case, the information will have been useful only to you, to your overall efforts at understanding him—and that puts a different cast on the matter. Without my minimizing this kind of usefulness and dismissing the likelihood that such understanding can play an important part in your future interpretations, I believe that when you actively gather information which you plan to use only at some future time, you necessarily incur the undesirable side effects of the interviewing format. The major one is the expectation on the patient's part that once you have amassed all the necessary information about him, you will proceed to give him useful interpretations. You are defining yourself as a repository of factual information and taking on the role of diagnostician. Consequently, using questions this way, though different from using them to insure that an interpretation is valid only in respect to time frame, makes a very significant difference for role definition.

My overall position with respect to offering patients explanations is also pertinent to this issue. The fact that you have an explanation in mind is never decisive; the fact remains that you aren't necessarily going to want to share it with your patient. You might judge that the *therapeutic process* won't benefit from it, and there is always the possibility that any explanation you could share would run the risk of interfering with, rather than facilitating, his work of exploration. So I have to consider the possibility that the question (''How old were you?'') will indeed have the desired result of facilitating the patient's exploration by drawing his attention to an important feature of what he is working on. It may well be ''useful'' in the sense that it might lead him to include a valuable feature of the event, thereby increasing the probability of discovery—and for him, not you. All you are conveying with the question is that it might be helpful to him if he took into account what his age was when the event occurred.

Before examining this possibility further, let me point out that a more direct (and directive) way to achieve the aim is to put it in the form of a suggestion (''Let me suggest to you that it might be helpful . . .''), and in that way you can shift the emphasis from ''useful to me'' to ''useful to you,'' which in turn might circumvent some potential complications of role definition as well as the implicit promise, ''If you tell me how old you were, I will be in a better position to help you understand the event.'' But let's suppose the question has that connotation, and that your patient construes it as nothing more than a suggestion that his age at the time might be an important thing for him to consider in his explorations. Two big questions now arise: (1) Is it an important consideration? (2) What makes you think so? Let's begin with the second question and imagine that the patient asks it. (''Why do you think it might be useful to take account of my age at the time?'')

You can answer by appealing to your psychological theory, or by justifying the opinion in terms of your experience as a therapist, or you can do both. Neither answer is optimal, in my estimation, but if I had to choose one, I would select the latter. To base your rationale on your theory would amount to sharing with the patient your belief in a certain conceptual point of view (for example, that developmental stages are important), which in turn would raise a number of issues that could have extensive implications—and at best would involve you in teaching him a lesson in psychology. There are several reasons why you should be loath to do this, and I'm going to discuss the one that's bound to be the most difficult and controversial.

To open a discussion with your patient on matters of psychological theory runs the risk of casting you in the role of an authority on psychology, an expert on human behavior—and that's a role you don't want to play. *Psychotherapy,* in my opinion and clinical experience, rarely requires that role of you; *Psychotherapy* (and again I'm appealing not to my theory but to my experience as a therapist) proceeds best when you don't wear the mantle of authority on anything other than the conducting of *Psychotherapy*—that is, when you don't wear the mantle of expertise on psychology in general, only on psychotherapy in particular. Now, I must hasten to add, lest this claim seem altogether impossible to entertain (if not altogether ridiculous), that I don't mean you should pretend to know nothing about psychology or to have no pragmatic, theoretical, and even scientific, knowledge about human behavior. What I mean is that you should try to avoid the position that you know more than the patient knows. He too has a theory of behavior, after all; he too has both pragmatic wisdom and an operating theory; and he might also know the science. At the very least, you should keep from teaching him what you know.

And another reason to be reluctant to invoke theory and/or science is that the didactic mode has a limited utility in therapy; its main function is usually to provide reassurance, and in this respect it overlaps with intellectualization (having the additional disadvantage of being your intellectualization instead of the patient's). Therefore, I regard it as generally useful to avoid any steps that would invoke, or seem to invoke, your knowledge of psychology in general—as distinct from your patient's psychology in particular—and for that reason, you shouldn't want to justify a question for information on nomothetic grounds.

Faced with the two options, I therefore advocate justifying a question (as well as a directive of any kind) not on your psychological theory but on your therapy experience. "It has been my experience that when patients take into account the age at which events in their past occurred, they can better explore it and come to a more complete understanding of it," is how the answer can be framed; and while it is clearly both a didactic remark and a normative formulation, insofar as it makes appeal to what is true for other patients, it limits your avowed expertise and avoids unnecessary complications of role definition. Notice also how it precludes the possibilities of argument and disputation, something always worth precluding.

Any intimation that you are comparing and contrasting your patient with others is bound to have subtle but important ramifications for the way he works. *Psychotherapy* proceeds best when it remains ostensibly ideographic and fully personal, when it restricts itself to evidence and observations that emerge from the patient alone. So even if it were true that every patient you ever had (or heard about) had experienced an improvement in his work of exploration and discovery when he took account of the age at which past events occurred, you shouldn't want to rely on that regularity because it is based exclusively on normative grounds. But this may be too ideal and un-realizable a position, too likely to be indefensible when taken to its extreme, so I have to avoid stressing it unduly here. To restore some balance, I can turn finally to the key question, the first one I raised a few paragraphs ago: Is it true that focusing on his age will help your patient in his explorations of the event?

My temptation is to answer no. I am tempted to insist that there isn't an *a priori* way of answering either yes or no, but that would be a gross overstate-ment and would only satisfy my need to win the argument. Instead, I can couch my answer in an it-depends context and concede that if the answer is a "likely-yes," then that might be judged to outweigh all the considerations I've examined. In other words, if chances are good that the *therapeutic process* will be significantly improved, then that could tip the balance in favor of the interviewing mode. And because my answer is not a yes but a "gener-ally no," I can maintain my fundamental opposition to it because I don't believe that factual information (the kind that is typically elicited by direct questions) will generally improve the level of a patient's work, especially when we have no idea about it (no interpretation in mind that requires the information for its confirmation). It can too easily amount to little more than a fishing for significance.

From another perspective, consider how easy it is to suppose that when we actively ask our patient questions, we are actively engaged with him in his work of therapeutic exploration. Indeed, many of you will insist that it's more than "easy" to suppose it, it's "essential" to do so. And the underlying spirit of the interviewing mode is this: "I will help you uncover and discover; I'll participate in your therapeutic efforts by pointing to areas you're overlooking, by drawing your attention to facts which may seem to you irrelevant but which may actually turn out to be both relevant and useful." Moreover, you can argue that many of the considerations I have so far examined apply mainly to a therapy in which you have used questions infrequently; and when your patient is confronted with a rarely asked question, he may well wonder why it was asked (what formulation you have in mind for which you need the information), but if direct questions are often asked him, if they are an integral part of your style and method, then he'll have no reason to wonder why for any particular question.

I would counter by again falling back on my familiar position: the spirit of inquiry that accompanies extensive reliance on interviewing differs fundamentally from the spirit of inquiry that occurs when there's little, if any, reliance on it, when it's used very infrequently and only selectively. It simply makes a profound difference to the way a typical session proceeds when you don't seek out information, but rely entirely on what your patient chooses to tell. And the kind of passivity on your part, which is embodied in working only with presented information, engenders a special quality of participation on his part. But I don't mean to contend that this kind of passivity necessarily causes him to be more active.

On the contrary, your passivity typically leads the patient also to take a passive attitude. Not, of course, a more passive attitude than yours, because he is thinking and talking, while you listen in silence and occasionally offer comments. But my experience has been that there's an important sense in which a patient who is working within the interviewing format is likely to be less passive than one working outside it. The latter's passivity will lead him into a relatively free kind of mentation, a kind of stream-of-consciousness modality that approximates the underlying spirit of the free-association method, and he will slip quite naturally into it without having been instructed to, without the disadvantages of taking it as an externally imposed task. This will secure for him the vital benefits of the modality, which include such therapeutically valuable features as a lowered level of defensiveness, an openness to spontaneous and fleeting thoughts and feelings, as well as the ability to listen to himself in the same way you listen to him. And for the patient to listen to himself, to observe his thoughts and feelings and actions, is most necessary, because important discoveries derive from such listening. Interviewing tends to prevent it; in certain ways it can obviate the necessity for such listening; and it can happen, paradoxically, that a patient will become even more passive than is optimal when freed from the necessity of observing himself, when you do that work for him.

But the issue of activity-passivity is more complicated than that, and I must resist the temptation to examine its complexities further. Suffice it to say that the optimal posture for a patient is probably not at either extreme of the activity-passivity dimension but somewhere in between. And without pursuing the topic further, I'll rest with the claim that when we ask questions and put probes, when we use the interviewing mode to any significant extent, we are likely to push him toward one or the other of the extremes.

The Explicit Directive

When your patient falls silent you have the option of asking, "What have you been thinking about?" I regard this to be another important exception to *Psychotherapy*'s general proscription of directives, and I'll try to explain why. To begin with, the gap in verbalization which occurs when a patient is silent isn't the same as the kinds of omissions I discuss in the foregoing section; and while there is a surface similarity between the directives, "Please tell me the following fact you omitted from your account" and "Please tell me the thoughts you had during your silence," there is a fundamental difference between them.

The former runs the risk of imposing a new topic, the latter doesn't. If you were to ask, "Why are you silent?"—which isn't the directive I'm discussing—that could amount to an imposition, insofar as it's quite likely he wasn't thinking about the reason for his silence. Moreover, even when the patient wasn't thinking about anything, when his mind was blank, so he answers, "Nothing," you haven't changed the subject or imposed a topic— unless he feels impelled to consider why, which wasn't really implicit in your question. Furthermore, asking him to verbalize his thoughts is significantly different from asking him to provide an omitted fact or feeling, because you aren't directing him to speak about something new and different, something he wasn't already thinking about.

But perhaps he was silent because he didn't want to speak his thoughts. Aren't you, then, violating the Basic Instruction by asking for them? He may well respond, "Look here, you said I was free to speak about whatever I wanted!—and I'm assuming that includes the freedom to remain silent. I was thinking about something I don't want to talk about. Are you directing me to speak about it anyway?" Whether the patient articulates the issue as clearly as this or not, the first thing you have to do is make it clear to him that he is free to remain silent if he wants to, and you didn't intend to imply that his silence wasn't all right. This has to be done when you first use the directive, and perhaps the first several times. The next thing to do is explain your reasons for having broken his silence. You can begin by reminding him that you had no way of knowing he was thinking about something he didn't want to talk about; then you can explain how you thought he might have slipped into a reverie-like mood, and there was the possibility he was experiencing some difficulty overcoming the inertia of the silence itself; consequently, you figured it might be useful to help him overcome the inertia by asking for his thoughts.

Notice how that explanation avoids the message "I am interested in your unspoken thoughts," which has certain overtones. But it fails to avoid the implication that reverie-like moods aren't useful and are not going to be allowed. Before examining that implication, I have to consider a more immediate question that the explanation is likely to raise in the patient's mind (and yours also): Why is it useful to have the inertia of silence overcome?

My answer is based on the premise that the *therapeutic process* is usually enhanced by verbalization, that exploration and discovery are usually best served when a patient is not only thinking but also verbalizing this thoughts, mainly because he is then in the position to listen to himself. Other things being equal, self-observation is facilitated by observing oneself in action; and for most people, most of the time, verbalizing thoughts improves the ability to observe those thoughts. If you judge that your patient is no exception, or that this particular silence is not exceptional, you can base your answer on such a rationale—"It's useful to overcome a silence's inertia because you may benefit more from the session if you spoke your thoughts." Notice, again, how the explanation avoids implying that your participation is at issue, namely, you have to know what he is thinking in order to help him understand and discover. There's no compelling reason to formulate it that way; you could take the position that the second part of the Basic Instruction requires him to speak in order that you can listen and try to understand, but that point is so self-evident that if the matter arose during the course of therapy I'd be inclined to focus on the first explanation.

That explanation, however, is potentially problematic, insofar as it can be adapted with only minor modifications to fit a variety of different directives. The *therapeutic process* could benefit, for instance, from the exploration of dreams, and this could justify the directive to bring them in. And suppose a patient is speaking about a symptom and focusing only on its current forms, and suppose you have reason to believe it might be useful if he were to consider its historical origins—why not simply notify him of that conviction in the form of a directive? Or conversely, if he is speaking only about the symptom's genesis, why not, "Please talk about the way the symptom happens now, because that might be useful"? In other words, if facilitation and promotion of the *therapeutic process* are your principal goals, why should you be prevented from following the most expeditious course of action across a variety of different areas?

Moreover, the Basic Instruction itself has not constrained you to the interpretive mode; as far as the patient is concerned you haven't ruled out the providing of directives and advice. Consequently, were you to give any of the directives I mentioned, he would have no reason to conclude you had departed from the conditions of the Basic Instruction, especially insofar as questions and suggestions pertaining to how therapy proceeds best are concerned. In view of this fact, you need to find an appropriate time and way to amplify on the matter. Once you've arrived at the clinical opinion that the patient is a suitable candidate for *Psychotherapy*, you have to look for an opportunity to enlarge on the Basic Instruction by notifying him that you will *try* not to give him any kind of advice—and you have to specify clearly that this means advice pertaining not only to behavior outside of therapy but also to his behavior during the sessions. He will likely understand why you refrain from advising him on courses of action to follow in his daily life, and the matter is easily explained in terms of your wishing to remain objective and neutral. But he might be puzzled, if not worse, about the restriction on advice as to how he should proceed in the therapy ("I can see why you wouldn't want to tell me whether I should change my job, or invest in the stock market, or even get married; but that's quite different from telling me what to talk about here, isn't it?") After all, insofar as you have experience and expertise in therapy, you should be able to give some useful advice in this area.

I have already examined the larger answer to this question. The answer you can give the patient is simply, "In my experience, what is useful is for you to speak about what you want to speak about," and you can amplify it by explaining that your wish to remain neutral extends to his behavior during the session because your ability to understand him will be enhanced if you haven't directed him in any way and have allowed him the freedom of deciding what to talk about. If he continues to press the question, you can introduce the distinction between short-term and long-term considerations; you can concede that a directive may be useful in the short run, but contend that it may impede the long-range goals of therapy. And there's no need to minimize the potential usefulness of certain directives; if the patient feels at a loss about what to talk about and says it would be "useful" for the moment if he got some directive from you, he may be perfectly right—it would be useful. But the question you ask yourself is whether it would be useful only in the short run, and therefore shortsighted, to fulfill his request, whether it would impede the optimal development of the *therapeutic process* in the long run. This doesn't mean there's a need for dogmatic rigidity, that your sole option is the long-range goal and you must under no circumstances opt for short-term benefits. All that's required of you is the awareness that these options exist, that they can be antithetical to each other, and that it might be more useful to your patient if you helped him explore why he feels at a loss over what to talk about and feels a need for direction (or why he doesn't bring in his dreams, or why he never speaks about the history of his symptoms). That's the option which has to be kept open at all times, and it requires a readiness on your part to frustrate his need for directives.

But I don't think these considerations apply equally to the directive, "What are you thinking?" I believe this is an exceptional case; the short-term benefits are very substantial, and they may not conflict so sharply with the long-term ones. Therefore, when a patient falls into a silence and needs your help to end it, I don't recommend frustrating that need, not as a rule of thumb. You can make an effort to distinguish between meditative or reverie-like silences, on the one hand, and transference or resistance silences, on the other; you can try to understand the nature and function of each silence; and depending on your understanding of it, you may choose to interrupt a silence either with the directive question or with an interpretation—or you may decide, of course, not to interrupt it at all.

The Confrontation

A traditional therapist's interventions generally fall into two major categories, confrontations and interpretations. The terms are somewhat misleading; *confrontation* connotes belligerence, a clash of positions and attitudes, and *interpretation* connotes translating a message from one form into another, elucidating meaning and resolving ambiguity. In practice, however, both categories encompass a much wider range of issues than their names suggest, and there can be a significant overlap between them. I'm going to begin by emphasizing their differences.

In an interesting essay, "Therapeutic Confrontation from Routine to Heroic," Howard Corwin stresses that the use of some forms of confrontation has always been a "routine" aspect of psychoanalysis, usually referred to as "helping the patient to see," "pointing out," or "calling to his attention." But there is another kind of confrontation, " . . . at the opposite end from the routine, which is distinguished in being considered something heroic, that which is perhaps a memorable part of the analyst's day . . . A heroic confrontation may be defined as an emotionally charged, parametric, manipulative, technical tool demanded by the development of an actual or potential situation of impasse and designed ultimately to remobilize a workable therapeutic alliance."[3] Such a confrontation is an emergency measure; its use is usually restricted to situations where the therapy itself is in serious jeopardy. My attitude toward it has to be obvious—if, indeed, it is ever used, it can only be used in extraordinary circumstances—and my discussion here is restricted to routine confrontations.

To draw a patient's attention to an aspect of his behavior or experience, requesting him to face himself in this or that respect, is to offer a confrontation. A confrontation is typically, if not essentially, a diagnostic formulation, a remark about the patient made from an outside vantage point. The message

3. Howard Corwin, "Therapeutic Confrontation from Routine to Heroic," in *Confrontation in Psychotherapy*, ed. G. Adler and P. G. Myerson (New York: J. Aronson, 1973), pp. 72–73.

is "I have observed something about you; I draw your attention to it." In certain contexts it can be forceful, even belligerent, and may impose an altogether new topic, but under other circumstances it can be supportive, even reassuring, and will be a minimal imposition because the patient is ready to consider the topic which is being drawn to his attention. It can be empathic when it applies to what he is experiencing phenomenally; when it applies to how he is behaving or acting, then little if any empathy is entailed. But in all contexts and circumstances, a confrontation points out a fact and doesn't explain it or integrate it with other facts—it "holds up the mirror."

The confronting mode is regarded by most practitioners and teachers as a valuable technical resource; many believe it can be the most efficacious aspect of traditional therapy. Patients too may share the opinion; many experience the confrontation as the most vivid aspect of their therapy and also the most moving one. Nevertheless, though I acknowledge its power and efficacy, though I am familiar with its special impact—its capacity for shaking things loose, stirring things up—I regard confrontations to be dissonant with *Psychotherapy*. At the same time, however, I cannot refute the contention that it's virtually impossible to avoid them altogether, that it is unreasonable to expect us never to use them, and that certain kinds of important interpretations (most notably, of resistance) cannot usually be made without first making a significant confrontation. Therefore, my position regarding the confronting mode is basically the same as my position on questions and probes: it should be used sparingly and judiciously, and mainly—if not only—when a full interpretation is at hand. But there is this difference: while I can conceive of our never putting a direct question and never probing, I cannot do the same for confrontations—for reasons I discuss soon.

A confrontation is a directive. ("Look at what you are doing!" "Please pay attention to this aspect of how you act or think or feel.") Insofar as the patient might be unready to face whatever he is being asked to face, the mode is, of course, risky; but it would be facile of me to denigrate it by giving examples that reflect poor timing or tactless formulation. When it's bady timed and poorly formulated, when it betrays the earmarks of an impulse to lead the patient and to force his hand, then confrontation needs no special condemnation by me. (After all, interpretation can also suffer from the same faults.) Instead, I'll try to explain why I remain skeptical of the confronting mode when considerations of timing and tact are optimal.

Consider this hypothetical illustration: "I'd like to interrupt you in order to draw your attention to something you may not be aware of. Do you notice that you tend to stammer whenever you speak about your brother?" If the patient were to respond, "No, I never realized that—But why do you draw my attention to it?" you could simply explain, "Because I believe it might be useful to consider it, useful to you and to the progress of therapy," and there isn't likely to be a clash of positions or any other interaction belligerent enough to deserve the label "confrontation." You have tactfully held up the mirror in order to show the patient something about his behavior that can be examined to good therapeutic ends and could result in important discovery.

Notice that your observation doesn't seem to contain the implicit message "So cut it out!" (which it would, had the topic been his regularly coming late to the sessions or his preoccupation with trivialities or something which could be construed as interfering with the progress of therapy), though it is, of course, conceivable that the patient could hear this message. What seems more likely, however, is that he will react to the fact that you've imposed a topic, the stammering. Still, if he were to react defensively, you could interpret that reaction as a maneuver to deflect attention from the phenomenon itself ("I believe you misconstrued my intentions in order to avoid looking at the fact that you stammer when you speak about your brother"), and that might also be a salutory development.

But it also might not be—and that, in my opinion, is the basic problem. Typically, there isn't a good way of telling in advance what the effect of a confrontation will be. This is chiefly because the patient's unawareness of the phenomenon being brought to his attention might be a defense mechanism. And when a defense is attacked without first having been weakened and analyzed, chances are good that another will take its place. For instance, it's easy to imagine that after he accepts the illustrated confrontation with no challenge, the patient will proceed to explain it (or explain it away) purely in the interest of intellectualization. Perhaps, then, it was not well-timed; since you had no reason to believe the defense against the awareness of the stammering was anything but secure, this was not the optimal time to bring it to his attention. So let's alter the illustration as follows: the patient is describing an incident in which he abused his brother cruelly but doesn't recognize the cruelty; you do recognize it, detect that he is very close to recognizing it also, and decide to offer the observation, "You were behaving cruelly to your brother," a simple confrontation ("Look here, don't you think your actions were cruel!"); the patient fully accepts the observation, saying, "Yes, you're perfectly right; I was very close to recognizing it; now I see it clearly."

How, when it had such a good result, when it helped him articulate something on the threshold of his awareness, could the confrontation be an error? It was an error because it circumvented the *therapeutic process*. Notice that you didn't say anything about the reason he needed your help in getting the cruelty out into the open, and (temporarily, at least) you participated in bypassing the reason that that awareness couldn't cross the threshold by itself, so to speak. (Bear in mind that the topic here isn't why the patient was cruel in the first place, it's why he defended against an awareness of the cruelty.) It should be amply clear by now that you did not supervise and promote the *therapeutic process* with that remark. There are subtle but vital distinctions in how I construe our participation in the process, and this is one of them. The threshold phenomenon—the reason the patient couldn't recognize the cruelty or the stammering without your showing it to him, his defense (or his resistance)—that's our first and our main order of business. (I made a similar argument about the use of questions and probes, and my distinction here is analogous to the one I drew between what-questions and why-questions.)

You might accept my basic premise and still argue that all you really have to do is be sure to follow up the confrontation with an appropriate interpretation explaining why the patient needs you to make it and couldn't do it himself. That, after all, shouldn't be so difficult; and chances are quite good that he will proceed to do it himself. Moreover, even if he doesn't, even if he needs to have the defense explained to him, the *therapeutic process* will have been temporarily bypassed, but it won't necessarily come to a grinding halt. And I wouldn't disagree with you, because I don't believe the *therapeutic process* is such a fragile phenomenon that a confrontation is likely to be so damaging to its integrity. But I would counter with the challenge, Was it necessary? Couldn't you have offered the observation together with an interpretation?

Why it might be better to do that is a moot question. You could contend that it's far better to offer the observation without any interpretation attached, because the interpretation might weaken its impact by providing an intellectual framework. Before I discuss that point, let's assume you couldn't offer any interpretation because you saw no reason for the threshold, and therefore had nothing more to say, at that moment, than you had said in the confrontation; moreover, you had reason to expect that the threshold (the defense) might be amenable to interpretation once the confrontation had drawn it to the patient's attention, because he was working well and not being resistive, and you had been tactful and free from all impulse to direct or judge him. Aren't you on safe ground? Yes, but only in the short run. You have resorted to an expediency which might have an immediate efficacy, but if you use it too early (because early in therapy, before its format and orientation have been securely established, it is especially risky and inimical), or too frequently, then it will have long-term consequences. So at the very least, I stress the necessity of being judicious and selective with the use of confrontations.

But my unwillingness to endorse the mode (given a reasonable choice and option, I rarely, if ever, use confrontations) is based also on the fact that it is dissonant with *Psychotherapy* in the following way: inherent in the confrontation is the fact that it entails, to some extent at least, a particular role for you.

It has a certain element of the taskmaster in it, a certain degree of evaluating and passing judgment, and a certain kind of authoritarianism also. True, they can all be mild and benevolent, but their presence will affect a patient in distinct if subtle ways. He is put, albeit temporarily, into a passive position; he is the object less of understanding and more of diagnosis, which casts him into the role of pupil as well as child.

This raises an important issue, the regressive aspects inherent in therapy. For a variety of reasons, but in differing degrees and ways, most patients experience a significant regressive pull during therapy. Partly because they recollect and reconstruct their childhoods, partly because infantile fantasies and conflicts emerge with fresh force, partly because of the dynamics of traditional therapy, with its potential for transference phenomena, a regression is experienced. Classical psychoanalysis, with its requisite prone position and free-associational abdication of ego control, elevates the regression to a *sine qua non*. But all forms of psychotherapy do engender some regression, and I believe it needs no special encouragement from the therapist. On the contrary, I believe the regression is therapeutically most efficacious when it receives no real (or "actual") support from our behavior, when it can therefore be explored and understood as a wholly intrapsychic phenomenon. A patient's wish to be a child, for instance, will be experienced in quite a different way when it cannot be tied to the reality of our actions and attitudes. At any rate, I mention this because the confronting mode can serve to foster and support a patient's regression in a way, and to a degree, that the interpretive mode may not.

For one thing, the sense of alert watchfulness which gets reflected in a confrontation differs qualitatively from the sense of attentive listening which gets reflected in an interpretation. Often, the difference is one of role definition: confrontation defines you as the one who diagnoses, interpretation as the one who understands. Since, however, you cannot always achieve the one without the other, because some degree of diagnostic observation is quite unavoidable and indispensable when we interpret, the best you can aim for is a balance substantially in favor of the interpretive-understanding role. I don't mean to suggest, however, that this role is wholly free from some of the same kinds of costs and pitfalls; there is an important sense in which also the interpretive stance can be inimical to the optimally functioning *therapeutic process*. But lest I appear to be headed toward an absurd conclusion, I hasten to explain that I have in mind interpretations which are fundamentally confronting in their nature and impact. The following discussion addresses this matter.

Consider the kind of interpretation that articulates the patient's experience. Not every interpretation offers an explanation or an integration, some offer only a simple articulation; and the difference between a simple articulation and a confrontation is sometimes insignificant. (For instance, there's no real difference between "Look at how guilty you are feeling!" and "I believe you're feeling guilty.") It isn't our tone of voice or our inflection that defines the articulation and distinguishes it from the confrontation. When the remark stops at identifying the patient's experience, when it doesn't go on to relate it to other experiences ("I believe your hostile remarks have made you feel guilty") or to a defense ("I believe you're feeling guilty, but you can't bear to acknowledge it because it doesn't fit your self-image as the carefree one"), then it is, strictly speaking, a confrontation. The central message of the interpretation *cum* articulation (which I usually refer to as "articulation") is "I know what you are experiencing, and I also understand why." The first part alone constitutes a confrontation.

Therefore, all other things being equal, a confrontation can be construed as a simple or incomplete articulation. As such, it can be viewed as an effective way of eliciting the complete articulation from the patient; instead of presenting the full articulation, you offer the first part and expect him to discover the rest of it. (The same can be claimed for the question and probe: they can serve as elicitors, ways to focus attention and permit a full articulation to emerge thereby.) In order for that to happen, however, you have to have a good inkling of what the full articulation is. To fish for significance, or rely completely on intuition as a guide to potential significance, is generally risky, because when your patient counters with, "Why do you draw my attention to this?" "Because I thought it might be important" merely begs the question. (The same is true when he responds to a question or probe with, "Why do you ask?") Therefore, a useful rule of thumb in deciding whether to venture a confrontation is to do it only with a full interpretation in mind, so that when the patient raises the counterquestion, the interpretation can be given. And if he goes on to ask why you didn't simply say so in the first place, you can explain that you weren't confident enough it was correct.

The essential property of an interpretation is its attempt to understand the what, how, and why of a patient's behavior and experience. The term can be misleading, insofar as it denotes, strictly speaking, only one aspect of our interpretive efforts, the translation aspect. However, if we take a broad construction of *meaning*, we can encompass the different kinds of work that interpretations may aim for. Insofar as they translate that which needs translation into a more meaningful form, they enhance the meaningfulness of experience and behavior. To resolve an ambiguity or solve a mystery may be construed in terms of enhancing its meaning; similarly, to elucidate the causes of an experience may contribute to its meaningfulness, and to draw connections between apparently independent acts and experiences may also enhance the meaning of each. Accordingly, the essential difference between an interpretation and a confrontation is that the one points and reflects and the other explains and makes meaningful.

But frequently, before we can explain, we need to point out; we must say what it is, after all, we're seeking to explain. For that reason, many of our interpretations may begin the same way a confrontation begins, and then they qualify as "interpretations" only because they go further and seek to explain the phenomenon they've drawn to the patient's attention. For example, consider your confrontation about the patient's stammering; all it may take to qualify it as an interpretation is to add, "And I think I understand why you stammer when you speak about your brother: you are overtaken with a deep and unexpressible rage at him, and it's that rage which interferes with your speech."

This appears to be an intellectually appealing way to resolve the problem, a way of integrating the two modes. And it makes a lot of intuitive sense. But my intuition (and my clinical experience) leads me to suspect it may be a false resolution and a poor integration, that the basic problem cannot be ameliorated in this way. Instead, my intuition leads me to defend the contention that any time an interpretation has to begin with a confrontation, it may remain a confrontation through and through. The fact that it ends with an interpretation doesn't automatically vitiate its confronting properties, because the hallmark of a confrontation is that it imposes a topic. It changes the subject from what the patient is talking about (to how he is talking, for example, or to feelings he's unaware of while talking); and anything that does that, in my opinion, merits being called a confrontation.

Since the term seems ill-suited to most instances of this kind of imposition, I'm tempted to substitute another that is more descriptive. But it may suffice if I'm careful to say what I mean by "confrontation" and emphasize that I mean it to cover a wide range of observations, all of which share the property of holding up the mirror. The confrontation says "Look, please, and notice what you are saying, doing, feeling, wishing, and the rest." And it can be said in a variety of ways: with a question, with an exclamation, and also with an interpretation. So instead of taking the position that a "confrontation" may masquerade as an "interpretation," and that a probe can be a confrontation in disguise, which implies that the categories are nonoverlapping and orthogonal, I prefer to construe "confrontation" as a single large category that can encompass every other mode of intervention. The critical criterion is context; what makes a remark a confrontation isn't its autochthonous properties, it's the background against which the remark is made. In short, when it imposes a topic or when it changes the subject in any significant way or when it subserves a diagnostic function, then any intervention is likely to be a confrontation.[4]

Consider once more the stammering patient. When you interrupt to draw attention to the fact that he is stammering because he's now talking about his brother, you're clearly resorting to the confronting mode, even though your remark has all the formal properties of an interpretation. But suppose he himself had raised the question, or wondered aloud, why he is stammering now; for you to offer the observation, "You are stammering because you're talking about your brother," is no longer a confrontation. Insofar as it seeks to explain the behavior he is seeking to explain, there is no change of subject; the topic is exactly what was on his mind, only the explanation is new. Similarly, if he goes ahead from there with the question, "Why do I stammer when I speak of my brother?" you can venture the deep speculation, "Because you wish him dead"—which may be faulted on several grounds but not because it's confronting. At any rate, the issue can now go in several different directions (Why does stammering occur with death wishes? Why is the brother the target of such wishes? and so on). What counts above all else is the direction the patient takes with it, what questions he raises; and whenever you follow him in these explorations, you are avoiding the use of confrontations.

Notice an important consequence of that formulation: your intention isn't the central criterion. You may have intended an interpretation, only to discover it was a confrontation because you were mistaken about the content or nature of your patient's deliberations. Conversely, you may have believed you were resorting to a confrontation, only to learn that it was entirely consonant with what he was thinking about (consciously or preconsciously), and therefore amounted to an interpretive act. The inescapable conclusion is that much depends on your skill in listening and your capacity for sensitivity and empathy, because in order to avoid confronting, it isn't enough to participate with interpretationlike observations; the criterion that counts is context—what the patient is actually thinking and feeling and wanting at the moment.

I can highlight the point by drawing an illustration from the realm out of which the term "interpretation" derives, dream interpretation. For most analysts the paradigm of the interpretive mode is the unraveling of a dream's meanings, the uncovering of its latent content. So let's consider how a dream

---

4. When I wrote *Letters to Simon*, I was not sensitive to this important issue. Many of the illustrations I composed contain interpretations whose timing is such that they impose a topic on the patient in a highly confronting way. Too often I appear to offer an interpretation when the patient isn't interested in having his behavior explained or when the context seems to define the remark as a confrontation.

interpretation can also be a confrontation. Your stammering patient recounts the following dream: "I was in a field filled with symmetrically placed rocks; my brother was with me; I began to say something to him, and I found I couldn't because my tongue was paralyzed." Then he falls silent, and you have no way of knowing what he's thinking during the silence. For you to offer any kind of dream interpretation at this point could amount to a confrontation if it happened that he wasn't thinking about the dream at all. Let's imagine he's completely disinterested in the dream's meaning; he recounted it because he wanted to get it out if his mind so that he could get on with more pressing matters, and during the silence he was trying to decide which of two events that had occurred before the session he should talk about. That's rather farfetched, I admit, but it highlights the point. A remark on your part, like, "What do you think of the possibility that the field with the symmetrical rocks represented a cemetery?" would amount to a flagrant confrontation.

Any efforts to elucidate the dream's meaning, if they are to reflect the interpretive mode exclusively, have to be made in the context of the patient's being interested in the dream's meaning. More than that, it's also necessary that he believe a dream has the same kind of meaning you believe it has. For instance, suppose he believes dreams are prophetic and that their function is to foretell the future; if he broke his silence with, "I'm wondering what the dream means," it would amount to a major imposition of topic for you to venture, "I think it could mean that you wish your brother dead." To characterize that remark as a confrontation seems peculiar, and here's where the term is quite inapt, but it has that important characteristic: you've imposed your own meaning on the dream, and you were mistaken about the nature of his concern and interest. Notice that correctness is not at issue; an interpretation doesn't become a confrontation because it is wrong in the sense of being untrue; it counts as a confrontation when it has misread the patient's state of mind, his interests and intentions.

Some useful technical guidelines can be deduced from this principle. For instance, if an explanatory remark amounts to a confrontation whenever the patient isn't interested in the meaning of his behavior or thought, it follows that we have to avoid responding to a direct question (like, "How old are you?") with an interpretation (like, "I gather you're wondering whether I'm old enough [or too old] to understand you") unless our intention is to be confronting. Similarly, when he is in the grip of an emotion but isn't sufficiently motivated to articulate or understand it, any attempt on our part to do so (for example, "I think I understand why you're feeling resentful toward me and critical of me; it's because I canceled our next appointment") is bound to be confronting instead of interpretive. Which, of course, doesn't mean there may not be very good reasons for us to make such interventions; it means only that we know the risks we're running, and we are sensitive to their impact and function.

This principle can easily be recast into the terms of the *therapeutic process* by stressing how the basic criterion is not whether our observation or explanation is intended to promote the process but whether it in fact does. And since it isn't always possible to know for sure at the time of our intervention, the best we can do is take the precaution of insuring that we stay in empathic touch with our patient's state of mind and affect, that we understand what he's intending and meaning; and then that we use our best judgment to steer a course which avoids undue risks in the confronting dimension, while at the same time keeping from avoiding risks that move in the interpretive dimension. The Scylla is risking too much (too confronting), and the Charybdis is risking too little (too noninterpretive).

6
The Interpretation
Paradigms

Consider the following narrative, which is Paradigm 1 of a study of how to formulate good interpretations.

[The patient is eighteen years of age.]

Yesterday afternoon my sister and her friend Pat ... I've told you about Pat, haven't I? [*Yes.*] They got sore at me because I had a fit of hysterical laughter at them. [pause] They were studying for an exam, but kept stopping to do their yoga exercises. They've been into yoga for over a month now, so I'm used to seeing them in these weird positions and everything—on their heads, in the lotus, and everything. But I still find it funny. [pause] I was supposed to be studying too, but they kept distracting me. [pause] I know what you're thinking: you're thinking, Why didn't I stay in my room if I wanted to work? Well, I did—for a while—but then they put on the stereo, one of my sister's Indian ragas, and it disturbed me. I hate those records, Indian music—I don't know why, but.... [pause] Anyway, since I couldn't get any work done anyway, I went back into the living room where they were, and sat around. [pause] Sometimes I'm ... I get sort of put off by Pat. She's an okay-looking girl, but she's too chubby, and she sort of sweats too much. [pause] Anyway, she went into this real far-out position, with her ankles up around the back of her neck, and all. And I just started in laughing hysterically. [pause] I couldn't stop, I was laughing so hard. [pause] I don't know why, because it wasn't all that funny, actually. In fact, you know, it was a bit disgusting to see her like that.

156

Listening to this account during a session, you'll think of an explanation—keeping yourself from doing so is virtually impossible. But what isn't impossible is to bear in mind that the explanation you've formulated is only one among many. It may, in your estimation, be the best one, but that's quite different from believing it's the "true" one. "The interpretation of an event is not a search for the true meaning of the event," writes Leon Levy in his excellent treatise on psychological interpretation. "Every event is subject to a vast range of interpretations."[1] Nicholas Hobbs puts the matter eloquently in the following way: "There is no way of establishing the validity of a particular order-giving structure independently of the individual who is going to use it. The concept of insight can have meaning only as a part of the process of elaborating on some particular system of interpreting events. There are no true insights, only more or less useful ones."[2]

The Good Interpretation

The good interpretation needn't be construed in terms of truth; it's quite sufficient to define it in terms of usefulness. "When I have something useful to say, I will say it," that's how our Basic Instruction is worded, and thereby it provides us with a utilitarian framework in which to evaluate the worth of our interpretations. Accordingly, there are these two bases on which to appraise how good an interpretation is: our clinical experience as therapists (interpretations that try to explain a patient's defensive needs and behaviors, for instance, are likely to be particularly efficacious), and the patient's mind (certain interpretations are more assimilative and meaningful than others, more valid for him in this sense).

Furthermore, before you offer your patient an interpretation, you have to have a clear idea about the purpose it can serve. "In psychological interpretation we apply that particular construction which we believe will best suit our purposes and which is consistent with the theoretical frame of reference we bring to the situation," is how Levy puts it.[3] Consider, then, your task of formulating an interpretation for the patient who narrated the above paradigm. If your chief purpose is to give him an understanding of his experience and behavior, then the narrative provides several options. For one, there's ample evidence to support an explanation of his uncontrolled laughter in terms of

1. Leon Levy, *Psychological Interpretation*, p. 10.
2. Nicholas Hobbs, "Sources of Gain in Psychotherapy," in *Use of Interpretation in Treatment*, p. 21.
3. Levy, *Psychological Interpretation*, p. 13.

anxiety; and the anxiety, in turn, can be formulated as a product of intra-psychic conflict. Accordingly, his feelings of disgust can usefully be explained as being the result of a defensive need to ward off unacceptable feelings and thoughts (of a sexual nature); and his hysterical laughter, the product of an imminent breakdown in the defensive posture. I composed the paradigm with exactly that formulation in mind, thereby inviting an interpretation that contains one, several, or all of its elements.

But even when your purpose is simply to proffer an explanation, you have to give serious consideration to its form. For in addition to content and timing, an interpretation has a form that is reflected in the way its content is formulated and inflected, its verbal structure. Form is sometimes referred to as "style," in order to take into account your personality. Levy, for instance, speaks of style as a personal element which " . . . may often count for as much as, if not more than, content in making the difference."[4] Emanuel Hammer goes further to implicate not only your personality but your mood of the moment. "Each therapist shapes his own style from the interaction of *his* personality and *his* experience," writes Hammer, echoing a point of view that is widely held by teachers.[5] But no matter how broadly construed, the form of an interpretation conveys significant information too.

Consider the following possibility for an interpretation. "You were feeling sexually aroused, but the feeling was unacceptable to you—because of your sister's presence, perhaps—therefore, you experienced instead a sense of disgust. But you caught a glimpse of your true feelings, and that threw you into conflict, which, in turn, made you anxious. It was that anxiety that caused you to laugh uncontrollably." Its definitiveness and explicitness, its certainty of voice, along with the overriding message "I can understand what you cannot" (perhaps also "Look how wise I am in the ways of men, listen to what good and complete explanations I have to offer you!")—these are its salient formal features. And they convey a good deal more than the interpretation's content alone. Notice also to what extent the interpretation is theoretical and normative. "People like you, in situations like that, when they behave the way you did, are most likely under the sway of this conflict and that defense; and when the defense breaks down, this is what happens" is one of its underlying messages. In that respect it is a diagnostic formulation, and that, too, is a formal feature.

But what alternatives are there? What formal features are possible and desirable? I mean the question in two respects: for a real patient who actually

---

4. Levy, *Psychological Interpretation*, p. 15.
5. Emanuel Hammer, "Interpretive Technique: A Primer, in *Use of Interpretation in Treatment*, p. 38.

recounts such an event, and for a simulated study in which the material is so meager. *Psychotherapy*'s central timing criterion provides us with a general guideline in the framework of its ruling question, What can you say to the patient that will result in his pursuing an exploration of the experience and discovering the factors that were significant in it? A full and diagnostic explanation clearly can't serve that purpose best. Since, however, the direct request that he explore and deliberate is not available to you (in actuality as well as in the study), it becomes equally obvious that some explanatory remarks may have to be offered, something he will find interesting, provocative, and useful, so that he will want to inquire further into the event and try to make fresh discoveries about himself. The solution for the problems posed by this study, given the substantial artificiality of the paradigms, may, therefore, have to entail certain compromises.

Before examining that solution, consider a further possibility for the paradigm: it may be that the patient is behaving somewhat disingenuously, that he isn't really so mystified by what happened. (He knew he was sexually aroused. Why else did he reenter the living room?) If that's the case, he is setting you up to say what he already knows, and this is basically a transference issue. The relevant remark might then be, "I believe you are not as mystified as you say, but you need for me to play the role of explainer."

Still another possibility, and a potentially significant one, is that he is being disingenuous not with you but with himself; he's being naive, or playing dumb, quite deliberately and purposefully. This possibility signifies a defensive process and permits the hypothesis that the same defense which operated during the event is functioning during the recounting of it; just as he defended himself against the recognition of his feelings, impulses, and conflicts then, he is defending himself against a similar recognition now, including a recognition of the explanation itself. This hypothesis has important ramifications; it focuses attention on the fact that the patient is mystified, that he can find no explanation even now for what happened then, which can mean that his work of exploration and self-inquiry is being impaired by an aspect of his personality that serves to defend him against self-knowledge. Insofar as this work is essentially what the *therapeutic process* means, and insofar as *Psychotherapy*'s central timing criterion is satisfied when you supervise the process, it follows that your active participation is called for.

The question remains, however, What kind of participation is most appropriate and useful? My general answer to this vital question, at the level of practice and in terms of technical application, is to accept the working hypothesis that the patient does "know" what he needs to know, that most of the articulations and explanations which are valid for him (useful, consonant, and resonant) are already present in his intrapsychic domain at some level, at least, and in some form. It follows from this working hypothesis that our most relevant and germane interpretations can be prefaced with "This is what is in your mind; this is what you feel, what you believe, how you see yourself and others, and how you explain your behavior."

My assumption derives in part from the psychoanalytic conception of the *system-preconscious*, and the proposition that interpretations address preconscious derivatives of unconscious mentation. Their function, accordingly, is to facilitate the emergence of unconscious ideas, memories, and fantasies. From another vantage point, interpretations make contact with the barrier (the threshold, the censorship, the countercathexis, or the defense), and in one way or another weaken it to permit not only the uncovering of unconscious content but also their reorganization. But psychoanalysis has, in addition to its topographic point of view, a structural theory, which speaks of interpretations addressing the ego. Insofar as ego serves three "masters" (id, superego, and reality), it must compromise on three fronts, and interpretations speak to its synthetic function. What complicates matters is that ego is at once the knowing agency and the defending agency, so that interpretations have to take account of its conflicting interests (when, of course, they are in conflict).

In terms of our working hypothesis, there is an important corollary to construing the process of explanation in therapy as merely uncovering what's already in the mental domain: the further question "So how come you are not aware of what's in your mind? Why [how] do you need to protect yourself against the knowledge?" This boils down to the widely accepted proposition that it is a patient's defenses, sometimes broadly construed to include his character traits, that require our diligent attention too. (Many would say our *most* diligent attention.)

The defense itself may lie outside the patient's mind, so to speak. At least intuitively, it seems quite necessary to construe the defense against knowledge at a different level of abstraction than the knowledge itself. Accordingly, therefore, a defense can't be addressed with "This is what is in your mind"; instead, it can only be articulated with an interpretation whose form is "This is how you behave: you avoid, obfuscate, cajole, forget, overlook, deceive." And therefore a defense would seem to be amenable only to a confronting and diagnostic interpretational approach, a "holding up the mirror," which is essentially a directive to stop and look, pause and observe, "Please notice what you do and how you experience events."

The problem we face, then, is how to interpret a defense without undue reliance on the confronting mode, how to formulate an interpretation when it cannot be prefaced with "This is what's in your mind." I'm going to examine this problem concretely during the course of this chapter and the next, but I can preface the study with two general guidelines. One is that we should address a defense only when the patient himself has already perceived or noticed it, and, therefore, when we can formulate the interpretation this way: "I believe part of you suspects that you are [avoiding, obfuscating, cajoling, forgetting, overlooking, deceiving]." The second is that we should address a defense not simply because it's there, and we observe it, but also because we have good reason to believe it is interfering significantly with the *therapeutic process*. This judgment rests on an estimation that the patient isn't likely to notice the defense himself, that his work of exploration doesn't warrant the expectation that, given more time, he will reflect upon the defense and come to see it in himself. In other words, our supervision of the *therapeutic process* may be relatively ineffective with respect to the defense.

But these guidelines may be too stringent and idealistic, and they can be softened. Moreover, as I already pointed out in chapter four, the supervision of the *therapeutic process* needn't be our sole concern—our principal concern, to be sure, but not the exclusive one. We can also take it as our function, when circumstances allow and warrant it, to participate in the process as a kind of partner. Occasionally, therefore, we can do some noticing for our patient. And that participatory function is also examined in the course of the Interpretation Paradigms. The nature of the study, because it presents such meager material to work with and because we have to assume that any interpretation is timely, sometimes mandates that we are seeking to arrive at an understanding of our own, at a discovery that we ourselves make; and our major technical problem is to formulate it in a way that can advance the *therapeutic process*. Most importantly, we have to guard against impairing the process, against risking its integrity, by resorting excessively to modes that violate or undercut our basic position as the neutral, nonjudgmental, nonreinforcing one, the one who seeks to understand in order to promote understanding, and who shares his understanding in an essentially nondirective way. The various aspects of the technical problem are examined in the light of my students' responses to the six paradigms of this study, as well as the four paradigms of the study presented in chapter seven.

The Interpretation Paradigms

Instructions: Here are hypothetical transcripts for which interpretations can be formulated. Your task is to formulate the best of all possible for each. In the interests of making your interpretation a full one, you may want to divide it into parts. If so, you will have to compose more dialogue for the patient.

For Paradigm 1—which appears above, on p. 156—students infer that the patient was sexually aroused, could not acknowledge the fact, and that his laughter was the product of conflicting feelings. Many also infer that he is a naive young man, and, therefore, that he has to be treated with special circumspection. How to maintain tact, keep from being insensitive, and at the same time avoid being gingerly, thereby participating in the repressive defense by conveying the message "There is something here to be apprehensive about," is a technical problem. Neither, "It seems possible that you may have some feelings about Pat that you are not quite in touch with," nor "You seem to be a little disturbed at your attraction to your sister's friend," which students suggest, solves the problem; they are too gingerly because they are too allusive and vague. Why not say what kind of "feelings" and "attraction" are being alluded to? It's clear enough that sexual ones are meant, and the fact that you don't say so can convey something which supports the patient's need for his repressive defense. On the other hand, "Maybe you felt as if you were watching Pat masturbate," epitomizes tactlessness for this paradigm; the patient is likely to be shocked by the idea.

Tact can often be preserved when we take a gradual or stepwise approach, dividing an interpretation into parts that gradually zero in on the issue and allow the patient to participate in its direction. A student gives a good illustration of this technique, as follows. We begin with, "I wonder if you weren't laughing because you were nervous and frightened." Then, when the patient picks up on the "frightened," asking, "But why should I be frightened? I'm not afraid of Pat," we have a good opportunity to explain, "No, but perhaps you were afraid of your own feelings." And when the patient falls back on his reaction-formation in a half-agreeing way, with, "Well, I was disgusted, seeing her like that—so . . . so exposed," the student has us offer the fuller explanation, "It could be that part of you found her attractive, or at least sexually exciting, and part of you was frightened and disgusted by these feelings." Notice how the patient was allowed to guide the dialogue.

But the technique of gradualness is easy to misapply. Its most appropriate use is for developing a single idea or theme, rather than introducing a number of separate ones. Here's an example in which the dialogue changes course after the student begins with, "I take it you were both attracted and repelled by Pat," and the patient both agrees and disagrees with, "Well, yes; as I said, she's not bad looking; but she just looked funny in those positions, that's all." The student persists with, "Seeing her in those positions made you feel uncomfortable, it seems. I'm wondering whether you felt sexually aroused by her, and part of your discomfort had to do with feeling aroused." So far so good! But the student has the patient take exception to the interpretation, saying, "That seems a little farfetched. I just thought it was hilarious the way they were carrying on; and I also said I wanted to study except for that damn music.'' Now, instead of ending the dialogue at this juncture, the student ventures an altogether fresh interpretation, ''I can see why you might find what I said farfetched. What do you think of the possibility that you were also quite angry at your sister?'' (Where did that come from?) The patient is appropriately puzzled—''Angry? Well, the music . . . But I don't know what else.'' Now the student demonstrates resourcefulness, if little else, with this final try: ''Perhaps because she had taken all of Pat's attention from you.''

Here's an example which uses the technique correctly, insofar as it amplifies only a single point, the patient's conflict, but remains quite tactless because it's not gradual enough and the student has us play too active and directive a role in the work of exploring and uncovering. We begin with, ''It sounds as if part of you found the scene exciting, and another part of you was disgusted at your excitement,'' and the patient responds with, ''I don't know. I had the feeling while I was laughing that it was just hysterically funny, but then when I stopped laughing, I didn't know why I was laughing.'' The student then has us offer a diagnostic interpretation, ''Perhaps your laughing was a way of trying to make them stop, while at the same time enjoying the excitement.'' (A more useful response, in my opinion, would be to wonder whether he was so thoroughly mystified—''I take it you had no idea then, nor do you have any now, what the reason could have been''—and if he insists on his mystification, we could repeat our initial interpretation and emphasize the unbearable conflict.) Now the patient hedges and backs off a bit with, ''I did feel excited. I don't understand that, because I really don't find Pat that attractive sexually. But the slow, repetitive pulsing of the music and the entwined way their bodies were really set me off.'' And instead of asking a clarification question (''Set you off in what way?'' or ''What do you mean by *set me off*?''), the student offers the provocative observation, ''You seem to be saying that it could only have been Pat to whom you were sexually attracted.'' The patient reacts with a frightened look and ''What are you suggesting?'' But the student has us proceed intrepidly with, ''It struck me that although Pat and your sister were there together, Pat is the only one you describe yourself reacting to. I am suggesting that perhaps some of your sexual arousal came from looking at your sister.'' ''Wow, that's pretty heavy!'' is how the dialogue ends. Taking my cue from the patient's frightened look, I would proceed by remarking tactfully that he seemed to have an inkling of what I had in mind, and then by giving him the opportunity to say it himself. Of course, if he refused the opportunity, then I'd be obligated to tell him; but tact can be maximized by putting it this way: ''I take it the possibility that you might be sexually attracted to your sister makes you feel disgusted.''

In my estimation, the best way gradualness can serve the interests of tact as well as promote the patient's exploration and self-inquiry is to begin a continuation to Paradigm 1 exactly where he left off. He had just said, "In fact, you know, it was a bit disgusting to see her like that," and the question that would occur to me is whether this reflects the way he felt then, or whether it just now occurred to him for the first time. That could be an important distinction, because if it's the latter, then the *therapeutic process* is already in motion—and I would try to get into gear with it. If I succeeded, I'd be able to steer clear of both diagnostic as well as tactless remarks. I would begin with the clarification question, "Are you saying you felt disgusted then, or are you realizing it right now?" If he answers that he was disgusted at the time, I would wonder aloud whether he himself is explaining his hysterical laughter in terms of that disgust ("I take it you're thinking that it was those feelings that brought on the hysterical laughing"), and it should be relatively easy then to wait for a suitable opportunity to suggest that the disgust stemmed from mixed feelings, and that one of them was sexual arousal. If he answers that it just occurred to him now, I might wait in silence for his further thoughts; but if he waited for mine, I would suggest that he is now realizing something in his feelings that he was only dimly aware of then ("I think you're now realizing that you had conflicting feelings; part of you found it funny and another part was disgusted—maybe that's why you lost control of your laughing"), and from there it might be only a short step to the insight that sex had reared its ugly head.

Tact is also served when you focus directly on what the patient is seeking to understand: why he laughed uncontrollably. "I'm wondering if you weren't somewhat aroused, and it was your own feelings that frightened and disgusted you," which many students offer, not only fails to take account of the fact that he didn't say he experienced any fright, it says nothing about what is mystifying him, the hysterical laughter. Similarly, he isn't wondering why he was distracted and fascinated by the goings-on in the living room, so to draw attention to that aspect of the event runs the risk of changing the subject. Changing the subject often amounts to imposing an idea that might be foreign to a patient, and there's a sense in which that can be classified as tactless. Consider the tactless, "You were angry; perhaps you were feeling left out," and "It sounds as though you were contemptuous of Pat" (and as if that weren't enough, the student adds, "Perhaps you have similar feelings towards me," which comes straight out of the blue). Notice how the following example manages to violate several principles at once. The student begins with this speculation, "Maybe you feel I'm making you do something like yoga exercises in here, making you do things to increase your self-awareness," and the patient's response nicely reveals how off base it is: "Well, I guess that's sort of true, but I never thought of it that way." But the student goes right ahead with, "And perhaps you feel that in the process I'm making you twist yourself into all sorts of distorted, disgusting positions."

Although it has an extreme diagnostic flavor, the following interpretation manages to address itself to the patient's concern, and at the same time offers an explanation that is tactful enough without being overly gingerly: "Perhaps you were laughing, despite the fact that you found the scene disgusting, to ease your discomfort at watching the two girls. You may have found it somewhat exciting sexually, and you laughed as a way of releasing the tension." I characterize that interpretation as diagnostic because it imposes an explanation from the outside, so to speak. The distinction between empathic and diagnostic can be subtle; it usually comes down to a difference between explaining with and explaining to, between an observation made from a kind of inside vantage point and one that seems to come from the outside.

Perhaps the clearest instances of diagnostic interpretations are those that attempt to point out the functional basis of the patient's behavior. Here are three good examples: "Your fit of laughter may have been a way of relieving frustration and dissipating your tension; at the same time it was almost like an attack on the girls too, a way of putting them down"; "When you laughed, you may have been expressing your tension; you wanted to belong to your sister and her friend but you weren't sure how to be a part of their situation or even if you should want to be; it was also a partial solution to your dilemma—you drew attention to yourself and got them to include you by getting angry with you"; "You indicated that besides feeling disgust you also found the situation interesting and distracting, and I wonder if perhaps your laughter was a way for you to deal with having those two different feelings at the same time, maybe a way to keep them hidden." Other diagnostic interpretations simply label the experience: "It seems that your sister and Pat have control of your behavior, and your laughter is a hostile reaction to that." Others spell out a possible consequence of the action: "I am thinking that the effect of your behavior, the laughing, had the effect of preventing all three of you from working." Such explanations are necessarily made from the vantage point of an outside observer. They have the advantage of inviting the patient to stand aside from himself, so to speak, and to consider his behavior from the position of an objective observer; but they tend to foster an intellectualized approach to his experience instead of an insightful one.

Finally, the form of an interpretation is determined by its choice of words, and these choices can sometimes be a crucial factor in the interpretation's impact. For example, a student includes the phrase, "her position triggered some sexual feelings in you," and the implications of "triggered" could be significant. The surplus meanings of words usually count, and only when they are intended should we resort to metaphorical language. Sometimes it is a theoretical (or jargonish) word that interferes, and here is an instructive example: the student begins by suggesting, "Your laughing sounds as though you were really feeling anxious about something," to which the patient responds, "Well, I don't know about feeling anxious, but I did feel sort of uncomfortable seeing Pat in that position." The student now ignores what he himself had the patient say, and continues intrepidly with, "You say Pat is a nice-looking girl and sometimes you like her, isn't it possible that seeing her in that position kind of excited you sexually and your laughter was therefore out of anxiety?" Why the stake in "anxiety"? Would it reduce the force of the interpretation to say, "Your laughter was out of discomfort"? At any rate, the important thing to pay attention to is the patient's clear statement that he doesn't know about "feeling anxious."

Paradigm 2

[During the previous session you notified the patient of a pending cancellation; he showed no significant reaction to the notification. He is a critical person—he's spoken about it and described it—but you have never been subjected to any criticism. The following is preceded by a long silence.]

I've been meaning to tell you this for a long time but somehow I haven't. This isn't the first time I thought it, but your clothes . . . the clothes you wear are awful. Don't you know anything about how to dress? [pause] I can't understand how you could choose that shirt you're wearing; it doesn't fit with anything else you're wearing. Not that anything else you've got on really matches, but you must be color-blind or something. [pause] And the way you speak, in that slow and halting way of yours; I meant to mention it before because it bugs me sometimes. You know, you never say a whole sentence right out straight. You always have to stop and find the right word, and that makes it so godawful slow. [pause] And another thing while I'm at it, you always speak so softly and so damned seriously.

This paradigm gives me the opportunity to examine, discuss, and fault what is probably the most popular of all interpretations, "You are feeling angry." I fully expect my students to infer that the patient is not only expressing "anger" but experiencing it and that they'd deem it altogether appropriate to say so to him. (My "data" amply confirm this expectation.) But I composed the paradigm with a patient in mind who was feeling nothing else but the need to criticize and the intent to hurt; he was giving in to the impulse to insult you, yet had no phenomenal experience of any anger at you. In fact, I imagined someone for whom anger was an unacceptable feeling, and what allowed him to give expression to such criticalness was the defense mechanism of isolation of affect. Therefore, to say to him, "You are feeling angry," is not only inaccurate—because he is not feeling anger, and that may be the crucial problem—it flies straight into the teeth of his defense.

His criticalness can be viewed as defensive in three ways: (1) it is a derivative or transformed expression of the defense; (2) it reflects a displacement of other impulses, wishes, and fantasies; (3) it represents a tamed or socialized rendition of primitive, probably unconscious, wishes. There are several implications of viewing his criticalness as defensive in these ways, and they all have bearing on the relevance of the affect-articulation. But I don't mean to imply thereby that the patient's criticisms are necessarily poorly founded; in fact, I would rather accept the assumption that they are quite accurate—because I also believe that's quite beside the point. At any rate, he is free to criticize as well as to verbally attack you, and *Psychotherapy* has to protect that freedom. The question of whether we ought to allow ourselves to be verbally abused is an interesting and debatable one, but I won't address it here.

Consider the question of motivation: Why is he verbally attacking you? Students answer this way: "I can understand your criticisms of my manner of dress and speech, but since you stated that you've been meaning to tell me this for a long time, I wonder if your reasons for criticizing me now may perhaps be due to your feeling angry at me," and "You've held off telling me the things you don't like about me, yet today you tell me. I'm wondering if the criticism is your way of telling me how furious you are at me." That, I submit, is no different than explaining a person's eating activity in terms of his feeling hungry. And what kind of explanation is that?

A disquisition on the psychology of affects doesn't belong in a book on form and technique, but I want to take exception to the theory that many practitioners seem to subscribe to in their clinical work. For one thing, I believe it isn't therapeutically effective; for another, it isn't widely accepted among academic psychologists and biologists. From a biological standpoint, "You struck because you were angry" is not a defensible formulation; instead, "You were angry in preparation for striking, or in order to signal an intention to strike, or in order to substitute for striking" is far more consonant. I am aware of the controversy surrounding the motivational properties of affect systems, and how a scholarly theorist like Silvan Tomkins regards them to be more likely instigators for a wide range of human behaviors than drive-impulse systems; but the question here is which conception is most efficacious for therapy, and I believe the former is.[6]

6. Silvan Tomkins, *Affect, Imagery, Consciousness*, vol. 1 (New York: Springer, 1962).

Imagine a patient who is thinking about succulent foods and appetizing dishes, reminiscing about meals he's eaten or fantasizing about meals he's going to eat. Which interpretation is better, "You are feeling hungry" or "You have a wish to eat"? Even if you agree with me that it's the latter, you may contend that the difference is entirely trivial. But your reason for doing so is worth considering: the difference is trivial because the formulations are functionally identical, and the patient will intuitively make the necessary translation from the one into the other. English makes it easy to translate affect language into impulse language: "I *feel* hungry" is equivalent to "I *feel* like eating"; "I *feel* angry" is equivalent to "I *feel* like striking"; "I *feel* happy" is equivalent to "I *feel* like rejoicing," and so on. Both in principle and in practice every affect statement can be transformed directly into a statement of an impulse or a wish, or of a conflict of wishes or impulses—with the conspicuous exception of anxiety (which I discuss later) and perhaps also of guilt. So instead of telling a patient he is "feeling" angry, we can tell him he "feels" like striking out; instead of saying he is hostile, we can say he wishes to annihilate; and we can also interpret most affects for their communication or signaling properties (for instance, to weep is to communicate helplessness and no intent to fight). Furthermore, and more germane to Paradigm 2, if a patient is actually engaged in eating food, it will seem pointless to offer him the interpretation, "You are feeling hungry," and that is not different, I submit, from saying to one who is attacking, "You are feeling angry."

I can think of two reasons why it may be better to interpret in the conative and cognitive spheres rather than the affective. The first is that affect language tends to be diagnostic. Affect words are essentially diagnostic labels and generally serve the same intellectual and conceptual functions that diagnostic formulations serve; they are essentially abstractions which categorize and organize experience into intellectually comprehensible forms. Of course, I'm not referring to affective experiences themselves, to their phenomenal and subjective modes; they aren't diagnostic and abstract, only their verbal expressions are. And the same isn't true for ideas and thoughts—what we want and what we think can readily be verbalized in relatively unequivocal and noninferential terms. But to say what we feel emotionally requires a fundamentally different operation. Affects and moods can be expressed by a wide variety of motor and action terms, but they are essentially communicated through empathy. And this has important implications for any therapy that is verbal: whatever their ontological nature, whatever their biological basis and function, whatever role they play in the determination of behavior and experience, affective experiences have to have a distinctive modality in order to be used psychotherapeutically.

The second reason it may be better to interpret in conative and cognitive terms is that when a person reflects introspectively on a pure affect state, that state diminishes in its intensity. (This was widely reported by the early Introspectionists, and for Titchener the affect disappeared so completely upon introspection that he was led to conclude it was not a basic element of consciousness.) And this has important implications for a verbal therapy: reflection and verbalization can diminish the affect under scrutiny. Perhaps this is just another way of saying that intellectual control over affects occurs in such a way as to diminish its intensity and vividness, and the implication for therapy is that intellectualization is a defense against affect. Therefore, to say to a patient, "You are feeling angry at me," could have the effect of diminishing the anger by bringing it under cognitive control. By labeling the affect for him (which is quite different from remarking, "I can feel the intensity of the anger you are feeling"), he is encouraged to experience it cognitively instead of purely affectively, and that often results in a diminution of the feeling itself. So if that's your purpose, then of course it's an altogether appropriate thing to do.

Returning now to the paradigm, we can assume that the patient is quite unaware of feeling angry (else why interpret it to him, except to make him stop feeling it?), and we can also assume he's unaware (or not fully aware) of a wish to hurt you. Based on these assumptions my thesis is this: you should aim at uncovering the wish; and if you try to deal with the affect as well, better to suggest to him, "You are angry at me because you wish [or need] to hurt me," than to suggest, "You wish [or need] to hurt me because you are angry at me." Bear in mind that his intent to be hurtful is apt to be closer to awareness than his feeling of anger, and it therefore requires less of an inference; it is certainly closer to the text and more available to you in countertransferential terms.

A similar argument can be made in respect to the question of the patient's motivation for choosing this time ("Why today?"). The paradigm contains only one piece of information that could be relevant to it, the cancelled session. Your only option, consequently, is to trace his behavior to the fact that a cancellation was made the session before, and your interpretation can take one of two forms: (1) "The cancellation made you angry, and you are now expressing that anger in the form of criticalness" ("Perhaps another thing which bugs you, that's been on your mind for some time," offers a student, "Is the fact that last time I told you I would have to cancel a session"); (2) "The cancellation hurt you, and you are now expressing that hurt by retaliating in kind" ("I think I understand why you are so critical of me today," suggests a student, "You felt I didn't care about you when I canceled the session, and, by criticizing me, you are saying you have reasons not to care about me either''). Again, the thrust of my argument is that the second interpretation is the better one to work with; it avoids the pitfalls of working with the affect itself, and it makes more psychological sense.

Some students offer sensitive and empathic interpretations which explain the patient's behavior in terms of a need to retaliate out of feelings of rejection or a sense of hurt or a feeling that the therapist doesn't care. A few focus on the fact that he can only express his reaction indirectly, an emphasis that can be useful insofar as it pertains to a defense. One begins, ''It seems to me that your criticisms may mask your anger at me for canceling your next session,'' to which the patient responds, ''But why wasn't I angry last time after you told me?'' So the student explains, ''I would guess you were, but to show it then would have been to say more directly that you need me.''

An attempt to interpret a defense head-on often runs head-on into the defense itself. You can, therefore, expect it to happen, and that should keep you from the kind of persistent approach (or call it attack) that is exemplified in the following dialogue, in which you insist on an interpretation despite the patient's clear disavowal. ''I wonder why you chose this particular time to find so many things wrong with me,'' you begin, ''Last time I told you I wouldn't be able to see you next session.'' ''So what?'' responds the patient. ''Well, you didn't seem to care one way or another, so I wonder if your criticisms today could be a disguised way of expressing anger toward me for the hurt you experienced but couldn't admit to me and maybe even to yourself.'' Now the patient disavows with, ''I didn't feel hurt—it didn't bother me at all.'' The correct technique here is to suggest that he is doing the same thing right now, defending himself the way you had just suggested. Instead, the student has you proceed insensitively and nonresponsively, ''And your finding fault with me would make the separation easier to bear; it might help you to feel that you were doing the rejecting.''

And you have to avoid being defensive yourself. Some students, in the interests of developing their interpretations gradually, betray the same kind of defensiveness that the patient does. A typical example is this: the student begins, ''I'm wondering why you choose this particular time to tell me all these things, since, as you say, you've been meaning to tell them for a long time.'' This gets him nowhere, insofar as the patient responds, ''I really don't know. You said I could talk about what I wish. I wanted to bring it up now.'' Then the student offers this coy piece of indirection: '' Could it be that you feel hurt by something else besides my clothes or my style?''

When you develop an interpretation gradually, you have to avoid a sparring interchange, or one in which you remain allusive. When the patient is critical and disgruntled, as he is in this paradigm, the risks of engaging him in argument are particularly great. You have to be especially alert to the possibilities both of defusing his criticalness and of intensifying it. Notice how the following dialogue succeeds in avoiding the pitfalls, and how well the student takes advantage of the technique of gradualness.

TH-1:   You seem annoyed with me today.

PT-2:   There you go again, with your serious remarks. Sure, I'm annoyed, but it's not just today. Like I said, I've been meaning to say this for a while. You just kind of bug me sometimes.

TH-2:   What made you decide to tell me today?

PT-3:   I don't know. Actually, I wasn't thinking much about you since last time, and I usually think of things I'll be wanting to tell you. But I do remember feeling sort of pissed-off at how slowly you talked last session.

TH-3:   It was during that session that I told you we wouldn't be meeting next week.

PT-4:   Yeah, but that's really okay, because I can always use the extra time. But . . . but I guess maybe it does bother me that you can sort of dismiss me so easily.

TH-4:   You were feeling sort of dismissed last week, and today you were sort of dismissing me with your critical remarks.

Finally, Paradigm 2 contains a potentially relevant piece of information, the fact that the patient is known to be a critical person, but few students make use of it. One does it this way: "You've told me several times that you consider yourself a critical person. I wonder if your criticisms of me now are related to the fact that I told you I'm cancelling a session, and you are angry with me for that; and instead of telling me you're angry, you criticize me for something else. And I wonder if this isn't what's happening when you're critical of other people, that is, you are angry at them for something but instead of experiencing the anger directly, you become critical of them." The interpretation would benefit from being divided into parts, which could be introduced one at a time. But it's an excellent illustration of how an interpretation can address itself to an aspect of character without at the same time being overly diagnostic. It remains sufficiently "personal" and free of didactic elements. The patient might resent the fact you're trying to take the heat off by implying that the criticisms themselves are unwarranted, as they may also be in the case of other people whom he criticizes. You could prevent this by first saying, "I don't mean to be saying that what you're criticizing me for isn't valid; instead, what I'm thinking about is why you haven't voiced the criticisms until today, and therefore what they might mean now." As I've indicated, I believe such a remark should preface any kind of interpretation you make to this paradigm.

The distinction between the *therapeutic process* and the patient's personality, between the act of exploration and the lay of the land, can be construed as a distinction between form and content. An interpretation can sometimes address itself to both aspects; it can explicate the form of a patient's work together with a relevant piece of content from his intrapsychic realm. Paradigm 3 provides such an opportunity.

Paradigm 3

I never told you this, but I always had a good singing voice. I still do. My mother used to say I should become a singer. [pause] I sang in the school choir in high school, but I quit. It was a big choir, about a hundred kids in it. [pause] The reason I quit was because it bothered me that I couldn't hear my own voice when I was singing in the choir. I remember telling the music teacher about it, and he told me that that always happens. You can't really hear your own voice when you sing in a choir, did you know that? I was surprised to find that out. But I don't think I could get used to the idea. I don't really know why. [pause] Anyway, I'm not sure that it was the real reason I quit. I quit so that I could devote myself to my studies. I was a very good student. [pause] I loved history best of all, and I always worked on topics that were different from the ones the other kids chose to work on. I remember doing a paper on Alexander the Great. I researched his childhood, I traced his education with Aristotle, and things like that. It was a great paper. [pause] My history teacher submitted it to the school literary magazine, and it was published.

As it stands, this paradigm provides you with the opportunity to give an explanation of what the patient is recounting but not of why. Students offer interpretations that are restricted to the personality implications—they point out that the patient is concerned about being different, feeling special, worthwhile; they speak of his being comfortable with himself only when he stands out or apart; they range from inferring a need to be different for its own sake, to its serving his sense of importance and self-worth, to its being essential for his very identity—for example, "It's as if you aren't really sure who you are unless you're someone special, apart from all the others."

However, the paradigm as I present it above is not complete. In order to permit an explanation of why the patient is recounting these aspects of his childhood, I included the following interchange as a preface.

PT-1:   Am I like your other patients?
TH-1:   How do you mean?
PT-2:   I don't know. It's a silly question. I take it back.
         [pause]

With this setting available, the question of why can readily be answered. You are now in a good position to understand the purport and meaning of the material and can infer that the patient is telling you why he is concerned with being like your other patients. Your interpretation can therefore explicate both the meaning of his concern (the form of his current work) as well as an important aspect of his self-image (the content). Furthermore, you can attempt to explain the past in a way that has great relevance to the present, and show how the present has connections with the past.

Students cast their interpretations in the form of "I understand now why you asked the question," and go on to highlight one or another aspect of the patient's personality and self-image. In a variety of ways they emphasize his need to be special and different. Some express it this way: "You feel you don't stand out from other people as an individual; you have to work extra hard to insure being noticed. When you ask if you're like my other patients, you're asking me if there's anything about you that's different, anything that marks you as an individual." Others say it this way: "It's important to you to stand out as someone special. Your question expressed a concern about how you are compared to my other patients. Here too, I think you don't want your voice to be lost in a chorus of a hundred voices, you want to stand out here with me as excellent in some way." Some introduce the element of worry and concern: "Perhaps you're worried that I don't perceive you as distinct from other patients, and this bothers you." Some infer that he needs reassurance and needs to be a "better" patient.

In my opinion, there isn't a need for such speculations; to explicate the self-image content, while at the same time focusing on the communicative aspects of the material, is likely to be quite sufficient. Here are two clear and excellent examples: "You've answered the question, haven't you? You've been telling me how important it is for you to feel special. Perhaps you asked me the question about my other patients because you'd like to feel special to me too," and "I think your asking me if you're like my other patients was really asking if I could hear your voice, or if all my patients blend together like a choir. It seems to be very important to you to feel special." And this one is interesting: "Perhaps you are trying to tell me, in a roundabout way, that you feel I'm not paying enough attention to you, or that I don't recognize your individuality; and unless you convince me of your special qualities, you'll remain an anonymous member of my *choir* of patients."

On the whole, then, this paradigm presents few technical problems. Students address both the content and form of the material, and their interpretations differ only with respect to whether they infer affect, how they construe the self-image, and how they formulate the communicative aspect. But few attempt something that can be attempted for this paradigm, and it's an aspect of technique that I regard as particularly important for *Psychotherapy*: we are in a perfect position to offer an interpretation whose form is not, "This is *my* explanation," but rather, "This is *your* explanation."

Since I have amply discussed the pitfalls of giving explanations, suffice it to say that the optimal way to work with explanations is not "Based on your account and your associations to it, I have come to the following conclusion about what happened and why you behaved the way you did" but "Based on your account and associations, I get the impression that the following is the way you explain what happened and why you behaved the way you did." And in addition to articulating the patient's explanation in this way, we might also be able to say something about why he doesn't recognize his own explanation, why he needs for us to make it.

Moreover, a number of possibilities can occur to us when we're thinking, not why did the thing happen, but why is the patient telling it as he is. For one, we may detect that he is setting us up to give an explanation he already knows well enough; for another, we may detect that he has a need to keep from confronting what he already knows well enough. Issues of activity and passivity may be entailed, issues of role definition (for instance, casting us into the role of parent-teacher who gives reasons), and they resolve into transference issues, in a sense, which always deserve our attention.

To return, then, to Paradigm 3, instead of saying, "I think I know why you asked me whether you're like my other patients," you can say, "Do you notice how you have explained why you're concerned about whether you are like my other patients?" If the patient is mystified by the question, you have two options: (1) address the defensive implications of the mystification (though there isn't anything in the material on which to base such an interpretation), and (2) spell out the explanation itself as he has given it in associational and reminiscence form. This is the optimal way to provide explanations without imposing them and/or casting them in diagnostic form, because the explanation remains the patient's; it's what is in his mind, and you're doing little more than articulating it.

I would begin by reminding the patient of his initial question and of how he dismissed it as silly: "I think you've been explaining to me why it was not such a silly question." I might even ask him at this point whether he has an idea of what I have in mind, and if he doesn't, I would put it this way: "What you've told me about your childhood amounts to an explanation of what your question meant to you; you've been explaining the question in the form of reminiscences about how important it used to be for you to stand out as someone different, perhaps special—Do you see what I mean?" I might add something about the details (the quitting choir, the special paper on Alexander the Great), but my overall emphasis would be on the fact that his reminiscences constitute an explanation that throws light on his original question. "I think you are telling me how important it is for you now, and how important it has long been, for you to see yourself as different and special." Two purposes will have thus been served: an aspect of his personality explored, and an aspect of therapy clarified—not only content but form as well will have been attended to. The next paradigm examines a further aspect of this important issue.

In Paradigm 4 there is again an initial question posed by the patient, which is followed by relevant associations. This time, however, there are additional considerations which mitigate against following the same line of interpretation I recommended above, because the relevant interpretation cannot address itself only to the initial question and the consequent reminiscences—it must take into account the fact that the patient is experiencing anxiety.

Paradigm 4

[The session is drawing to a close; it has been a good one.]

Why do you sit so far from me? Your chair could be closer, you know. [pause] Somehow, the distance between us seems greater now than it usually is. That's crazy! [pause] Sometimes I feel like speaking softly here, but I can't because then you wouldn't hear me. [pause] My kid brother always yells. It used to be funny when he was little, and my parents would tease him about it. He just couldn't say anything in a nor- mal voice—always at the top of his lungs. [pause] He was a cuddly little butterball of a kid, always smooching up to people. But the minute he opened his mouth . . . [smile] It was hilarious. My mother is sort of a yeller too—always at the top of her dear lungs. But not my father; he never, ever spoke loud. He was always sort of calm and . . . you know, sort of removed from people. He loved to sit off by himself and read or watch TV. He liked to be left alone. [pause] When my brother or I hurt ourselves, or something like that, we never went to him, only to my mother. She just loved to cuddle us. A lot of times we would both climb on her together. [pause] I don't know why I'm thinking about all that now. [pause] You know, I'm feeling a bit anxious—sort of funny, in a way. [pause] I don't like the feeling one bit.

An impulse threatening to overcome defenses against its conscious recogni- tion and expression—that's the formulation I had in mind when I composed this paradigm. I tried to depict a patient wishing for physical intimacy with you. But instead of being aware of that wish, he conveys it through asso- ciations and reminiscence; and when it comes too close to awareness he experiences a pang of anxiety. My chief purpose was to exemplify a situation where a brief and pointed interpretation that simply focuses on the patient's impulse or wish can be the most efficacious kind of interpretation to make. Though the widely accepted rule of thumb "defenses before impulses" is generally a good one, there are occasions when the impulse itself can be addressed first, and when anything else could amount to an evasion of the issue, perhaps a flight into intellectualization.

The technical question, therefore, is whether it would be better to offer the articulative interpretation, "I believe you have the wish to be cuddled by me," or the explanatory one, "I believe you are feeling anxious because you have the wish to be cuddled by me, and that wish is unacceptable to you." The difference between the two is significant in principle but not necessarily in practice, because if you were to say the second, the patient would hear the first—all that would really matter is the articulation of the wish. This, of course, is not a strong argument in favor of elucidating the impulse alone; if in fact it won't make a difference to the patient whether the anxiety is interpreted as a defense and whether his associations and reminiscences are used as evidence for his wish, then it follows that you may as well go ahead and interpret that way—unless, of course, it weakens the effectiveness of the interpretive act. The chief consideration is whether it makes a significant difference to the patient; even if all he hears is the articulation of the wish, he might hear it better when it's unencumbered with explanation.

To elaborate with, "I think I know why you asked why I sit so far from you," and/or "I think I know why you've been reminiscing about your kid brother and your parents the way you have," could dilute the impact of the interpretation by providing a kind of intellectual superstructure within which to elucidate the impulse. Now, if such a superstructure is judged desirable for one reason or another (to furnish a cognitive control over the anxiety, to strengthen the patient's synthetic-function, or to teach the kind of lesson about therapy that I discussed in connection with Paradigm 3), then it is of course appropriate to give. Again, however, he may only hear the impulse part and react only to the uncovering of his wish to be cuddled by you.

Therefore, I think the best approach is to articulate the impulse and the wish alone, and follow it later with the affective defense. One student comes close with, "Do you think that this feeling may have something to do with the wish to be cuddled again?" But the student imagines that the patient will respond, "How so? I don't see that," and thus provides this elaboration: "Well, that was the last thing you were speaking about when you started to feel that way, anxious and sort of funny. Maybe you'd like me to be more nurturant with you, less distant, so that you could feel free to express those needs to be cuddled here." Notice how intellectual and somewhat tangential the explanation is. Here are two examples that are more direct and less encumbered: "Perhaps you want me to comfort you; you'd like to sit closer to me, maybe even climb on my lap; but you feel anxious because you think I'd react like your father did and prefer to be left alone," and "I think you're feeling anxious because the thoughts you had about my sitting so far from you reminded you of the feelings you used to have as a child. Perhaps you'd like to climb on my lap now and be cuddled, but that feeling makes you anxious."

Unnecessary elaboration spoils the following line of interpretation. The student begins, "I think I know part of the reason for your anxiety; you feel a wish to be cuddled," but instead of stopping there, continues with "And dependent, and a contrary wish to be independent. And you fear that either or both of your wishes may be granted." Interestingly, the student has the patient continue in this way: "I don't think I understand all that. I can see how I want to be cuddled, taken care of—after all, doesn't everybody?—but what about the rest of it?" Now the affective situation has changed markedly, and what ensues is an intellectual discussion whose usefulness must perforce be of a different order. Perhaps recognizing that it's something of an argument, the student ends the dialogue with this remark: "And finally, that part of the anxiety is due to your rage at me and your father for not being as supportive as you sometimes want." And here's a good example of how an accurate and perceptive interpretation can be spoiled by overelaboration and a stilted intellectuality: "I think you are uncomfortable because a part of you would like to ask me to draw closer to you; you spoke of this on a physical level—moving the chairs closer—but I think you'd also like an emotional closeness, the kind your mother shared with you when she would cuddle you. But another part of you is unwilling to acknowledge this desire for more closeness with me, and so you're feeling anxious, because of this conflict between the two parts of yourself."

Many students choose to deal immediately with the transference issue, therapist equals father. Some do no more than mention it (for example, "It's possible you feel anxious because in certain ways I remind you of your father," which leaves itself open to the question "In what ways?"); others offer some explanation ("Perhaps you'd like to be close to me in the same way you were close to your mother, and instead I'm distant like your father," and "Maybe a part of you wishes I was like your mother who cuddled you when you were hurt"); and some provide excellent exemplification of the fact that even a transference interpretation can be a highly intellectualized kind of interpretation to make, as this one does: "Are you feeling that I too am like your father, removed and distant? You would like me to hear your request for cuddling and are afraid both that I won't hear it and that I will."

When a patient experiences a painful affect like anxiety we are likely to have the impulse to make it go away, to comfort him and make it better; and we may want to offer an interpretation based on these concerns. Clinical experience suggests, however, that affects such as anxiety—and especially anxiety—can serve a valuable signaling function, signaling the activation of a conflict that may involve a burgeoning wish or fantasy which cannot be safely countenanced. Consequently, it becomes somewhat shortsighted to explain the anxiety itself without exploring the impulse and conflict that generated it. (For example, a student suggests, "Perhaps you see me much as you saw your father, as calm and removed. Could it be that the anxiety you're feeling stems from the fear that I won't be there when you hurt? Perhaps you'd feel more comfortable if I were more like your mother, loud and cuddling.")

I don't mean to imply that the signal theory of anxiety has to be subscribed to. Consider this student's way of construing the anxiety: "Maybe you're anxious because you miss that, being able to climb into your mother's lap and be comforted, and that upsets you," and when the patient responds, "Yes, I guess so; I just can't have that anymore, I guess, that kind of closeness and support," the student articulates the impulse clearly and sensitively with, "But you'd like to have it still; that's perhaps why you feel the distance between us is greater today, because you're feeling that need to be held and comforted, to be close."

Here's a well-articulated alternative to the signal theory which begins with, "It seems you see me as being quiet and removed like your father. I wonder if you wish I were closer and more affectionate with you, like your mother was, and this wish makes you feel anxious." "Why should it make me feel anxious?" asks the patient, and the student suggests simply, "Perhaps you have had a similar wish about your father." "I guess I have," says the patient, adding, "But he never paid any attention to what I wished." The student offers, "I guess that made you angry," and the patient agrees with, "Yes, it did, but I never could do anything about it. I felt so frustrated by him! I just couldn't reach him." And now the student offers a certain theory of anxiety with, "And when I remind you of him in that way it makes you anxious, because you still don't know what to do with that frustration and anger."

And yet another interesting alternative is the following. "It must have hurt you not to be able to get close to your father," begins the student, "I wonder if you're feeling close to me now, and you're conflicted over how to get me to respond—and that's what you're anxious about." The patient says, "I'm tempted to really come on strong, like my mother or my brother, but I'm afraid that might just put you off." The student then continues (perhaps with a bit too much), "I gather you never really found a way of reaching your father, and you're afraid that same dissatisfying relationship will repeat itself here, and that instead of giving you the consideration and understanding you need, I'll remain cold and aloof."

Finally, the ubiquitous question "Why now?" may be asked. The preface to the paradigm mentions the fact that today's session has been a good one, and that provides a basis for answering the question. A few students include that answer in their interpretations, and here's a particularly sensitive example of how it can be formulated: the student begins a dialogue with, "I have an idea about why you may be feeling anxious: your earlier comment about my sitting so far away from you sounds similar to your description of how your father loved to sit off by himself, he was distant from people, he liked to be left alone," to which the patient responds, "Yes, I can see that. But why would that make me anxious?" and then gets this answer: "Perhaps you're feeling that you've been *cuddling up* to me. But instead of reacting with warmth, as your mother would have, I chose to remain distant and aloof, like your father." That's a piece of good technical work.

Paradigm 5

[The patient has never expressed any hostility toward you—nor toward anyone else, as far as you know—but he does have a big tendency to tease, which he chalks up to a good sense of humor.]

You have a supervisor, don't you? I know you must, so you don't have to answer that question. [pause] Yes, I'm sure you have a supervisor and you discuss these sessions with him. And he tells you what you did wrong, eh! [broad smile] That's cool! [pause] Sometimes I have the impulse to fool around here, maybe make things up—like tell you something that happened to Peter as if it had happened to me, or tell you one of his dreams. [smile] Give you and your supervisor a run for your money. [pause] I wonder how much he criticizes you, like tells you you shouldn't have said something you said to me. That must feel crumby when he does that. [pause] Hey, you know what!—let me talk to him. Yes, and I'll tell him how great you really are. [friendly smile] Don't worry, I'll do right by you!

The preface informs us that the patient likes to tease, and it suggests that he is probably unaware of its hostile aspect; he chalks it up to a good sense of humor. The paradigm presents a piece of good-natured teasing, and your chief problem is whether to suggest the underlying hostility of it, and how to do it in a way that is sufficiently empathic and tactful. If you decide to opt for an interpretation of hostile fantasy and intent—and the transcript itself in the context of this study strongly implies that you should—you want to formulate it in a way that preserves your regular neutrality. You might have to throw some cold water on the patient's teasing, but you must avoid any sense of scolding him for it and any hint of retaliating.

First a word about the advisability of responding with some humor of your own. I believe we should resort to humor rarely, if ever. Moreover, in a situation like this one, where the humor is of a teasing kind, any attempt to respond with humor is likely itself to have a teasing component. I'm sure an inventive therapist could come up with a humorous response that doesn't tease, and highlights the underlying intent of the patient's teasing, but it takes a special knack and skill. So at best it's risky to try to respond in kind. To retort, "So will I," to the patient's, "Don't worry, I'll do right by you!" is safe enough, but it isn't clear what purpose that would serve. To retort, "Thanks! I won't worry," or "I'll make sure to tell him," is merely sarcastic and could amount to a kind of put-down. Therefore, I believe the most prudent approach is to stick with your usual way of responding and not try to match (or compete with) the patient's humor. At the same time, however, you should try to respond not only to the content of his remarks but to their form as well; you needn't overlook the humorous cast nor the teasing intent.

But most of my students not only steer completely clear of the teasing and make no mention of the humorousness, many also steer clear of the hostile elements and implications. Instead, they offer serious and sober interpretations that focus on a variety of possible meanings of the patient's thoughts and impulses. (The paradigm provides plenty of content to work with.) Some construe the patient's remarks as reflecting a concern over their competency as therapists (for example, "I'm wondering if perhaps you're having some doubts about whether I'll do right by you"); some focus on the patient's need for control and power ("Perhaps you're enjoying the thought that you have power over me via my supervisor," and "Do you by any chance wish that you can control me because you are afraid of being controlled by me?"); some speak of helplessness, of concern over doing well, and the like. I find it difficult to imagine that such interpretations would evoke a useful response from the patient. I can only picture him insisting that he was just teasing, that's all—so why are you so uptight?

Some students infer that he is feeling critical; for example, "I'm wondering whether it isn't easier for you to think of my supervisor being critical of me than to consider the possibility that you might have criticisms of your own toward me." And consider this interesting, if farfetched, formulation: "I wonder if your impulse to fool around here might be due to your fear that if you really told me how you were feeling I would criticize you and then you would feel crumby," which at least makes allusion to the teasing. A surprising number infer that he is retaliating for some perceived criticisms. Here are two examples: "Yes, but maybe you also have some critical feelings toward me, some feelings that I've said or done a wrong thing; and perhaps your impulse to fool around expresses a wish to get back at me for it"; "Could it be you sometimes don't like the things I say to you, that you take my remarks as criticisms, and therefore the idea of someone criticizing me—as well as your *putting me on*—is a way of getting even?"

It isn't so surprising that students infer that the patient is angry ("I wonder if kidding around isn't a way of expressing anger towards me"), but without suggesting a reason for his anger, such interpretations run the risk of being simple scoldings and put-downs. The material provides for this kind of explanation: "Perhaps you are angry because you feel mistreated and used. You may believe my performance in here is more important to me than my understanding what you say." Notice how it differs fundamentally from the diagnostic cast of the following explanation, which is the finale of a dialogue: " . . . by joking about it you are able to convey your anger while at the same time not taking full responsibility for your angry feelings." That remark is likely to have a squelching effect. (Diagnostic interpretations often do.)

And finally, some students try to touch all the bases. "I get the impression you're really angry at me, and you'd like nothing better than to be my supervisor, as that you could have authority over me and feel safe in expressing your resentment"; as if that weren't sufficient, the student continues with, "Becoming pals with my supervisor would really give you control over me, so I would become impotent, and you could determine the course of therapy." How is the poor patient to respond to all that? Similarly, of what possible use is it to his therapeutic work to be told all this?—"You are both imagining that my supervisor is highly critical of me and reassuring me that I'm really great. It sounds as if you're not so sure about how good I really am, you're debating it inside, and it makes you somewhat angry."

Despite the preface's clear hint, only a few students infer hostility in the patient's remarks. And those who do, find it difficult to keep from being flagrantly diagnostic, if not also didactic. For example, "You seem to be teasing me," begins a student, to which the patient responds, "I hope I haven't made you mad." The student then lectures, "Whether I am mad or not is not at issue here; I would like you to understand that a lot of hostility can be expressed through humor." Another student winds up a dialogue with, " . . . nevertheless, humor does frequently have an element of hostility, and words have effects as well as causes." ("No fooling!")

To interpret hostility without being confronting, diagnostic, or didactic, isn't easy at all. In my experience the best way is to wait and listen for something in what the patient has said that could provide a basis for suggesting that he himself suspects he's being hostile. Such an approach requires first acknowledging the fact that he may have no clear awareness of hostility (it could begin with a remark like, "I appreciate that you're teasing and fooling around"), then pointing to something he had said which could suggest he has a glimmer of some hostile feelings or intentions (for instance, "I wonder if you yourself suspect something about the way you're teasing me; what you said about my supervisor's criticisms suggests to me that you may sense there's a streak of hostile feelings in it"). This approach may be too indirect; the patient might recognize that you have something in mind but you're being gingerly about saying it. Nevertheless, the approach remains quite empathic insofar as it alludes to what he is experiencing rather than to the impact or intent that you experience. A student captures its spirit in the following interesting dialogue.

TH-1:   For a moment it seemed you were seriously trying to imagine being in my position, and then you continued joking. I wonder if perhaps you needed to get away from your feeling of identifying with me, because it made you feel too close to me.

PT-2:   Yeah, that sure didn't last long. It didn't feel too good. But too close? I don't know what you mean—at least, I don't think I do.

TH-2:   One thing which occurred to me was that perhaps you wanted to get away from your feeling of identifying with me because it gave you a different perspective on your joking here, that from that point of view it seemed more hostile to you than it usually does.

Several students solve the problem by construing the patient's remarks as indicating concern that you will judge him for being hostile. An interesting example is this: "I wonder if you think I might feel you are being hostile when you show amusement at the thought of my being criticized and made to feel crumby. What do you think of the possibility that your joking offer of a testimonial in my behalf is a way of making amends for your thoughts?" And the following example scatters its shots, makes too many speculative inferences, but ends up with a good focus.

TH-1:   You seem to feel the need to stay on my good side, while at the same time poking a little fun at me.

PT-2:   I do like you, you know, even if you do make a lot of mistakes, and do have big feet.

TH-2:   I think there is another reason why you feel the need to stay on my good side, over and above the liking of me; and this other reason is fear that I may become angry at your kidding.

PT-3:   Some people do become angry; and besides, if my therapist were to become angry then I would be stuck—he couldn't help.

TH-3:   I feel the major reason for your fear of making me angry is that it would lead you to feel the hostility implicit in your comments, and perhaps become aware of great but unacceptable feelings of hostility within yourself.

That *TH-3*, however, is a diagnostic formulation. Students who address the patient's hostility find it hard to avoid being diagnostic. Consider this flagrantly diagnostic interpretation: "I wonder if what you call teasing isn't partly a wish which becomes frightening to you soon after you express it. Any time you catch yourself sounding angry or hostile you hurry to make things all better again." Even if we overlook its speculative zeal, even if we accept its diagnostic cast, and even if we recognize it as an interesting formulation, it's not easy to see what the patient can do with it. The following dialogue offers the same kind of interpretation, but by developing it gradually, and keeping things clearer, the student manages to allow the patient some room to maneuver. (And also gives him some options for a response other than "That's interesting!")

TH-1: You seem to be teasing me, by describing a trick you might play, and suggesting you might go and talk to my supervisor about me.

PT-2: Yeah, but it's all in fun. I always did have a nutty sense of humor.

TH-2: But perhaps there are some mischievous elements in your teasing too—as if you'd be a little bit glad to confuse my understanding or to know what criticisms my supervisor makes. As if you'd almost enjoy seeing me at a disadvantage, or in a bad position.

PT-3: Oh, no! You don't have to get paranoid. I was just kidding around. I wouldn't feel that way at all if you got into trouble—I mean, I'd feel terrible probably. I wouldn't want anything bad to happen to you.

TH-3: Well, while you are reassuring me now that you don't feel any hostility toward me, still in "teasing" me you set up situations which might reflect a somewhat hostile intent. Maybe that's what your "good sense of humor" is really about; you bring up situations in which you might hurt people, even indirectly, and then you can reassure them that you didn't mean it, and don't feel any hostility at all.

Again, however, notice the recourse to the diagnostic and confronting modes. To avoid them and still draw the patient's attention to the hostility that underlies his teasing is obviously difficult, because the impulse to be confronting with him can be strong ("Look here, don't you see how hostile is your teasing!"), and the way to soften the blow is to explain things diagnostically. Thus, even a rather tactful formulation like, "I know this feels like good-natured teasing to you, but I wonder whether you also feel some of the hostility in it; I think you may be feeling an impulse to hurt me in some way, but that feeling is unacceptable (or dangerous) to you, so instead you tease,'' falls back on the diagnostic mode to lessen its confrontational nature. But it may be a reasonably good compromise solution to the technical problem, insofar as it avoids the pitfalls of gingerliness, which the approach I recommended seems to have.

Paradigm 6

[This is the same patient as in Paradigm 5. He's an only child, and his father is a successful lawyer who doted on him. In the following account he is revealing something about an underlying fantasy he has long had.]

I can make you laugh whenever I want to. I like that. [pause] Peter has a stoneface for a shrink, who never even cracks a smile. Poor Peter! [pause] Remember a couple of weeks ago when I was kidding you about you and your supervisor? Well, I was lying in bed one night, having my usual trouble falling asleep, and I was thinking about that. I was thinking that you're a student, so you're being evaluated on how you perform as my therapist. [pause] If I was your supervisor I'd give you an "A." I really mean it, you know—no kidding. At first I thought you were too inexperienced and young to be much good, but then I saw that wasn't true. Hey, I hope it doesn't embarrass you, but I think you're terrific! [pause] Anyway, while I was waiting to fall asleep I was thinking that how I do here as your patient makes a big difference in how your supervisor evaluates you. I mean, if I get better, then you get your "A." [broad smile] I know that's not really true; it's a crazy idea. But it's cool. And it helped me fall asleep.

What does the fantasy mean? The answer is likely to help explain why it helped the patient fall asleep. The preface suggests an important historical basis, and the fantasy I had in mind when I composed the paradigm can be described as "the power behind the throne." But the technical question, the one that addresses our intentions and goals, is not answered by figuring out the fantasy.

Consider this fine example: "Maybe what helped you fall asleep was the idea that you could have such power over me. For instance, you mentioned your power to make me laugh, and then you had the fantasy of being able to control the kind of evaluation I'll get from my supervisor by determining whether you'll get better or not, and thinking that that would influence how successful I seemed as your therapist. Maybe this is a fantasy you also had about your father—that however successful his career might be, you still had the power to control his success, or even his appearance of success, according to how well you turned out as his only son." This is certainly a well-formulated interpretation—only it fails to satisfy some of the chief technical requirements of the interpretive mode. It's too long and too complete, and thereby offers the patient too full an explanation. And it fails to enlist his participation in the process of explanation, not to mention discovery; he will probably find it an intellectually interesting and personally illuminating explanation—from the passive position of audience, however. It seems to assume that the patient was wholly unaware of the fantasy's nature and ramifications, and therefore was incapable of exploring them himself.

I suspect that the student who wrote the interpretation didn't ask the question, What purpose do I want to achieve with it? Or if he did consider that question, the answer was not *Psychotherapy*'s—to promote the *therapeutic process*. Notice how the process appears to be in good shape in the paradigm, how there aren't any signs of resistance. In fact, there isn't anything to indicate that you need feel called upon to offer a remark. But since the study requires you to participate at the end of the transcript, and it's an Interpretation Paradigm, you have to formulate an interpretation (or a line of interpretation), and not only its content but its form and function must be carefully considered. With that in mind, let's examine some interpretations students give.

Many focus on the patient's need for control and power. For example, "The fantasy that you can help me get an 'A' evidently pleases you. Feeling I am dependent on you for a good grade is a little like being able to make me laugh, it gives you a sense of power and control," and "Perhaps your believing you have some control over my fate makes you feel less vulnerable to what I say to you here." Some introduce the theme of feeling important. Some extend their interpretation of the need for control to cover the patient's problem with falling asleep, for example, "I think I understand why you often have difficulty falling asleep. Could it be you're hesitant to give up conscious control to sleep, just as you wish to feel totally in control here in therapy?" Some generalize in a diagnostic way to all of his interpersonal relationships, for example, "It seems you need to feel you have great control over people and situations; perhaps this helps you maintain control over yourself." Many include the patient's father, for example, "I think you want to be as important to me as you were to your father," and "You seem to feel my success depends on you; perhaps you felt that way about your father," and "You think your behavior here would affect my supervisor's evaluation of me as you used to think your behavior would affect other people's evaluation of your father," and "I think a part of you would like to see me as similar to your father, someone who is really terrific and who you can help by performing well, in this case by *getting better*." The following dialogue puts it all together.

TH-1:   That would make you very powerful in a way; by get-
        ting better or not you would have great control over
        me, and, in a sense, by feeling good or bad you could
        control me.

PT-2:   I know it's a crazy idea. I said that, but the very
        thought of having such power over you is really rather
        neat.

TH-2:   Going to sleep is a kind of losing control, of letting go
        of control. So I wonder if the need to have control is
        not a major issue with you.

PT-3:   I always just sort of thought of myself as an insomniac,
        one that good old Sominex didn't help. But it is possi-
        ble. I just never thought of it that way.

TH-3:   Further, it's a very specific kind of fantasy of power and
        control; it's the kind that a child might have to control a
        father. And knowing you're an only child and that
        you've said that your father always doted on you, I
        wonder if you might not have done something similar
        with your father, and it worked to a degree. And if all
        that is true, then it might very well be frightening to a
        child to have such power.

Here's an interesting example, which takes a speculative step away from
the material (like *TH-3* in the above dialogue), but which succeeds in enlisting
the patient's active cooperation in the work of exploration (a point I return to
shortly).

TH-1:   You seem to like the idea of your performance determin-
        ing my evaluation.

PT-2:   Yeah. I know it's not true, but I do. It gives me a feel-
        ing of control, sort of. I mean you're good, but ...
        [falls silent]

TH-2:   I wonder if you feel as though it's your turn to have
        control, to tell people what to do.

PT-3:   Maybe. I mean, I was always having to meet standards.
        Like my father, he really loved me, but I always had to
        do things just right for him or he'd sort of sulk. And I
        would feel hurt and a little mad.

TH-3:   So perhaps you are angry at him, and would like to
        turn the tables and be the controller?

The same student offers a second dialogue, in which the form and function of his work is good and appropriate, though it takes matters far afield and
can be faulted for excessive speculation.

TH-1:   Your pleasure at my success, won with your help, was what helped you fall asleep.

PT-2:   Yeah. You know ... [pause] It's sort of like when my father would come in at night and tuck me in. [pause] He always said "we," you know—we did this today, and we did that, and we will, and like that. It always felt good, and I'd go to sleep.

TH-2:   So your feeling of togetherness and friendship with your father was very pleasurable.

PT-3:   Uh-huh. In fact, I sometimes wondered if maybe I wasn't a little weird for feeling that way. I mean, he's my father! I don't know ...

TH-3:   I wonder if you had a fantasy of sexual relations with your father, which you found very pleasurable.

PT-4:   [Taken aback] I think I did! You know, I sometimes would masturbate after he left the room, and then fall asleep.

By taking a speculative step (or call it leap) away from the material, by falling into the category of plausible but unfounded, an interpretation runs a number of risks. The main one, of course, is that the patient will be puzzled; but together with that may come other implications, and the one that pertains most directly to the present material is that he will feel chastised and put-down. Consider this interesting example: "It seems hard for you to believe that anyone would be interested in you for any other reason than to enhance his prestige," and notice how, even if it were altogether accurate, it could be a subtle put-down; and I believe that its speculative nature contributes to its evaluative edge. The same is true for this interesting example: "I think that a part of you still wants an 'A' from your father, just in the same way that you want me to get an 'A' from my supervisor. You see, it sounds to me that thinking of yourself as so inexperienced and young in relation to your father made you feel as if you were no good." Since the patient said none of these things, he might wonder why you say them, and that could readily lead him to infer a criticism.

Some students give him a verbal rap on the knuckles. "It seems to me as though your being able to please me and give me an 'A' as a therapist is more important to you than how you're doing and what you may be getting as a patient," is an example; and even this one belongs, I believe, in that category, "You were able to fall asleep after you had thought about how you could help me and please me, about how you could be a good boy. But somehow it's not acceptable to you to think about what pleases and helps you—you even see your getting better in terms of my getting an 'A' rather than in terms of what it will mean for you.'' These interpretations can be justified on the basis that they focus attention on the way the patient is viewing therapy, and whenever we see the opportunity to articulate a transference reaction we should take it. Moreover, it is especially the kind of transference motif that he is expressing in Paradigm 6 that is of paramount importance to fully uncover and thoroughly explore. But I am not criticizing the intent of these interpretations, only their form. Compare them with the following example, and notice how this one manages to strike a much less critical tone: ''You seem to be implying that we can make a deal: an 'A' for me and getting better for you. I wonder if you are assuming that you'll get better because it will be I who will work hard—because an 'A' is important to me.'' This kind of interpretation has intrinsic merit and great value; in fact, there is reason to contend that it can take priority over addressing the patient's need for control, his attitude toward his father, the new version of his old fantasy, and the like.

Some students address their interpretations to the central transference issue, but few develop it adequately. For example, one begins appropriately with, ''It seems as if you feel a pressure to get well; you have to get well for my sake,'' but then distracts the patient from the issue by continuing with, ''I bet it's similar to other feelings that you may have experienced before.'' Thus, when the patient responds, ''Well, I did feel pressure at times; my father was a big one for achievement, he was pleased when I did well, like in school,'' the transference motif has moved into the background—and the student keeps it there with, ''So maybe you felt a pressure from him when you were growing up, a pressure to live up to his expectations, lest he be disappointed in you. Failing him would make you feel bad because you would be letting him down and would feel bad.'' And consider how this dialogue misses the point: the student begins well with, ''You could relax and fall asleep when you thought that I would be paid back with a good grade for the good that I may do for you,'' to which the patient responds simply, ''Yes, I just thought it's good that I can sort of help you while you are helping me.'' But then the student draws an oversimplified parallel with the father: ''I wonder if this might be related to your feelings of wanting to pay your father back for the things he did for you. You can relax when you think you're not getting something for nothing from me, like you felt you did from your father.''

The best approach to Paradigm 6, in my opinion, is to work with parts of a complete formulation and to structure each part in a way that invites the patient's active participation in the exploration and uncovering. I would try for interpretations and articulations that are simple and open-ended, that are more evocative than fully explanatory. I would begin with a remark like, ''I think you understand why the fantasy helped you get to sleep—It's a comforting and reassuring one, isn't it?'' If the patient didn't deal with it spontaneously, I would show interest in the idea that my success is dependent on his getting better, perhaps simply by articulating the idea with some emphasis. Afterward I could suggest that the fantasy probably goes back to when he was a child and his father was such a powerful man in his eyes. (For instance, ''What do you think of the possibility that you used to have this kind of fantasy about your father?'') And finally, I would hold in reserve my key interpretation—''Your fantasy is that you have a lot of power over him, that you are the power behind the throne; and now with me too you have that kind of fantasy''—until I am sure I need it to help the patient achieve a valuable piece of understanding. The transference motif can be kept in the foreground, and it will have served a double function: to bring to the surface and clarify an important way he is viewing therapy (as well as me), and to expose for exploration an important fantasy about himself that he has probably long nurtured. The *therapeutic process*—not to overlook the patient himself—will have been well served by such a use of the interpretive mode.

7
The Alternative
Interpretations Paradigms

Paradigm 1

I was thinking about the vacation. I'm not exactly sure
when we're going to resume here. You said it would be two weeks,
didn't you? [*Yes, that's right.*] So that means we resume on Tuesday the
fifth? [*Yes.*] [pause] You said it very clearly, but I never remember dates
and figures. I'm one of those people who rely more on intuition than on
calculation. [pause] Vacations are a drag. Most people don't know what
to do with them. Like Veblen said—was it Veblen?—leisure is a
privilege of the idle rich because they're the only ones who study it.
People get conditioned by our society into their daily routines. That's
because our society regiments us, makes us dependent on its institutions.
But I guess I'm doing what you pointed out to me last week, intellectualizing. [small smile and long pause] My plans for the next two weeks are
still up in the air. Joan wants us to go camping, but I dread being stuck
with her all the time. I need to be alone a lot; Joan doesn't understand
that. And I'm a terrible camper; she's very good at it; so everything will
be up to her. [pause] She's such a fusspot too, and that drives me crazy.
She just doesn't understand me . . . [pause and smile] I was going to say
"like you do." But women are biologically incapable of understanding
men. I really believe that. Actually, the same is true for most men.
Anyway, you're practically the only person I know who does, and I
don't know how you do it. [pause] I think it's because you're independent
and sure of yourself. I picture you as someone who knows who he is, so
you don't have to step on people and smother them. [pause] Freedom is
as vital as air is. You can smother if you don't have enough of either. I

190

can't stand to be smothered, you know. [fidgets and frowns] That's because I'm an existential being. I need to be *in* the world and not *of* it.

Idealization is the transference, intellectualization the most prominent defense, the issue centers on a pending separation, and the patient is struggling with feelings which are at variance with his self-image as the independent one. Consequently, you have several options for an interpretation: you can address the transference, point out the defense, articulate the feelings, the self-image, and also try to integrate several or all of them into a single, coherent, and "complete" interpretation.

In the opinion of many analytically oriented teachers and practitioners, the complete interpretation must address the defense-impulse (or defense-conflict) aspect of a patient's experience as well as its transference and resistance implications, and it should also include the genetic and dynamic dimensions. To the extent that any of these elements are omitted is the interpretation "incomplete"—and "the more complete the better" is a good rule of thumb. Others stress the self-image (or "ego") component, the affective involvement, and one or another aspect of character. But in my opinion, the desirability of completeness has to depend. Whether a simple and focused interpretation will be most useful depends on the patient and the context; sometimes it can be more effective to deal with one issue at a time.

While complete interpretations are liable to be closed formulations that wrap things up too neatly, they have the important advantage of minimizing unwanted reactions (such as embarrassment, shame, and resentment). They can be maximally tactful insofar as they offer such a many-sided and full explanation that the patient will feel understood and not judged or censured. For instance, to draw his attention to the fact that he is intellectualizing, without offering a reason why he needs to be doing it, can be perceived by him as both a criticism and a directive to stop doing it. Similarly, simply to point out that he is overidealizing you, without at the same time offering a reason why he wishes to do it and suggesting the historical and dynamic basis of that wish, can be misconstrued as a simple admonition.

And I agree with the point of view that a transference interpretation, to be most effective, has to include an emphasis on the fact that the patient wishes it (that it reflects, as a dream does, a wishful fantasy). Accordingly, to articulate the distortion or the defense involved may be insufficient; what's often required is an articulation of the wishful or functional nature of the distortion and defense. To make the wish plausible, it is sometimes helpful, and sometimes necessary, to offer some genetic and dynamic reasons. But this needn't be done all at once, in one step; usually the articulation can be offered and the rest deferred, for the moment at least. And that, in my opinion, is the more effective way to proceed. For one thing, the patient's reaction to the articulation can be very significant; he may complete or extend it himself, he may want to explore its explanation, or, of course, he may reject it altogether. If he does the last, or if his reaction is one of shame or resentment or perplexity, it can be useful and necessary for you to work with that reaction, unless—and this is the crucial point—you believe his reaction was legitimately evoked by the incompleteness of your interpretation. And, as I've indicated, there's a school of thought that holds we must offer the complete interpretation in order to prevent him from reacting in these ways. At any rate, when you choose to run that risk and offer only the articulation, you should have in mind the complete interpretation and be ready to give it.

Transference reactions are often accompanied by strong emotions, mainly because they entail profound distortions based on profound unconscious images (*imagos*). They may evoke deep feelings of awe as well as apprehension, perhaps a sense of the uncanny as well as of revelation. For those reasons they have to be approached with special care and understanding. I recommend that early transference interpretations be introduced or accompanied by a statement indicating that you appreciate what your patient is experiencing, how powerful and awesome his feelings can be. It's very useful to look for the opportunity to express an empathic understanding of how the intensity of his reaction to you frightens him, especially since he knows how irrational it may be. After all, a genuine transference reaction is intrinsically a deep distortion of reality, and he may sense it. We should too.

If we appreciate the distortion and its dynamic bases, we won't be so prone to take it "personally." Moreover, when we are the object of an idealized transference, we're likely to have some reactions ourselves; we may want to shake off the idealization, insofar as it makes us guilty, embarrassed, and so forth, perhaps evoking our narcissistic fantasies and conflicts. Furthermore, when the idealization is accompanied (as it is in Paradigm 1), by dependency feelings on the therapy, we are prone to additional misgivings and guilt. So not only must we take special pains to keep such feelings well under control, we have to be especially diligent to keep from conveying a sense of defensiveness, a wish to push the patient away, to disavow and disclaim responsibility for his dependency, and to rapidly dissipate the transference.

For such reasons perhaps, some students offer remarks to this paradigm that are snappish, curt, and sarcastic. "Perhaps if I were as understanding as you suggest I would not be so inconsiderate as to take a vacation," for example, is a sharp remark that can be dramatic and incisive, but in my opinion it runs the risk of having no other result than that of putting the patient in an embarrassed and defensive position. (Moreover, it's also ambiguous: Do you mean you really aren't "understanding," or are you implying that he has been saying you really aren't?) Note the underlying sarcasm of "wonderfully" in, "I wonder if, to flatter me, you are telling me how wonderfully independent I am, while really you wish I were not so independent of you—especially at vacation time,'' and also the moot question of what function the flattery serves, how it is connected with the wish. And above all, note its cleverness. I see no value in being curt and clever, ever, but especially when addressing a transference issue.

When an interpretation is simple and to the point, it can either be succinct or curt. Its content and context determine whether its form is appropriate or not. In the context of the patient's anguished intellectualizations, as depicted in Paradigm 1, the simple and direct "I'm wondering if you'd really like to go on vacation with me" is apt to be curt and harsh, because it cuts beneath his defense and lays bare what he "really" wants. Even this gentler, more modulated and qualified rendition is likely to be too curt: "I'm not certain but I think you are flattering me today because part of you wishes you could come with me on vacation." There is also a special hazard in telling him what he "really" feels, especially with an interpretation whose form is simple and direct. Though the word *really* is not mentioned in the following example, notice how clearly it's implied: "I wonder if you are feeling that if I knew how much you needed me I would not abandon you for the next two weeks." And bear in mind how strenuously the patient has been stressing his need for freedom and independence.

Consider this relatively direct and sensitive rendition of the transference: "I wonder if in ascribing special powers of understanding to me you're not viewing me as someone special with whom it's all right to allow yourself to become dependent." This interesting interpretation raises another kind of problem, and a potentially important one. I have in mind its reference to "special understanding," which I believe can be ambiguous, perhaps with serious consequences. After all, insofar as *Psychotherapy* entails a unique relationship with your patient and a unique role definition for you, you are "special"—you do show "special understanding." Therefore, his regarding you as the one who understands in a special way is based on an important element of reality. That fact should not be overlooked, and it poses certain technical problems in any attempt to articulate an idealized transference.

One way to approach the problem is by centering on the act of generalization and drawing a distinction between your specialness as a therapist and your specialness outside of therapy. The patient provides for such a distinction when he implies picturing you as quite perfect in your everyday relationships. Therefore, you might say, "I gather you picture me not merely as a perfect therapist but also as a perfect human being, someone completely sure of himself, who treats his family and friends in a perfect way." If the patient concurs, you could offer an interpretation which begins, "I think I understand why you need [wish] to see me that way.'' Without losing sight of the fact that he has no way of knowing for sure what your ordinary behavior is like, and that for him to make a simple generalization is not so irrational, you can probably suggest to him that he could have inferred instead that only your behavior in therapy was ''special.''

Thus, an interpretation's context and content has an important bearing on its optimal form—and to find the optimal form in the light of its context and content is the main purpose of this study. I call it the Alternate Interpretations study because each of the four paradigms is designed to permit at least three different types of interpretation: a transference, a defense, and a self-image interpretation. (And because I tried to include material for the three kinds of interpretation, the transcripts themselves are somewhat more contrived and ''unreal'' than those in the previous studies.) The instructions call for three separate interpretations for each paradigm: a transference interpretation (to therapist and/or therapy), a defense interpretation (against impulse and/or affect), and a self-image interpretation.

Many students choose to interpret not intellectualization but disavowal in their defense interpretations. A good example is, ''I wonder if the vacation hasn't aroused feelings of dependency and helplessness in you that you are trying to deal with by denying that they exist, and instead insisting on your need for freedom and your fear of being smothered''; another is, ''I think part of you feels frightened of the vacation separation, and part of you feels frightened of how dependent you feel on the therapy—and you are denying both of these feelings.'' Some students stress the fact that the patient is strenuously asserting his independence; for example, ''I have the idea that your reliance on me makes you feel vulnerable, so you are reasserting your need for independency''; and several include the suggestion that he is feeling ashamed of it. Some interpret the transference reaction as a defense, as these examples do: ''By seeing me as perfect, you don't have to look at how my going on vacation hurts you, that you are stung by the rejection you experience in my going away,'' and ''I believe you are beginning to feel dependent on therapy and on me, and these feelings seem irrational, frightening, and unacceptable to you. To cope with them and protect yourself, you speak rationally and abstractly about independence and freedom, as if to convince yourself and me that the more mundane human needs don't apply to you.'' They are all good interpretations, and their only problem is their diagnostic texture.

But when you choose to address the defense of intellectualization you face an interesting technical problem: whether to regard the intellectual content of the paradigm as a reflection of the patient's beliefs and opinions, or whether to construe them merely as his attempts to use intellectualization as a defense. It seems to me you have to make a choice between the two, and not attempt, as many students do, to have it both ways. Consider this interesting example: "I agree with you that you're intellectualizing, but I think it would be useful to look at the content of it"; and when the patient responds, "I don't know what you have in mind," the student explains, "Well, I think you see me as one of society's institutions that has conditioned you into a routine of dependency on me and on therapy." The interpretation is a good one, but the patient may be left in some doubt about whether he is intellectualizing or not. The following example makes things clearer, but its tone is critical: "It seems far more acceptable for you to speak in general terms of how society conditions people, regiments them and makes them dependent on institutions, rather than accept your own dependency on the therapy institution and the feelings that the pending vacation may engender in you." And notice, also, the intellectuality of the interpretation, which may actually serve to support the defense.

As I've already emphasized, the optimal way to interpret a defense is to suggest that the patient has an inkling of it, that "Part of you suspects that what you're doing may be a defense." It isn't often you can formulate it that way, but this paradigm provides you with the opportunity to do so. The fact that the patient has said he was intellectualizing enables you to offer a simple and direct interpretation about it. But, "You say you're intellectualizing; I wonder if that's done in an attempt to avoid the anger you feel at me for leaving you," makes the mistake of inferring a specific affect for which there isn't any evidence. "What anger?" he may respond. Better, therefore, to refer to the pending interruption in therapy and allow the patient to speculate about the feelings—that's likely to be sufficiently simple and direct.

Consider, "It seems to me that your awareness of the fact that you intellectualize gives you a label to rely on in order to explain away your feelings of uneasiness." That may be quite valid, but it's also quite tactless; so completely lacking in empathy is it that he may experience it as little more than a rap on the knuckles. Or else he may welcome it for its intellectual elegance and include it in his own armory. Similarly, notice the intellectual and lofty stance you seem to take with this formulation: "It strikes me that your confusion about the dates and your very independent stance today may be a reaction to feelings of loss and disappointment about my going away. Perhaps even your impatience with Joan is a reflection of some anger at me for putting you in this predicament."

As I have also already mentioned several times, the optimal way to interpret a defense is to articulate the way it is currently in operation. A student attempts it, with fine form but poor content, this way: "It seems you were about to say you preferred me to Joan when you began talking about freedom again and frowning. So I wonder if perhaps your praise of me makes you

uncomfortable, makes you feel smothered, because you suspect it's preventing you from thinking about yourself.'' One student has the idea that what the
patient intends with his intellectualization is to confirm an interpretation that
had already been given him: ''Perhaps your use of intellectualization today
may in part be serving to confirm what I pointed out to you last week. And it
may further confirm the idealized picture you have of me.'' I find that rather
farfetched, and I suspect the patient would find it ''very interesting.'' My
preference would be to begin quite simply by suggesting to him that he was
about to say he preferred to be with me rather than with Joan, and I'd be ready
to continue with, ''That idea might have upset you, so you slipped back into
intellectualizing about freedom, and also into idealizing me as someone who
is perfectly independent and free.'' Another possibility is to point out that the
idealization, both of me and of freedom, occurred immediately after he experienced the impulse to express his need, which conflicted with his self-
image.

Paradigm 1 provides for a straightforward way to use the patient's self-
image in conjunction with his defense, and students use it. Many, however,
construe the self-image itself as the defense, or imply that it is serving little
more than a defensive function—and that, in my opinion, isn't the most
effective way to formulate it. ''Your need to see yourself as free and independent may be an effort to fend off your fears of both aloneness and relationships,'' and ''Perhaps your image of yourself as an independent, existential
being helps you to cope with feelings of dependency and helplessness,'' are
good examples. Not only are they highly diagnostic, they seem to back the
patient into a corner. Similarly, consider, ''By thinking of yourself as a
person who smothers easily from overprotection and who needs a great deal of
freedom, you protect yourself from feeling lonely and lost when you are left
alone.'' How is he supposed to respond?

He can be given some room, some paths to consider and explore, when the
formulation stresses his current dilemma—as these two examples do: ''It
seems that being independent is very important for you now. I wonder if
perhaps you must see yourself as so independent now in order to protect
yourself from feelings which have arisen as we are nearing my vacation,
feelings of dependency and vulnerability,'' and ''It's important to you to see
yourself as particularly independent right now, I think, because the idea that
you might be dependent on therapy and resentful of my vacation is unacceptable to you.'' The disadvantage of these formulations is that they seem to cast
doubt on the validity of his self-image. At best, they suggest that the patient is
using the self-image to ''protect'' and ''cope,'' which implies that he and his
self-image are quite separate.

A few students speak of a conflict within his self-image, or a contradiction in its basic structure. Consider this interesting example: "So you are clearly letting me know that you see yourself as a person who wants to be free, who needs to be independent; but at the same time you describe yourself as in fact being controlled by various external forces—biological rhythms, Joan—sort of viewing yourself in two ways: as you feel you need to be [free and independent], and as you feel you are [externally controlled]." I can't see how he could use it to further his work of self-inquiry and exploration. "Yes, I guess I am complicated, and perhaps also a bit mixed up," is easy to imagine for a response. Similarly, "I hear you saying that you are dependent on others to allow you to be free, that there's nothing you yourself can do to be free; you depend on others even for your independence," is certainly interesting and provocative—but what will it provoke?

It is far better, in my opinion, to keep the self-image formulation simple. The patient can be counted on to complicate it by himself, and his intellectualizing needs little support from you. Therefore, this example, "You see yourself as a person who can't be easily understood," is apt to be quite sufficient and effective. Its form takes full account of its context.

Paradigm 2

[The patient is in his late thirties. Jimmy is his roommate and is also his lover.]

Jimmy is such a bitch! The dinner party last night was a fiasco—a *miserable* fiasco! Nothing went right, nothing! And it was his fault. [pause] I told you how we planned it: we'd do everything together this time. I guess that was a *big* mistake. He's so damned unreliable! We shopped in the afternoon, and he chose the vegetables. Well, the lettuce was limp and the tomatoes tasteless, so the salad was simply awful. And the roast I prepared the evening before wasn't heated through enough because Jimmy didn't turn the oven on high enough. And the soufflé—my god, the soufflé! It never rose. I did it just the same way I always do, and I don't know why it didn't rise. [pause] I think he must have slammed the oven door when he took out the roast. He's so damned careless!— thoughtless! And I was a nervous wreck during the dinner, but not him. He couldn't have cared less. All chirpy and gay as if everything was peachy. [pause] I broke one of our best glasses. [pause] And then the after-dinner was deadly, just deadly! Nothing but a lot of inane chatter, with Jimmy right in the thick of it. I don't think anyone was amused. They all left early. [pause] It was such a fiasco! I felt awful about it. It was all Jimmy's damn fault. [pause] This therapy is something of a fiasco too. When—oh, when!—am I going to start getting better?

The defense is externalization of blame and responsibility, the self-image is the blameless one or innocent victim, and the transference is a combination of the two. Each of the three interpretations I had in mind when I composed the paradigm shares the same motif, but each has to be formulated in a different way.

The transference interpretation can be formulated simply and succinctly in the form of a direct response to the patient's final question (or call it a complaint). "When I start doing my job right?" can be your remark, and it captures the point quite fully. It qualifies as an "astringent" formulation, but it's far from "tender";[1] it may embarrass the patient, and also may strike him as defensive. Still, it doesn't exceed the tactlessness of this student's remark, "It sounds as if you're angry at me for not making the therapy go just as you'd like." Another student's, "I take it that part of you would like to blame me for that," is a nice compromise that makes the point as succinctly and maintains a certain tenderness.

Here is an interesting interpretation, not succinct or astringent, that epitomizes tenderness: "It sounds as if your disappointment over the dinner party has disturbed you so much that other experiences, such as your therapy, seem like fiascos too. Perhaps you blame me as you blamed Jimmy for not caring enough, and you don't feel you can rely on me to help you either." Its emphasis on caring is important; that is a transference motif that always deserves special attention, especially in a form of therapy which is marked by your extreme neutrality and impersonality.

Another example that underscores the motif of caring is, "Perhaps you are saying that just as Jimmy didn't care about how the party went, I don't care about how the therapy is going, and that in some way my not caring is responsible for its being a fiasco." Notice how the externalization of blame is integrated with the theme of caring. That's a far more effective way to handle

---

1. I am referring to Emanuel Hammer's recommendation that, "The style of interpretation is often best when both astringent and tender, astringent in content and tender in manner" (in *Use of Interpretation in Treatment*, p. 34). However, after adding the recommendation that an interpretation be offered tentatively, in the manner of one of several possibilities, Hammer writes the following: "Similarly, if a patient gives a rationalization, the therapist might say, *'Yes, and for what other reasons?'* or *'Yes, and what else?'* " And the rationale for saying it this way is, "This doesn't make the patient feel he has been called a liar, and yet shows the therapist not to be naive. At the same time it moves the patient forward towards the more basic reason behind the secondary or 'good' reason he initally offered." It should be clear why I disagree with that technical suggestion. I regard it as a confusion of tenderness with disingenuousness; and it's apt to be a naive way to demonstrate a lack of "naivete." The average-expectable patient is just as likely to respond with "No, there is no other reason. But you wouldn't have made your remark if you thought my reason was good and sufficient, so please tell me what you have in mind instead of directing me to come up with the *real* reason."

the defense, in the context of the transference, than the way this example does it: "I appreciate the fact that you're very upset about what happened. But I wonder what you think of the possibility that you want me to be as unreliable and as thoughtless as Jimmy, because then you could blame me for therapy being a fiasco." It is tactful enough, and it has the advantage of suggesting that the patient "wants" you to be responsible, but I believe the formulation would be improved if it implicated the theme of caring—which it could easily do.

Here's a good example which focuses on caring: "When you said how Jimmy seemed so unconcerned and nonchalant during dinner, while you were upset, it occurred to me that you might be expressing some of your thoughts about how things are here"; the patient then asks, "What do you mean?" and the student continues, "That perhaps you see me as being indifferent, or unconcerned, at times when you feel like a *nervous wreck*"—the implication being that the transference reaction is a defensive distortion stemming from the way he is feeling about himself. But notice how you haven't committed yourself to a cause-effect formulation, and the patient can still insist that it is your "indifference" that causes him to be a "nervous wreck." If he did insist, then you mustn't say anything which could be construed as disputing his formulation, especially if he seems adamant and certain about it. You have to proceed carefully and accurately, and patiently. Your aim should be to exploit the dinner-party event, insofar as it provides a vivid analogue to the therapy situation, to probe (gently, tactfully, and "tenderly") for some evidence that he is externalizing the blame—and it will have to be evidence that he can accept without undue embarrassment or defensiveness, so that he can begin to take some of the responsibility for at least the defense itself. How that can be done is examined below.

The following example is not the way to do it—not all at once, in any case: "I believe you are thinking that I, like Jimmy, am causing your failures and confusions. From what you've told me, though, I get the impression that at least a good part of the failure of the party was your own doing, that you tried to undermine the party because you weren't in stage-center of it. Similarly, you feel therapy is a failure because you are only partly in control of its outcome." Notice its three distinct and separate parts; they should be developed distinctly and separately. Notice also how the third part is a non sequitur, and how the second part is highly judgmental.

Judging from my students' work, it seems more difficult for us to maintain tact and tenderness when addressing a patient's self-image. For example, the same student who gave the "tender" transference interpretation I cited above gives this self-image interpretation: "You seem to see yourself as surrounded by incompetent people, who you blame for any failures. That way you can think of yourself as being able to do a really great job at anything were it not for the interference of others." Such challenging, refutation-begging, and fighting words—what could be less tender? Moreover, while students interpret the transference in a rather uniform way, that isn't true for their self-image interpretations. Many opt for a formulation based on the patient's seeing himself as the perfect one, rather than the blameless one, and those formulations tend to be very tactless. Consider, "It sounds as if you see yourself as the only one who does everything right," and "I wonder if you're not also upset because your image of yourself as someone who does things *just right* has been tarnished." Such remarks are obviously difficult to make while still maintaining an empathic and nonjudgmental position.

Here's a way of formulating the self-image that's somewhat more tactful, but it misses the point in a way that may be construed by the patient as little more than a challenge: "The fact that you were so nervous at dinner because everything wasn't absolutely perfect tells us something, I think, about the way you think of yourself and about the standards you set for yourself in life: things have to be either 100 percent okay or else they're 100 percent awful, a miserable fiasco." It's too easy to imagine him objecting to the "absolutely" and the all-or-nothing characterization.

Students also attempt to go beneath the surface and explain his self-image as a cover for quite the opposite image, which is always risky and usually inimical. "It seems imporant to you to see everything as someone else's fault. Perhaps you are afraid of how you might feel if you felt responsible for things going wrong," is also a feeble attempt because it's so vague. (How might he feel?) This one spells it out: "You seem to feel that you're a competent, capable person, and it's other people's fault if things go wrong. Maybe this is your way of avoiding other feelings which you can't face in yourself, feelings of inferiority, failure, and helplessness." (But it has to be obvious by now why I don't like it.) Explanations of his self-image can wait until the patient himself wonders why it is what it is; otherwise, the explanation runs the risk of being either evaluative-critical or an explaining-away. Therefore, the following example strikes the best compromise, and shows how a self-image interpretation can be maximally useful: "I appreciate how upset you are, including your pessimism about therapy; but I feel that one of the reasons for your despair lies in your intense feeling of being the helpless victim—doomed to be hurt and misunderstood by others, and yet unable to do anything to make things better." I would substitute "need to see yourself as" for "your intense feeling of being."

The defense interpretation—aside from its implication in the transference (that is, discounting the final sentence of the paradigm)—is perhaps the most problematic of all three. For when a defense like externalization occurs in the context of an account that a patient has given, when it lies outside the therapy itself, it cannot be explored and analyzed without his active cooperation. Bear in mind that you are in no position to make an independent judgment of the degree to which Jimmy was in fact responsible for the "fiasco." You have little choice but to accept the patient's word for the reality, and you want to preserve your neutrality. "Perhaps by blaming Jimmy for the entire fiasco you can absolve yourself of all the blame," is an exampe of what many students suggest, and it fails to satisfy the criteria of neutrality, not to mention empathy and tact. Similarly, "It seems to me that you are getting angry at Jimmy to avoid getting angry at yourself for your own contribution to the evening's problems," is risky because the patient may have no sense of his own contribution. Such interpretations seem to imply that you are challenging his reality testing and taking on the role of skeptic.

In order to minimize that implication, there must be some basis to infer that he was in fact partly responsible, and you must be prepared to say on what basis you're making such an inference. The following example has good form, insofar as it suggests to the patient that he suspects the defense, but it makes no reference to any evidence for the claim: "I understand that you are feeling very upset right now; but I think a part of you suspects that by being so upset about Jimmy's shortcomings you're avoiding any painful realizations about what might be some of your own." He is likely to appreciate your tact and care, but may wonder what makes you think he "suspects" the avoidance—just because he's "so upset"? Similarly, "I wonder if by being the one to worry and suffer you are alleviating guilt about your own responsibility for things going badly," implies a logic (or psychologic) that may be puzzling to him, and he may wonder what makes you think so.

The matter of evidence is also germane to a formulation's diagnostic form. A good measure of how diagnostic it may be is how you could respond to the patient's rejoinder "What makes you think so?" If your answer had to resort to normative or theoretical considerations, it was a more diagnostic formulation than one based on evidence that he had already provided. For example, "I sense that your vulnerability to what others think of you is so great that you defend yourself against the possibility of pain by blaming them before they can blame you," is highly diagnostic in several respects, one being the fact that no evidence is alluded to—nor is it easy to see how you could provide any were the patient to ask, "What makes you sense that?" Similarly, "I realize you're very upset about the party, but do you see perhaps that your blaming Jimmy is one way that you avoid responsibility? If you allowed yourself to think that the fault may be partially yours you would then have to face certain feelings about yourself that are unbearable, feelings of failure, incompetence, and helplessness," is a tactful and altogether plausible formulation, and he might well accept it, but the risk is that he can't (or won't); he may require some evidence. Similarly, "It seems to me that you are getting angry at Jimmy to avoid getting angry at yourself for your own contribution to the evening's problems," may evoke the querulous challenge, "What contribution?"

But the paradigm does contain some evidence—for instance, the fact that he felt like a "nervous wreck" during the party and the fact that he broke a glass (perhaps also the fact that he only "thought" Jimmy didn't turn the oven on high enough or that he slammed the oven door). This evidence can be pressed into service to suggest that he included it in order to hint at his own part in the fiasco. "You tell me in great detail what Jimmy did to make things go wrong, and how things are wrong here too," begins a student, but instead of making reference to the patient's contribution, he simply continues with the flagrantly judgmental remark, "Perhaps by focusing on what others are doing wrong you avoid looking at how you feel about yourself."

I would structure a defense interpretation around the evidence the patient has given which suggests he played a significant part in spoiling the party. My main point would be that the evidence seems to undercut his contention that it was all Jimmy's fault, and perhaps the patient meant it to do exactly that. In other words, he intended for me to tell him he was externalizing all the blame because part of him suspects that fact. Why he needs for me to tell him is certainly a germane issue; it can be viewed as an integral part of the defensive strategy, insofar as my interpretations reflect the way I am accepting blame and responsibility; but it can wait until the externalization onto Jimmy has been explored. I would begin, therefore, by drawing attention to the parts of the patient's account where he alluded to his own culpability—his being so nervous and worried, his breaking the good glass, perhaps also his not participating in the conversation—and the parts where he had no direct proof of Jimmy's dereliction but only inferred it. Then I would suggest that he included them because part of him suspects that the blame was not all Jimmy's, but it is painful for him to acknowledge that suspicion. I would then look for an opportunity to say, "I think you realize that you are blaming him too much, that you are overdoing it—and I think you want me to say that to you; I think you need for me to tell you that you're defending yourself against accepting any of the blame and responsibility."

A student approaches the issue somewhat along the lines I am suggesting, by pointing out, "Right now you seem most angry at Jimmy, but during the dinner party you took most of the responsibility on yourself"; and when the patient asks, "How do you mean?" the student explains this way: "Well, you said you were a nervous wreck during dinner; it sounded as though you might have been blaming yourself quite a bit then, and it seems as though now you're focusing that blame on Jimmy. Maybe you changed the direction of your criticism because of how painful it was when you directed it at yourself.'' Notice how this line of interpretation succeeds in elucidating the defense in a way that is tactful and nonjudgmental, and at the same time doesn't have a strong diagnostic flavor. The diagnostic element is there, of course—it's virtually impossible to avoid it altogether when offering such an interpretation—but it is held to a minimum. And above all, notice how you aren't pussy-footing around the issue; you are addressing it directly. Being nondirective does not mean being indirect.

Paradigm 3

[The patient is in his early twenties.]

Jayne and I were alone then. [pause] She was beside me on the sofa, and I'm sure she was waiting for me to make an overture—she was expecting me to. But I couldn't. I couldn't make myself do it. I just sat there as if I was frozen. [pause] All I had to do was put my arm around her, make some sort of a move. I knew she expected me to, and I knew she would accept it, but it was as if I was waiting for her to make the first move— even though I knew she wouldn't. She expected *me* to. . . . Oh, God! [tone of anguish] I wanted to be close to her, I really did. But I couldn't start. [pause] I just can't understand why not! [long silence] [*What are you thinking about?*] How I used to fight with my cousin Ellen when we were little kids. I've told you about that, haven't I? I don't know why it comes to mind now. We fought in anger sometimes, but sometimes we weren't so angry. [pause] I guess we just enjoyed it. But whenever my mother caught us, she would give me a long lecture about how it's bad to fight. A gentleman never fights! And she expected me to be a perfect gentleman—perfectly gentle all the time. To be rough was the biggest sin. And all of us—not just me, my father and brother too—were always models of good manners and breeding. Never say anything critical to anyone! Never hurt anyone's feelings! Never impose yourself! The Jews, you know, were bad because they were so pushy. The Catholics were too uncouth, the Blacks too aggressive. We were the perfect Protestants, WASPs. [long silence] I assume you are Jewish, and I feel bad I said that about Jews. Look here, I don't really believe it. I'm no bigot—just a damn mouse! [pause] I really wish you wouldn't just . . . I wish you'd tell me why I couldn't make a simple pass at Jayne.

If you wanted to tell him why, you could do it easily; he has spelled it out clearly enough. His apparent equation of sex and aggression, together with his mother's insistence on nonaggressive gentlemanly behavior, provides ample basis for an explanation. Consequently, the paradigm invites an interpretation that is both gratuitous and diagnostic. I count as too gratuitous such examples as, "It seems you feel to be assertive and aggressive is bad, so when you're in a situation that arouses such impulses you freeze," and "Perhaps you feel that a sexual advance is like a fight ...' '; and I regard these three as too diagnostic: "In making a pass you would show you can be assertive, but displaying this kind of behavior might cause you anxiety because to act that way might be to impose yourself, and it's against what your mother taught''; "I wonder if perhaps the feeling of being frozen and unable to move farther was in one sense a way of keeping in check your desire to be rough and tumble, just as you had been with your cousin Ellen''; "Your sitting *as if frozen* seems to have been a way of insuring that you don't get carried away." And even a well-formulated interpretation, like this one, has an excessively diagnostic texture: "I wonder if you become passive and freeze when you feel anxious about what you might do; perhaps you become passive when you feel like being more aggressive, but this frightens you." Students speak of the patient's "protecting" himself, of "fearing" aggression, or "fearing" the enjoyment of it; one writes, "Perhaps you experience yourself as impotent because it would be so frightening to allow yourself to really feel the full strength of your sexual or aggressive impulses''; and one focuses on the unacceptable impulse with, "Perhaps you use your gentlemanly behavior to hide feelings of aggression; maybe you are afraid that if you assert yourself you will hurt someone." All of these interpretations may be valid enough, but the question is this: Should you elect to explain matters in that way? (And would I have raised the question if my answer were yes?)

Now, I may be giving the impression that we ought never to comment on past events being recounted by our patient, so I want to make it clear how that impression is inaccurate. We aren't limited to silence, or to clarification questions, when he is working on an event that occurred in the near or remote past, when he's recounting and reliving the event in order to understand what happened and why he did and felt what he did and felt. We are only constrained in offering him the explanations he is seeking; we may have to frustrate his wish for our explanations. But that doesn't mean we can't participate usefully in the *therapeutic process*, that we can't offer remarks and observations that may help him arrive at his explanations and might facilitate the process of exploration and discovery. For instance, suppose that instead of asking, "What are you thinking about?" after the first long silence in Paradigm 3, you wanted to make a useful observation; you could say, "You emphasized how much she expected you to make the first move; I gather you're thinking that may have been why you couldn't." Or you might remark, "I gather you felt something inside you holding you back."

Or suppose you felt the need for a useful remark after the second long silence, before the transference issue got raised; you could articulate the self-image, without at the same time implying that it served any defensive function. But even that restriction needn't be so stringent. When we judge that a defense interpretation may be useful, and we have no option but to interpret it in the then and there (there is no here-and-now analogue for it), we can do it in the context of the patient's self-image, by formulating it the way Freud originally construed defense (as a way of protecting, maintaining, and supporting our "egos"[2]). To be sure, this lends the interpretation a distinctly diagnostic cast, but there's a significant difference between "This behavior serves the function of defending you ..." and "This behavior fits your self-image as the ..."; the latter is more empathic, and can be more useful for a patient's work of inquiry and exploration.

Here's an example which puts it succinctly, though perhaps also gratuitously: "Perhaps it was impossible because it was something a perfect gentleman wouldn't do." I think the remark could benefit from the addition, " ... and you need to see yourself that way." Similarly, this one, "I wonder if you see sex as some kind of struggle, some kind of aggressive imposition, something a gentleman doesn't do," would benefit from, " ... and it doesn't fit your image of yourself." A well-articulated, though somewhat curt, self-image interpretation is, "I think you would prefer to see yourself as a mouse who is unable to take initiative rather than risk being pushy, uncouth, or aggressive." And another student offers this interesting speculation: "Perhaps being a gentleman—though it paralyzes you in some ways—helps you preserve the idea of being special, being better than other people."

Self-image interpretations are usually most effective when they remain simple and focused, when they do not offer dynamic and functional explanations until the patient shows interest in exploring them. Nevertheless, in this case it might be useful to emphasize that he may be struggling to shake his mother's values or her role in his self-image. However, "I believe you're afraid to see yourself as strong and aggressive because you feel you might risk losing your mother's love," doesn't achieve this end, partly because it's too explanatory and partly because the explanation is vague and abstruse. Some students speak of a conflict among his self-images, which is generally a useful kind of formulation to make—but only when there's some evidence for it. Here's one that's quite excellent, were it not so speculative: "Is it possible you choose to think of yourself as an ineffective mouse because you're in conflict about whether you have the right to experience and act on the same feelings of anger and aggression and sexuality that other people have?"

---

2. Freud's first conception of *ego* was simply the individual's values, ideals, and standards of conduct. Accordingly, the chief function of defense was to protect and maintain his sense of who he was and what he ought to be, his self-image. "A person like me ought not to have such ideas and feelings, therefore I couldn't have them—therefore I don't," is the paradigm of defense and conforms with the topographic point of view.

Notice how the self-image interpretations I've cited speak only of the patient's "viewing" himself as unaggressive and inoffensive. I believe it's important to keep from suggesting to him (as this formulation seems to, "It's important to you to see yourself as a mouse because then you must be too innocuous to offend anyone") that he was in fact unaggressive and inoffensive. Maybe he did, after all, hurt Jayne with his passivity? Maybe that's the reason he felt guilty?—not because his impulse was sexual-aggressive. This intriguing and potentially insightful possibility is bolstered by the fact that he is feeling guilty right now, for having insulted you, and perhaps also because he is again taking the passive position. "I think a part of you is feeling guilty now," suggests a student, "Maybe you think you have hurt my feelings and that I am angry with you." But then he continues in a way that misses the point, "And now you may be anticipating a scolding or lecture from me, believing that I, like your mother, only expect you to be a polite good boy." Better to suggest that he also felt he'd hurt Jayne.

He may also be feeling guilty because he is asking you to do something he himself should be doing: explaining his behavior with Jayne. Since he has already provided ample material to explain it, he has put you in a perfect position to say, as one student does, "I think you've already partly answered the question, and it has to do with the way you think of yourself—as someone who was taught never to impose, not to be pushy, aggressive, and so forth." Another student puts it succinctly, "So you think it's possible that you couldn't make a move because you were afraid of being aggressive." In other words, you can observe that he already has an answer; many students include that suggestion in their interpretations.

This raises a further question: Why does he need you to give the explanation? And many students answer it by suggesting that he needs you to take the initiative in therapy in the same way he needed for Jayne to take it. For example, "You want me to take the initiative here, the way you wanted Jayne to take it on the sofa; maybe it'd be *imposing yourself* into my work if you took the initiative in explaining why you couldn't make that pass."

On the other hand, when things are as obvious as they seem to be in this paradigm there is the temptation to look for the nonobvious. Though he has given a perfectly good explanation for his inhibition, the patient claims to be mystified; perhaps he's right, the real explanation has not been given. "Perhaps you are living up to your mother's expectations—with a vengeance," suggests a student, and then continues with the nonobvious possibility, "By acting the perfect gentleman too well with Jayne you may have hurt her; yet you don't experience any anger that you may have toward women." In other words, he may actually have been behaving hurtfully, while protecting his self-image as the nonaggressive one.

When we venture a nonobvious interpretation, we run the risk of defining ourselves as shrewd and clever ones who don't take things at face value. Such a role definition has to be avoided, and therefore interpretations which raise nonobvious possibilities have to be given with special care and circumspection. If I thought it useful to ferret out a nonobvious explanation for Paradigm 3, I would go about it slowly and gradually. "I take it one reason you felt bad was because you sensed that Jayne felt hurt," is a good and tactful way to begin, simply drawing attention to the effect his action had on her. Of course, the fact that she was hurt doesn't meant that was his intention, but such an approach might lead him to consider the possibility that it was. If he is taken aback by the suggestion, and if he wants some evidence for it, I would offer two points: that he stressed how much she expected him to make a sexual overture, and that he believed I was hurt by his remark about Jews.

Consider, however, nonobvious interpretations such as these: "I think that here you have an urge to be closer to me, to put your arm around me; and you're waiting for me to make some kind of overture, to be the aggressive one," and "It sounds to me as if you're not sure now whether it would be fun to fight with me, like with Ellen, or whether I'd lecture you about it like your mother." More than nonobvious, perhaps, they are overly literal and far-fetched. Given the patient's anguish, such remarks are likely to be jarring; and they have the quality of hoisting him on his own petard. Notice how much more sensitive and empathic is this rendition of the same theme: "I wonder if you aren't doing in therapy what you describe yourself doing with Jayne, feeling yourself to be frozen and unable to express what you really feel. Similarly, you want me to make the first move, to be the assertive one. One way you would like me to do it is by providing you with the answer."

Many students make similar transference interpretations. Some simply stress his need for them to take the initiative, as this one does, "Now you want me to make the move, or be a little pushy." Some address themselves to his expectation that they will react either like his mother used to or in the opposite way; for example, "Perhaps you feel that I, like your mother, expect you to be a perfect gentleman, so when you are pushy or critical here you feel the need to retreat and call yourself a mouse," and "I take it you want me to play the role your mother used to but you want to change the outcome; this time you want permission, you want me to encourage you to have physical contact with women," and one student puts it more generally, "You seem to be having difficulty living up to the expectations of women; Jayne expected you to make a pass, your mother expected you to be a perfect gentleman; perhaps you're concerned about what I expect of you." And some speculate that he wants them to tell him how to make a sexual advance "like a gentleman." These, on the whole, are good and potentially useful interpretations.

Paradigm 4

[The patient, in his late teens, has recently been coming late to his sessions.]

I don't know why I came late today again. I could've made it on time, but I just didn't try. It somehow didn't seem worth the effort. [pause] I bet you're angry at me for coming late. [pause] I'd ask you, but I know you won't answer—probably throw me an interpretation, [slightly mimicking tone] "So you want me to be angry at you, eh!" [pause] Maybe I do, I don't know. [pause] Everything stinks these days. I seem to be getting worse and worse. What's the use! [sighs and lights a cigarette] I had another big fight with my father. This time it was about my sleeping late. It really bugs him when I sleep till noon. He gets all hassled. [pause] And I'm really getting fed up with it. I wish he'd just resign himself to the fact that I'm an adolescent, and that adolescents like to sleep late. [pause] He really blew up when I told him that—flew into a rage. And I got a bit scared at how furious he got when I said "Tough shit!" You know, I was afraid he was going to hit me. [pause] But what does he expect? Ever since I was little, he always treated me in such an offhand way, as if I didn't matter much to him. And he'd make all these big promises to me and then never keep them. So naturally I wasn't going to be his good little boy. I mean, what'd he expect! [pause] He always wanted me to do well in school, but I guess I wasn't as smart as the other kids. [pause] And he wanted me to learn to play chess, but I hated it. And the piano too. [puts out cigarette and begins to weep] God, I'm such a . . . such a mess!

With respect to a self-image interpretation, this paradigm raises the question whether it's likely to be sufficiently useful to offer the patient a simple articulation, or whether some elaboration and explanation is called for. Perhaps because the material provides the opportunity, the majority of students opt for more than a simple articulation. But there are specific risks in doing that at this moment, risks of amelioration and exoneration, as well as of criticism and faulting, and there is also the risk of shifting the scene to an intellectual plane. Therefore, for the moment at any rate, while he is feeling acutely distressed and is weeping, I believe it's quite sufficient to suggest to him that he believes there's no choice but to see himself as the bad and disappointing one, the one who has to provoke anger and disapproval.

But a simple articulation needn't restrict itself to the form of "This is your self-image." It can be embedded in a formulation that takes account of what the patient is feeling and what issues he's exploring. Consider how this tactfully formulated example restricts itself to articulation and uses the self-image to explain his despair: "I appreciate how upset you are, including your pessimism about your therapy. But I feel that one of the reasons for your despair lies in your intense feeling of being the helpless victim—doomed to be hurt and misunderstood by others, and yet unable to do anything to make things better.'' Another student finds an interesting and sensitive way to formulate his simple articulation, with, ''You know, I think you're beginning to explore that aspect of yourself which feels you never lived up to your father's expectations,'' then he adds, taking into account the patient's weeping, ''And it hurts.'' Such a direct and unencumbered interpretation is relatively free of unwanted implications, and it's likely to be effective.

This succinct interpretation, ''I think a part of you gets pleasure from feeling like the hopeless one who can't be helped,'' is actually not so simple, and it might prove provocative in suggesting that he enjoys his self-image, even while he's feeling so distressed about it. And here's a curt one that's also not simple and is bound to be provocative: ''I'm wondering if perhaps, while you seem to be the poor little oppressed one, another part of you is very angry and provocative.'' And some students cast their simple articulation into a form that makes it sound like a fatherly lecture. Here's a flagrant example: ''Sometimes it's tempting to give in to feeling like a hopeless mess and unable to do things, because it's hard to always stand up for yourself and insist on your rights in the face of other people's anger,'' and here's one that is subtle: ''I understand that you are distressed by feeling like such a mess, but perhaps it is more acceptable to you to see yourself as incapable of doing anything about it than as unwilling even to try.'' This, surely, isn't the moment for such remarks, even though the patient has ''transgressed'' by being late again and has given in to feelings of hopelessness about therapy.

Some students construe the self-image as the blameless one (''It's not my fault,'' ''It's only natural''), and some emphasize his sense of unfairness over expectations he couldn't meet. That, of course, has to be done carefully in order to avoid seeming to blame him or implying that there's no good basis for his self-image. But what also has to be avoided, in my opinion, is doing the opposite—implying that he has every reason to feel about himself the way he does, that it's perfectly ''natural.'' That, it seems to me, is the main danger in any explanation given in conjunction with the self-image interpretation. For instance, many students suggest to him that his self-image is in effect a way of punishing his father for the offhand treatment, and for his being disappointed by the father. I see little merit in offering such a tit-for-tat kind of intellectual formulation, and it might only serve to buttress the self-image. Thus, even a shrewd explanation, like the following, can be overly intellectual and serve the interests of further defense: ''I wonder whether you need to think of yourself as someone who is messed up and bad because then you can protect yourself from being disappointed by others by disappointing them first.'' And what else but grateful acceptance can follow an explanation like, ''It is safer for you to feel like the bad boy than to feel like the good boy who deserves to be loved and still gets treated in an offhand manner''?

An interesting kind of self-image formulation, which deserves a closer examination than I'm going to give it, is exemplified by the following: "Perhaps in order to explain your father's offhand treatment of you, you need to see yourself as a mess and a failure." This cognitive formulation, construing the patient's self-image as a measure to reduce cognitive dissonance, is favored by many teachers and practitioners. Commonly it's done simply by suggesting, "You behave as you believe you are expected to behave; your self-image conforms to the image you believe others have of you," and in our patient's case it can be put in terms of his father having long expected him to be the failure. Without questioning its validity, I want to question its utility. Not that the patient isn't likely to welcome the formulation; chances are, however, he'll use it in the interests of intellectual defense rather than for making useful discoveries. In my opinion, it runs the risk of explaining things away. It may provide some useful structure for his synthetic-function, but it may also provide too much; it may be too purely a cognitive and intellectual construction. Therefore, I prefer the way the following example articulates his belief about his self-image: "I think you very much want to believe that you were forced to be rebellious and to do badly at school, but a part of you fears that it is all your fault—that you are a bad person, that your father rejected you because there was something wrong with you." Perhaps I am relying too much on intuition when I judge that such a formulation, if it happens to be valid, can have a kind of impact which isn't purely cognitive-intellectual. Notice how it implicates the volitional and affective realms of experience, even while it does speak to the patient's synthetic-function. Notice also how free it is of nomothetic overtones.

Paradigm 4 provides for a transference formulation which draws a direct parallel to the patient's father. The emphasis can be on the theme of indifference—for example, "Perhaps you're thinking that I too treat you in an offhand way, and so you aren't going to be my *good little boy* and come on time or get better." It can include anger—"It occurs to me that your wish that I be angry with you for coming late would mean I care for you, just as you attempted to get your father to stop treating you in an offhanded way by doing poorly in school or hating the piano." It can speculate that a reaction of anger is better than nothing—"I think you're feeling so sad and discouraged about therapy because you expect I'll be like your father, that you'll have to be a good boy here too, and that it still won't matter, that I won't care about you. Perhaps you come late to try to provoke my anger because you feel that the anger would at least show I care about you—just as your father notices you only when you can provoke his anger." Several students infer a motive—for example, "I think you want me to comfort you and show you I really care about you, just like you would want your father to do." Some infer an affect—"I wonder if you could be feeling angry at me because I am becoming important to you, and you are afraid I'll disappoint you and let you down as you say your father does." And a few formulate the transference in terms of their being a figure whose expectations are so high they can't be satisfied—for example, at the end of a long and rambling interpretation, a student says, "Part of you, however, believes you can only disappoint me if you *do* try—that you can never live up to my expectations anyway, as you felt you couldn't meet your father's—so why bother." All of these, in my estimation, are bound to be good interpretations, though they may also be quite superficial.

To be sure, transference processes needn't be complex, and certainly it's good technique to formulate them as simply and parsimoniously as possible. But there's a distinction between simplicity and superficiality; a formulation that extends to an underlying level needn't be complex; in fact, when we seek to understand at a deeper level, matters often become less complex. Consider, then, the likelihood that the patient has a need to cast you in the same image as his father, as the one who disapproves and disappoints, who breaks his promises and reacts in anger. But consider further the fact that you don't disapprove and disappoint, you don't break your promises and react in anger—and the patient senses that. This raises the possibility that he is experiencing a fear, not of your being like his father, but of your being exactly unlike him. Moreover, the transference he's experiencing has a distinctly resistive cast; it seems to be serving the need to withdraw from therapy. (In fact, this paradigm might well be included in the next chapter, among the Resistance Paradigms.) This suggests that the patient is experiencing some danger in the therapy, and wishes to flee. The question becomes, What is it he's afraid of? And one potentially intriguing and useful answer is that he's afraid that you're not going to fulfill his transference "needs," you're not going to be like his father.

A student formulates this idea in an especially tactful and sensitive way with, "I know you're feeling very upset, and I think you're telling me that if I expect anything of you, just like your father, I will only be disappointed and angry because you're such a mess. I wonder, however, if you don't need to see things that way because the possibility that I won't react as your father has is even more disturbing to you." Though I didn't have this formulation in mind when I composed the paradigm, I'd like to think that in practice it would occur to me, and I'd share it with the patient.

A handful of students infer from his tears that the patient is feeling afraid. "Your tears suggest that maybe you are afraid that I will be angry, so you are telling me not to hurt you now," says one, and continues to spell out the transference implications (perhaps quite unnecessarily, because the interpretation already says a good deal) with, "I have an idea about the reason for that feeling, which is that you see me like your father, whose anger when you are a *bad boy* frightens you." Another interprets the tears as a signal: "Your crying might be sort of signaling me that you don't want me to hurt you—for coming late, or for sleeping late" (which draws an allusion to the father). And one ends an interpretation of the patient's efforts to provoke anger with, "So in order to nullify my anger, you cry."

These formulations overlap with the defense interpretation I had in mind when I composed the paradigm, except that I construed the weeping as the patient's defense against his own rage. Of course, since he isn't wondering why he's crying, it's bound to be an imposition to tell him; and chances are he'd either be perplexed or enraged by any suggestion that his tears were anything but expressions of despair. Still, he might be able to work with the idea that his despair was related to self-criticism and derogation, that he was defending himself by internalizing the blame or turning aggression back on himself. How to say this to him is a big problem, and the following is a poor solution because of its flagrantly diagnostic form: "At first you were criticizing your father in what seemed to be an angry way, but then you turned the criticism on yourself, saying what a mess you are. That self-criticism, which makes you feel bad enough to cry, seems to be your way of preventing yourself from getting really angry or critical towards your father, and perhaps towards other people too" (meaning, of course, "me"). Better to try a more succinct remark, like, "You were furious at your father a moment ago, and now you seem to be furious at yourself," and see if he uses the help. Another example, "It sounds as if you are very angry at your father for treating you as he did, and what you do with the anger is turn it against yourself and say you're just a bad boy, someone who isn't good enough to live up to your father's expectations," is considerably less diagnostic but could benefit from further simplification.

Students' defense interpretations reflect a lot of unclarity, and more frequently than for the other three paradigms, I had recourse to the comment, *What's the defense?* For example, "I wonder if you use your anger at your father to cover up that you feel bad that you don't seem to matter much to him"—What's the defense? Similarly, "It sounds as if it hurt you when he didn't seem to care, but that was such an awful thing to feel you provoked him to anger, and when he was angry you at least felt he cared"—What's the defense? Many speak of his making others angry as a way to secure their love or as a means of avoiding disappointment or as a wish to be taken care of. In other words, the defense is provocation to anger. Some construe the being bad as a defense—for example, "I believe that you avoid being the good boy now so as not to be hurt all over again,'' which sounds like an interesting variation of avoidance. And, finally, a few formulate a purely resistance interpretation, like this one, ''You seem to be saying your performance in school and with the piano was a way of paying your father back for his indifference. I wonder if a part of you would like to fail at therapy because you believe I too am indifferent.'' Which is a good place to end this discussion, because resistance is the subject of the next chapter.

8

The Resistance Paradigms

Though a patient's motivation to change is likely to have a significant influence, and sometimes a most profound effect, on the course and outcome of his therapy, we can usually take it for granted that he feels deep conflict about changing. In fact, I believe it is always a good and prudent assumption that, no matter what his stake in making changes (overcoming his painful symptoms, his debilitating inhibitions, his intolerable condition), he also has a substantial stake in staying the way he is. The motivation not to change can be conceptualized in a variety of ways and can take a variety of different forms; but however conceptualized and whatever its form, it can be so powerful a force that to lose sight of it and fail to give it the active attention it deserves—by articulating and formulating it at every turn, by analyzing and explaining it in every form, and by working it through and reformulating it in every way—is to place the patient and his therapy in several kinds of peril. *Resistance* is the broad clinical rubric under which this ''negative'' or ''inertial'' motivation is commonly classified.

There is, however, a narrower and more circumscribed definition of resistance, which reserves the term for episodes of what can be called ''flights from therapy.'' This narrow definition will serve my purposes in this chapter better than the broad one because, while a nondirective therapy has no special technical problems dealing with resistance in the broad sense of the term, it does when dealing with resistances that are directed against the therapy itself. Those problems are serious enough to merit special attention, therefore I designed a set of paradigms to study them exclusively.

214

Resistance

An intimate relationship obviously exists between the narrow definition of resistance and the broad one, and we could easily formulate the latter in terms of the *therapeutic process* by defining it as the defensive measures a patient takes against the process itself.[1] That definition, however, is likely to be of little practical utility unless we can specify criteria by which to identify defenses which also threaten the integrity of the therapy as a whole—the narrow definition. Otherwise we would have to contend—as many psychoanalysts do—that, since the *therapeutic process* (in psychoanalysis the *analytic process*—more specifically, the quality of free-association) never achieves its full potential, our patient is always in a state of resistance. Not that this point of view is devoid of practical significance: it reminds us what a high priority must be given to resistance and insures that defenses will remain a principal focus of our attention. But it fails to distinguish those departures from optimal state of affairs that demand our special attention and active intervention: empirical manifestations of a serious withdrawal both from the work of therapy and from the therapy itself.

The most commonly encountered resistances are not difficult to identify. Their characteristic feature is withdrawal or evasion, and for that reason the term *flight* is commonly used to denote their different forms; sometimes they are referred to as impasses. When a patient becomes preoccupied with quitting therapy or experiences a strong sense of detachment and uninvolvement, it is obviously a resistance of this kind. But it can also be a resistance, or the manifestation of a resistance, when his thoughts become blocked and scattered, when he falls into protracted silences, experiences a loss of interest, a reduction of urgency to speak, or the sense that there is nothing worth speaking and thinking about. Furthermore, it can also be regarded as a state of resistance when there's a sense of things having slowed down or of having reached a plateau, when he is speaking freely enough but not about what is most vital and meaningful to him. Since the hallmark of the well-functioning *therapeutic process* is not a continuous stream of speech (such a criterion will not satisfy anyone familiar with what is called "resistance in the form of free-association"), since its essence is best captured in the phrase *It is a striving after self-revelation*, it doesn't stretch matters too much to expect that a patient speak of things which are meaningful to him and that his attitude be

---

1. The broad definition, which construes resistance as synonymous with any major defense against significant change and growth, derives from the way the psychoanalytic conception of defense originated. It was the clinical phenomenon of resistance, as well as the subsequent observation that the forms of a patient's resistance tend to correspond closely to his major defensive proclivities, that led Freud to give "defense" a metapsychological status.

one of inquiry and exploration. Qualities such as lack of involvement, activeness, and reflectiveness are not so difficult for us to identify, they are only difficult to deal with and still preserve the spirit and format of *Psychotherapy*.

The most serious difficulty arises when we have sufficient evidence to know that resistance is taking place but our patient is unaware of it—and this, unfortunately, is a fairly common characteristic of resistance. It is often unaccompanied by any phenomenal counterpart. This can apply to the more obvious manifestations as much as to the subtle ones; often a flagrant resistance will occur without his being aware of its resistive function. Ideally, we should wait until he at least catches a glimpse of that function; we shouldn't impose the idea (by making interventions that are necessarily confronting and diagnostic). But usually we cannot wait for that recognition because the therapy itself may be in jeopardy. The danger of a serious impasse is always great when resistance is high, and a resistance that begins with a withdrawal from the *therapeutic process* can grow into an intention to quit altogether; the theme "I need no longer *work* in therapy" is easily and logically transformed into "I need no longer *be* in therapy."

The Resistance Paradigms were designed to examine some of the more common manifestations and the ways they can be dealt with in *Psychotherapy*. I regard this study as the most problematic of this book, chiefly because it can be enormously difficult, and often it is practically impossible, to deal adequately with resistances without a substantial reliance on confrontations, without resorting to diagnostic and highly speculative interpretations, without sacrificing tact and empathy, and without our assuming a role posture that is inimical to the unique definition that *Psychotherapy* strives for.

Before turning to the study I want to emphasize that when a patient makes a comment like one of those I have written in the four paradigms, he isn't necessarily in a state of resistance. It's quite impossible to lift material out of its clinical context and assign it an invariant meaning or fit it into a conceptual category. However, the content of each paradigm is specifically designed to exemplify a resistance; I composed each one by first formulating a particular resistance, and then, with that formulation firmly in mind, writing a brief exemplification or rendition of it. And since their only purpose is to provide a means for studying purely technical problems, certain assumptions I made in composing the paradigms have to be accepted. The chief assumption is that the patient is manifesting a resistance, and it is a condition which has to be resolved; if it isn't, it may lead him to terminate therapy prematurely. Your chief technical problem is how to take steps to resolve that resistance, how to translate the latent theme into an effective therapeutic intervention that remains fully consonant with the principles of *Psychotherapy*.

The translation of a thematic formulation into a therapeutic intervention always requires great care, but when the subject is resistance—and the "subject" is in a state of resistance—it requires a very special care. The pitfalls and dangers, the likelihood of unwanted implications and dissonant attitudes, are greater for resistance interpretations than for any other because, for one thing, the patient is in a highly defensive posture (and sometimes in a fighting mood). What is especially problematic is how to maintain an empathic sensitivity to what he is experiencing, while taking active steps to open up for exploration the resistance factor itself. When the patient has no direct experience of the resistance, which happens to be a fairly typical concomitant of resistance, it falls to you to introduce the topic and raise the possibility, and that's practically impossible to do without resorting to confrontations and slipping into the roles of skeptic, judge, diagnostician, and defender of the faith. Moreover, attempts to use interpretations are bound to require substantial amounts of speculation, and while speculation in itself is no special problem, there is the special danger of seeming to use it against the patient, so to speak. Breaches in your neutrality may be difficult to avoid during states of resistance—and sometimes it isn't altogether possible—because, for one thing, you have an ulterior motive: your goal is not merely to understand but to prevent a premature termination.

Nevertheless, I believe the problems posed by resistances can generally be solved within the constraints of *Psychotherapy*, that "flights from therapy" can usually be dealt with interpretively, with a degree of empathy and tact that may not be perfect but still sufficient, and with a neutrality that may be strained but nevertheless adequately maintained. It requires, however, great technical care and facility. It usually puts our craft to its severest test.

The Resistance Paradigms

Instructions: In each of the following extracts from hypothetical therapy sessions, there is an underlying theme that reflects a resistance phenomenon. What's involved in each case is a defensive move directed against the therapy and/or the therapist, you. The assignment is to identify the theme and then write an intervention that can be given to the patient. Each paradigm is drawn from a different patient, and each occurs after the opening stages of therapy have been completed.

Paradigm 1

Boy, am I ever feeling great these days! I don't know what I'm doing here any more, everything is going so well. You know, I've been getting to all my classes, even the morning ones, I finished the

Socio. paper yesterday, handed it in right on time, and I'm working on the English assignment too. For the first time in a long time I can actually sit down like a person and apply myself without getting all restless and jittery. And I can get my ideas down on paper; the words come, they feel right. Boy, is that ever a good feeling! [pause] I spoke to my father on the phone last night, and for the first time in a long time he didn't hassle me. You know something, it was practically a human conversation. I didn't get the usual feeling he was bugging me about every damn thing. He made only one remark that got to me: when I told him I was working on the papers he said his usual thing, "You're a real *macher* [achiever], eh!" [pause] But you know what, I just brushed it off, didn't let it hassle me at all. I felt like saying back, "And you're a real *shlemihl* [loser], eh!" —but I didn't. I just shut up. [pause] I was rapping with Henry a couple of days ago, and he said he never saw me so cool, so relaxed. You know what he said?—therapy has done me a lot of good. I'm a new man. [pause] I'm not so tense and so worried anymore; I can laugh and fool around. [pause] And it's really true. It's marvelous!

If this transcript reflects or depicts a resistance—and that is our ruling assumption—it can only be what is usually called a "flight into health." "Because I am doing so well, because I have improved so much, it is pointless to continue with the work of therapy or the therapy itself" is the logic of the patient's narrative. Many students formulate an interpretation that articulates the logic; here are two representative examples: "Things in your life are going the way you want them to, and you say you don't know what you are doing here. Could it be that you are wondering whether to continue in therapy, whether there is any more to be gained from therapy?" and "You are telling me how well everything is going and how great you feel; I think you're saying that we have nothing left to do here." Their main shortcoming is that they make no allusion to resistance.

Articulating the patient's message can be regarded as only your first step, perhaps as a necessary preliminary step, in exploring the resistance itself, because when the patient simply concurs with the articulation (as he probably would) you will have to continue toward the resistance. Even the following example, which takes matters somewhat further by inferring conflict, remains little more than a good articulation: "I understand you've been feeling good about yourself, but I wonder if perhaps your emphasis on it is a way of saying you feel you don't need therapy anymore. Perhaps you couldn't come right out and say that because a part of you thinks you still need therapy." All it would take to transform it into a resistance interpretation is to add, " . . . and that part of you thinks [or suspects] it is a resistance—in other words, that its purpose is to enable you to feel you don't need therapy any longer." The problem, of course, and it's the key problem of this paradigm, is that there simply isn't any evidence that the patient thinks or suspects it.

However, since you do, and since you're already well familiar with the phenomenon, you have the option of simply apprising him of the fact, perhaps with a few didactic remarks by way of tactful introduction. And that is what many practitioners would do. To do otherwise, they might contend, is to deprive the patient of their professional expertise. Basically I don't disagree with them. But I would not take the didactic approach before I had attempted a purely interpretive one. My initial goal would be to help the patient recognize for himself that his condition is serving a resistive function, to discover the phenomenon rather than learn about it. To be sure, I may have to speculate more than I usually do, I may have to resort to confrontations more than I ordinarily do, but I would proceed with the conviction that an interpretive approach will be more advantageous in the long run than a didactic one. And Paradigm 1 invites a number of different interpretive approaches.

Consider, first of all, the most direct, most no-nonsense and no-beating-around-the-bush, approach: to convey the message "Look here, your remarkable improvement is serving the function of getting you to quit therapy prematurely!" That epitomizes the confronting mode, and it is risky. In fact, any attempt to meet the resistance head-on is too likely to promote an impasse, which will just as surely bring therapy to an end. Some practitioners would venture a tough line that conveys the challenge "So how come you're still here?" A student comes close to it with, "I hear a contradiction in what you're saying; on the one hand, you say nothing is bothering you and everything is fine, but on the other hand you have come to therapy. Perhaps you do realize that you have problems, things you would like to say but don't, things you try hard to *brush off*." It should be obvious why I reject such an approach.

"You are making a point of talking about how well everything is going," begins one student and then he suggests simply, "I wonder if you are trying to avoid talking about some of the things that are bothering you." I suppose such a speculation can be justified as an attempt to promote the *therapeutic process*, in the sense that it enables the patient to get back to work on his remaining problems, which after all he must still have; but the attempt has a substantial risk of failing—it can just as likely promote an impasse. Even a more tactful formulation, like the following, runs a similar risk: "I can appreciate the fact that you are pleased because you are feeling happy and productive; but just as you brushed aside your father's comment so that you wouldn't be hassled, I wonder whether you find it easier to brush aside therapy for the same reason." It isn't easy to imagine the patient's responding in a useful and productive way to such fighting words; given the fact that he is in a state of resistance, he is apt to resist such a suggestion.

A second approach, which isn't much better, entails doing something we should try not to do: suggesting to the patient that the improvements he has described are not genuine and/or permanent. Now, to be privately skeptical of a patient's experience is one thing, but it quite another to lose sight of the fact that for him it can be entirely authentic and have no phenomenal counterpart even to its potential impermanence. In this paradigm I carefully avoided including any evidence that the patient regards his condition as anything but genuine and stable; my main purpose was to make it difficult for you to introduce an element of doubt. Had I ended the paradigm with an expression on his part of some doubt, or some awareness that he was exaggerating, you could simply support it with, "I take it part of you suspects that the way you're feeling may not be altogether genuine; it may be serving some other purpose, some ulterior motive perhaps." But as it stands there's no reason to infer any doubt, and you must therefore take care not to disbelieve, or seem to be questioning the authenticity of, his experience as a whole. In practice, you might choose to wait for an opening, for some evidence that the patient himself has some doubts.

Therefore, "I get the feeling you are trying to convince yourself and me that you no longer need therapy—everything is rosy," and "It seems you're saying you have no problems anymore, perhaps because this is easier than having to talk about your problems," which are flagrantly tactless versions of a kind of remark that many students suggest, are without foundation and are poor kinds of interpretations to make. They say little more than that the patient's claims are not to be believed and that he should come off it; the message is "Who are you trying to fool?" which is not the way to invite useful doubt—it's more likely to provoke resentment and defensiveness. Even less challenging and more tactful interpretations like, "I can appreciate that you are feeling good, but I wonder if a possible reason for your general good feeling is that you want to leave therapy," and "You are feeling good now, and I think you would like to stop coming to therapy before you encounter more changes that will involve greater risks and possibly be painful," run the risk of seeming to cast doubt on the authenticity of his experience. They do so, in part, because they are too blunt—and resistance is not the best issue to address bluntly. The patient is obviously unready to give the idea thoughtful consideration; he's apt to be taken aback and perplexed by it. Therefore, and at the very least, a gradual approach is called for, a stepwise form that can allow for some modulation of the doubt and some tempering of the challenge.

Some students cast their doubt by suggesting to him that not everything in his life is as good as he is claiming, that he must still have problems. Such speculations are likely to intensify the resistance instead of opening it up for exploration. Not only do they draw a big inference for which there isn't any evidence, they also have a somewhat self-serving texture. "Why such a speculation?" the patient may wonder, "For my sake or yours?" Consider the following example in this light. The student begins with this preface: "It is marvelous that you are feeling so good today," a remark apparently meant to underscore the patient's insistence on how good he's feeling, but which runs the risk of being perceived as patronizing, if not sarcastic. Then the student articulates an interpretation in two sentences, framing the first in an interesting kind of passive disavowal, as follows: "Although I can't help wondering if there aren't some things causing you problems that you are overlooking." This sort of passive formulation is well worth avoiding, assiduously. In fact, I believe it's good technique always to speak to patients in the active voice. Instead of "The thought occurs to me . . . ," we should say, "I am thinking that . . . ," and we can altogether avoid such formulations as "It struck me." At best, "I can't help wondering" has an apologetic undertone, and when you feel the need to apologize you can do so directly. At worst, it is an attempt to sweeten the bitter pill, something that is rarely necessary and useful. Finally, the student suggests, "Perhaps by telling me how great you feel and how you don't need therapy, you hope to avoid exploring areas that might cause you pain." Such a confronting, speculative interpretation—especially when the patient is in a state of resistance—can only put him on the defensive.

Similarly, those formulations that express their doubt by restricting the focus to therapy suffer the same shortcoming of making a big inference from no evidence. Here are two good examples: "You seem to be experiencing less anxiety and feeling more in control of your life; yet I am wondering if you are trying to stay in control here by declaring yourself cured and therefore not having to look at some of the unresolved and more painful issues," and "What do you think of the possibility that you are telling me how well everything is going and how great you feel in order to show that we have nothing left to do here, and you won't have to talk about things that are still distressing you?" What will you say when the patient asks, "What makes you think so?"—What evidence can you appeal to? And some students speak of his feeling "uneasy" about therapy—again, out of thin air. Given his great optimism and enthusiastic gratitude, that's likely to make him feel second-guessed, put-down, and otherwise misunderstood, even chastised.

In short, it seems clear to me that you have to fully accept the patient's claims and not challenge the validity of his documentation, with one possible exception: the telephone conversation with his father. The patient's description of that telephone conversation is of a somewhat different order than his description of his other gains. Although he intends it to be no different, his conclusion that it reflects an improvement is open to question in a way that his other claims are not. He brushed off his father's denigration; he had the impulse to engage him in a familiar way, but he simply "shut up." That solution seems forced and artificial; it may be flawed. And therefore you may be tempted to exploit it and press it into the service of articulating the resistance and defending your inference that all is not so well. Moreover, even without the flawed solution, the interchange with the father has dynamic content, which offers you something concrete to work with. From several vantage points, then, it is a tempting target, and many students aim their interpretations at it.

Again, I regard that as an error—or at least, as a potentially basic error. In fact, I believe that the temptation to exploit the interchange with the father is one that should be resisted altogether. Short of that, it must be used with special care and extreme circumspection. For one thing, you have to be especially careful not to hoist the patient on his own petard, thereby making him regret having described the interchange. (When I composed the paradigm, I had in mind that students would misuse this material and, thereby, give me the opportunity to teach a lesson on how not to exploit it.) The crucial point is that the patient views the interchange in a particular way: for him it represents a success. You cannot ignore that view, and neither should you undercut it by simply reformulating it into something less than success.

Many students, in their eagerness to suggest a transference implication, show little sensitivity to the implications of having challenged the patient's attitude toward the conversation; they proceed too rapidly without first giving him a chance to consider the fact that a different way of construing the interchange is being suggested to him. Here are two examples of good interpretations that suffer from this shortcoming: ''I can appreciate your feeling marvelous and finding yourself more productive at this point, but I wonder if perhaps these good feelings are in part serving to enable you to brush off things that bother you—as you did with your father's sarcastic remark last night—rather than deal with, or understand, them,'' and ''It seems to me you might be handling your feelings here in therapy the same way you handled your feelings last night with your father: that by not saying what you really want to, by brushing things off, by shutting up, you will avoid feelings that might hassle you.'' Notice how these interpretations seem to brush aside what the patient has claimed—and this, by the way, is what his father did too. (Patients are adept at provoking this kind of correspondence, which is what countertransference is about.)

The situation can be ameliorated if you proceed slowly, taking pains to explicate and amplify. One student begins with the pointed remark, ''I wonder if you are more bothered by your conversation with your father than you say,'' apparently taking advantage of the patient's remark that one of his father's comments did ''get to'' him; but instead of taking pains to allude to the basis of this speculation, and perhaps amplifying on it, thereby allowing the patient an opportunity to react (and himself the opportunity to gauge the reaction), he continues right ahead with, "And perhaps you feel that you won't allow yourself to be hurt by me that way," and thereby runs the unnecessary risk that the patient will respond by insisting that his father had not hurt him (". . . he just got to me, that's all"). A flagrantly high-handed attitude is exemplified in, "It seems to me you are saying, 'Things are so good, let's not rock the boat by doing anything more,' at the same time as you are telling me that you still have trouble dealing with your father in an active and self-respecting, rather than a passively compliant, way." Such an interpretation bespeaks a judgmental, nonempathic stance that can only have an abrasive and punitive effect. It is certainly an astringent and direct observation which defines you as the one who isn't afraid to call things the way you see them, but it simply isn't the way to deal with resistance—in the framework of *Psychotherapy*, that is.

Whether the patient's response to his father represents an improvement is, of course, open to question, and I don't mean to imply you shouldn't be alert to it. There are, however, certain ways to press the matter into therapeutic service without challenging it. For one thing, the father's attitude toward his successes has a potential bearing on the transference, and you can suggest it. You can draw the inference that he is intending to provoke you to challenge and disbelieve in the same way the father does; you can speculate that one of the reasons he described the father's sarcastic mocking of his successes is to provoke a similar (or perhaps dissimilar) reaction from you. And many students formulate their interpretations around this kind of transference theme.

Before I examine them, two points are worth stressing: (1) strictly speaking, such interpretations avoid the resistance factor itself, or at best they approach it in a roundabout way; (2) the fact that the patient intended the interchange mainly as an illustration to demonstrate the validity of his improvement makes it likely that he will resent having it used as evidence against that validity. Therefore (1) you must take pains to allude clearly to the resistance factor; (2) you must remain alert to the possibility of an argument and the likelihood that he will react with a sense of having been misunderstood.

Very few students meet both those requirements, but this one comes closest: "Are you trying to tell me that, since you can do your work and handle your father now, maybe you do not need to look into yourself anymore? Are you a little afraid, perhaps, that I may bug you about every damn thing, as he did to you?" Notice how you acknowledge the sense of success without really depreciating it, and how the interpretation manages quite well to capitalize on the interchange in order to draw attention to the resistance. The resistance factor itself, however, remains poorly articulated. In the following example it isn't even alluded to: "You were telling me of the many things you're doing now and finding satisfaction in, then you told me of your father's sarcasm at hearing about them. Perhaps you feel I will put you down for your attempts also.'' Nevertheless, that's a nicely formulated interpretation with a clearly articulated focus.

Some students emphasize not only that the patient expects a reaction like his father's but that he may actually intend it. One puts it clearly with, ''I wonder whether you are trying to find out whether I will react to you as your father did''; another spells it out with, ''I wonder if you expect me to undermine the new changes in you, as your father did.'' This one formulates it carefully, ''It seems to me that you are setting up a situation with me in which I could easily disagree with you and underevaluate your progress, as your father did.'' And several students suggest that he expects an opposite reaction—for example, ''While I understand and appreciate that you feel better about yourself and your behavior, I get the impression that you want very much for me to give you the praise that your father withholds,'' and ''I think you want me to agree with you as to how well things are going, and it seems to me you were doing the same thing with your father.'' All of these are sound articulations of a potentially important transference issue, and they can be regarded as preliminary steps to the resistance interpretation itself, which none of them alludes to. Strictly speaking, therefore, they fail to meet the study's requirement. But since the hallmark of resistance is the impulse to flight, and since flight is commonly motivated by fear or apprehension, all it might take to qualify them is to add, as one student does, ''Perhaps a part of you is afraid to go on and wants to quit now.'' That, however, is a pure speculation; there is no hint of any fear or apprehension in the paradigm—there is anything but—and neither is there any hint as to what the patient might be afraid of.

Nevertheless, students do infer that he's afraid to continue therapy; some attribute it to feelings of anger, others to a conflict over dependence and independence; and they seize upon the one piece of evidence that might support such a theory, the interchange with the father. Not only does this lead them into the error of casting doubt on the goodness of the interchange, it tends to lead them into a provocative kind of formulation. Consider this example's way of using the ''evidence'': ''You report good feelings in general and that your father didn't hassle you; but when you describe the conversation it seems as if you didn't notice the fact that his comments were as sharp as ever. What I'm wondering is whether your general good feelings are the result of such not noticing.'' How is the patient supposed to respond, ''Yes, now that you mention it, I see your point; I was closing my eyes to the truth; your observation is most useful because it helps me question the validity of my general good feelings—which I will now proceed to do''? Surely, any positive response, unless given the heavy sarcasm he learned from his father, is hardly expectable. Instead, what will likely ensue is an argument and an impasse, and the *therapeutic process* will fall by the wayside.

To be sure, the *therapeutic process* will just as surely fall by the wayside if the patient's resistance is not resolved and he quits therapy. Your key problem, therefore, is how to protect and maintain the process—how to remain empathic, nondiagnostic, nondidactic, and neutral—and at the same time take a sufficiently active approach to the resistance. The approach will necessarily have to be confronting; the patient has no idea that resistance is afoot, so the idea will have to be imposed. But it needn't challenge the validity of his claims and documentation. Instead, in my opinion, what it can challenge is his optimism.

The way I would approach the resistance is to start from an empathic understanding of what the patient is feeling—and that, it seems to me, is optimism. His optimism is intense and pervasive, and its basis is not only the current excellent state of affairs, it is also a wishful assumption, namely, that the state of affairs will continue. The underlying logic is that of the optimist, and I would try to use that logic as a point of leverage in uncovering the resistance.

The question that would occur to me is, "Things are going very well, yes, but what makes you feel so sure they will continue that way?" I wouldn't put the question to the patient, in part because it is too blatantly a challenge, and in part because I have the answer, "You need to feel so sure because it subserves your need to be finished with therapy." Notice how it isn't necessary to doubt whether things are indeed going so well in order to justify the challenge—the basis of his optimism is clear enough. But the logic is moot (or vulnerable), and I would use it as an opening into the resistance. This comes down to leveling a challenge, not at the basis of his optimism, but rather at its form and function. My approach can therefore be schematized as follows: the patient is feeling optimistic and therefore is questioning the point of continuing the work of therapy; his optimism is also subserving a need to be finished with the ordeal of therapy, or an impulse to flee from it (or from me).

To put this formulation into practice, I would begin with a remark that focuses on the optimism and articulates his feelings in this way: "You are feeling very well, doing very well, and it's making you very optimistic. I gather that you're feeling so optimistic that you are thinking you don't need to work any more in therapy." After he has responded (presumably in the affirmative), I would venture a doubt-casting remark, directed not at the improvements (or at the interchange with the father) but at the optimism. It is necessarily going to be a confrontation , but it can be formulated in a way that minimizes the pitfalls and side effects of that mode in the following way: "I want to raise a question about the way you are feeling optimistic; I appreciate that the changes you've been experiencing feel marvelous, and I know it may seem foolish to be questioning the way they've made you feel so optimistic. But what do you think of the possibility that your optimism is so great because you wish no longer to work in therapy [or be finished altogether with it]?''

I wouldn't be surprised if the patient heard me challenging his gains and documentation, and I would take pains to make it clear that I wasn't. Neither would I be surprised if he misunderstood the resistance formulation and I had to explain that I meant to be suggesting that his wish to stop is what's causing some of his optimism. But notice how my interpretation also takes pains to provide him a way out: he can agree that it is foolish to question his optimism. ''Yes, I do think it's foolish,'' he might say, ''But since it obviously is not foolish to you, would you please explain yourself!'' Or he might react with a baffled, ''You are asking me to consider the possibility that I've gotten better only in order to be finished with therapy, and I find that an extraordinary idea—frankly, it seems crazy to me—so I wish you'd tell me how that could be.'' At this juncture I have two options: one is to emphasize that I was speaking about his optimism and raising the question whether it might be serving a wish to be finished with therapy; the second is to go the didactic route by notifying him about the ''flight into health'' phenomenon. Notice how the didactic explanation, since he has literally asked for it, won't be construed as a gratuitous act of supportiveness (perhaps the chief pitfall of the didactic mode); but it does cast me into a teacherly role. Therefore, if I had so far avoided didactic explanations, I would want to choose only the first option, though it may turn out that both will have to be done. To be sure, the first option transforms the resistance from a ''flight into health'' into a ''flight into optimism,'' but the transformation might be little more than a temporary expediency.

If the patient reacts with a feeling of resentment that I've thrown cold water on his improvements, then it may be possible to point out to him that he himself probably has some doubts about them—Why else would he accuse me of something I didn't do? If, on the other hand, his reaction is little more than obstinate, if he has no sense that his optimism is suspect and refuses to entertain the possibility that his wish to withdraw from therapy reflects a resistance, I may be able to prevail on him to suspect the intensity of his obstinacy. Then again, of course, I may not. But bear in mind that if my efforts fail, the outcome will be no different than if I had said nothing to begin with—he may quit therapy—and I will at least have done what I could within the limits of tact and judiciousness and professional responsibility.

Paradigm 2

I can't see what good therapy is doing me. I just can't see how it can really help me. [pause] I talk about my hang-ups here, and

I get to understand them better, but nothing really changes. [pause] Last
night I was lying in bed, unable to get to sleep, as usual, and I was
thinking about therapy and about you. [pause] You know, I think you're a
decent person, and you're very smart, and you listen all right. And I'm
not saying that you tell me things that aren't true, because they are.
Like when you said I was angry at my father because he wouldn't let me
grow up and be a man—that's exactly the case. And I really didn't know
how angry I was at him, and you helped me to realize it. [pause] But so
what? I mean, what good does it do me? Nothing has changed—I still
can't talk to him without getting stomach cramps. [pause] And I still can't
sleep like a normal human being. And I'm still self-conscious with
people; I can't talk to anyone for more than five minutes without getting
anxious. [pause] So this . . . this is not helping me. And I don't see how
it can. [pause] If anything, you know, things are getting worse instead of
better.

My intention in this paradigm was to duplicate the structure of Paradigm 1
with the obverse resistance. There isn't a commonly used name for it; it might
be called "flight into misery," but I prefer "flight into despair." The
patient's logic this time is "Because I am doing so badly, because things are
getting worse, it is pointless to continue with therapy." Again, many students
simply articulate the logic and not the resistance; and again, many find a way
to cast some doubt on the authenticity of his experience. As in Paradigm 1,
there is a documentation of claims—which can only be taken at face value and
should not be challenged—including an interchange with his father that can
be pressed into the service of articulating and then defending the resistance.
For these reasons, both paradigms entail the same kinds of technical problems, and I believe their solutions are formally similar. This time, instead of
optimism, it is pessimism that provides the key point of leverage for the
resistance interpretation.
   "You say the discoveries you've made here have not helped, and the things
I tell you are true but they don't do you any good; so you're feeling convinced
that anything you may discover here, or anything I may say, is doomed to be
useless; in other words, since things are getting worse, you don't see how
therapy can possibly help you." That's how I would begin my articulation of
the patient's pessimism. Then I would use the pessimism to address the
resistance, with this speculation: "I wonder whether your pessimism is also
based on a desire to stop therapy." I would probably want to emphasize that I
wasn't challenging his condition ("I don't mean to be saying that your experience of therapy's not helping is not true"), and I would not put all the onus on
the resistance ("I'm suggesting that your pessimism is partly due to something other than the fact that you're not getting better and even getting worse").
   If the patient asked me why I thought he was resisting the therapy (what I

had in mind with the "something other," for instance), if he wanted to know what else besides his poor condition was making him want to stop, I would say I wasn't sure, and that there are several possibilities. One has to do with the way his father wouldn't let him grow up and be a man: perhaps he mustn't let me be so different from his father, perhaps there's a danger in allowing me to be the agent of his independence and maturity. A second possibility, which is at once more specific and vague (and also more purely a speculation), is that there are certain things he wants to avoid talking about because they are so painful. But I would hold both of these possibilities in abeyance, and offer them only if his reaction to my resistance interpretation required them.

Two students offer interpretations that center on the patient's pessimism, and each includes the nonspecific speculation that I mentioned. One puts it this way: "It sounds as if you are experiencing that nothing has helped, and you seem to be implying that nothing can. Perhaps you are taking this extremely despairing position because it is your way of not facing some painful matters," and the second this way: "You say I tell you things that are true and which you didn't realize before. Could it be you are afraid of what other things I might tell you, and therefore you are expressing the doubt that therapy will help you?" In my estimation, they are too premature and too abrupt; they should first articulate the resistance itself. As they stand, the speculation is highlighted, and this invites the patient's challenge, "What makes you think so?" Or he might wonder what "painful matters" and what "other things I might tell you" you had in mind. The fact that the speculation is a pure one (that is, one based on no available evidence) may be quite unavoidable in this case, there may be no other way to formulate the resistance, but it can at least be embedded in a clearly articulated resistance formulation, and it should be clearly defined as an act of speculation.

Only two students do it my way. How do the rest do it? A good way to begin an examination of their interpretations, and thereby the technical problems posed by Paradigm 2, is with the following example, which manages to incorporate different themes that occur separately in many of the students' interpretations and omits only the resistance idea itself. "I think a part of you is very disappointed and angry with me for not being able to magically solve your problems. I believe you may find it difficult to accept the fact that change takes time, and that I cannot supply you with immediate answers; and I get the feeling that you want to punish me in some way—by saying, *Things are getting worse*." This interpretation is fully cast in transferential terms; therapy is the principal subject, and you are the main object. It begins with an articulation of the patient's feeling of disappointment, but adds anger as well, and then proceeds to speculate that the basis of those feelings is a set of unrealistic (and immature) expectations, nothing more. Not only is the interpretation unresponsive to what the patient has said, it clearly implies a disbelief or minimization of the genuineness and legitimacy of his despair. Its overall tone is judgmental and confronting, and it has a kind of defensive, if not retaliatory, tone. And where is the evidence?

A surprising number of students infer that he is feeling angry. He is expressing disappointment, he is certainly complaining, but does that provide an adequate basis for inferring anger? One student offers this interesting interpretation: "It sounds as if you should be feeling pretty angry that things aren't getting better, particularly since you are doing everything expected of you here." Does that mean that the patient is angry because he "should be" or are you suggesting that he isn't angry but "should be"? The patient has taken special pains to exonerate you from blame (that is, I took those pains when I composed the paradigm), yet students infer that he is angry at you—and they say so in their interpretations. What they achieve thereby is a transformation of his message from "I want to quit because therapy is not making me better, in fact worse" to "I want to quit because I am angry at you for not helping me get better, in fact worse."

Consider, then, the inference that he chose the illustration of his anger at his father because he wanted to convey the message that he is angry at you. Such an inference may make good theoretical sense, but in practice it is an unwieldy and difficult inference to use. Let's suppose you explained that you think he's angry at you because he mentioned his anger at his father; he might protest, "But I meant it merely to illustrate that knowing what I really feel is not helping me overcome my problems," and, "Why do you use it in a way that I did not intend it?" And suppose he says, "I am wholly unaware of any feelings of anger at you. As I said—or don't you believe me?—I think you are a good person and a good therapist. So not only do I not feel anger at you, but since I feel no sense of holding you or the therapy to blame for my failure, I have no reason to feel any." How would you now proceed? Would you back down with a tactful apology or press ahead with your original formulation? I think you'd have to do the former, because the latter requires taking his painstaking exoneration as evidence—and you could only claim, "I think the fact that you took such pains to exonerate me from blame is an indication that underneath you do feel I am to blame, and therefore that you do in fact feel angry at me." But if he now asks for some explanation of how that works and how that could be—and he has the right to have the matter explained to him—you would have to give a normative and/or theoretical answer, like this one, "Because in my experience, and according to my theory of human behavior, when a patient does what you have done, he is resorting to the defense of reaction-formation or disavowal"—and it's generally unwise and therapeutically ineffective, in my opinion and experience, to use this kind of

basis as evidence for an interpretation. Normative and theoretical formulations, after all, brook exceptions; and just because there is a probability that
behavior X is a cover for experience Y doesn't necessarily mean it obtains in
any particular case and instance. So I believe this entire approach is likely to
lead to an untenable and difficult position, and, given the patient's state of
resistance, it may achieve less than nothing.[2]

Some students formulate the resistance according to its broad definition,
and their interpretations tend to be too general and too diagnostic. A succinct
example is, "I think part of you fears changing and becoming independent." I
find it hard to imagine how such a remark could enhance the *therapeutic
process*; even if the patient accepts it, and even if it comes to him as news, he
will most likely simply add it to his list of complaints ("Yes, that too—And
how is therapy going to cure me of that ailment?"). Here's a more complicated
version of the same theme, which is still too general and too diagnostic to be
useful: "You're discouraged and feeling helpless, and I think I understand
why. Feeling helpless is a way of saying to yourself that you can't change,
and I think a part of you is very afraid of changing and wants you to feel
helpless so that you won't have to change." ("Yes, I feel helpless, and I
guess I am afraid to change—so I guess therapy is not for me.") The theme
can be formulated in a more specific way, by including a reference to the
father, the way this example does: "Perhaps you prefer to see the therapy as
useless and ineffectual because you may find it difficult to face the growth that
your father did not allow." That may be a better way to do it, because it
invites the patient to consider the role that his father's attitude toward growth
and independence may be playing in his conviction that therapy is useless. But
in view of the fact that he is under the sway of a resistance, it seems to me that
any interpretation that has a diagnostic form runs the risk of being perceived
as a scolding. Moreover, the patient may also have the sense that the scolding
stems from a need on your part to defend the therapy and yourself.

Since it challenges the efficacy of the therapy, and indirectly also their skill

---

2. I cannot resist the temptation of footnoting the following complete response to Paradigm 2,
because it illustrates so vividly the great gap that can exist between theory and practice.
(Remember that the instructions call not only for an intervention but also for an identification of
the resistance theme.) "*Theme:* This is what Freud calls *transference resistance* and Menninger
calls *frustration resistance*. The patient is beginning to react to the growing frustration that his
therapist is not kind, rewarding, and loving, in the same way as he reacted to his father when
frustrated as a child. He is attempting on one level to gain love through pity and helplessness.
Underlying this childish maneuver is a tremendous amount of mounting anger towards the
therapist, repressed anger that the patient felt towards his father. However, he is resisting his
negative transference; he cannot accept his feelings of anger, and therefore denies them and
displaces them onto the therapy situation in general in the form of resistance. *Interpretation:* You
are angry at your father because he wouldn't let you grow up and be a man. And yet at the same
time you are angry and discontent with therapy, and perhaps me, for not helping you feel better."

as therapists, since it attacks them where they are apt to be most vulnerable by calling into question the efficacy of their treatment method, the nature of Paradigm 2's resistance shakes students from their neutral position, and more than other paradigms, causes them (1) to shift the blame onto the patient's shoulders in a defensive way, (2) to counterattack in an aggressive way, and (3) to offer interpretations that make little sense.

Defensiveness. A representative example of what too many students choose to say is this: "You are feeling helpless and also feeling that therapy is not helping. Perhaps you would like therapy to change you in spite of yourself, that is, without your actively changing." The message is "Look here, don't blame me! It is you who is not trying hard enough." And consider, "The goal of therapy is for you to develop self-awareness. This requires that I assist you in the process of self-understanding by listening to you and trying to make useful interpretations. But the basic responsibility for change is yours, not mine." What else can the patient now experience but a sense of having been reprimanded, even rejected? Notice how it adds yet another item to his list of failures. And notice also how you've broken the very promise being enunciated. Even a gentler version, like the following, is open to the same criticism: "I think one of the reasons you feel things aren't getting better is because a part of you still construes therapy as a place where you come to tell me about your hang-ups and problems, and then expect me to solve them for you, to point things out to you."

Offensiveness. "You know, I bet this complaint about my not really helping you is a lot like your anger at your father. Part of you is saying, 'Help me, damn it!' while at the same time another part of you is saying, 'Stop the therapy, let me do something by myself, leave me alone!' " I regard this as an example of aggressive counterattack. Its style is consonant with the tough confronting approach that is espoused by many contemporary therapists who believe it can be useful to shock a patient into self-awareness and reality-testing, and who argue that gingerliness and indirection must be avoided at all costs. Moreover, it's probably a resistance like the present one that seems most suited for a tough, countering stance, because the nature of the patient's complaints cries out for a firm reaction (like a parent's, for instance). And I also regard this one, "Perhaps you are focusing on the fact that I haven't helped you get better rather than thinking about how you can work to change yourself," which is representative of what a number of students give, as belonging in the same category.[3]

Fuzziness. "Things do seem to be getting worse for you, and you seem to

---

3. Knowing I would disapprove, a student puts this in a footnote: "Tough! I guess you'll have to really do some things for yourself for a change, if I'm not helping you and Dad isn't."

be telling me how miserable you are and how ineffectual I am, though I'm a
decent and smart person to you. But how can I be decent and smart and at the
same time useless in your eyes? You seem to be in a bind in which you need to
see yourself as miserable so that you can avoid helping yourself change. After
all, if I can't help and you can't help yourself, you needn't experience your
feelings toward me.'' That epitomizes the convoluted, illogical, and obtuse
kinds of remarks this paradigm evokes from students. Here are two somewhat
more intelligible ones, but notice how hard they are to figure out: ''I believe
you are struggling with the idea of growing up. Part of you wants to grow up,
so you are angry at your father for not letting you; but part of you doesn't want
to, so you are angry at your therapy and at me for allowing you to grow up,''
and ''Rather than utilizing your increased understanding to change outside of
here, you are protecting yourself against further exploration by blaming the
therapy for your problems.'' And what are we, not to mention the poor
patient, to make of this one? ''I'm thinking that you feel that being in therapy
makes matters worse because therapy allows you to avoid standing up to your
problems.''

Now, the question of efficacy itself is a difficult and complicated one, and
especially difficult and complicated is the attitude we should take toward it
when we conduct *Psychotherapy*. This isn't the best place to discuss the larger
question, but I can mention how I believe we ought to approach it in the short
run. I believe that our patient's well-being is best served when we calmly
accept the working hypothesis that our method is the optimal one for him. Not
that we blithely ignore the advisability of introducing modifications, or even
the possibility of an entirely different form of therapy for him, but our short-
run attitude can be one of giving *Psychotherapy* the benefit of any doubt. We
can maintain a full faith in the method, a sense of optimism that includes the
patient's ability to use it beneficially, which means we proceed for a time with
a business-as-usual way, doing nothing differently until we have reasonably
exhausted the interpretive approach. And this also means we don't have to
take time out to defend the therapy itself.

Some students offer the patient an interpretation that amounts to little more
than a defense of the therapy, insofar as it suggests that therapy is actually
working. Here's a particularly interesting and instructive example: ''I am
wondering if your feeling that things are getting worse is related to the fact
that you are more in touch with your feelings—your anger at your father, for
instance—and that makes the repetition of the same old patterns more uncomfortable.'' A similar, though less subtle, formulation is, ''You say things are
getting worse rather than better. Perhaps that's because you're beginning to
experience a lot of negative feelings you weren't aware of having. Therapy is
not necessarily supposed to make you feel good, but help you be in touch with

all your feelings, whatever they are." And a student adds the following remark to an interpretation which had suggested that the patient wanted to quit therapy because it, in fact, had been proving effective: "But isn't it possible that we are actually getting close to an awareness of the conflicts that are causing you to feel this way, and you feel like running in the other direction?"

There are several risks inherent in these interpretations, though also some benefits which I don't want to minimize. For one thing, they suggest to the patient that it isn't true he's getting worse or not improving, he's merely feeling "uncomfortable" or "not good" as a result of the therapy's effectiveness. The implication is that that's how it has to be; getting in touch with one's feelings, for instance, is necessarily a mixed blessing. That may be quite true, though in this case there's no evidence of it, and still be quite self-serving. Moreover, if you have been avoiding didactic lessons up to this point, his resistance may be intensified rather than lessened. His pessimism might be reinforced by the fact that he was successful in shaking you from your usual stance; he may hear reassurance instead of explanation; he certainly won't learn anything about his resistance. To suggest to him that he's experiencing no gains from therapy and feels he's getting worse precisely because that's what therapy entails is quite different from suggesting that a resistance to therapy is at work, and that that's what is responsible for his lack of improvement; or, more precisely, that his condition is serving the prior and more basic need to be out of therapy; and even more precisely, in my opinion, that his condition is serving to bolster his pessimism, and it's his pessimism that is subserving the resistance.

Paradigm 3

I didn't feel like coming today. I don't know why not, but . . . I just didn't feel like it. [pause] Henry asked me to go downtown with him today, and I was really tempted to. But I figured I'd better not, I'd better keep my appointment with you. [pause] Anyway, he's a drag to go anywhere with. He's always late and always making phony excuses. Like he'll say he'll meet me at two o'clock in front of Macy's, and at two o'clock I'll be waiting for him, and then he shows up at two-thirty and makes a phony excuse—like he thought we were supposed to meet then, or else he thought he said some other store. [pause] It gets me depressed when he does that—when anybody does that: doesn't keep their word. [pause] Not that I don't really expect it to happen to me, because somehow it always does, you know. I don't know why. But I get to thinking I must be sort of a bad person, in a way. Not a bad person; it's more like sort of . . . evil. Yeah, like someone evil who should be avoided, or something like that. [pause] There must be a reason why people don't keep their word to me. You know, my father used to make promises all the time that he didn't keep. That didn't used to really bother me so much, though, because I expected it from him. He was a kind of weak person, you know, and he could never say no to me. Anything I asked for, he would say he'd get it for me. And then of course he wouldn't. [pause] He once promised to buy me a big train set, and I knew he wouldn't because it was expensive and he didn't ever buy expensive things for us because he didn't have enough money, really. So I didn't really feel so bad when he didn't. [pause] And then when I grew up I just avoided him all the time. [pause] We became like strangers because I knew he would always disappoint me. [pause] I guess people just do.

This paradigm, which purports to embody a resistance that can be called "flight into distrust," seems to pose fewer and less serious technical problems than the first two. Nevertheless, no student responds with a resistance interpretation that, in my judgment, is complete and adequate, that provides a sufficiently articulated or focused formulation of the resistance. And I think there are two main reasons: (1) the fact that the patient has acknowledged a wish to miss the session invites the complacent assumption that he is aware of the resistance; (2) the material invites a good and sound interpretation that is not, strictly speaking, a resistance interpretation.

Consider these two similar examples, one a succinct version and the other a more articulated version of the kind of interpretation that most of the students make: "You wished not to come today because you feared that I would disappoint you," and "I think you didn't feel like coming today because you're beginning to wonder whether I can be trusted, whether I will keep my word, or whether I'll disappoint you like Henry and your father. And as you've said, when you begin to wonder about that, you get depressed." They seem simple and clear enough, they focus on the "resistance" and offer a motivational basis for it. But, assuming that the patient is in a state of resistance, they are, in my judgment, not the most effective interpretive responses to the paradigm. As resistance interpretations they have a number of serious shortcomings.

First of all, do they articulate the resistance? I think they don't. The patient's wish to miss the session is not the resistance; it may be the manifestation, but the resistance itself is the underlying wish to stop therapy altogether. My contention here is not merely theoretical or abstract, it can have important practical implications. The patient may well respond to those interpretations as if he were fully aware of the resistance ("Yes, I didn't feel like coming today"), but if you were to suggest that he wanted to quit altogether then his response might be quite different ("No, no, I just didn't want to come today"). For that reason the first step has to be, "You didn't want to come to today's session because you wish to stop therapy altogether." I believe such a resistance articulation is a critical step to take, even though it reflects an act of speculation based only on the assumption of the study. The next step, after the idea has been discussed and explored, is the resistance interpretation proper, which could take the form, "You wish to stop therapy [not merely miss today's session] because you are afraid to trust me not to disappoint you."

But is that actually the most cogent, most potentially effective, resistance formulation? Again, I believe it isn't. I can imagine the patient's having no qualms accepting it ("Yes, I'm afraid you will disappoint me like Henry, my father, and everyone else does"), and I can also imagine his welcoming the help you have given him to bolster the resistance ("Yes, you're right, I guess I want to quit because I'm afraid you're going to disappoint me too"). That, however, isn't the only reason I think the more cogent, more potentially effective, formulation is to reverse the cause-effect sequence, namely, "Your fear that I will disappoint you too is not the cause of your wish to stop, it's the other way around: your wish to stop, to flee therapy, is what's causing you to feel distrustful of me and to fear disappointment." In fact, I would not speak of "fear," I would use the word "expectation," because I don't think he fears disappointment so much as he expects it, and perhaps even welcomes it. And I would try to make it very clear I was suggesting that the expectation was serving him as the vehicle for his wish to stop therapy. This formulation is bound to be provocative and tactless (therefore it has to be conveyed carefully, gradually, and sensitively), but at the same time it is likely to be powerful and insightful.

The point I'm making here is partly theoretical and partly empirical. It has to do with a way of construing resistance and giving it the importance and weight that it deserves in most forms of traditional therapy. Just as the patient in Paradigm 1 is using his optimism, and the patient in Paradigm 2 is using his pessimism, as the vehicle (or instrumentality) for his wish to stop therapy (and the *therapeutic process*), so the patient in this paradigm is using distrust and the conviction that he is doomed to disappointment. In other words, the resistance proper is not explained by the distrust, it has to be formulated with respect to the therapy as a whole and especially the *therapeutic process*; the therapy and the process contain the seeds of their own resistance—they have an indigenous inertia, an inherent counterforce against self-inquiry and significant change—which enlist a variety of mechanisms to serve the underlying purpose. As a working hypothesis, this way of construing resistance is likely to be particularly effective in therapy, and in my opinion and my clinical experience it's often a requisite one if the phenomenon of resistance is to be resolved adequately.

For that reason, resistance has to be approached with diligence and patience, and usually with a gradually evolving sequence of steps. A terse and succinct interpretation will usually not suffice, an incomplete formulation will prove inadequate. We have to be especially alert to the dangers of premature closure, of explaining away the phenomenon instead of opening it up for further and deeper exploration, of oversimplification and minimization. Resistance is probably the most crucial and sensitive issue in long-term psychotherapy, and in the interests of efficacy, it must be treated as such.

Virtually every student opts for a single interpretation to Paradigm 3. The material is so clear and apparently simple that it seems to invite no extended dialogue. Within the limits of a one-shot interpretation, however, the pitfalls of oversimplification and minimization can be avoided by a more complete interpretation, by at least incorporating the self-image theme of the unworthy and "evil" one, as this example does: "Could it be you didn't feel like coming today because you are afraid I might also see you as someone evil, and therefore I'd become one more person who would disappoint you." A student writes, "I wonder if you are afraid I am going to let you down as other important people in your life have, as your father did," then adds, "Perhaps you feel you must have been a bad person for him to have done that, and it's risky to take a chance again on having those 'bad-person' feelings reinforced." Another implicates the self-image by rounding off an interpretation with, " . . . and that it will be your fault since you think you must be some kind of evil person who really should be left alone." Another does it subtly, perhaps a bit too subtly, with, "It seems that you're saying that I shouldn't be concerned that you considered canceling because you're not really worth my trouble." And here's one that is most complete and explicit, a well-formulated one-shot interpretation: "In telling me you don't expect people to keep their promises to you, I wonder if you're letting me know that you're expecting me to break my promises to you also, because you think I'll find you unworthy, evil, and then you're expecting to avoid me for it. Maybe that would partially explain why you didn't feel like coming today."

I've already indicated why the emphasis should be on the patient's expectation of disappointment rather than on his fear of it, and his self-image as the bad and evil one lends itself well to that emphasis. I would reserve the affect of fear for the resistance itself, the wish to stop the therapy and the *therapeutic process*. In fact, if the final sentence of the paradigm had been accompanied by a smile or by a look of victory, my impulse would be to say, "Isn't that lucky! It enables you to be in the enviable position of the one who is always disappointed, and this nicely reinforces your self-image as the evil one." Of course I wouldn't say this aloud, but I'd use the response to help formulate the theme in my mind. A student comes close to articulating the theme with this interpretation: "I am wondering if perhaps this feeling—that people let you down because something is wrong with you—does not allow you to feel disappointment and perhaps anger over being let down.'' As a preliminary step toward the resistance interpretation, I believe that kind of interpretation can be good and useful. I like the way it formulates matters in the active voice instead of the passive, and suggests that the patient may secure gratification from his distrust. It's a short step from that to the possibility that he is using the theme in the interests of bolstering and making sense out of his resistance.

Another step that can be interpolated is to raise the question ''Why today?'' Why is he now feeling so mistrustful and anticipating disappointment? A few students pay attention to that question by inferring that there must be some topic on his mind that he fears discussing, perhaps because it will reflect badly upon him. My inclination would be to add a remark to that effect, perhaps in these words: ''And what you said a moment ago suggested that it [the topic you want to avoid talking about] has something to do with the fact that you are feeling unworthy these days, or *evil* as you put it.''

But Paradigm 3 invites some further complications. Is it merely an expectation of being disappointed that is at issue? What about the possibility that beneath this expectation lies the expectation that you will in fact not disappoint him in this respect? If I were you, I'd take that possibility very seriously, and infer that the patient may be apprehensive because he senses that I'm not going to be another person who lets him down—and therefore his experience in therapy is going to threaten the integrity of his self-image. Now, there are two ways in which I can let him down, two ways to construe the ''promise'' I have made in the context of therapy: one is that therapy will cure him, the other is that I will understand him with compassion and neutrality. I would assume that he is apprehensive about both these promises, perhaps because they each threaten his self-image. So I'd be inclined to formulate an interpretation along these lines: ''What you are saying is that you didn't feel like coming today because you're afraid I will disappoint you, as your father did. But I wonder what you think of the possibility that it would not upset you very much if I really did that, and what would upset you is that I won't—and that is what you fear.'' From there I could go on to point out that it's the trusting that he fears, the sense of unconditional acceptance that he finds threatening; that he needs to feel bad and unworthy, misunderstood as well; and because he senses that therapy will not fulfill those needs, he is experiencing the wish to withdraw and stop. Such an interpretation has the potential for important and profound insight and discovery; and it also has great pertinence to therapy, insofar as it touches on a central feature of the *therapeutic process*.

Paradigm 4

I went shopping for a new suit. Yesterday afternoon it was, and ... [pause] I couldn't decide where to go. [pause] Henry went to Macy's last week and got an imported suit from Italy for only half-price. It was ... [pause] It was originally marked at $125 and ... uh, he paid only $70. [pause] But when he got home he found a small rip, about an inch or so, in the right armpit. He took it back but had a lot of trouble over it. [pause] Anyway, so I decided to go to Orbach's. But I didn't get there because on the way I passed a shop on Fifth Avenue, just off Fifth, and in the window I saw this beautiful suit, dark green with a fine yellow stripe. It was marked down from $95 to $49.95. Henry has one almost like it, except his ... uh, his is gray with an orange stripe. [pause] Anyway, I tried it on and it fit perfectly, except the jacket was about an inch and a half too long, but it can easily be shortened. [pause] The salesman was a tall, skinny guy, he must have been over six-four, with big thick glasses. And he kept smiling all the time, and he had buck teeth. [pause] And the reason I mention this is because he reminded me of a fellow named Allen who was in my class in the eleventh grade. Everybody used to make fun of Allen because he had big buck teeth and lisped badly. He had braces for his teeth, but ... [pause] I used to feel sorry for Allen, though God knows he was better off than I was. His father was an executive in the telephone company, a vice-president I think, and they were richer than anybody else in our school. I remember how impressed we all were with the fancy telephones in his house. And he was the first person in the class to get his own telephone. That was when colored telephones were a new thing. It was a red one, his. And he could make all the calls he wanted because his father got the service for nothing, I believe. Or maybe at a discount. [pause] Allen had a girlfriend who was in boarding school in the Midwest, somewhere in Illinois, I can't remember the name of it. And he used to just call her up and talk for hours. [pause] He once talked to her for a solid hour and forty minutes.

This was a difficult paradigm to compose, and I hesitated to include it in the book because it fails in certain ways to exemplify what I intended, a "flight into trivia." By packing in as many irrelevant details as I could, I produced a caricature that is so extreme as to be ambiguous. Moreover, not only is the patient unaware that he might be resisting in any way, he gives no hint that he's speaking in a way that is unusual for him. (That, despite my having tried for a crescendo of circumstantiality to suggest that something special was up.) But instead of relying on the presumption that therapy would not have gotten past the beginning stages with this kind of obsessional attention to irrelevant detail, and therefore that it represented not a style but a resistance, I should have included something in the paradigm to suggest that the patient knew he was speaking in an unusual way, that the mentioning of all the details was remarkable.

So it's no surprise that only half my students recognize the form of the resistance. By giving the benefit of doubt wherever there was any doubt, I counted precisely half of their formulations as having recognized that the trivia reflects the resistance. However, a majority of that half fail to use the resistance in their interpretations and make no mention of the patient's way of speaking. The main reason, I suspect, is because this resistance is especially difficult to interpret without resorting to a flagrant confrontation, and at the same time not directly, or even indirectly for that matter, criticizing the patient for it.

My reluctance to delete this paradigm is based on the fact that it deals with a resistance which relates in an essential and vital way to the basic orientation and format of *Psychotherapy*. This resistance also clearly points up an inherent paradox (or dilemma). The Basic Instruction, after all, grants a patient the full freedom to speak however he wants to, and that freedom may not be abrogated. If he decides to speak trivia, even in the service of avoiding the *therapeutic process*, that decision has to be explored without at the same time restricting the freedom. The technical problems, therefore, are especially delicate and difficult insofar as they touch directly on an aspect of the method that is both basic and potentially paradoxical.

The problems are compounded for this paradigm because it differs from the others in that the patient shows no awareness of any derivative or manifestation of a resistance. Not only is there no allusion to stopping therapy or withdrawing from the work of therapy, there isn't any allusion to therapy at all. Therefore, you have no choice but to introduce the idea of a resistance, and that demands a confrontation. You will have to interrupt and draw attention to the way he is speaking (probably ignoring the content, though you might be able to use the content in some helpful way), as the first step in beginning an exploration of the resistance. This can only put a strain on your tact and neutrality, and necessarily entail some compromising of your basic role definition. There is no way to be fully empathic and purely interpretive and still address the resistance, and short of waiting for a suitable opportunity, you have to resort to confronting with all of its potential for tactlessness, directiveness, criticism, and the rest. In a sense, then, this one is a study of compromise, an exercise in how to maintain sufficient tact and neutrality and how to use confrontation in a way that minimizes its unwanted implications and side effects.

I would do it this way: "I want to interrupt you in order to draw your attention to the way you are talking today." Then I would pause briefly to see whether the patient recognizes what I'm referring to. If he doesn't, I'll spell out the form of the resistance in this way: "Do you notice how much detail you are going into about things?—the exact price of the suits, the color of the telephone, and so on." But I wouldn't want to pause again and await his response, because if I stop here I am left with all the risks that attend the use of confrontation, the chief one being the message "So please cut it out!" In order to disavow that message I would go right ahead with a remark that has an interpretive cast to it, that seeks to offer an explanation. And I have two main options: one is to say something about the resistance itself, perhaps by suggesting the possibility of an underlying wish to withdraw from therapy; the second is to say, in effect, that it would be useful to explore the reasons behind his speaking this way today.

The first option is riskier than the second, because it's bound to strike the patient as farfetched that he is expressing a wish to stop therapy altogether. He might be prevailed upon to accept the possibility that his circumstantiality is interfering with his work of self-inquiry and exploration, but anything more is hardly imaginable and bound to be premature. I would therefore choose the second option. However, instead of saying, "I believe it would be useful to explore the reasons behind your speaking this way today," and thereby compounding the violation of the Basic Instruction with a directive to explore, I would cast it in the form of an interpretation, as follows: "I am wondering why you feel the need today to go into such details, whether it might be a way of avoiding talking about something that you fear might be upsetting to talk about." This way of solving the technical problem is unsatisfactory on several counts. First of all, my interpretation is perhaps not a simple directive, but, insofar as it "asks" the question, it is directive nonetheless. I am clearly suggesting that the patient should consider the possibility of some specific evasion. Thus, I am imposing a new topic; and though I do it with some tact, I cannot undo that fact. But short of not intervening at all, and waiting for him to notice the resistance himself, I cannot see what other choice I have.

Secondly, my interpretation entails a speculation wholly unsupported by any evidence. There isn't even a reference to any evidence in my remark. It would obviously be better if I could suggest to him what topic it is he's avoiding, but I purposely didn't do that. Why not?—because there is a fresh risk involved in picking something out of the material to serve as possible evidence: that of grasping at straws. (Some students do that, and I discuss their choices below.) I regard it as important to try and avoid even giving the impression to a patient that I selected something from the content of his narrative for the sole purpose of backing up an interpretation—and more precisely in this case, for the purpose of transforming a confrontation into an interpretation. There's a subtle but significant difference between using evidence to justify and using it to rationalize.

A student offers a solution quite similar to mine, but finds a clever way—and perhaps it is too clever—to integrate it with the paradigm's content. "I think you're having to do the same thing here with me, because a part of you is afraid of what might happen if you stop talking solidly," is how you begin, picking up nicely from where the patient left off; then, after allowing him to ask, ''What do you mean, what might happen?'' you continue with ''Well, two things occur to me: talking solidly might be a way of keeping the unexpected or troublesome thoughts from occurring; it also minimizes the opportunities for me to say something. Perhaps either of those possibilities makes you anxious, and talking solidly is a way of avoiding that anxiety.'' That, I'll confess, is an attractive possibility.

Another student who comes close begins, ''I wonder whether you are talking about these remote details in order to prevent yourself from getting into other things that might be more disturbing to you.'' However, not only is there an insufficient focus on the resistance, but the student doesn't stop at this point, and continues with a blatantly diagnostic formulation, ''I think that when you feel threatened by some thought you tend to go into elaborate details about something else, as a way of stopping yourself from having to confront whatever you are afraid of.'' In a similar vein, a student begins with an unnecessary and imprudent apology—''Please don't take this as a hostile criticism of you, I don't intend it to be''—which the patient may take as nothing more than kind consideration; but it has at least two big faults: it gratuitously suggests that what's coming can be taken as a hostile criticism, and it sweetens the bitter pill artificially—so it's far better to let the chips fall, and then work with the pieces. Then the student proceeds with an interpretation which captures the spirit of my solution, ''But I was impressed by the amount of detail in what you've told me so far; and yet all of it doesn't seem to relate to you on anything but a kind of superficial level. I am wondering if you're talking on this level because talking on any other level now might make you more anxious.''

A student offers the curt continuation, ''It seems to me that you too would like to just talk for hours,'' and then invites the patient to recognize what he has in mind, ''I wonder if you see what I mean, or suspect what's behind this.'' That's an attractive possibility, though I doubt whether the patient is going to get the point. I am certain he would not get the point—unless the point was to chastise him—of this version of the formulation: ''You seem to feel you can talk on and on here, like your classmate did on the phone, without using the time meaningfully—as if the opportunity was worth nothing.'' And here's one that can only amount to a rebuke: ''It seems that you are looking for a bargain in the therapy sessions; perhaps you feel you can get something out of them without really putting anything into them—that is, you seem to be talking about things that don't require any effort on your part to say.''

It's no surprise that students betray an irritation with the patient's chatter. Here's an example which may reflect an undercurrent of impatience: ''I find myself wondering if there is some point you are trying to make, or if there isn't something you want to talk about with me more directly." Notice how the student has accused the patient of being indirect, and done it so indirectly, without offering any basis for the charge. Another does exactly the same thing, but then provides a basis by drawing some content from the material— "I wonder if what you are saying is that everyone is better off than you are." I doubt whether that lessens the sense of irritation.

When I composed the paradigm I made the mistake of deliberately avoiding any usable content because I was trying to present a pure form of "flight into trivia." Nevertheless, many students do find material in what the patient has said and press it into service for explaining the resistance. "I have the sense that what you've just told me bears on something you fear about therapy; that you fear scorn and rebuke for the specialness of this relationship, and that you avoid that feeling by getting lost in detail," is an example of an interesting speculation. Another is, "Your talk today seems indirect and full of unnecessary detail; possibly this is the way you choose to speak about issues of value and about the question of whether therapy is worth all this time and money." Several students go further in their speculative zeal; for example, "I have the sense that you are feeling today very much like that guy with his red telephone, who'd call his girlfriend and talk for hours. You seem to be in the mood to chat with me, much as you might with a friend over the phone, moving from one subject to the next, nothing too serious." And here's a succinct interpretation that implicates the transference (but not the resistance): "Perhaps you want to do much the same thing here—you seem to want to just talk for hours to see if I'll allow it."

And perhaps I should heed a similar message and bring this chapter to a close. But before I do, an epilogue which is pertinent both to "flight into trivia" and resistance in general.

An Epilogue on Resistance

I can summarize my views on resistance by exemplifying them in an imaginary dialogue that conceivably could occur during a session. If it seems like a Talmudic disputation, and if the patient seems too legalistic, it is because I have in mind that PT is you—and TH, of course, is me.

> TH: I want to draw your attention to the way you are talking today. Do you notice how you are speaking of things that are unimportant to you?
>
> PT: Yes, I'm fully aware of that. But why do you want to draw it to my attention?—To get me to stop doing it?

TH: No, that's not my conscious intention. You see, I intended to ask next whether you are aware of doing it out of a wish to avoid talking about something that is important to you.

PT: Yes, of that I am also aware. But look here, you said at the beginning of therapy that I was going to be free to talk however I wanted to. And this is the way I really want to talk today: about things that are unimportant to me. Are you implying I shouldn't—that it's not all right?

TH: Again, that wasn't my intention. I can see where you draw that inference, but I didn't mean to imply that you have to talk about important things. I decided to raise the issue, and find out whether you are aware of it, because I thought it would be useful.

PT: I see. I remember you also saying at the beginning that you would be saying "useful" things. You didn't explain how you construed "useful," so what I'm wondering now is, What makes it useful to raise the issue you've raised? Assuming I was not aware of it, why is it useful for you to point out to me that I am avoiding talking about things that are important to me? I can think of only one answer: to get me to stop doing it, and to get me to speak of things that are important to me.

TH: I can think of another possibility: to help you discover why you want to avoid talking about things that are important to you.

PT: Sure, but that amounts to the same thing, doesn't it? If I were to discover why, then I would stop doing it. What other reason is there for trying to discover the motive?

TH: Here's one: if you felt compelled to talk about unimportant things, understanding why might free you from that compulsion; and then you'd be free either to do it or not.

PT: I see. You have a point—understanding can increase a person's freedom of choice. But I felt today that I was in fact freely choosing. So, if I had let you know I was doing it knowingly and deliberately, if I'd begun the session by notifying you that I was planning to talk about unimportant things out of a conscious wish to avoid something important, then you wouldn't have had anything useful to say about it. Is that so?

TH: No. In fact I might not have said anything, but in prin-
      ciple there is always something useful to say, because
      there will be aspects of your decision that are outside of
      your immediate awareness. For instance, I might have
      judged it useful to wonder aloud whether you were chal-
      lenging me to a confrontation, or whether you were
      doing it out of a wish to withdraw from therapy.

PT: Hello! Then we're right back where we started from.
      What other message could that have than "Stop chal-
      lenging, and stop withdrawing!"? Am I not free to do
      those things?

TH: Yes, you are. I don't intend to abrogate that freedom
      either. But once again, you see, there is the question of
      whether or not you are aware of wishing to do those
      things.

PT: Okay, so let's go around once more. Suppose I was
      fully aware of avoiding talking about important things
      out of a wish to challenge you and/or withdraw from
      therapy—What useful remark could you make to me
      that would not simply request me to stop what I was
      doing?

TH: I can imagine a number of different possibilities, all ad-
      dressing the question "Why do you have these wishes,
      and why do you have them now?" And chances are that
      some of the answers lie outside of your awareness.

PT: And so what if they do? Are you implying that they
      would be useful for me to know?

TH: Yes.

PT: Useful to me in what respect?

TH: In respect to discovering things about yourself that you
      weren't fully aware of, or didn't fully understand.

PT: I see. I appreciate how you put it in terms of knowledge
      and self-understanding. But even if I grant you that that
      would be intrinsically important to me, even "useful,"
      it would also go counter to my conscious decision to
      speak today of unimportant things. So you would have
      forced me—as in fact you have—into speaking of im-
      portant things. What happens to my big freedom to
      speak as I choose when you force me to widen the
      scope of my self-knowledge?

TH: That's an important and difficult question. In a sense,
      your point is irrefutable, though the word "forced" is
      perhaps too strong. I prefer to put it this way: I would

have encouraged you to stop acting on your decision, and instead to explore the reasons for your decision. After all, if your talk was unimportant, as you agreed it was, what harm is there in encouraging you to make it important? And furthermore, you would remain relatively free to resist my encouragements if you wished. I don't believe I've forced you into this discussion we're having.

PT: All right, say I agree with you on the distinction between "forced" and "encouraged"; the fact remains that it was you, not me, who encouraged the discovering; it was you who moved me in the direction of understanding why I made the decision.

TH: And that's one of the chief ways I construe the word "useful"; it's a principal way I try to be useful to you. I assume, you see, that one of your reasons for coming to therapy is to make discoveries about yourself. I further assume that you are likely to have conflicted feelings about it, and part of you doesn't want to discover anything new about yourself because it might be painful and upsetting. But I regard it as useful to ally myself with the part of you that does want to discover and risk the consequences.

PT: I've noticed how you tend to parcel me into parts. That, I gather, is your favorite way of articulating my conflicts. But I won't quarrel with it; I'll even agree that there's a part of me that wants to discover, widen the scope of my self-understanding, and the rest. I'm not sure, however, what it means concretely for you to "ally" yourself with it. It's a nice metaphor, but what else does it entail other than encouraging me to explore and persuading me that it's a beneficial activity to engage in? And isn't there a paradox in that?—that you necessarily infringe on my freedom of choice in order to enlarge on it.

TH: Yes, I fully agree. That paradox is real. But let me make two points about it. First, I try my best to keep such infringements on your freedom to a minimum. Second, I make a distinction between short-term and long-term freedom, and it's only the short-term one that I violate—hopefully, in the best interests of your long-term freedom. It's a matter, really, of balance and judgment, when you come down to it.

PT: Point well taken! Okay, so I guess I should now talk

about the important thing I was consciously planning to avoid.

TH: "Should?"

PT: Look here, it's going to take some time!

TH: I appreciate that. But the reason I repeated your "should" is to suggest to you that you are still in a state of resistance.

9

On Neutrality, Impersonality, and Consistency

Can we participate effectively enough in therapy without contributing a significant source of extrinsic reinforcement? Can good interpretations be made without judging, valuating, criticizing, and advising—if not overtly and explicitly, then covertly and implicitly? Can the stringent kind of impersonality that such a neutrality requires be established and maintained at a sufficiently rigorous level? And can it be sustained throughout the entire course of an average-expectable therapy? These questions—which comprise the components of the larger challenge, Are *Psychotherapy*'s technical requirements feasible?—have to be considered carefully, closely, and concretely.

For if the requisite impersonality cannot be established and sustained at a sufficiently rigorous level, then our efforts to achieve it are not only bound to be futile but will be perceived as forced and artificial, and so too will be our efforts at neutrality. Moreover, and perhaps this is a more fundamental problem, if reinforcement concomitants lie implicit in every kind of interpretation that is therapeutically effective, then there's a serious dissonance between *Psychotherapy*'s basic goals and its chief technical resource.

I frame these problems and questions in pragmatic terms deliberately. The concept of neutrality has repercussions into profound issues having to do with human interrelatedness, with caring and loving. For that reason it isn't easy to examine it without taking account of basic human needs and emotions, and without engaging in questions and considerations that are fundamentally philosophical and ideological. Nevertheless, I'm going to restrict my definition of neutrality to the circumscribed context of one-to-one psychotherapy, and thereby keep my discussion close to the level of pragmatic feasibility. I don't intent to offer a defense of neutrality beyond the bald assertion that it is therapeutically efficacious, and my discussion is largely focused on its practical ramifications and limitations. The following introductory paragraphs contain as much theory as I deem necessary for those purposes.

Since communication is an intricately complex and many-faceted process (messages always abounding in messages, connotations and denotations multiply layered and intertwined), any remark we make—even discounting its nonverbal accompaniments—will inevitably convey meanings which are consciously unintended. To offer the explanation, "You berated your wife because you were humiliated by your boss," may be to scold our patient for it, or else exonerate him from blame ("So it wasn't really your fault"); to remark, "Your feelings of unworthiness are an incorporation of the feelings you were convinced your father had toward you," may be to imply that we don't share such feelings, or that the patient should try to be rid of them. There is a body of informed opinion which holds that these "unwanted" messages are actually what make traditional psychotherapy work; it isn't the content of our interpretations but rather their reinforcement concomitants that result in whatever psychological change occurs.

Nicholas Hobbs, in an essay called "Sources of Gain in Psychotherapy," gives a strong and thoughtful expression of that point of view—" . . . namely, that insight may have nothing to do with behavior change at all, or is, at best, an event that may or may not occur as a result of more fundamental personality reorganizations."[1] Hobbs defends the opinion that all methods of psychotherapy are efficacious insofar as they provide " . . . an opportunity for the client to experience closeness to another human being without getting hurt, to divest symbols associated with traumatic experiences of their anxiety-producing potential, to use the transference situation to learn not to need neurotic distortions, to practice being responsible for himself, and to clarify an old or learn a new cognitive system for ordering his world."[2] While it isn't easy to see how all this can be achieved without insight, the principal instrument is apparently reinforcement, broadly construed. Thus, what I am calling "unwanted" messages and concomitants are precisely what Hobbs, and others, believe are necessary and efficacious.

Without minimizing the fact that such reinforcement effects can and do lie implicit in each and every kind of interpretation we can offer (even those

---

1. Hobbs, in *Use of Interpretation in Treatment*, p. 14.
2. Ibid., p. 21.

which aren't so blatantly diagnostic as the two I mentioned above), I am convinced, for one, that their therapeutic efficacy is merely short-range, and for another, we aren't helpless against them. There are effective steps to ameliorate them, and when taken with diligence, sensitivity, and tact, those steps can reduce the reinforcement effect to a point of relative insignificance. I examine and discuss those steps under the rubric of "neutrality."

I also believe the requirements of neutrality can adequately be satisfied by a fully relevant and feasible kind of impersonality; and I am convinced that all of the technical principles can, and should, remain rigorously in force throughout every stage of *Psychotherapy*. Only when a patient is suffering a crisis, when his well-being is seriously at stake, do we need to abandon or modify our efforts to maintain the unique role definition that *Psychotherapy* entails. I examine and discuss the first belief under the heading of "impersonality" and the second under "consistency."

The Nature and Limits of Neutrality

To develop the *therapeutic process* takes time as well as work; and a significant amount of that time and work is devoted to establishing the fact that our behavior as therapists can have a variety of unintended meanings and unwanted implications. The paramount lesson our patient has to learn is that we mean never to advise him, judge him, valuate, scold, exonerate, and the rest. And it's obviously insufficient for us simply to have told him of that intention. "When I say things to you, you might hear things I don't mean to be saying. For instance, when I comment on an argument you had with someone, you may hear me taking either your side in it or the other person's; when I try to explain why you feel or felt a certain way, I may seem to be giving you an excuse for it; when I suggest that a habit of yours is due to this or that reason, I may seem to be blaming or scolding or exonerating you. I want to make it clear, however, that I don't ever intend to be doing those things." This message has to be conveyed, probably repeatedly, but it must also be actualized—to the limits of our capability and sensitivity. It has to be conveyed and actualized in a variety of different ways and contexts because it's a lesson that takes time and much experience to learn. But, short of an ideal extreme, the achievement is altogether possible.

In order to establish our neutrality we must first be sure we don't, in fact, intend anything more than exploration, understanding, and discovery; we have to be confidently free of any impulse to advise and guide our patient in any extra-therapy ways. Our second requirement is to remain alert to the likelihood that he prefers to be advised, guided, valuated, and the rest, and therefore may hear such messages in everything we say (as well as don't say).

Consequently, when a patient does respond to the unintended message, we have to bear in mind that his response was determined by at least these two factors: our interpretation's actual implication, and his underlying motivation. We have to keep from losing sight of the fact that interpretations are likely to imply both advice and criticism; we must listen closely for those implications (both in our formulations as well as in our patient's responses) and take active steps against them. I can best explain how by means of illustration.

Suppose you have offered the interpretation that your patient is behaving cruelly toward his brother out of feelings of envy for him. Even if your timing was optimal, you should have been aware of having implicitly scolded him for it, and also of having implicitly advised him to stop behaving that way. Sometimes these implications will be apparent in his immediate response and can be dealt with directly. Suppose that's the case: after accepting the validity of your interpretation, the patient says, "So I guess I should stop behaving that way toward my brother, shouldn't I?" and he persists in asking for your opinion. "I take it you want me to advise you what to do, or at least endorse your new way of behaving," is your optimal rejoinder. This kind of interpretation is far more valuable for the *therapeutic process* than anything you might be able to say at this juncture about his envy. And if he persists further, exclaiming, "Yes, but what's wrong with your doing that?" you can remind him of your promise to give no advice.[3]

When the implications of advice aren't so apparent, they have to be listened for. And you'll find it especially helpful to be on the alert whenever a patient reports a significant action that was different or new for him, or when the action is clearly related to the topic of a recent session, because it may have been motivated by a desire to conform or not to a piece of advice that was latent in an interpretation you gave. Often he reports that action with an attitude that reflects the fact—a note of stubborn defiance, perhaps, or an air of resigned compliance, or a "look what a good boy I am!" or something indicative of the fact that your reaction is involved. But even when such signs are not evident, it can be useful to raise the issue because it has such an intrinsic value.

So suppose the patient in the illustration had accepted your initial interpreta-

---

3. The rationale: "Because then, if you chose not to follow my advice, I would find myself in the position of being disappointed in you. Or if you did do it, then you would expect me to be pleased with you. And those are feelings that I don't want to have toward you, because that would mean I was judging you. You see, if I did judge you, or have feelings of disappointment, or anger, or whatever, then that would interfere with my ability to help you to understand your behavior. In any case, I don't think it would be helpful to you to behave in ways that are meant to please me or to displease me" (Paul, *Letters*, pp. 89–90).

tion and then gone ahead to explore the basis of his envy, and now, during a subsequent session, he is telling you (with a tone of some defiance, let's say) that he has again behaved cruelly toward his brother. Two possibilities might cross your mind, and both might be equally valid: (1) he is telling you your interpretation was wrong (or, if not wrong, ineffective); (2) he is saying he didn't follow your "advice." The second possibility has the greater priority, and therefore I advocate you take the opportunity to explore it with him.

The straightforward way to initiate such an exploration is with a confronting articulation, "I gather you're feeling defiant right now, both toward your brother and toward me." You could formulate it this way: "When you told me how you behaved cruelly again, you seemed to be experiencing a sense of defiance about it; I gather that reflects how you feel about your brother, but I think it also has to do with similar feelings you are having toward me." If the patient acknowledges defiance toward you, you can go ahead to suggest that he must have thought you'd given him a piece of advice when you made the interpretation in the previous session—and you can point out that that was not your intention. If, however, he acknowledges the defiance only with regard to his brother, you can still press the point, as follows: "I have a hunch your feeling is also directed at me; what I have in mind is this: last time, when I said I thought you were behaving cruelly out of envy, you may have taken that as a piece of advice, as if I was really advising you to stop behaving that way; so the fact that you're feeling defiant today here could mean that you thought I wanted you to stop it." If he accepts this formulation ("Yes, I guess I did think you were sort of saying I should cut it out"), you can continue to clarify the issue by pointing out, "So it might be that part of the reason you decided not to change your behavior is you didn't want to do what I seemed to be telling you to do," or you can try to clarify the general issue by saying, "It is reasonable for you to hear a piece of advice when I make an observation or tell you what I think your motivation is, but I don't intend ever to tell you what to do or give any kind of advice"—or you can do both.

The same considerations apply to criticism. But criticism is more complex and subtle than advice, with several different shades of meaning as well as dimensions. The basic dimension pertains to value judgment, which overrides all of our attitudes and every aspect of the way we live and relate to people. And nevertheless, despite the fact that moral values, whether broadly or narrowly construed, can be said to provide the framework for all human experience and behavior, the only value judgment that *Psychotherapy* permits us is the one that attaches to full and authentic understanding, to rigorous self-examination and exploration. All other values based on moral precepts are stringently excluded. Maladaptive behavior, too, is not to be regarded from a value-judgment standpoint, and the same applies to self-destructive behavior.[4] And if I am to claim, as I mean to be claiming (but I soon qualify the claim by excluding intrapsychic events from our neutrality), that maladaptive and self-destructive behavior is neither "good" nor "bad," I must recognize that to discover with a patient that a certain action of his, either by design or not, leads him into maladaptive and self-destructive ways, is bound to convey the implicit message "This action is bad for you," which, in turn, can be little different from saying, "It's bad."

Consider the illustration: Isn't there a value judgment attached to your patient's cruel behavior? Isn't envy a bad feeling? (Isn't it good to be kind and sympathetic?) And don't you, as a human being, for yourself and in your personal relationships, have values and attitudes based on moral considerations? Of course you do—and so does your patient. The point is not whether you have them, or even whether you happen to share his; but as his therapist, the only system of values and morality you recognize and work with is his. You do not impose your moral code, your values; you work exclusively within the framework of his.

But is that really possible? If his moral code differs sharply from yours, if he has a positive valuation of cruelty and envy, for instance, can you simply accept it and not work in such a way (subtly and insidiously) so as to alter his valuation in accordance with yours? That's a moot and a difficult question. My position on it, however, is clear and simple: the goal of neutrality is so vital that the only question becomes whether you can realize it. And in those cases where you have reason to suspect you cannot, when a patient's moral code is too repugnant and unacceptable to you, then your only recourse is to abandon any attempt at conducting *Psychotherapy*—because you won't be able to maintain the kind of neutrality that's essential for establishing and developing the *therapeutic process*.

I am skirting a profound and difficult subject, whose implications, when taken to extremes, may render my position untenable. But rather than examine extreme cases (suicide, for instance) and try to establish limits to my position on neutrality that way, I restrict myself to the more typical and less extreme forms of the problem. I want to stress, however, that it is only *Psychotherapy*, not necessarily psychotherapy, that may need to be abandoned. This circumstance is one of several that rules out the advisability of *Psychotherapy* as a method of choice.

A useful way to realize the goal of not criticizing and valuating is by

---

4. It is tempting, but misleading, to sidestep the issue with the kinds of value judgments that the medical model provides, by claiming that maladaptive behavior is "bad" according to a biological criterion. All moral values can be reduced to such a criterion.

listening hard for the patient's reaction to the latent or implied criticism and valuation in each of your interpretations. You can safely assume the reaction is there (especially when therapy is in its early phases), and you should welcome every opportunity to articulate and discuss it. You should want to follow up an interpretation with, "I believe you're taking my remark as a kind of criticism of you [as if I'd made a judgment of you and had accused you of being an unworthy person]." Or if not directed at him personally, the same kind of remark can be made with respect to the experience, the action, or the affect that was involved—"I believe you're taking my remark as a criticism, as if I'd said the action you took [or the feeling you had] is a bad one."

Suppose he acknowledges the fact, and then goes on to challenge your claim that you didn't mean to criticize him. "Sure, I feel you've criticized and judged me by saying I feel envious of my brother, which is a terrible way to feel toward anyone, especially one's brother, and it makes me a terrible person; so what you've done is imply that I am terrible—and if that's not a criticism and value judgment I don't know what is!" The crucial issue is joined, and you have a valuable opportunity to clarify it by making a vital distinction. Not only do you need to be utterly clear about the issue and the distinction, you must take pains to make them equally clear to the patient, which usually requires both patience and perseverance; so you shouldn't be eager to be rid of the issue or approach it with a once-around-is-enough attitude. You can continue as follows: "I do appreciate that you can hear a criticism and a value judgment when I observe that you are envious. But when I say you're feeling such-and-such, I mean only that I believe it, I don't mean it's a bad way to feel or that it means you're a bad person." And if he responds, "Fair enough, but do you mean to say that envy is not bad? It's good, then!" you can reply, "I mean to say nothing at all about whether it's good or bad." If he pursues the point by exclaiming, "But surely you recognize that envy is a bad and unworthy way to feel!" you have to keep from making the error of saying anything about the morality of envy. The temptation to be resisted here is to go into why he regards envy as so morally reprehensible, because at this point it might have the distinct implication that you don't share his attitude, and he ought not to feel that way. Another possibility, the interpretation, "It may well be that one of the reasons you haven't been able [or willing] to recognize the feeling of envy in yourself is because you have such a strong negative value attached to it," is an error for three separate reasons: (1) it deflects attention from the vital issue of neutrality; (2) it imposes an explanation on the patient which he isn't interested in right now; (3) it seems to be using the interpretive mode for the purposes of winning an argument.

I want to stress what a serious error it can be at this juncture to challenge, or even seem in any way to be challenging, his conviction that envy is bad and therefore he's a bad person. This is the wrong moment to deal with that issue—and the right moment will come in time, no reason to doubt it. At this juncture, however, during the kind of exchange I'm describing, the salient issue is your neutrality, and the patient needs to be persuaded that you can work free from moral judgments—or, if not "persuaded," he must at least be clear what your avowed intention is.

Therefore, the most useful rejoinder to his exclamation is to say you understand his valuation of envy, and you empathize with his feelings about it. You can point out that you too have a personal position on the morality of envy ("along with a position on the morality of a lot of other matters as well"), and then this crucial message: "But as your therapist, during our sessions, I try to steer completely clear of such value judgments; I try not to let myself have them here, or at the very least to let them matter to me, because my only aim is to understand and help you understand, and that precludes passing judgment on you and evaluating the things you speak about." Now, if the patient expresses incredulity, saying something like, "I don't see how that is humanly possible," you needn't make any further response. That exclamation, after all, is an eminently fair question, but all you could claim is, "I do my best"—and that much can be taken for granted.

You can also take it for granted that he will be listening for the implications of criticism in your remarks because he needs, wants, and probably dreads them. Given the power of transference and influence of regression to distort and magnify your meaning to him, a patient is likely to react to those unintended aspects of your remarks even when he disclaims any interest in your criticism. And this, again, requires of you a diligence in detecting and interpreting these aspects of his reactions. Moreover, in addition to articulating the wish and need, in addition to making it clear you never intend to gratify them, it may be necessary to point out to him that such implications are manifold and subtle, and for that reason you're going to try and show him how they are at work whenever you detect them.

Here are several illustrations. (1) When you've had occasion to remark that he wants a scolding from you, you remain alert to the patient's response insofar as it may reflect the fact that he experienced the remark itself as a scolding ("You wanted me to scold you, and then when I pointed out that fact to you, it felt as if I was actually doing it, didn't it?"). (2) When you've made a remark which may contain an implicit exoneration, as if you were excusing his behavior or taking his side, you want to detect in his response some evidence of it so you can point it out: "You feel warmly toward me right now for two reasons, I believe: one, I helped you understand why you were cruel to your brother yesterday; and two, the explanation lets you off the hook; it implies I'm taking your side against him, maybe also that I'm excusing your behavior.'' (3) When he grows resentful after you've interpreted his overreaction to his brother's provocation, you may choose to explain his resentment in terms of your having implicitly sided with the brother against him. Such possibilities abound in the course of therapy, and each provides a valuable opportunity for establishing—and reestablishing—your neutrality, while at the same time acknowledging and exploring your patient's wish and need for your partiality.

However, though we can take some clear and effective steps against the unwanted but unavoidable implications of criticism and advice, we face a more difficult problem with respect to a certain implicit value judgment and directive that inheres in the act of interpreting, the message "This is important, so pay attention to it!" I have already discussed this potential contradiction between the interpretive mode and the *therapeutic process*, and when it comes right down to it, my resolution is a species of hedging. The value judgment can probably never be entirely eliminated, but with careful technique this breach of neutrality can usually be reduced to a point of relative insignificance. Ideally, the spirit with which to make an interpretation can be expressed in these two sentences: (1) "Here is a piece of understanding [an observation and/or an explanation] that I think may be useful for you to consider in your deliberations." (2) "You are free to consider it or not." The first sentence is no problem, the second is. It says, in effect, "Though I believe this is useful I nonetheless remain neutral on it." But the question becomes, In what way and to what extent can a patient remain free from considering an interpretation's content?

At the very least, I believe it's possible for us to maximize our neutrality with respect to interpretations by avoiding any sense of ego-involvement in them, any hint of chastising the patient for ignoring them, and also any hint of satisfaction when he takes them seriously. But it would be disingenuous of me to claim that it's likely a patient will ever feel perfectly free to ignore an interpretation. From his vantage point, after all, if you'd decided to make an observation or offer an explanation, then it must be "important," and you must therefore be expecting him to take it seriously. To simply disavow any such expectation can do little good, and there are circumstances where any attempt on your part to do that would only confound the issue. There are, nevertheless, certain circumstances in which effective steps can be taken against this reinforcement effect. For one, early in therapy it is quite common for a patient to feel that each and every interpretation demands a response from him; he will feel called upon to "deal with" its content, to validate or invalidate it, and occasionally he will have the need to express gratitude. These reactions can usually be subjected to interpretative work; you can articulate and discuss them, while at the same time pointing out that you don't intend any of them and that what you're striving for is a condition in which he feels just as free after an interpretation as he did before it. You have in mind, of course, that he should feel more free afterwards, freer to express his mind and experience his feelings. To be sure, while it isn't so difficult to interpret the fact that the patient feels you have a stake in your interpretations (and the fact that it gets done with an interpretation may seem to make this claim absurd, but in practice it doesn't), it is far more difficult for you to actualize that aspect of your neutrality. For that reason it remains an ideal state of affairs that can only be approached and approximated.

Furthermore, the inescapable fact that every remark we make, not excluding interpretations, has to some extent the effect of directing our patient's attention remains a vital consideration in the timing of all our remarks. And insofar as the well-timed interpretations are those which satisfy the criterion of resonating with the ongoing *therapeutic process*, they are the only kinds of remarks whose directive effects can be minimized. The good interpretation, formulated empathically and personally, is one that enables a patient to say what he wants and needs to say, rather than directing him to say it; its facilitating effect is substantially greater than any other of its effects. Accordingly, insofar as it remains relatively free from coercive and directive effects, it remains the ideal instrument for protecting and promoting our neutrality as well as his freedom.

Now I have to consider a potential danger that can result from the intensity of our neutrality, the fact that it can shade into indifference. It goes without having to be said that if our neutrality amounted to indifference, then it would be entirely untenable, because indifference implies noncaring, and our professional service is without ethical foundation if we don't care that our patient is suffering—and care profoundly. But not only shouldn't neutrality entail indifference, it needn't, and for several important reasons which *Psychotherapy* shares with psychotherapy at large.

Psychotherapy provides us with many opportunities—which, in turn, provide for many ways—to show a patient that we care. The principal opportunity emerges from his need to be understood, and the way we gratify that need reflects a profound aspect of caring. We care to know his suffering, to understand and empathize. But our caring needn't stop there. A deep respect for his needs can be shown in such actions as being accommodating about appointment times, fees, extra-session attentions, and the like. A willingness to be "manipulated" for the sake of our patient's well-being can be a tangible expression of our caring attitude. And there's no need for stringency in regard to such actions, so long as the first priority remains with the principal process of therapy. A substantial flexibility can be maintained to meet the needs of particular patients, and where we "draw the line" should be based on their particular requirements and conditions in conjunction with ours. We are indifferent to their "real" needs only when, and to the extent that, what we could do to meet them would seriously interfere with the essential work of therapy. That rests on a judgment we must make for each individual patient, and he must concur in it. If he cannot, whether for reasons that are substantially transferential or not, we may have to make certain compromises to insure that our neutrality is not perceived as indifference—for I cannot see how psychotherapy can be effective when our patient perceives us as indifferent to him.

But—to repeat—it is the very intensity of our interpretive stance that guards us against both the appearance and substance of indifference. And I believe it's vital to define our neutrality as limited to the act of understanding; we can then construe our position this way: we remain so neutral in that respect *because* we care about our patient's well-being.

From the perspective of caring, indifference can be construed in terms of taking sides. One of its dimensions in psychotherapy has to do with taking the patient's side vis-à-vis others with whom he is related. When there is interpersonal conflict, neutrality means taking a position neither for or against him in that conflict; it means avoiding both the laying of blame and the exoneration from blame. Blame, however, is not the same as responsibility; or if it is, then a distinction has to be drawn between ethical responsibility and causal (or objective) responsibility. To lay responsibility in the latter sense doesn't necessarily mean to be partial; responsibility can imply only cause or determination, while blame implies fault. Still, however, the distinction between assigning responsibility and laying blame is easier to draw in theory than in practice.

If your patient was wondering why his brother is unfriendly to him, and you offered the explanation that he is hostile toward his brother, or behaves cruelly toward him, you may have intended only to point out a determinant, to explain that the hostility and cruelty is objectively responsible. But he may construe the explanation as a laying of blame and finding of fault, and he isn't unjustified in that construction. To try and persuade him that there's a subtle but real distinction between what he apprehended and what you intended could be quite futile, and might only provoke a philosophical dialogue. Moreover, it might be quite impossible to convince him that you had remained neutral when you offered the explanation. Does this mean, then, that it is impossible for you to maintain the requisite neutrality? Yes, in fact it may mean exactly that—but only if and when you make such interpretations.

The direct and inescapable conclusion is this: when you want not only to remain neutral but also to maintain a neutrality in your patient's eyes, you have to keep from making those kinds of explanations. (And that's easy enough to do, because those kinds of explanations tend to be poor technique from other considerations as well.) In other words, if you have any reason to suspect that an interpretation you are considering will have strong implications of fault-finding—or exonerating, scolding, advising, and the rest—then it isn't a good interpretation to make, and you should avoid making it. The key word in the foregoing sentence is "strong," and the opening phrase is crucial.

Several technical rules of thumb can be adduced from the general principle that before you venture an interpretation you should feel secure in your neutrality. For one, you should never interpret out of emotional arousal, when you're feeling irritated or defensive, and the like. Neither should you use an interpretation during anything like an argument, or when you're caught off guard by a direct question. Chances are too great that under such conditions any interpretation will carry a heavy burden of unwanted implications, it's purpose won't be merely to understand.

This guiding principle doesn't rule out all interpretations of interpersonal events and conflicts, even early in therapy before your neutrality has been well established. If the patient is wondering why he gets hostile toward his brother when his brother does little to provoke it, to suggest a reason for his hostility (for example, "What do you think of the possibility that you have old and unresolved feelings of rivalry with him") is not necessarily to have taken sides. In practice it's usually easy enough to distinguish between blaming, on the one hand, and explaining, on the other. And if the patient responds with, "So it's really all my fault," you could try to clarify the distinction by inquiring into what "my fault" means to him. Furthermore, even when he accepts the distinction you can remain alert to occasions in which this kind of issue might arise, and unless you could first achieve a resolution of the issue itself—unless you could really convince him that you weren't laying blame or finding fault when you sought to explain his interpersonal conflicts—you can (and you probably should) avoid interpretations of that kind. The same is true, of course, for all the manifestations of neutrality I have so far discussed.

The same is not true, however, for a second dimension of neutrality: a more difficult, and perhaps also more vital, dimension to conceptualize. It has to do with taking a patient's side against his suffering, against his psychological problems, his neurosis or symptoms. To side with "part" of a patient, with an aspect of his self (no matter how conceptualized), is often a tacit and subtle kind of position for us to take, but I believe it's quite accurate to characterize our fundamental position in those terms. The question, for me, is whether this is a fair way to construe "neutrality."

It is certainly problematic, and perhaps also unwarranted, to contend that neutrality requires of us not to take sides in that way where the patient's intrapsychic life is concerned. I could resolve the difficulty by again distinguishing between blame and responsibility, by contending that we remain neutral, insofar as we never imply an ethical injunction when we "blame" his harsh super-ego or his neurotic habits, we only lay objective responsibility at their doors. But perhaps it would suffice to claim that the question of neutrality does not apply in this, the intrapsychic, realm. For in a vital sense we must take the patient's side against his problems; to do otherwise is to fall into an indifference that could undercut the very nature and purpose of our service.

I'm going to examine the nature and limits of this kind of intrapsychic side-taking with the help of two illustrations. The first deals with a particular instance of suffering that has an external source, the second with a longstanding problem of an intrapsychic nature.

Suppose your patient is in a state of distress; he barely manages to tell you that his lover has abandoned him, rejected him in favor of another, and then he bursts into tears. You can hardly help empathizing with his anguish and wishing there was something you could do to ameliorate it, but let's suppose that anything you think of saying will either violate the principles of *Psychotherapy*, or will be ineffective, or both. You have reason to judge that an interpretation is untimely because understanding (as distinct from "There, there, I do understand!") will not prevail against the intensity of his suffering. At the same time, your business-as-usual stance may make you feel uncaring and callous, so your temptation will be strong to abandon, at least temporarily, the principles of *Psychotherapy* and offer the patient some sort of relief based on principles of healing. You might, of course, try to disguise such an effort by formulating a remark in terms that at least sound like an interpretation; for instance, "You're feeling devastated right now because", not only are you feeling the hurt of rejection, you are also feeling rage"; but that would actually convey little more than the message "You will feel better by and by." Even, "You're feeling especially devastated because you cannot imagine that you could lose your love for your lover and find it in another," might amount to the same underlying message, "Patience and fortitude! Be strong! Endure your suffering and you will prevail!" But what other alternative do you have?

Do I seem to be implying that you are helpless in the face of your patient's suffering? Is your experience of helplessness nothing more than an empathic recognition of his? And do you in fact believe he is actually so helpless? These questions are pertinent insofar as they suggest a possible line of interpretation which can focus attention on the intrapsychic issues. You can articulate his helplessness with, "You're feeling utterly helpless, as if there's nothing you can do about your anguish," and if he agrees, but asks, "So is there?" you can respond with, "I have no way of knowing, but I think your sense of helpless-ness is so deep and pervasive right now that it is contributing to your suffer-ing." If you already know a good deal about his intrapsychic realm, you may have some basis to be specific about how and why his sense of helplessness is contributing to his suffering; for instance, you might be able to suggest it is making contact with feelings of impotency, or redintegrating memories of his father's having left him, and the like. The point I'm stressing is that you can address yourself to the sources of his suffering which are internal and idiosyn-cratic to him—there are bound to be some.

If the patient accepts your suggestion, and if he goes on to reflect upon it, then the *therapeutic process* will be brought into work. If he cannot make that switch, cannot consider the possibility that his helplessness is not a function, even in part, of his inner reality, you cannot press the issue. But neither do you have to abandon your characteristic role posture until and unless you judge that he is experiencing a serious crisis, that he is plunged into a danger-ous depression, that he is now a suicide risk, and the like. If that becomes the case, then anything you can do to help must, of course, take precedence over maintaining the integrity of the *therapeutic process*.

It goes without saying that there is no sense at all in protecting long-range benefits when short-range problems are so severe there may never be a long-range. When the therapy itself is in jeopardy, not to mention the patient's existence itself, then all short-term considerations have priority, and whatever measures we can take must be taken. And there is always the danger that we will hold back too long and allow a situation to deteriorate too far before we take appropriate action. Here, of course, is where clinical wisdom and experi-ence count for everything, where rigor can become insupportable rigidity, and neutrality nothing short of indifference.

But I believe it's important to bear in mind what enormous benefits a patient can gain when we show him, with our business-as-usual equanimity, that we have faith in his ability to endure and overcome. I discuss this matter in the final section of this chapter, under the heading of "consistency" and in the framework of considering modifications of technique. Suffice it to say here that your neutrality with respect to real events, combined with your focus on intrapsychic determinants and conditions, can have a profound kind of therapeutic value both in the short and long run.

The second illustration involves a patient who comes for therapy suffering from a disabling symptom, say a phobia, that is seriously disrupting his life. (I am assuming he is well informed, and has decided he wants a traditional therapy, knowing that it isn't likely to be the most economical method for ameliorating his symptom; in other words, you've taken pains to rule out all doubts about his decision and willingness to delay a quick relief from his disability.) Under such conditions you have to work, I believe, with two timing criteria: the fundamental one I've been describing in this book, and a special one which has the short-range goal of achieving as rapid as possible an understanding of the symptom. This special criterion entails actively offering interpretations relevant to the phobia, and in this way caring about it—caring to explore its causes, its meanings, its ramifications, and to achieve discoveries thereby which may help to ameliorate it.

I don't believe you have to assume that an active exploration of his symptom must await a full uncovering of the patient's life history, his personality, or whatever; I don't believe it's necessary to assume that the symptom must take a back seat until therapy has achieved some of its other goals, nor must it be delayed until the *therapeutic process* has been fully established. Not that it may not have to do that, for it well may; my point is that you needn't make such assumptions in advance. Furthermore, if you believe you can give the patient advice or guidance that could significantly affect the symptom, then you may choose to introduce a "flaw" in the therapy; and you can readily explain the departure to him in terms of the need to overcome his disability as swiftly as possible.

But what if the patient prevents you from doing any of that by beginning therapy in a way that seems oblivious of the disabling phobia, making no direct references to it and few if any allusions to it? That should strike you as noteworthy, and you should want to understand the meaning and function of his avoidance of the subject. If you think you understand it, and even if you aren't so certain your understanding is correct, you can venture to share that understanding with him, using the special timing criterion as your justification. Here, of course, you'd be taking the risk of harming the *therapeutic process*, insofar as you'd be steering him toward the subject of his phobia. But you can prudently take that risk, because he may be proceeding with the belief or fantasy that the symptom will dissolve if he talks about his early childhood, for instance, or his sex life, his interpersonal relationships, or whatever. He may also presume that after he's given you all the facts, you're going to formulate an interpretation for him that will cause the phobia to vanish. Whatever the case, it can count as a piece of useful understanding to uncover and examine the patient's assumptions, beliefs, and fantasies vis-à-vis the disabling symptom, and for that reason you will want to achieve that goal. Therefore, I recommend taking special pains to find an opportunity to say something like the following: "I believe you're deliberately not talking about your phobia because you believe that that will do no good; instead, you believe it might be more helpful to work on your early childhood [sex life, interpersonal relations, etc.]."

Now, suppose the patient agrees, "Yes, you have understood me well," and continues with, "Now I'd like to understand you. Are you implying that my belief is wrong, that working on my early childhood isn't the best way to overcome my phobia?" The subject is now your neutrality with respect to the content of the sessions, a subject I discussed in chapter three in the context of the Basic Instruction. What you say in answer has to steer a very delicate course between the neutrality to which you've committed yourself in the Basic Instruction and the way in which that neutrality may not extend to the disabling symptom itself. I believe the appropriate answer can be formulated this way: "No, I didn't mean to imply that—I can see where you draw the implication from, but I didn't intend to challenge your belief. The reason I drew your attention to it is because I was distracted by the fact that you weren't talking about the very thing that caused you to seek therapy, and it's something that's causing you so much suffering." The point of formulating your decision in terms of "distraction" (rather than saying simply, "I was wondering why . . .") is that it stays consonant with the spirit of the Basic Instruction. After all, if you are distracted by your patient's behavior, and that distraction is interfering with your ability to listen and understand, then you are justified in doing what you can to remove it.[5]

Let's suppose the patient appreciates your rationale and doesn't quarrel with your formulation, but he wants to know whether you were distracted because his avoidance was surprising, and that meant his belief was mistaken; or suppose he simply asks to know whether you disagree with his belief that the appropriate way to approach the symptom is via his early childhood. You now have to decide whether to tell him that you believe (if in fact you do believe) that it might be better if he spoke about his phobia, or whether to say, no matter what your belief is, "I'm not sure what would be more useful for you and more helpful for overcoming your disability, whether as you believe it would be more effective to talk about your childhood or whether it would be more effective to talk about your phobia." Either response, in my opinion, is likely to be useful, though the second has the added advantage of avoiding a didactic discussion. In any case, however, chances are now good that he will go on to examine both his assumptions about therapy as well as about his symptom—and you have acted in a way that isn't indifferent to him and his suffering.

There is more to be said about the two illustrations (and I return, at the end of this chapter, to several of the issues they raised), but I intend them only to

---

5. This rationale is so elastic, and so easily stretched to cover a wide range of directives, that it has to be used sparingly and judiciously—only when the issue at hand is of major import. It should probably be reserved for issues like the one I'm examining, where your distraction is based on the fact that you care about the patient's well-being.

exemplify an important limitation on our neutrality. Before I move to the subject of impersonality, a third aspect (or meaning) of neutrality must be considered and distinguished from indifference; it is reflected in the fact that you don't gratify your patient's interpersonal needs vis-à-vis you as a person. You do recognize and acknowledge the full gamut of needs and wishes that come to be directed at you—needs for support, for nurturance, dependency, love, and the like—but you rigorously avoid gratifying them for the patient. That you frustrate these basic needs invites the charge that you are indifferent to him. Furthermore, in a certain sense, you are also "indifferent" to what he tells you, insofar as you avoid reacting with approval or with disapproval, with pleasure or displeasure, with gladness, sadness, excitement, disgust—at least, you carefully keep from revealing or conveying such reactions when you have them. But I believe the term "neutrality" remains fully appropriate here, because you aren't indifferent to what he tells you, insofar as you strive to apprehend and comprehend his messages and meanings. You don't frustrate his need to be understood, which is a vital ego function and a basic human need.

Its emphasis on understanding may leave the impression that *Psychotherapy* is mainly an intellectual experience for the patient; he works with his cognitive processes at the expense of his affective and conative ones; your neutrality extends to everything except intellectual events, and those are all you care about. There is actually a certain sense in which this impression isn't altogether inaccurate. But first it bears mentioning that intellectualization can be a defense and a resistance, and often it is. Therefore, to draw a patient's attention to the fact that he's resorting to intellectual constructions in order to avoid experiencing the full impact of his affects, impulses, and conflicts, can serve the interests of the *therapeutic process* (as well as his synthetic-function). Moreover, when intellectualization isn't implicated, there can be value in articulating those affects, impulses, and conflicts. A significant kind of interpretation takes the form, "I think I know what you are feeling" (for instance, "You are ashamed, I believe, but you cannot bear the feeling, and so you ..."), by which you attempt to foster in the patient a readiness to confront and acknowledge his affective experiences and also to allow such experiences their full effects.

> Much of the transaction in *Psychotherapy* commonly has to do with nonintellectual aspects of behavior. At the same time, however, the transaction itself is largely in verbal and cognitive terms. When your patient feels angry you will not give him license to throw ashtrays, instead you will encourage him to talk about it (not, mind you, to talk himself out of it). When he attempts to provoke you into some emotional state, you won't permit yourself the emotion—at least you will not express it to

him. Instead you will interpret (again, in verbal and cognitive terms) his intention. Thus, not only is there a steady translation of experience into verbal-cognitive discourse, but you will not engage your patient in anything like a direct encounter.[6]

We don't discourage affects, of course, and the fact that we never react in kind (or, for that matter, in opposite kind) enhances our patient's freedom to experience and express his feelings. But the therapy's format—the fact that verbalization remains the chief currency of expression—does have a constraining influence both on the range of his feelings as well as the modes of their expression. Moreover, while he may be encouraged to experience his affects and impulses, there is an undercurrent in the session that flows in the direction of cognitive control over such experiences. The overriding goal is to gain control over them, which needn't entail any stifling or inhibiting of affects. What it means to "gain control" deserves more discussion, but I'll only emphasize how it very often leads to a release of affects, a freeing of emotions from the grip of cognition, and how the patient typically gains in his sensitivity to affective experiences.

The reason that happens is because cognitive control is a two-way process, and because ego-autonomy is fundamentally an intrapsychic phenomenon. But theoretical speculations aside, it is clear to me that *Psychotherapy* can heighten and intensify the patient's emotional life. At the empirical level it typically does. Faced with a therapist who is protecting his neutrality, and therefore behaving in an emotionally nonresponsive way, it's easy to suppose that a patient will remain equally nonresponsive, either as a result of a modeling process or because his emotions fail to have any real impact on us. But this needn't happen, and won't if we stay alert to the possibility and take appropriate interpretive steps with respect to it.[7]

The Nature and Limits of Impersonality

A neutrality so stringent as I have outlined for *Psychotherapy* mandates, it seems to me, an equally stringent impersonality. I can see no way around the conclusion that when we intend never to evaluate and pass judgment, when we try to keep from being a source of extrinsic reinforcements, from taking sides, then we must also remain as impersonal as we can possibly and feasibly be. Because if a patient knows you are a pacifist,

---

6. Paul, *Letters*, pp. 18–19.
7. I can refer you to *Letters* 22 and 23 (pp. 232–47) for a discussion of the issues I raise in this paragraph.

how can he persuaded that you're not judging him when he advocates war? If he learns you believe in the sanctity of marriage, how can he behave adulterously without incurring valuation? And if you tell him that your tastes in music range from the Renaissance to the Baroque, he may have to defend a love for Tchaikovsky.

You may challenge my thesis by contending that being personal need not, from your vantage point, prevent neutrality, that you can maintain a thoroughgoing neutrality despite anything your patient may know about you personally. After all, you do have attitudes, opinions, values, and tastes—How could it humanly be otherwise?—so your task remains the same whether or not he knows what they are. In either case, after all, you're going to have to make it clear to the patient that your intention is to be neutral, and you can do that from a personal position no less than from an impersonal one.

This argument is necessarily made from your vantage point, not from his. Two questions, therefore, remain: (1) Of what value is it to your patient to know personal things about you? (2) Won't knowing them complicate and encumber his task of accepting your neutrality and working securely within it? My answer to (1) is, Little-if-any; to (2) it's, Yes—and unnecessarily.

Since you don't "use yourself" when you conduct *Psychotherapy*, since the *therapeutic process* provides no way for your "personality" to serve any useful function, there isn't any significant benefit to being personal. Consequently, insofar as it does facilitate neutrality, impersonality is the optimal position to strive for. And the two interlocking questions—How impersonal *should*, and how impersonal *can*, we be?—therefore reduce to one. Only the *can* question is germane, because the method requires you to be as impersonal as possible.

This is an aspect of *Psychotherapy* that typically evokes the most protest from my students (but not, I hasten to add, from my patients) who challenge it with some heat. And when I spell out the full extent to which I believe you must strive for impersonality, some students give expression to outrage. For I don't stop at refusing to divulge such things as whether you're happily married or your taste in movies; you may choose not to tell a patient whether you are married, and might refuse to divulge whether you've seen a particular movie, even if it's a movie to which he had an important reaction that he plans to explore during the session. It would, after all, economize on time if he didn't have to describe the movie and could devote all the time to his reaction. However, for you to tell whether you saw a movie would be to have revealed something personal about yourself, and therefore you can choose not to. Your intention to remain impersonal can extend that far.

But I have already overstated the matter. The fact that you've seen a movie differs from the fact of your marital status insofar as it pertains to knowledge;

and your store of factual information may be personal, but it can have different implications for your neutrality than other aspects of your life and personality. So when your patient asks if you have seen a particular movie, or if you are familiar with *King Lear* or with Mahler's Ninth Symphony, you may give a direct answer if you have reason to judge that it was not a "loaded" question. And what I mean by "loaded" is the extent to which its intention and function is to learn something about you personally.

However, the problem of knowledge and neutrality is not as easily resolved as that. But before I examine it more closely I need to draw a distinction between our personality features which have a direct bearing on our ability to understand a patient and those which do not. The patient's personal questions, especially at the beginning of therapy, are generally directed at our credentials and suitability. Competency and compatibility are basically at issue, though it will often be accompanied by a concern over whether his particular life-style and experiences will be comprehensible to us. Discounting questions about professional training and orientation (which must, of course, be answered), a variety of questions can be asked about our personal status, questions such as "Do you have children?" "Are you a devout Catholic?" "Are you knowledgeable about music theory?"—and they may be interpreted as questions about special competency. If a patient is having difficulties with his children, he might believe that a parent is likely to understand him better than someone who is childless; if he is a devout Catholic, he might believe that only a devout Catholic would comprehend his feelings and experiences; and if he is a composer having problems with his work, he may want his therapist to know something about music theory.

These are clearly fair questions, up to a point, but they can readily be answered in a way that preserves our impersonality. The underlying question is all that needs to be addressed, and it is, "Will you understand me sufficiently?" And since understanding is such a crucial aspect of *Psychotherapy*, this is really a key question that deserves our greatest consideration; so in the interests of making the best possible judgment, it will be necessary to investigate matters carefully. Such an investigation, in fact, is necessary whether or not the patient brings it up. The fact remains, however, that it can be done in a way that preserves our impersonality—at least in one important sense of the term.

Consider the three questions I used for illlustration. Suppose your patient believes that a childless, non-Catholic, and unmusical therapist is not likely to understand his problems. Whether or not you believe this is likely to be true, you have to acknowledge his underlying concern; and therefore you have to take pains both to articulate it fully and to explore it carefully. You can do both, however, without taking a position on the question itself—without, on the one hand, denying that his concern may be intrinsically valid, and also without losing sight of the fact that your being a parent doesn't insure your ability to understand his particular problems, that your not being Catholic might have little bearing on your ability to understand his religious experiences, and that you may know a good deal about music theory but your knowledge might be insufficient for the level of complexity that he will bring to bear on it. Thus, the personal facts about you will not, not in and of themselves, that is, have served their intended purpose, and the question at issue may remain unanswered.

This issue, special competency and suitability, is rarely a simple one. Ideally, both you and your patient ought to share equally in making the determination, Are you the right therapist for him? Generally, a trial period, a relatively brief course of therapy whose principal function is to determine whether you can work together and understand each other, is the best and most appropriate way to arrive at the determination. But while trial periods are good standard practice, they may not always resolve the issue because certain aspects of special competency will not become significant until later on. In cases where a trial period is not likely to suffice, the problem can be dealt with by encouraging the patient to inquire into specific areas of knowledge. You can submit to an investigation which has the purpose of determining whether there is a sufficient body of shared knowledge to insure adequate understanding. While this can be awkward, it needn't be especially problematic.

Bear in mind that for you to tell a patient that you're quite well acquainted with the problems of parenthood, that you're familiar with the rites of communion, and that you know what species-counterpoint is, is not, after all, to have told him anything that is "personal." The distinction between saying, "Yes, I know what the four species of classical counterpoint are, even the difference between Fux's and Schoenberg's treatments of them," and saying, "I studied counterpoint for four years during the time I was a music student at McGill Conservatory," is a meaningful one. It's the difference between what you know and how come you know it. Both are personal, but the former remains exclusively in the domain of factual knowledge. The same is true for, "I know the problems of parenthood" versus "I know them because I have four children of my own," and "I am not a Catholic, but I grew up with Catholic friends."

Thus, "Where do you draw the line?"—a challenge I have grown well acquainted with, having heard it often from students and colleagues—can be answered this way: we draw the line at the boundaries of our store of factual information or knowledge; we define our impersonality as therapists in a way that limits it to our opinions and beliefs, our social attitudes, our value judgments and tastes, and the like. Our main rationale is this: those aspects of our personalities are generally irrelevant to our effectiveness as therapists for the average-expectable patient; they need not interfere with our ability to understand him and with our capacity to supervise the *therapeutic process* for him. The same isn't true for our knowledge, because our ability to understand can be significantly enhanced or impaired if we are, or are not, sufficiently informed about aspects of our patient's experiences. Up to a point, therefore, it can matter substantially what we happen to know.

Where is that point? It can only be located ideographically, with respect to the individual patient. If your patient has a psychological problem with counterpoint and needs to explore the problem in depth (drawing on dynamic factors, genetic factors, and the like), you will have to understand what counterpoint entails. To the extent that you don't, you will have to ask him to clarify what the musical and technical issues are. In itself this isn't necessarily a handicap for him, because a patient can benefit during the course of his explanations by discovering things he was taking for granted, if not some new things altogether. Explaining things to us, something that goes on a great deal during psychotherapy, needn't be a necessary evil; it can clarify things for a patient and sometimes leads to genuine discoveries. But the possibility remains that your grounding in music is so lacking that his explanations don't suffice, and that possibility has to be taken seriously.

I don't want to overstate the problem. The illustration is highly specialized, and I chose it because counterpoint is a subject few nonmusicians are likely to know very much about. Similarly, I could draw an illustration from the field of mathematics, where few of us would have much knowledge and understanding. The average-expectable therapist can be expected to have a fund of common knowledge (operationally defined as whatever is fit to print in the *New York Times*), but will be uninformed about a wide range of topics that are known to the average-expectable patient. This doesn't obviate the fact that what we know can matter, and therefore it represents a personal area of potential relevance for our understanding of a patient. My point, however, is that it can have little to do with neutrality.

But unfortunately it also can have a lot to do with neutrality. The problem isn't fully resolved by drawing the line at knowledge—distinguishing between a familiarity with the writings of Thomas Pynchon, for instance, and a personal opinion of those writings—because it isn't true that all matters of knowledge are irrelevant to neutrality. For one thing, knowledge is selective, and thereby it implies values and interests. You can no longer expect to know everything (not even everything in the *Times*), and the selections you make are therefore revealing. If you've read *Gravity's Rainbow* but not *Airport*, if you know who John Cage is but not John Lennon, you've revealed something about your reading habits and given a clue to your taste in music. In short, that you know something says something about you no less than that you don't know it; and if you're prepared to inform a patient about what you do know, you must also be prepared to inform him about what you don't know.

But notice that I'm no longer writing about the issue of special competency and suitability. My illustrations are now drawn from questions a patient is likely to ask you during the course of an ongoing therapy. The problem can therefore be dealt with by exercising judgment in each instance, rather than by obeying any hard and fast rule. You can weigh each question to estimate whether the balance is on the side of divulging personal information for the sake of insuring a level of understanding, or whether it's more on the side of learning personal things for purely transference purposes. Moreover, it's helpful to bear in mind that a personal question can usually be translated into the form of "Do you understand?" That translation can be useful. And since it's inevitable that you'll often have to ask your patient for informational clarification, instead of answering his personal question you can tell him that when you haven't understood you'll ask. This won't apply across the board, of course, and there are bound to be instances when he will need to know in advance whether you'll be understanding him—so you'll tell him whether you're familiar with the book or movie and run the risk of a "flaw" in your neutrality. The same "flaw," after all, will develop when he speaks on a subject, in a way that presumes your familiarity with it, and you don't ask for clarification.

This leads us into the question of feasibility—How impersonal can you be?—which raises different problems. There are obvious limits here, and there has to be a substantial artificiality to limits which are based exclusively on what you choose to divulge. To refrain from telling the patient whether you're married is one thing, but do you not wear a wedding ring? And how about your clothing, the way you cut your hair, and decorate your office, don't they reveal a great deal about you? And isn't your personality reflected in a wide range of nonverbal behaviors, expressive gestures, and the like? To argue that you can know for certain what your stimulus properties are isn't germane here. Every therapist must take pains to know them, the one who doesn't strive for impersonality no less than the one who does. You can, of course, try to keep them as minimal and as blandly nondescript as possible—you can remove the wedding ring before sessions, wear nondescript clothes and hair, decorate blandly and conventionally—but there are limits. And the question remains, "Where can you draw the line?"

Furthermore, if a patient wants to learn about you personally, there are ways he can: he can look you up in the directories and professional literature, he can query your colleagues and friends. So why not simply spare him the trouble? Isn't it artificial to insist he must find things out for himself? That merely tests his resourcefulness. The paradigm is this: when he asks if you are married, you won't tell him, but he has a way to find it out—he can notice the wedding ring. What could be more artificial? And when he asks if you saw the movie and gets no answer, he can know if by chance he happened to see you at the theater. So why make it hinge on happenstance? If you wanted to take all necessary steps to protect your impersonality in these respects, you'd have to take extraordinary and impractical measures. You'd also have to lead a sequestered life to insure never crossing paths with the patient outside the office. Fortunately, none of that is actually necessary because again (and still) the line can feasibly and sensibly be drawn at what you choose to divulge verbally.

Before I explain why, it's worth mentioning that we have to do as much as we feasibly can to protect our patient's sentiments. We needn't dress in ways offensive to him, or behave in ways disturbing to him, and we can avoid unnecessary social encounters which are likely to evoke affective reactions. There are a variety of judicious and feasible measures which serve, basically, to insure tact.

My reason for drawing the line at what we tell a patient rests on the distinction between being impersonal and being personality-less. The term "personality" can be construed broadly—to include attitudes, opinions, values, tastes, even interests and hobbies—and narrowly. In its narrow sense it encompasses only our behavior as it is presented to the world—appearance, manners, demeanor, emotionality, and the like. To be personality-less in the narrow sense would entail a kind of blandly nondescript appearance and manner along with an affectless facade. There can be little merit in attempting such a posture; not only would it take an extraordinary effort (which is bound to show), it would necessarily fall short of any useful standard (which is nothing more than my personal opinion).[8] Moreover, the requirements of neutrality alone, as distinct from the requirements of other rationales (the "blank-screen" one, for instance), do not entail such a posture and facade. The requirements of neutrality are fully and adequately satisfied by maintaining a nonselective position—not by being personality-less, but by refraining from using our personalities in discriminating and selective ways.

Here's an important illustration: if you are emotionally warm and expres-

8. If your rationale is based on the so-called blank-screen theory, if you're striving to provide an optimal projection object in the interests of maximizing and purifying the transference, then you do need to minimize your personality features, narrowly defined. You need to avoid the expression of mood and emotion, you need to strive for detachment and opaqueness. The fact that real limitations exist doesn't in itself vitiate the value of the effort, it only limits the scope of your blank-screenness; and you need only be cognizant of where the boundaries lie so that you can discriminate between the "pure" transference and the "real" relationship.

sive, if that's an aspect of your personality, you can behave warmly and expressively towards your patients without at the same time violating your neutrality. The critical point is this: you remain uniformly and unvaryingly warm and expressive throughout, without regard to what they are saying and how they are behaving. When a patient is despondent, when he's elated, when he's angry at you—no matter what he is feeling—you are warm and expressive. In other words, you avoid variations that are reactive. Now, in order to achieve that kind of uniformity and nonreactiveness, it will generally be necessary for you to temper your warmth and expressiveness, for it is bound to be more difficult to achieve uniformity when its level is too high (and also, to be sure, too low). The same is true for other expressive aspects of your personality; if you are enthusiastic, you need only make sure to maintain the same degree of enthusiasm throughout—and too much of it, as well as too little, can make the task more difficult. I select these illustrations deliberately, because I believe a degree of warmth on our part, along with a degree of enthusiasm, can be beneficial to the *therapeutic process*, and I see no reason why these attributes need have implications for our neutrality, provided they aren't used in a selective and reinforcing way.

But the principle of nonselectivity by no means provides us the license to divulge personal information, and neither does it obviate the goal of maximizing our impersonality; it simply provides us with one basis for making a judgment in a particular instance or for a particular case. The criterion of feasibility remains the chief basis for answering the question, How impersonal should we be?—that is, As impersonal as we feasibly can. And feasibility is specific not only to you, but also to your patient.

On your part, if you could keep him from knowing your gender, you would; but since any attempt to conceal it would obviously create fantastic problems, it has to be judged unfeasible. The same is true, in different degrees, to everything about you that shows: your approximate age, your speech dialect, your expressive gestures, and the like. On the patient's part, the limits of feasibility may be broader than that which shows; your marital status may not show, but he may have a way to find it out (by looking you up in a professional directory). And suppose, for instance, he puts it this way: "I have a need to know whether you are married, and I don't care to understand that need or make it go away. If you refuse to tell me I'll go to the library and look you up; therefore your refusal will cost me time and effort. And I realize this is a kind of ultimatum, but I don't care." You may judge that it isn't feasible not to comply, because the practical implications and side effects would be too far-reaching. That, of course, is largely a matter of judgment, and it's going to depend on who the patient is and what stage therapy is at—but it can be formulated in terms of feasibility, which is my main point.

Similarly, with respect to the movie illustration I gave earlier, he may say, "If you don't tell me whether you've seen it, I will listen very carefully to your remarks about my reactions to it in order to discern whether you're familiar with the movie. I don't care to understand why I'm going to do it, but I'm going to do it; I will be preoccupied with your remarks, and unless you are able to choose your words so carefully—which will put a big constraint on you—I will be distracted. So it would save me time and effort if you simply satisfied my need to know whether you saw it." And even if he didn't articulate all those different factors, you might judge that feasibility required you to tell him whether you saw the movie. It comes down to a matter of judgment, and no general principle can dictate whether we divulge information or not, even though it necessarily reveals something personal about our tastes and values. It has to vary from therapist to therapist, from patient to patient, and from instance to instance.

A useful guideline is to take account of the public record, which encompasses not only factual information about us but also information about our opinions and attitudes. If, for instance, your views on social and political issues are in any significant way public (if you have written and spoken out on subjects), you may no longer claim that this personal information can be feasibly withheld from your patients. Insofar as they have access to those opinions and facts, you may choose to regard them as no more confidential than your gender. And the same can be true for information which is public in the sense that a particular patient can readily have access to it. In other words, whatever patients can readily learn about us is information we cannot protect, and therefore we may not feasibly withhold it.

There may be a point beyond which the minimal requirements of neutrality cannot be satisfied, when this patient knows too much about you and therefore will be unable to work effectively enough within the structure of *Psychotherapy*; but that point, too, is a matter of judgment. Just as neutrality is a relative achievement, an ideal position at best, so is impersonality—which doesn't justify abandoning all attempts at it. To argue that since it is practically unfeasible to achieve it perfectly, we may as well give it up altogether strikes me as tantamount to arguing that since a germ-free operating room cannot be perfectly achieved . . . or since empathy with another human being is never complete and perfect . . . Granting that the line has to be artificial and arbitrary is not the same as contending that it's futile to draw it. Moreover, the matter can be fully explained to each patient, and he can even be told there is a significant arbitrariness to the degree of your impersonality, that you're using the criterion of feasibility.

Neutrality and impersonality differ in the degree to which they can strain a patient's sense of credulity. Despite all your efforts to maintain your neutrality, despite the care you take to time and formulate your remarks so that they remain empathic and nonjudgmental, he may find it difficult if not impossible to really believe it, and he will cling to the conviction that you are valuating and criticizing him, only hiding the fact. Even when he comes to appreciate the profound advantage to him in having such reactions hidden from him— and the average-expectable patient does come to appreciate it—he may be unable to shake the conviction that the reactions are there. He is, in a sense, quite correct. You can hardly be expected to remain perfectly neutral throughout; even when taking pains to conceal it you are subject to personal reactions. The critical point, however, is not whether you react in such ways, but whether you are able to keep from allowing those reactions to influence your work with patients. But the fact that you are deliberately being impersonal is quite different. For one thing, its achievement is not so difficult—it's easy, at least, at the level of not divulging personal information. Moreover, that you have a personal life, with convictions and opinions, tastes and values, is never really in question; and patients will accept the fact that this aspect of you is going to be kept from them. They may balk at it (especially at the outset of therapy); they may not see how and why your impersonality will be of any special benefit to them, and therefore may protest it; but my experience has been this: (1) The central issue entailed by impersonality generally has to do with special competency and compatibility, and it can be dealt with at that level ("Are you the right therapist for me?" is the basic question). (2) Once that issue has been resolved, a patient will gradually come to appreciate, and also value, the benefits and advantages of your impersonality.

Inherent in the dynamics of *Psychotherapy* is the fact that your impersonality comes to serve a vital function for your patient. His not knowing you in a personal way provides him with a profound freedom from external constraint. He is free to admit every shameful secret, every painful experience, every embarrassment and debasement, without knowingly running the risk of incurring any criticism and censure. And the same also applies to "good" experiences (for instance, feelings of pride and victory), they too can be inhibited from full expression when another person's interests are at play. In short, the extent to which the naturally functioning *therapeutic process* depends on freedom and autonomy is the extent to which we have to remain both impersonal and neutral.

Do I mean "remain" throughout the entire course of an average-expectable *Psychotherapy*?—yes. Do I advocate that the technical principles and requirements remain unvarying from the beginning stage until the termination across every turning-point?—yes. In fact, only when a patient experiences a crisis, only when his well-being is in serious jeopardy, do I acknowledge the necessity and value of doing something different. But perfect consistency is another of our unattainable ideals, and there are circumstances in which you can prudently relax your rigorous stance and behave with a certain degree of flexibility. What those circumstances are is difficult to specify in a general way; nevertheless, I have some general views and opinions, which are heavily weighted on the side of technical purity and rigor, and I present them in a loosely knit way in the next, and final, section.

The Nature and Limits of Consistency

Our work as psychotherapists, and our patients' work too, would be far easier if the requirements of consistency and rigor were congruent with the requirements of flexibility and resourcefulness. To the extent, however, that they aren't—and I believe the two sets of requirements are likely to be negatively correlated—we have to make a fundamental choice. When we opt for consistency and forego flexibility, and when we maintain our inflexibility with the requisite rigor, we incur problems that are technical as well as emotional in nature. For one thing, rigor shades easily into rigidity, and consistency into dogmatism; for another, a rigorous consistency runs the risk of being perceived (both by our patients and our consciences) as inhumane and mechanical.

Many therapists nowadays prefer to view themselves as serving their patients' best interests by doing whatever they ethically can. Flexibility and resourcefulness are central values, which generally entail a willingness to use a variety of quite different approaches and techniques; and this, in turn, precludes an adherence to a single or "pure" method. Even those who aren't eclectic and who don't take a wholly pragmatic approach will readily deviate from their normal procedures in the interests of maintaining flexibility. And their rationale—based, of course, on their clinical judgment and experience—is that the patient and his circumstances require it of them.

Now, who is to gainsay that rationale? And who is willing to take issue with flexibility and resourcefulness? Anyone who is skeptical of the rationale insofar as its potential elasticity makes it prone to becoming a rationalization (after all, it's usually possible to justify having deviated from regular methods and practices by laying the onus on the patient and his special circumstances), and someone who is as convinced as I am that consistency has a greater therapeutic efficacy than flexibility. Furthermore, not only do I believe that efficacy is likely to be strongly correlated with rigor, I am also convinced that when the going gets rough, so to speak, when therapy is in a state of impasse, for instance, that is precisely when a rigorous consistency can have an especial therapeutic efficacy.

Before I defend that conviction, I need to distinguish between ad-hoc modifications and systematic changes, between short-term shifts made in response to particular developments and exigencies and systematic shifts made on the basis of a preconceived rationale which pertains to all patients and circumstances. I will first examine the latter and single out two possibilities: one occurring at the very beginning of therapy, during its diagnostic-consultative phase, and a second that takes place during the termination phase, when separation is the major issue. Since I examined these two possibilities in considerable detail in *Letters to Simon* (pp. 167–68 and 311–35), and my views haven't changed since then, I will do little more than summarize my position.

To begin psychotherapy with a structured interview whose main purpose is to assess the patient's suitability, is commonly regarded as good and necessary clinical practice. This may require an interviewing mode and a diagnostic attitude, and you may have little choice but to define yourself as the troubleshooter who is directing and evaluating, at least to a certain extent. When you are satisfied that he should have *Psychotherapy*, the necessity for a radical change in your attitude and stance needn't require a referral to another therapist; you can explain matters carefully to the patient, and then define your new role in terms of the Basic Instruction. Simply informing him may not be enough; he will have to be gradually convinced of your new and unique role, and it will take some time because he will have to experience it in all its ramifications before he can fully accept it and use it. But the same, of course, is true when you begin *Psychotherapy* right away. The only disadvantage can be a waste of precious time. I don't want to minimize the value of assessing patients' suitability—we have a clear obligation to determine the optimal form of treatment. But I don't believe a routine diagnostic interview is always, even usually, necessary for that determination; I believe the initial sessions of *Psychotherapy* can often serve adequately enough. You can begin by giving the benefit of doubt, with the assumption that this is the treatment of choice. Then you can pay close attention to the patient's behavior and verbalization, watching and listening for evidence of a serious thought disorder or character deformation, of schizophrenia or psychosis, or a symptom neurosis which might respond better to a different form of therapy. If the evidence raises questions in your mind, throwing your initial assumption into doubt, you should not hesitate to act appropriately even if it means slipping into the role of diagnostician. But if the evidence all points to his being suitable for *Psychotherapy*, then you've gained the significant advantage of needing to make no changes in your role posture, and no extraneous burden has been placed on the optimal development of the *therapeutic process*.

However, while it is entirely feasible to shift out of the role of diagnostician into that of therapist, especially at the beginning, it should be clear why I believe it's impossible to return to it later on, to alternate roles and attitudes during the course of *Psychotherapy*. It's one thing for a patient to become convinced over time that you've stopped giving directions and making evaluations, it's quite another for him to be convinced that the change is only temporary and will be undone whenever you choose to undo it. If he has reason to believe that you're steadily forming a decision whether or not to reverse your role, and that shift can come about any time, then he will be distracted from his work by the anticipation of such a shift, and he may also be motivated to search for ways to control it. ("What must I do," he will ask himself, "To maintain his role? What must I do to bring about a desired shift back to the role of the interviewer, the helpful one who directs me, the good doctor?") To be sure, you can interpret those efforts and concerns, you can articulate and explain his motives; but if, in fact, you are keeping open the option of changing into the role he desires (or perhaps fears) then the force of those interpretive efforts will necessarily be weakened. At any rate, you've placed an unnecessary burden on the *therapeutic process*.

The second form of role shifting is also unidirectional, but goes in the reverse direction, moving systematically away from the regular therapeutic position into something familiar and congenial. Many practitioners and teachers advocate a gradual shift when therapy is into its termination phase. Most commonly, this entails a relaxation of neutrality and impersonality, and they recommend giving expression to personal feelings and opinions, even advice—you behave more like a friend or a mentor would. The main rationale for advocating these changes is to weaken or loosen (or "dissolve") the transference, and thereby facilitate the separation from therapy and therapist.

Once you've relinquished your regular and unique stance you have given up the possibility of returning to it; so once termination has been effected, you cannot consider it advisable for this patient to resume therapy with you. The shift is necessarily unidirectional—you can hardly expect to return to a position of neutrality and impersonality once you've abandoned it. Thus, he is being eased out of therapy (if not necessarily out of therapy in general, then out of therapy with you). The change in role is designed to prevent interminable therapy, or else it's based on the conviction that he has had a sufficient experience of one kind of relationship with you, and he now needs another. This kind of shift is obviously free from technical problems, because it simply takes a unique relationship and transforms it into a familiar one. The main question, then, is whether it is in the patient's best interests, and I believe that, as a rule, it isn't.

I have several reasons for believing that the average-expectable patient stands to benefit when we eschew any changes in our regular stance. The main one is this: the vital issues that can be evoked by the termination are best dealt with in the same way therapy has dealt with all of his vital issues. The psychological problems of separation don't require, in my opinion, any special handling; they are not ameliorated by removing them from the intrapsychic realm and making them "real." Moreover, it isn't necessarily the case that a patient will find it easier to separate from you when you've become something like a good friend or mentor; one's attachment to friends and mentors is of a different nature and intensity than one's professional attachment to a psychotherapist. To separate from a neutral and impersonal professional can be freighted with fewer concomitants than to separate from a friend and mentor. A friendship, after all, unlike a therapy, doesn't necessarily reach a point of diminishing returns.

Consider, however, the transference and its requisite dissolution. Clinical experience has taught us that transference feelings and fantasies can be relatively unyielding and recalcitrant to a full and complete analysis. Consequently, their dissolution can be facilitated by the therapist's actually moving out from behind his "blank screen" and offering himself as a real transference figure in order that the actual (or "neurotic") transference can be weakened by a confrontation with reality. I have already mentioned the reasons why *Psychotherapy* doesn't require you to be opaque and ambiguous, that your reasons for being neutral and impersonal are not to facilitate a patient's projections and redintegrations. Therefore, this rationale needn't apply to us at all. Nevertheless, your patient can be fully expected to form a transference relationship to you—often as intense and deep as anything he would experience in a classical psychoanalysis—and that transference has to be resolved. Completely?—I believe not. In fact, I am convinced that a patient's transference feelings and fantasies are never entirely dissipated, even long after therapy has been discontinued. And I also believe they needn't be entirely dissipated or even fully resolved.

Perhaps I should now draw some distinctions between types of transference as well as among its component parts, because the phenomenon is complex and multifaceted. But my basic point doesn't rest on such distinctions, or, if it does, they aren't germane to the termination phase of therapy. Certainly, the termination does evoke fresh and powerful transference fantasies and conflicts, and they can be as "neurotic" as any of the previous ones. My basic point is that they can be subject to the same kind of therapeutic work as the previous ones, and the termination phase needs to be substantial enough in time to achieve those goals. At the same time, however, and insofar as complete resolution is always an unattainable ideal, we always have to judge the sufficiency of its achievement. And according to my clinical experience, we can prudently terminate a course of therapy with a substantial transference still in bloom, so to speak. Time alone, or the absence of therapy sessions, can be expected to further reduce the intensity of a transference; and a certain degree of it will probably linger on, without our patient's experiencing any deleterious effects from its presence. Accordingly, only when his condition requires it of you, when you judge that his well-being depends on a substantial dissolution of his transference feelings and it cannot be effected within the constraints of your regular role posture, should you consider the kinds of shifts and changes I have been discussing. In the case of the average-expectable patient, and the average-expectable course of *Psychotherapy*, you need do nothing different for termination—and you most likely shouldn't.

Now I turn to the question of ad hoc changes, and I'm going to approach it from a broad perspective. Most professionals, ranging from pure scholars to pure practitioners, will experience, at different times and with varying intensity, doubts and misgivings about their conscientiousness. The nagging doubt is familiar to most of us over the spectrum of our professional work, and it's likely to be especially prominent in our work as therapists—"Am I doing enough for my patients?" Therefore, the claim that there's more we can do has a powerful intrinsic appeal; "Don't just sit there, do something!" is a challenge that's hard to dismiss (especially when it's made by our colleagues); and anyone who purports to show us what more can be done in the interests of speeding and enhancing our patients' improvement gets himself listened to. We are constantly prey to the nagging worry that we have fallen into complacency and smugness, and we must always contend with the aphorism that tradition is laziness. Moreover, since nobody likes to believe, or even give the appearance of believing, that he has all the answers, that his is the perfect method, any innovation will have intrinsic appeal. There's a kind of security in change for change's sake, in following a leader into fresh territory in order not to be left behind, in doing what's new and up-to-date; our professional super-egos will be mollified, and we can escape some of the guilt-provoking recriminations—we aren't being unconscientious.

The challenge, "Are you doing enough?" will also be made by our patients. Psychotherapy, and especially *Psychotherapy*, is a frustrating experience for them; it can be painful and anxiety-provoking too. And insofar as its uniqueness is unfamiliar and strange, it tends to evoke in patients the conviction that it isn't (or can't be) enough. Most traditional forms of therapy evoke a variety of resistances, and it's far from uncommon that it should take the form of "This is not enough; I need something more." And even the most committed practitioner who has great faith in his method's validity may experience a pang of doubt which is not altogether empathic. (Maybe the patient is right? Maybe this isn't sufficient to his needs? Maybe I ought to do something more? How long can I doggedly stick to my guns in the face of slow therapeutic movement and apparent absence of improvement?) And the temptation will be strong to do something more.

Commonly, that temptation will be accompanied by a change in the patient's diagnostic evaluation. We may come to see him as perhaps a bit more borderline than he first appeared to be, or as having a more severe character deformation than he seemed to have at the outset. Such a reevaluation can serve as a handy rationale, if not a rationalization, for doing something more in a way that retains our conviction in the validity of our method. (It simply wasn't right for this patient.) But the complaint and challenge "You aren't doing enough!" is fully expectable, and we have to be fully prepared to deal with it, both in ourselves and with our patients. The big question is how.

It would be facile of me to spell out the many ways in which the complaint can be based on neurotic processes. No one will seriously argue that for certain patients at certain times it can reflect little more than a kind of transference resistance fully deserving to be classified and dealt with as such. And I could readily appeal to our basic concept of ego-autonomy in order to deflect all argument. The patient, I would claim, is doing nothing more than defending himself against the fundamental human condition of separateness; he wants you to be mother, father, teacher, mentor, helper, and not leave him so alone. But my position is based on some further considerations, and it has an important positive aspect.

I prefer to conceptualize the positive aspect as integrity, because I believe that when our consistency is both a function of and a reflection of our integrity, then it can have a substantial therapeutic efficacy in itself. I cannot, of course, overlook or minimize the possibility that consistency can be conceptualized and perceived in terms quite different from integrity—in terms of callousness, indifference, or obstinacy. But we have a variety of ways to insure that the principal basis of our consistency remains integrity, and therefore my thesis is this: when your faith in your method's validity is not only firm but also accompanied by actions that are clearly designed to promote and protect your patient's well-being, rather than serving your own convenience, then your rigorous consistency is likely to resolve into integrity instead of an empty kind of rigidity. And perhaps the most fundamental issue that underlies your consistency, and therefore your integrity, is that you keep your promises.

Consider the two basic promises you make to the patient when you conduct *Psychotherapy*. One is that the therapy will be effective, the second is that you will try to understand him. These two promises are related to each other, but only in principle; they are not equally under your control, and they differ in other ways as well. Therefore, I have to consider them separately. I'll begin with the second.

Insofar as you can eschew all interventional modes which aren't directly in the service of understanding, you can have full control over the promise to understand. But consider what this promise does and doesn't entail. It does not entail, and needn't necessarily entail, such actions as making appointment changes to meet exigencies and making up for missed sessions; neither does it necessarily imply anything about allowing fees to be lowered or deferred, or accepting phone calls, or writing to insurance companies and draft boards, and the like. In other words, it says nothing about a range of ways in which you can be of practical help to your patient. To be sure, the illustrations I've used can be construed in terms of maintaining the therapy itself, and that, too, can be viewed as ultimately in his best interests, but I have in mind a variety of actions which don't have that immediate function.

Before I discuss them, however, I want to mention that the basic criterion for taking actions which are not directly in the service of the *therapeutic process* but which contribute importantly to our integrity is this: they shouldn't interfere with our capacity to understand the patient, to listen to him free from distraction, and to help him freely explore his mind. This criterion is quite elastic to be sure; it requires a weighted judgment that balances short- and long-range implications and benefits. But I want to stress how it also requires of you a substantial degree of tolerance and generosity, so that you can be resilient against feelings of resentment and imposition when you have "put yourself out" for the patient. Ideally, your decision whether or not to take a certain action ought to be based entirely on his well-being, so that considerations of your convenience play a minimal part. In practice, how-ever, you'll have to place limits on your willingness to ignore your own personal needs; you can't overlook the fact that your neutrality may be strained when his requirements of you exceed a certain threshold. But I believe you have the obligation to keep that threshold as high as possible, and also to avoid taking a rigid, preconceived stance with respect to being "ma-nipulated." The Basic Instruction commits you to a neutrality that is only limited to the act of understanding, and it limits all other actions only to the extent that they may interfere with understanding. The degree to which you can tolerate "interferences" can be the degree to which you actualize your integrity, especially when your patient's well-being is at stake.

Thus, I see nothing intrinsically wrong in lending a patient a book, or acquiescing to his request to remove a painting from the office wall, or giving him a piece of information without at the same time giving advice. What I mean is that these actions aren't proscribed in principle, but have to be individually weighed in each particular case or circumstance. Only if and when it runs the risk of undermining the *therapeutic process* and you have good reason to judge that your integrity is not at stake in some tangible way (that is, it's truly in your patient's best interests), do you have to keep from taking an action. Otherwise, you will not have broken your promise to understand him; you will have shown him that your rigor isn't rigidity and your consistency isn't indifference. And in either case, of course, you can carefully explain why you did, or didn't, take the action he requested or needed. I can imagine a situation in which such explanation may not suffice, and he will have questions about your integrity if you fail to take the action; and you may therefore choose to risk a potential impairment of the *therapeutic process* in order to avoid an extraneous impasse. Even then, I would contend, you haven't broken your promise to understand, and you may have strengthened the *therapeutic process* indirectly.

To keep the first promise, however, something more than integrity is required of you. This promise is not under your control the way the second one is. For one thing, you might be quite wrong, insofar as *Psychotherapy* may not prove to be efficacious for this patient. Precisely stated, the promise is this: "Everything being equal and optimal, this is a method of therapy that stands a good probability of achieving for you a substantial improvement and benefit." Therefore, to live up to its terms, you need to be vigilant with respect to the "equal and optimal," and beyond that you have to add something important to your integrity, faith.

Faith isn't easy to conceptualize and discuss in purely psychological terms, it carries such multifarious connotations. On the one side stands the kind of magical trust which the medical model categorizes as the placebo effect; on the other side stands the kind of passive submission to authority which the priestly and healer model categorizes as faith. There is, however, something vital in the middle: the kind of position that can best be expressed by the term *courage*. The psychotherapy model requires a conception of faith that is based on a realistic estimation of a patient's adaptive capacities along with the courage to struggle against his problems and disabilities. I suppose I could formulate these issues in terms of *Psychotherapy*'s basic concepts, namely, ego-autonomy and self-determination, and enunciate the thesis that the process takes courage, that your patient's courage needs to be supported and strengthened. And then I could simply declare that when you make modifications you can undermine his courage. I believe that's true, but I know it's far from being so simple.

Nevertheless, I do contend that a certain measure of "keeping the faith" is indispensable for us. Whenever our faith wavers we can expect our patient to notice, and then he will most likely experience a sense of apprehension. This sense of apprehension can be present even when it is accompanied (and perhaps masked) by a sense of victory, a victory for the forces of resistance to change. We can always assume that he has conflicting feelings about psychotherapy's efficacy and that "part" of him will be gratified by a no-change outcome. For you in any way to gratify the interests of that "part" is to undermine the other one which is yearning for positive results—and it is that "part" which needs the support that comes from our keeping the faith. Bear in mind that the faith I'm referring to is not exclusively in the therapy but also in the patient himself. Therefore, it can be enormously encouraging to him when you stick to the promise, "This treatment will be good for you."

Just as a patient will be deeply frightened when his physician begins to doubt the efficacy of his treatment, so will the patient undergoing psychotherapy be frightened if you are doubtful; but just as a physician must judge whether the treatment will be deleterious to his patient's well-being, so must you. There is, however, this important difference: in psychotherapy it needn't be the treatment itself that is deleterious; for I'm not considering the situation in which your regular role posture and technical procedures are harmful to your patient, but where you come to doubt their sufficiency—when you must decide whether he should be given advice, instruction, emotional support, and the like. My point is that any time you depart from the promise (*"This* treatment is good for you"") you will also frighten him, and this can set in motion forces which may overshadow and undermine whatever benefits might accrue to him from the changes you're considering.

The paradigmatic situation is this: the patient is experiencing a crisis and asks you to do something more than you're doing, something different, in order to help him weather and overcome the crisis. Up to a certain point, your response is to deny him his request; you maintain your regular position and stick to your promise. However, as I've already discussed under the heading of "neutrality," you now work with a new and critical ingredient in the therapy, and you make it the focus of your interpretive work. You are far from indifferent to the crisis; you actively strive to understand it and share that understanding with him. Thereby you communicate the conviction that your method will be effective against the crisis.

The ruling rationale is based on considerations of the patient's well-being. Were you to respond to the crisis with a basic change in technique, you'd be putting him and his therapy into several kinds of jeopardy. One of them is the fact that he has discovered a way to shake you from your position, and that can provide him the incentive to experience further crises whenever he finds the pressure of the therapy too intense. The change you make may actually promote further crises. Another stems from the fact that he wasn't able to weather the crisis alone, so to speak, he needed your special assistance, and therefore he's going to need such special assistance for future crises. If he were given the chance to discover that he can, in fact, weather it alone—at least, alone in the sense that the basic therapy situation remained unchanged—he stands to benefit enormously. Not only will he gain a significant measure of faith in the therapy itself, he will also gain a significant measure of faith in his own adaptive powers. You helped him understand the crisis, but he was the one who overcame it. Such experiences can only strengthen a patient—unless, of course, the crisis has a deleterious effect.

This caveat is, of course, crucial, and it's bound to be complicated. The average-expectable patient can be expected to go to various lengths, wittingly and unwittingly, to promote situations which test your consistency and courage. Basically, such tests belong in the category of acting-out, and they can optimally be dealt with by a careful and sensitive and diligent application of interpretations. Within the format of *Psychotherapy*, you cannot proscribe acting-out; the best you can do is clearly articulate and explain it and actively share your understanding of it with him. But, like all resistances, acting-out is rarely pure and simple; typically, it integrates aspects of reality (both outer and inner) in a way that obscures and complicates matters. The element of the real with the fantasied, of an actual problem or crisis with a resistance test, is usually present, and the balance can be tipped in favor of the one or the other. When it is the one, then you face no special need to do anything differently; but when it is the other, you may have to act as though no acting-out were involved. You may have to say to yourself, "Sure there's an element of acting-out here, but the situation is such that interpretations won't suffice against it, and I must do something more because the situation is potentially of such danger it will seriously endanger the patient's well-being if I don't." So you'll go ahead and give the advice, the instruction, the admonition, or the emotional support, or whatever is required of you, and you'll accept the danger to the integrity of the *therapeutic process* as the lesser of the evils.

But a caveat is such a poor cadence, better to end on a positive and optimistic note, so I return to the benefits a patient can enjoy when you can maintain consistency and rigor. When you convey a sense of equanimity and faith, when you show him you aren't easily rattled by his unsettling experiences, or even by his psychological changes for the worse, he's likely to take courage and strength both from your faith in him and in the therapy. And it does take courage to be a psychotherapy patient—to struggle against the recalcitrant organization of one's character and experience, to withstand the pressures of one's life circumstances and history, and to grapple with the forces of resistance. It takes courage also to be a psychotherapist.

Index